THE GREAT AMERICAN BROADCAST

THE GREAT

AMERICAN BROADCAST

A Celebration
of
Radio's Golden Age

LEONARD MALTIN

A DUTTON BOOK

DUTTON
Published by the Penguin Group
Penguin Putnam Inc., 375 Hudson Street, New York, New York 10014, U.S.A.
Penguin Books Ltd, 27 Wrights Lane, London W8 5TZ, England
Penguin Books Australia Ltd, Ringwood, Victoria, Australia
Penguin Books Canada Ltd, 10 Alcorn Avenue, Toronto, Ontario, Canada M4V 3B2
Penguin Books (N.Z.) Ltd, 182–190 Wairau Road, Auckland 10, New Zealand

Penguin Books Ltd, Registered Offices:
Harmondsworth, Middlesex, England

First published by Dutton, an imprint of Dutton Signet,
a member of Penguin Putnam Inc.
Distributed in Canada by McClelland & Stewart Inc.

First Printing, October, 1997
3   5   7   9   10   8   6   4   2

REGISTERED TRADEMARK—MARCA REGISTRADA

LIBRARY OF CONGRESS CATALOGING-IN-PUBLICATION DATA
Maltin, Leonard.
The great American broadcast : a celebration of radio's golden age / Leonard Maltin.
p.   cm.
Includes index.
ISBN 0-525-94183-5 (acid free paper)
1. Radio broadcasting—United States—History.   I. Title.
PN1991.3.U6M35   1997
384.54'0973—dc21   97-11490
CIP

Printed in the United States of America
Set in Janson Text
Designed by Jesse Cohen

This book is printed on acid-free paper ∞

Contents

Introduction and Acknowledgments

I am a child of the TV generation. I first learned about radio from my parents, who tried to explain that there was no such thing as television when they were young. I remember my response quite clearly: utter bewilderment.

"You sat and listened to radio? What was there to look at?"

Radio, to my way of thinking, was something you listened to while doing something else: making breakfast, eating dinner, riding in the car. The idea of *concentrating* on a radio broadcast seemed very strange indeed.

Most of what I heard, while growing up, was the chatter of disc jockeys and the playing of records. I dimly recall some quarter-hour *Amos 'n' Andy* shows that played right around dinner time, and I remember stumbling onto *Don McNeill's Breakfast Club*, a cornball show (to my teenage ears) from Chicago that appeared rather incongruously every morning on WABC, which was otherwise a rock 'n' roll station! Neither of these living anachronisms endeared me to radio as it had been.

But I do remember one experience that gave me food for thought. Our family was on vacation, driving in some distant state, and on the car radio we picked up Arthur Godfrey's daytime program on the CBS network. Like any kid, I'd gotten bored during the long ride, and my parents had tried to find something interesting on the radio, to no avail. There were none of the personalities we were used to hearing at home ... and then, just by chance, we came upon Godfrey. There was something comforting about hearing that familiar voice, so far from home, and it made an impression on me. I had my first hint of the power of radio.

I was in my teens when I was first exposed to "old-time radio." I liked some of what I heard, but I pushed it aside, to focus instead on my growing interest in movies. Yet it was that movie buffery that led me back to radio. My old friend Alan Barbour, knowing that Ronald Colman was my wife's favorite actor, gave us some radio tapes of the actor in his prime. That was all it took. We especially enjoyed the Jack Benny shows on which Colman and his wife, Benita Hume, played themselves, as Jack's long-suffering next door neighbors. They made us laugh out loud. (Of course, the Benny program represents the zenith of radio comedy. Had we started out with *The Sealtest Village Store*, I might not be writing this introduction today.)

Another factor in my transformation into an old-time-radio nut was moving from New York to California and spending more time in my car. There is no pleasanter way to pass the time while driving than listening to radio shows. One Sunday night in the early 1980s, my wife, Alice, and I came upon a local radio personality, Bobb Lynes, who played old programs every week on a public radio station. Bobb promoted the activities of SPERDVAC (The Society to Preserve and Encourage Radio Drama Variety and Comedy), and we decided to attend a meeting where an old-time radio show would be re-created by some of its original participants.

Not only did we have a great time—and make new friends—but my interest was fired until it became a passion . . . and when I develop a passion for anything, I feel compelled to write about it. I knew I couldn't do a definitive history; the subject is simply too big. (Radio's news coverage, sports programming, soap operas, and game shows could fill large volumes all by themselves.) I didn't want to compete with existing reference books, like John Dunning's *Tune In Yesterday* or Frank Buxton and Bill Owens' *The Big Broadcast*. Those are standard works that belong in any radio buff's library and provided many vital facts in my research. Nor did I want to attempt a chronological history of the medium.

I wanted to present my own interpretation of radio's great achievements, within the mosaic of an anecdotal history. That meant conducting lots and lots of interviews. In this, I was especially fortunate, for two reasons: When I embarked on this project in 1985 many of radio's leading lights were still alive; but even better, they all loved talking about radio. Radio represented, for most of them, a very happy time in their lives and a rewarding facet of their careers. (How often, since then, have I watched old-time-radio re-creations and marveled at the skill of the actors involved—actors who ought to be employed every day of the year, but who, thanks to rampant ageism in our society, aren't called on very often. I count myself lucky to have seen and heard them at their best.)

As soon as I started on this project, I had wonderful encounters. Television writer-producer John Wirth set up my first official interview, with radio's renaissance man, actor-writer-director-producer Elliott Lewis. Elliott, at the time, was a story supervisor on the *Remington Steele* TV series, where, John explained, he'd been hired to help give the series some old-time style and panache. We all had a wonderful lunch at the Warner Bros. dining room; then I returned with tape recorder in hand to Elliott's office, where he gave me a lengthy and incisive interview about working in radio, on both sides of the mike. It may be the best interview I've ever had.

Jeanette Nolan wanted more than anything to have her husband and partner, John McIntire, talk to me about his early radio career, but John, in failing health, was reluctant to wax nostalgic. (It seems he associated reminiscing with drinking, and he'd given up the latter.) Then, one day, when they were visiting my neck of the woods, Jeanette told me to drop by their motel; she thought John was in the mood to talk. It was true, thank goodness. His memories of early days at KMPC Los Angeles, dating back to the 1920s, were priceless, and his observations, along with Jeanette's, gave me a real understanding of the territory I was trying so hard to learn about.

William Conrad turned down all requests to attend SPERDVAC gatherings, even those proffered via old friends and colleagues. But my good friend, actor James Karen, offered to act as go-between to see about an interview. Conrad replied that he'd see me *if* I could get him a video copy of the 1939 movie *Of Mice and Men*, which he'd been searching for in vain. I had it within a day and had my interview several days later; we spent two glorious hours together. (His home was filled with sailing paraphernalia, but behind him at his desk stood the Maltese Falcon prop he'd taken home from Warner Bros. years ago. After his death it went up for auction and brought a small fortune.)

I had a fabulous afternoon with Arch Oboler, as feisty and as articulate as ever, at his sister's home in Studio City, and began a long friendship with the great Norman Corwin, who seems to me incapable of uttering an inelegant remark. These men were giants of radio; how lucky I am to have known them. (I just missed out on Orson Welles, but asked a reporter friend who was going to interview him to serve as my proxy and ask some radio-related questions, which he very kindly did. So I *do* have some exclusive quotes from the Great Man in my book after all.)

Over ten years' time I conducted scores of other interviews, both in person and on the telephone. I also took advantage of my far-flung assignments for *Entertainment Tonight* to collar a number of Hollywood contemporaries, from Jack Lemmon to Lauren Bacall, whom one wouldn't immediately think of as "radio veterans," but who did have interesting experiences to share from their brief sojourns in that medium.

I decided early on that I would try to build this book around my own interviews, rather than digging into the clipping morgues. I made only a handful of exceptions. Karen Everson was kind enough to loan me the interviews she and Annabelle Sheehan conducted for an NYU Orson Welles project, including a valuable session with the late William N. Robson. Similarly, Frank Beacham gave me access to interviews he'd transcribed for a Welles audio documentary that I narrated. Chuck Schaden, Chicago's reigning king of radio nostalgia, was generous enough to pass along his interviews with two key figures of the past, Harry Von Zell and Lurene Tuttle. Anthony Tollin sent me his taped interview with Paul Stewart, as well as precious paperwork relating to sound-effects pioneer Ora Nichols.

My friend Keith Scott, a walking encyclopedia of old-time radio, also loaned me source materials galore, then fact-checked the entire manuscript to save me from public embarrassment.

Backing me up, every step of the way, have been John and Larry Gassman, the remarkable guiding spirits of SPERDVAC, whose knowledge is exceeded only by their generosity. Whatever I needed, from a phone number to a vintage radio episode, or just a sounding board for my developing ideas, they've been there.

I especially wanted John and Larry to review the manuscript, but this presented a challenge since they are blind. Enter the indefatigable Tracey Campbell, who volunteered to read the entire book into a tape recorder! God bless you, Tracey (and thanks, too, for introducing me to Jeanette Nolan and Elliott Reid).

For the best transcripts imaginable, I'm grateful to Spencer Green. For always being willing to field a new (and oddball) research request, I thank my assistant, Cathleen Anderson. For other favors and moral support, I want to acknowledge Skip Craig, Alex Gordon, Howard E. Green, the late Larry Kiner (and his son David), Miles Kreuger, Gene Lees, the late Gene Lester, Bobb Lynes, Bill Oates, Morlene Rouse, George Sidney, Barbara Watkins, Marc Zicree, and all the folks at SPERDVAC.

And of course, my interviewees (including those who are no longer here to accept my deepest thanks): Harry Ackerman, Mel Allen, Don Ameche, George Ansbro, Eve Arden, Gene Autry, Hy Averback, Lauren Bacall, Parley Baer, George Balzer, Andre Baruch, Jackson Beck, Milton Berle, Murray Bolen, Ray Bradbury, Himan Brown, Les Brown, George Burns, Raymond Burr, Gaylord Carter, Ray Charles, William Conrad, Norman Corwin, Joseph Cotten, Dresser Dahlstead, Rosemary De Camp, Frank DeVol, Howard Duff, Herb Ellis, Ray Erlenborn, Lucille Fletcher, June Foray, Fred Foy, Stan Freberg, Larry Gelbart, Art Gilmore, Jerry Goldsmith, Gale Gordon, Jerry Hausner, Skitch Henderson, Ruth and Paul Henning, Bob Hope, Bill Idelson, Raymond Edward Johnson, Jack Johnstone, Hal Kanter, Ray Kemper, Jerome Lawrence, Peggy Lee, Robert E. Lee, Jack Lemmon, Sheldon Leonard, Elliott Lewis, Jerry Lewis, Art Linkletter, Peg Lynch, Fletcher Markle, Mercedes McCambridge, John McIntire, Tony

Martin, Billy May, Sidney Miller, Carlton E. Morse, Ross Murray, Frank Nelson, E. Jack Neuman, Jeanette Nolan, Arch Oboler, Margaret O'Brien, Norman Panama, Roger Price, Elliott Reid, Kenneth Roberts, Adele Ronson, Terry Ross, Mel Shavelson, Ann Sothern, Arnold Stang, Barbara Stanwyck, Leonard Stern, Bud Tollefson, Bea Wain, Sylvester "Pat" Weaver, Peggy Webber, Richard Wilson, Robert Young, and Fred Ziv.

Even casual conversations with John Astin, Alice Backes, Harry Bartell, Ralph Edwards, Marcia Mae Jones, Casey Kasem, Norman Lear, Patricia Hitchcock O'Connell, and Dick Tufeld yielded valuable nuggets of information.

Many of my interviewees were just as generous about loaning me precious photographs from their private collections. I am grateful to them, as well as Dick Bann, Conrad Binyon, Janet Waldo Lee, Millie Morse, Rita Perrin, Shirley Robson, George Sidney, Steven Smith, Anthony Tollin, Lou Valentino; and Erin Coughlin of Bob Hope Enterprises, Stanley S. Hubbard and Connie Eckert of Hubbard Broadcasting Inc., Debbie Spatafora of WWJ Michigan, and Martin Halperin, Ron Wolf, and Ken Greenwald of Pacific Pioneer Broadcasters for their kindness. At the eleventh hour, when I needed specific pictures to complete this book as I envisioned it, Howard Mandelbaum, a true radio buff, and his brother Ron of Photofest, came through with the goods. And I'm delighted that Carl Amari of Radio Spirits, Inc., was so eager to participate in this book by providing a compact disc of great radio broadcasts.

Sharing this adventure with Alice has made it all the more enjoyable; I am blessed to have found a partner in life who gets just as big a kick out of delving into show business history as I do. We are both fortunate to have a daughter like Jessie, who took to *The Jack Benny Show* the first time she heard it.

For a variety of reasons, it took me eleven years to complete this book. That's a long time by anyone's standards (certainly mine), but it's been a wonderful journey. I've had great experiences getting to know a lot of talented people, and I've had fun listening to hundreds of shows. What's more, I'm just as enthusiastic about old-time radio today as I was the day I started listening to Ronald Colman in the car with my wife.

There is something about these shows—about the medium of radio itself—that I find compelling, even addictive. As many shows as I've logged, there are thousands more I've yet to hear. And you know what? I can't wait.

—LEONARD MALTIN
Los Angeles
January 1997

Signing On . . .

"A Boy In Kaki and A Girl In Lace"

"Kate Smith Program"

June 12, 1942

Re-recording

PART   OF

MADE IN U.S.A

Think about the enormous impact videocassette recorders had on our lives in the 1980s. Compare that to the introduction of television in the 1950s. Then try to picture a younger nation in the early part of this century, a society still giddy with changes wrought by the industrial revolution. Bear in mind that movies, phonographs, and even comic strips were still in their infancy when radio came along.

Radio was the culmination of a communications explosion. The concept of wireless communication was in the air, no pun intended, in the last two decades of the nineteenth century; a number of scientists approached the idea from varying disciplines, including the German physicist Heinrich Hertz, who quantified crucial information about electromagnetic waves and ether. An ambitious young Italian named Guglielmo Marconi ventured to England in 1896, and at the age of twenty-two managed to secure the first patent in radiotelegraphy. His Wireless Telegraph and Signal Company, Ltd., was an instantaneous success and opened divisions around the world, followed quickly by a number of rivals. American Marconi Co. was incorporated in 1899.

But radio, as we know it, still didn't exist. The medium was seen as a substitute for telegraphy only where wires couldn't be laid down. Its usefulness seemed limited to matters of seagoing safety and international security; accordingly, its development was accelerated because of radio's strategic importance during World War One. During that period, and for several years to follow, it was seen by most businessmen as a means of sending wireless communication, not as a medium of entertainment.

Even in the late teens and early 1920s, radio listeners were referred to as hobbyists, and at first, radio was just that: a pastime, a novelty. Many enthusiasts built their own radio sets, and mail-order businesses thrived selling crystals, tubes, headphones, and related paraphernalia.

Radio magazines and newspaper columns kept eager readers apprised of the latest developments in the field, while manufacturers competed in the superlative sweepstakes to boast that their receivers brought in the clearest signals, the least static, the longest distances.

And America responded. The man generally credited with transforming radio into a mainstream phenomenon is David Sarnoff, the former wireless operator who rose to the presidency of the Radio Corporation of America. Sarnoff saw the radio's potential—if it could be made affordable. In a 1916 memorandum, the then-assistant chief engineer wrote to his superiors at the American Marconi Co. (later to become RCA), "I have in mind a plan of development which would make radio a 'household utility' in the same sense as the piano or phonograph. The idea is to bring music into the home by wireless." In 1922 he introduced the Radiola console, which sold for $75—no small sum, but within the reach of the country's middle-class citizens during that prosperous decade. In its first year the Radiola racked up $11 million in sales. Three years later the total was $60 million.

This was no fad. With astonishing speed, radio became a permanent fixture in the American home, and in American life. It brought new meaning to the term "home entertainment," the apex of which (up to then) had been the record player.

Advertisements of the day made clear the radio's appeal. "Sitting comfortably in an easy chair you forget dull care. The magic wand of the radio sends worry scurrying," read a pitch for Crosley consoles.

"It doesn't matter where you live," boasted another Crosley ad. "Tampa or Portland—it's all the same with the Ace Type 3C Consolette. If you don't care for the Programme in San Francisco, the turn of a dial wafts you and your family as tho by magic to New York, Detroit, Wichita—all in the flash of a second."

If Sarnoff was the standard-bearer for radio sales, the Westinghouse Electric and Manufacturing Company, headquartered in Pittsburgh, Pennsylvania, may be credited with the earliest commitment to building and operating radio stations. It was an engineer at Westinghouse, Dr. Frank Conrad, who in 1920 began sending transmissions of phonograph records from a transmitter in his garage over the makeshift "station" which was then known only as 8XK. When a Westinghouse vice president discovered an advertisement in a Pittsburgh newspaper offering

radio equipment for sale "for those who want to tune in the Westinghouse station," he realized for the first time the impact these modest broadcasts had made in the community. Westinghouse then moved forward with plans to formalize the station, which adopted the call letters KDKA.

(KDKA's longtime boast of being the first commercial radio station in the country has been challenged many times. WWJ in Detroit was doing similar broadcasts prior to November 1920; so was KCBS in San Francisco. According to historian of popular music Gene Lees, "In 1918, the Canadian division of Marconi's company established the first regularly operated broadcasting station in the world, licensed the following year as CFCF. In May, 1920, CFCF made a broadcast with a full orchestra, which was received by men on ships in the St. Lawrence River and a few others. The station has been on the air ever since.")

As with television a generation later, cable TV thirty years after that, and today's Internet, there was a kind of "gold rush" to establish footholds in this new, mushrooming field. Industrialists and entrepreneurs saw the medium as a voice for special interests—and a lucrative vehicle for advertising.

Newspaper owners were attracted to radio as a companion form of communication, so a number of early stations were connected to major papers, like the grandly named WGN (an acronym for World's Greatest Newspaper, the *Chicago Tribune*). Other outposts were established by various media empires, like the Hearst Corporation, which named New York's WINS for Hearst's International News Service, and Loew's Theaters, which went on the air as WHN. On the West Coast, the Warner brothers set up shop as KFWB even before *The Jazz Singer* put them in the talkie business.

Media barons weren't the only ones who were jumping into the radio field. Owners of department stores, such as Gimbel Bros. in Philadelphia operated WIP (Watch Its Progress!) and L. Bamberger & Co. in Newark, New Jersey, owned WOR. In smaller towns,

The first transmitter installation on the fourth floor of the *Detroit News* building in 1921. WWJ is still on the air today.

stores and hotels found broadcasting a natural way to attract customers and gain local notoriety. Electrical companies considered radio a natural extension of their ongoing activities. In fact, businessmen of all kinds got involved in this exciting new medium. WPG of New Lebanon, Ohio ("The Pulse of Miami Valley") was owned by the Nushawg Poultry Farm. KPOF in Denver was the communications arm of a religious cult; its call letters stood for Pillar of Fire!* Churches set up their own broadcasting headquarters in many cities; so did colleges and universities.

* Many stations had evocative call letters, for decades to come. KPOL played nothing but polka music. WMGM identified itself as "the call letters of the stars." And the name of New York's WNEW reflected the initials of one of its backers, comedian Ed Wynn.

Murray Bolen, later to become a major radio producer and advertising agency representative (associated with, among others, *The Jack Benny Show*), started his radio career at a college station in Northfield, Minnesota, in the 1920s.

He recalled, "At Carlton University, Dr. Charles Culver, who had worked with [radio pioneer] Lee De Forest, came there to teach physics. He decided that

A young announcer (possibly the engineer as well) mans the operation at St. Paul's KSTP in the 1920s, which resembles nothing so much as a telephone switchboard, with record turntables on either side.

with my talent I should help him put the parts together and be part of the station, so I was. I was his helper, soldering iron, putting together small parts. Dr. Charles was the engineer, and he got the design for the transmitter which was a low-power 250-watt grid-modulated station. I knew about grid modulation because I was already cheating on my ham station, grid modulating and talking to Europe, when you weren't supposed to. . . . We were supposed to use only code in those days; dot-dash. But I was cheating, so I knew about that.

"He kept pushing me along. When we got ready to get the transmitter on the air, we didn't have a fully licensed operator, and by law you had to have it. So they let me out of going to college to go for a week to Minneapolis and study, and take the examination that you had to for an operator. . . . Any radio station that went on the air, according to FCC rules, had to have a licensed operator standing by at all times. So I became that guy. Dr. Charles would cheat and send me out to do the announcing, then [I'd] go to the music conservatory and set up the mikes, go to chapel services and monitor them, while he watched the transmitter. Then I'd run back and sign the log that I was there."

Stations like Carlton's were designed to reach only their immediate communities, and scheduled to function for just a few hours a day. Others boasted transmitting power of up to 50,000 watts, which meant they might be heard (on a clear night) across the country; their daily schedule started at sunup and ended at midnight.

In Yankton, South Dakota, the Gurney Seed and Nursery Company (established 1866) launched its own 1,000-watt station, WNAX, in 1921 and soon became a hub of activity in that Northwest community. Various members of the Gurney family, who ran a vast agricultural business, appeared on the air and became friends to their listeners. One such listener won a poetry contest with the following verse:

> *The Gurney's are the farmer's friend,*
> *They always will be to the end.*
> *Phil mentions several times a day*
> *About the worth of alfalfa hay;*
> *George tells them, in his daily talks,*
> *The wonders of their nursery stocks.*
> *They can fit you out with all the seeds*
> *You are sure to want to fill your needs.*

WNAX signed on every morning at six with Variety Entertainment including Bill's Harness Makers, Master Co. Music Makers, the Battery Boys program, the Sunshine Paint Orchestra, and Welk's Novelty Band, led by a young accordionist named Lawrence Welk. (He and the band were back on the air daily at 2:00 P.M.) Other acts on the station included Gurney's Hawaiians, Happy Jack's Trio, and the Sunshine Cord Tire Orchestra. Farm and grain reports were interspersed throughout the day until sign-off at 8:30 P.M. Regular listeners came to realize that despite the many names attached to these programs and entertainers, they all drew from the same small talent pool. Esther Smith, Contralto, was also Aunt Esther on the Children's Hour. J. V. "Dad" Barborka, harp soloist, also led the German Band. The Battery Boys ("A" and "B") were also members of the Sunshine Cord Tire Orchestra. No one minded; judging from listener response in a gala anniversary booklet published in 1929, they reveled in the familial feeling engendered by this hometown station. Such feelings were echoed a hundredfold at similar operations around the country.

Small-town stations weren't the only ones to adopt a small-town flavor. Los Angeles (or Low-se Angeleeez, or Laws Angle-es, depending on the announcer) had much the same feel to its early broadcasting as any one-horse town. John McIntire, destined to become a top radio announcer and actor (with a long screen career ahead of him), got his start in radio at KEJK in Beverly Hills when he was still a college student in the late 1920s. He got the job as part-time announcer at their headquarters at Wilshire Boulevard and Western Avenue, and was the first to announce the station's new call letters when it was purchased by the Macmillan

Petroleum Company. He later recalled, "I pushed the button and I said, 'This is KMPC, the Macmillan Petroleum Company station, Beverly Hills, California.' And that was all the advertising. [The owner] didn't have any idea about plugging Macmillan Petroleum products or anything. His sister was managing the station and she was a professor at University of California, and was interested, more or less, in classical stuff."

The staff consisted of three people: an engineer who operated the transmitter, which was located in the same building as the studio, a station manager, and a secretary. At first, McIntire was the entire broadcasting staff, for which he was paid $25 a week, then $50, although a woman came in once a day to do a domestic-type program for the ladies.

Advertising first reared its head at KMPC in the form of a colorful character who was carrying on the tradition of the medicine show. McIntire recalled, "I was in the control room playing records, and there was a door with a big window in it; I saw this fellow come in. He had a kind of a flowing tie and a morning coat; he had spats and striped pants. He said, 'Hello, John, I'm your cousin Maurice. I'm worth a million, you can have me for a dime.' Then he laughed and said, 'I just made it up, John.' "

This was Dr. Maurice B. Jarvis, a snake-oil salesman of the highest order. McIntire and his colleagues were so taken by him that they put him on the air every day at noon. He had a formidable gift of gab; he greeted his listeners in five languages, then said, "I'm your cousin Maurice; I'm related to everybody in the world." People were mesmerized, so much so that when he started pitching things—from a memory course to a red liquid you could pour in your bathtub to cure a variety of ailments, people bought what he had to sell.

"He also had an insurance deal for drivers called S.O.S.—Safety or Sorrow. He originated that. So when this money would come in—it would be a dollar to the station and a dollar to him, split right down the middle—it was a pretty good deal for the station," McIntire recalled.

Cousin Maurice took a powder one day when something from his past caught up with him, but there were others to take his place, including Dr. Johnson, with long hair, flowing tie, and a black, formal suit. He taught at the school of religion at U.S.C. and had the idea of talking to insomniacs at midnight on KMPC, soothing them and offering helpful advice for coping with life. He was so effective that he branched out by selling pillow speakers. He, too, simply disappeared one day. Then there was Matt Murray, "the poet and philosopher of the common-place," who turned out to be a disbarred attorney. And there was the preacher Daddy Rango, "a hellfire and damnation guy who would spit into the microphone and just raise hell." He would ask for a dollar from his radio constituents, entreating them, "Keep us on the air so that we can spread the word of God." KMPC took a fifty-fifty cut.

But the station's greatest success came with the formation of the Beverly Hillbillies. Long before the TV comedy of the same name, McIntire and his crony Glen Rice thought of this appellation for a group of cornpone entertainers. It wasn't just their music that attracted listeners: it was the mythology that these were genuine backwoodspeople who lived up in Beverly Glen, behind Benedict Canyon, and just happened to wander down to the station to perform. The five-piece group was such a hit that they started making personal appearances, with McIntire as their interlocutor, Mr. Fancypants. Soon the personal appearances were such a hit (they even headlined a stage show at Grauman's Chinese Theatre that accompanied the hit movie *Hell's Angels*) that McIntire had to cut back on his announcing duties at the station.

～

At least one municipality decided to run its own "public" radio station: New York City, which put WNYC on the air in 1924. This was but one of the city's unique claims to fame in radio history. As radio chronicler Robert Landry reported in 1946, when the population of the city alone (not counting suburbs and surrounding communities) was seven million, "New York has many audiences, many levels of culture and income, interest and appeal. Hence New York is unique in supporting what may be described as 'neighborhood' stations, as in the Bronx and Brooklyn. It is unique in having foreign-language stations broadcasting in as many as ten different tongues. It is unique in having one station, WQXR, which frankly caters to 'high-brows.' It is unique in having, alone among the bigger cities of America, a municipally owned station."

But all these stations shared one thing in common: the need for programming to fill up time.

At first, the thrill of sending and receiving signals was so great that it almost didn't matter what the actual content was. But as radio began to establish itself, and listeners had more choice, competition spurred station owners and managers to find the most interesting material available to them. In the early years, there was a cavalcade of "firsts." KDKA of Pittsburgh went on the air in November of 1920 with the Presidential election returns (Warren Harding won); a year later New York City's WJZ broadcast the 1921 World Series between the Giants and the Yankees (the Yankees lost). It wasn't until 1924 that microphones were allowed to be installed in the House of Representatives so that a Presidential speech to Congress (in this case, one by Calvin Coolidge) might be broadcast to the nation at large.

Various celebrities were lured before the microphone to perform, deliver speeches, or sometimes just say hello. One day in 1923, news-paperman Alfred J. McCosker of the *New York Morning Tele-graph* brought Charlie Chaplin to the studios of WOR in Newark, New Jersey, to make his radio debut. Chaplin was arguably the most famous man in the world at that time, but

WWJ made news—and won friends—by broadcasting the inning-by-inning results of the World Series over loudspeakers at Grand Circus Park on October 9, 1922.

his voice had never been heard by any of his fans. He was noticeably nervous.

"This is quite an ordeal, you know," he told WOR's director. Then, grimly, he approached the microphone. A reporter was there to cover the event.

"This is the first time I have spoken over the radio," he declared. "It is, to me, ghastly to think of you out there in your homes with Tom, Dick, Katherine, Harry and the baby all gathered around, and me here by this funny little thing perforated with holes (the thing, not I), my knees trembling, my hands tightly clasped."

As he went on, he seemed to gain confidence, and after a few more prelimi-naries, he announced that he would imitate a violin; at that point, a studio violinist played a passage. Then he volunteered to imitate a saxophone, and a sax player took his cue. Finally, Chaplin declared that he would imitate an entire jazz band, and the musicians played a brief number.

When the routine was over, Chaplin concluded by telling his listeners, "If you have nothing else to do, go to see my new picture, which I directed, *A Woman of Paris.*"

Thus was cemented another media institution, the movie plug.

While novelties like guest stars and coverage of events helped establish the importance of radio—and the desirability of owning a home receiver—stations needed regular, reliable programming to fill their broadcast day. The answer came in a mixture of three elements which remain the foundation of radio programming today: music, talk, and sports.

Music was performed live in the early days of radio, so every station built studios large enough to accommodate orchestras, and learned how to engineer and relay remote broadcasts from nearby auditoriums, nightclubs, and hotel ballrooms.

With so many stations on the air, and so many hours to fill, radio offered incredible opportunities for musicians and entertainers. Salaries were often modest, sometimes minuscule, and in many instances nonexistent. What radio offered in lieu of cash was exposure to an audience (which might pay to see the same performers at a local nightclub or dance hall) and the opportunity to do whatever they pleased. Thus, everyone from cosmopolitan string quartets to down-home jug bands found a home on the radio. Pianists and organists, glee clubs and choirs, classical soloists and dance bands all had their place. Amateur shows made a successful transition to the airwaves, and Robert J. Landry remarked of this period in his book *This Fascinating Radio Business* (1946), "As with amateurs, so with minstrels—radio resurrected the forgotten and the obsolete." The performers that proved most popular earned regular time periods, from fifteen minutes to one hour in length.

Andre Baruch, soon to become one of the best-known announcers in America, was in college and walking along the boardwalk in Coney Island when he literally stumbled into his new career. "At the base of the Half Moon Hotel on the boardwalk were some storefronts," he recalled, "and on the window of one of them were the letters WCGU. I looked at it and said, 'I wonder what that is.' And my friend said, 'I think it's a radio station.' At that point somebody came running out and said, 'Can anybody here do anything?' My friend pointed to me and said, 'He plays piano.' So this fellow grabs me by the back of the neck, and practically pushed me into a room that was surrounded by red velvet drapes and a piano in the center and an old carbon mike. And you had to tap it to make sure it was OK. He opened the mike and said, 'Ladies and gentlemen, we now present that distinguished concert pianist Mr. Paul Hart.' And I looked around; I didn't know who he was talking about. So I played, and when I was finished he said, 'Do you want a job?' I said, 'I can't, I go to school.' He said, 'What time do you finish?' I said, 'Somewhere around 1:30 usually.' He said, 'We don't open here until 3:30 or 4:00, and then we close at 11 or 12.' I said, 'What does the job pay?' 'Twenty-five dollars.' Well, twenty-five dollars in those days was like twenty-five hundred today. I said fine, so I took the job, and I played piano as a studio pianist. I was Paul Hart playing classical music; I read the news under the name George Stalling. I did many things, and then worked at a lot of little Brooklyn stations as a pianist and part-time announcer."

Show business headliners, for the most part, stayed away from radio at this time. No radio station could afford to pay a proper fee to a stage star like Al Jolson or an orchestra leader like Paul Whiteman. This was one reason the networks were formed in the coming years, to bear the expense of hiring such big-time talent, and then amortize the budget by collecting a fee from each subscriber station. Musical stars may have been discouraged (or even barred) from working on radio, as well, by angry record companies, which feared that the upstart medium was encroaching upon their business.

Indeed, at the depths of the Great Depression in the early 1930s, record sales plummeted. People had little if any "disposable" income and couldn't justify spending 75 cents for a phonograph record when they could get their fill of music on the radio for free. Records made a comeback in the latter half of the decade, spurred in part by the introduction (by Decca) of a low-priced disc retailing for 35 cents.

The music industry never completely made its peace with radio, however. Well into the 1940s there were major battles between the networks and ASCAP, the American Society of Composers, Authors and Publishers, over fees to be levied for blanket music licenses. ASCAP had a virtual monopoly on the licensing of popular music, and the radio industry felt that it was being blackmailed into paying ever-increasing sums of money. When the stations finally stood up to ASCAP in 1940, the resulting song "strike" meant listeners could hear only Stephen Foster tunes, and other aged songs in the public domain. After eighteen years of battling with ASCAP (and paying many millions of dollars in fees), the radio industry invested $2 million to form a rival copyright clearinghouse entity called BMI (Broadcast Music Incorporated). New and untried songwriters were lured to BMI and their Tin Pan Alley creations licensed to stations across the country. In time, the ASCAP songs returned as well, but it was an uneasy truce at best.

Likewise, the newspaper industry was never sure whether to treat radio as an ally or an enemy. The fact that major newspapers *owned* radio stations only muddied the waters. This was a time when every American hamlet had its own daily newspaper, and residents of major cities had many to choose from. Big-city papers had several editions during the course of the day, to keep up with breaking news. Radio represented a genuine threat to their economic survival.

In the early 1920s, the Associated Press warned subscribing papers not to use its wire copy over the air. The American Newspaper Publishers Association spent the better part of the next decade debating the issue of radio: whether to allow or encourage broadcasting of newspaper-generated copy, whether to bar election returns from being read over the air, and whether to publish daily program logs as news or charge for it as advertising. Eventually, the public had its say; there was no need for warfare. Newspapers and radio prospered side-by-side, until television threatened them both in the 1950s.

In the earliest days of broadcasting, there were no rules, and there certainly were no precedents. No one had ever devoted themselves to the purpose of providing hours of daily entertainment—and those who came closest, from the world of the theater, were accustomed to providing the *same* entertainment to a *different* audience every day, be it a play, a vaudeville show, or even a circus. A vaudevillian who perfected his act might use the same ten minutes of material for years. If the entertainer used that material one night on his local station, he couldn't very well repeat it the following evening. What's more, radio had no use for dancers, jugglers, acrobats, animal acts, or anything that depended on making a visual impression. (In later years, radio scored one of its most amazing triumphs in making a star of a ventriloquist, Edgar Bergen.)

On the other hand, radio was less demanding for a performer than any other form of show business. As George Burns later noted, "Radio was so easy; if you could read your lines without rattling the paper, you were a great star."

Public speakers were also in demand for the "talk" part of the radio mix. Distinguished visitors were often asked to deliver lectures on their most recent travels, while experts in subjects ranging from astrology to philately had programs of their own. Taking a cue from contemporary newspapers and magazines, many radio stations invited commentators to broadcast their views and reviews. (As early as 1923 there was even a movie critic on the air; WDAR Philadelphia offered one James A. Nassau with his "moving picture review" on Monday nights at 7:45.)

It didn't take long for novel ideas to hatch. An antecedent of the quiz show can be found in the early 1920s, when KYW Chicago broadcast its "Musical Guessing Contests," inviting listeners to send in their guesses about the names of songs performed. KFI Los Angeles offered Nick Harris reading detective stories every week at around the same time.

The first radio "institution" seems to have been the reading of children's stories at bedtime. Dozens of stations seized upon this idea, and boasted of their "story ladies" with velvety voices who would help put the toddlers to sleep.

But the October 27, 1923, issue of *Radio Digest* (a direct predecessor to *TV Guide* in its format of articles and program listings) primed its readers for something new and different:

"The radio play, a new form of dramatic interest, is increasing rapidly in popularity. Go to a movie and then come home and listen to a Radario and you will have received two exactly opposite theatrical effects. Perhaps, in the near future, you may have both movie and Radio broadcast to you.

"Of course, scenes and acts from current plays are often broadcast, but many eastern stations now have their own theatrical groups and give plays especially adapted for Radio use. Pretend you are blind and listen to these plays. The better your imagination, the better the play."

This, of course, was the key to making radio a medium of expression all its own, and not just a parasite dependent on other forms of entertainment. But it took time for original radio drama to catch on, with radio stations and listeners alike. Such an endeavor required a major

Musical entertainment at Kansas City's KMBC studio: The Tattler and his Four Little Gossips, aka Milt Mabee, Willie Gang at the piano, Eddie Edwards at guitar, Paul Henning and The McCarty Sisters lending an ear.

commitment on the stations' part, to hire an entire troupe of actors, not to mention writers and directors, who could broadcast on a regular basis. It had yet to be determined whether listeners would tune in to a specific program of this kind week after week—or night after night—to justify the expense and effort involved. And it wasn't yet clear how listeners would respond to radio drama, a medium in which they would have to visualize everything they were accustomed to seeing on the stage or screen. (Isn't it ironic that the 1920s saw the coexistence of radio drama, which offered words but no images, and silent films, which offered images but no voices?)

For now, radio drama consisted of groups such as "the WJZ Players" performing old stage warhorses like *The Passing of the Third Floor Back*, a British stock-company staple about a boardinghouse tenant with curiously Christ-like qualities. Other favorites from the repertory of America's many stock companies filled the airwaves, and once again begged the question of how quickly radio might eat up all existing material. It seems clear that original radio drama was born of necessity, not inspiration.

⌒

There were other, practical hurdles to be cleared. Radio reception in the 1920s was damnably unreliable, especially in the summertime, when thunderstorms wreaked havoc on broadcasters and listeners alike. Another annoyance was the tendency for signals to fade, without warning, in the midst of a broadcast. Finally, hobbyists complained about the inability to tune and lock in one station precisely, with other stations crowding the dial and causing "spillage" from one signal into another. (The peccadilloes of radio broadcasting became fodder for magazine panel cartoons, popular songs, and even movies. In a 1928 comedy short, a young man remarks—via title card—to his brother, "Mama's acting like she has birds on the aerial!" As late as 1930, Laurel and Hardy got big laughs out of the wholly recognizable premise of Ollie having to climb onto the roof to readjust a radio aerial to suit his wife. "Mrs. Hardy wants to get Japan," he explains sarcastically to his friend Mr. Laurel.)

But Hugo Gernsback, the popular scientist and pundit who edited the best-selling monthly *Radio News*, predicted in 1925 that "revolutionary changes will be effected in many phases during the next

Stunt broadcasts were staples of any enterprising station. Here, preparations are made for an airborne wedding to be broadcast over KSTP in St. Paul, Minnesota.

year . . . Little by little we are learning how to overcome a great many natural defects of radio broadcasting."

By far the greatest advance was made in 1926, when through the use of telephone lines, the National Broadcasting Company went on the air. This was history in the making. George Kent recalled the momentous events of November 15, 1926, in the January, 1935, issue of *Radio Stars*:

"Graham McNamee was the announcer. He spoke into a WEAF mike hung, if you please, in the Grand Ballroom of the Waldorf-Astoria. Everybody in Who's Who was there! Radio had come a long distance from the day when studios were squeezed into cloakrooms or at the junk ends of factory buildings.

" 'Good evening, ladies and gentlemen,' said Graham when the white light flashed. Historic words! Thirty-six hundred miles of telephone wire carried his greeting to nineteen stations extending as far west as Kansas City, thence out over the air to 10 million listeners. If you were one of them you must remember your excitement when he introduced Mary Garden, singing from Chicago, and then Will Rogers, doing a monologue from Independence, Kansas. These great swoops of radio, commonplace today, were brand new in 1926. This, you and the rest of us decided, was romance, adventure, a new world."

Overnight, radio was no longer a hobby, and broadcasting was no longer strictly a local concern.

The formation of NBC was followed several years later by the creation of CBS, the Columbia Broadcasting System. Then in 1934, four powerful stations, WOR New York, WGN Chicago, WLW Cincinnati (each one a 50,000-watt giant), and WXYZ Detroit banded together to form "The Quality Group," which later changed its name to the Mutual Broadcasting System. By the end of 1935 they had nineteen stations. Then the West Coast's Don Lee network joined up in 1936. By the mid 1940s Mutual would number more than three hundred affiliates, including small ones in towns that couldn't boast an NBC or CBS station.

But the networking of radio was more than a matter of business consolidation. It had a profound effect on the culture of our nation.

One day in the 1930s, entertainer Al Jolson went to visit his aging father, the cantor of a synagogue in Baltimore, Maryland. Jolson was full of himself, as always, and anxious to tell his father of the great things he'd been doing. The old man seemed distracted. "Almost seven," he said repeatedly, checking his watch. "Almost seven o'clock." Jolson continued to beg his father's attention, but the cantor was more concerned about the fleeting minutes. "Almost seven o'clock," he said again.

Finally, Jolson could stand it no more. He walked closer to his father's chair. "Pop, what is this with the seven o'clock, seven o'clock?" the son demanded.

"Time for *Amos 'n' Andy*," said the aged cantor.

The story may sound apocryphal, but it's true, told to show-business historian Max Wilk by Jolson's colleague, songwriter Irving Caesar. Just about everything else you hear about the impact of *Amos 'n' Andy* on American life is also true: movie theaters actually did pipe the show through their brand-new speaker systems (installed for the benefit of talkies) so that patrons wouldn't stay home. And, as it's often been said, one could walk down the streets of American towns and hear an entire *Amos 'n' Andy* broadcast without missing a line, as the sound of the program filled the air through the windows of every house on the block.

Amos 'n' Andy was, in its earliest incarnation, a serial, a hybrid of soap opera and folk humor. Freeman Gosden and Charles Correll created a complete, rounded world on their nightly quarter-hour broadcasts that drew listeners in and kept them in cliffhanger suspense at the end of every installment, waiting to see how the latest scheme or misadventure of these two mishap-prone pals would turn out.

This was heralded as the first photograph that Freeman Gosden *(left)* and Charles Correll allowed to be taken during an actual broadcast of *Amos 'n' Andy* in September 1935.

This was something new in our country: a shared, common experience that came right into one's living room, night after night. Readers had enjoyed serialized stories in newspapers and magazines before; moviegoers had returned to theaters week after week for installments of the latest serials since the days of Pearl White; children had waited anxiously for the continuation of comic strip adventures in the daily newspaper. But there was nothing to compare with the impact of radio, as exemplified by the continuing saga of *Amos 'n' Andy*. It was immediate. It was real. And it called on the most powerful tool of all to make it work: the listener's imagination.

This was the magic of radio; it was, as the eloquent writer-director Norman

Corwin puts it, "at once both public and private." Television has never had the same kind of impact. Corwin explains, "Radio is much more direct; it's one to one, whereas [with] television you're talking not to an ear, you're talking to an eye—a mechanical eye. Also, the eye is a very literal organ and the ear is a part of the senses. The ear is the organ through which we receive, after all, the music of Beethoven, Brahms, and all the great composers, who don't speak a word to us. It's all said in symbolism, in symbolic harmonies and symbolic melody; even symbolic cacophony does something which enlists our collaboration, to the extent that we are required to collaborate as we are when we read a book. Then we are giving something. We are not just taking. Television, too often, puts the reader in the position of a passive receptor, of a spectator. This is less likely to happen in radio.

"There's no set designer like your own self; you furnish the mise-en-scène, the wardrobe, the physical proportions of the actor, and the setting. Then radio is doing something that television very rarely achieves."

Corwin achieved greatness on the CBS radio network, but he began, as most people did, at the local level, reading the news at 10:45 P.M. in Springfield, Massachusetts.

Local activity—and ingenuity—continued to thrive during the 1930s and '40s. The networks may have had nationally known stars, but millions of listeners still turned to local stations on a daily basis, not only for news but for an array of homegrown entertainment. America was a less homogeneous place in those days, and people clung to their regionalism.

In Kansas City, an enterprising young man named Paul Henning (who would go on to write for Rudy Vallee and

KMBC's jack-of-all-trades, Paul Henning, interviews Hollywood star Lupe Velez during her visit to Kansas City. He later went to Hollywood himself, became a writer on several popular radio shows, and eventually made TV history as the creator of *The Beverly Hillbillies.*

Burns and Allen, and, much later, create and produce a number of TV series, such as *The Beverly Hillbillies*) fell in love with radio. At KMBC, "I did everything," he recalls, without exaggeration. And he seized every opportunity that came his way. "For an example, I wanted to take Ruth [his girlfriend, and later his wife] to the movies, but I couldn't afford it, so I became the Movie Editor, thereby getting passes to all the movies in Kansas." What's more, he arranged to interview all the Hollywood stars who passed through town, which many of them did in those days before nonstop air travel.

"I promoted a pass on TWA, which had just been organized, and which had its home office in Kansas City. So I got a pass and I could fly to the West Coast 'dead head' anytime. The trouble was that between Kansas City and Glendale, where we landed in those days, there were five stops. Now if they took on enough paying passengers, I [had to get off]. . . . I have been stranded in every airport between Kansas City and Glendale—Albuquerque, Amarillo, Texas . . ."

His boss wrote a letter of introduction to all the movie studios on CBS stationery, since KMBC was the local CBS affiliate, saying that Henning was visiting Hollywood to gather material for his broadcasts. "We had a due bill at a hotel, so I got to stay for free. It was really a shoestring operation, but the studios would always send a limousine. I'll never forget, the first fellow was RKO; they sent a limousine, picked me up and brought me to RKO. I was probably eighteen or nineteen years old, but I looked thirteen. I walked into this publicity office, and the fella looked at me and said, '*You're* the Movie Editor of the Columbia Broadcasting System?' It was great."

(Being enterprising never hurt. Several years later, after Henning and his wife had moved to Los Angeles, they found themselves destitute. Ruth Henning remembers, "The first Christmas we were married, Paul wasn't working and neither was I. We wanted to go home for Christmas. We were very homesick and very broke, and by this time, we had a car; his brother helped Paul get a car for almost next to nothing. We thought we could drive back home for Christmas if we just had a little bit of money. So we were both out pounding the pavement, and I think Paul sold a couple of ideas—for $25 an idea—to Don Quinn, and I went up to one of these cheap recording studios, trying to get a job as an actress. While I was waiting, I heard them talking about how they had to record some episodes of a cheap imitation of *Dick Tracy* called *Dan Dunn, Secret Operative Number 13*. They had to have the scripts by Monday and the writer disappointed them so they didn't know how they were going to do it. So I marched in and I said, 'My husband and I are both writers; we'll do it for you by Monday.' I think I went home on Thursday and said, 'Paul, can we write thirteen episodes by

Monday?' And so we did. They were going to pay us $15 per episode and they never did pay us for all of them, but they paid about half of it and it was enough for us to get back home.")

San Francisco, then as now a cosmopolitan and culturally rich city, was a hotbed of nascent talent in the 1930s. Meredith Willson later wrote in his memoir, *And There I Stood with My Piccolo* (1948), "San Francisco was the key radio town of

Local radio at its grandest: "Natty" Max Dolin conducting the NBC Firestone Group in San Francisco, complete with vocal soloists and a double quartet, circa 1930.

the Coast in those days and had lots of potential stuff simmering. Al Pearce had a daytime show at KFRC. Over at the St. Francis Hotel a curly-haired drummer by the name of Phil Harris of the Loughner-Harris orchestra was causing talk. . . . Not only Phil, but Art Hickman, Paul Whiteman, Ted Fio Rito, Tom Coakley, Carl Ravazza, Jim Walsh, Horace Heidt, Anson Weeks, and Tom Gerun either got their start or became famous there . . .

"Over at NBC down on Sutter Street they had a fine radio stock company, including an ambitious writer named Carlton Morse, who wrote practically everybody at the station into a serial called *One Man's Family*, which later moved to Hollywood with the whole original cast. Bill Goodwin was one of the staff announcers at KFRC and up on the Hill at the Mark, a Latin fiddler named Xavier Cugat was playing intermission solos for Anson Weeks' orchestra.

"But the big show in those days was *The Blue Monday Jamboree*, a two-hour clambake every Monday night from eight to ten, and you could shoot off a gun in any street in California on that night and never hit anybody on account of they were all home listening to *The Blue Monday Jamboree*. I can't think of anything that's ever been done on the radio that we didn't do first on that program."

Others, ranging from John Nesbitt to Jack Webb, got their start in San Francisco, but when mini-mogul Don Lee moved his headquarters down to Los Angeles, it signaled a change that proved to be irrevocable.

⸏

Even in the 1940s, local initiative won out over network-show dominance. Parley Baer, on the verge of a prominent and prolific acting career, got his start in Salt Lake City at a major station, KSL. "KSL was noted for its production," he says. "At one time when I was on the staff there, I was doing twenty-two shows a week, and I was writing eleven of them. And of the eleven, six were half-hour shows. I was special events and drama supervisor. We had a staff orchestra. We had about eight or nine really fine announcers; a lot of them went on to do network duties. We had a large sales staff and we used to do audience shows at the women's club with the KSL Players. Then we had a murder mystery that was on for years, literally years, called *Deathwatch*. We used to go on at 11:30 to 12:00 on Friday nights. Then we had a number of local soap-opera strip shows that went on [around noon].

"KSL, if it could get out of it, would not take advertising for liquor or tobacco because of the church influence; they were the CBS station there, a 50,000-watt clear channel station [but] if they could get out of taking those kinds of programs or could eliminate the commercials, they would do that. So sometimes we filled in locally when the network was not up to KSL's standards.

"Salt Lake's a great cultural city; I think our staff orchestra was about twenty-four pieces. I did a show that I directed and wrote called—it had a highfalutin title—*The Inner Mountain Empire March of Progress*, and it was sponsored jointly as a public service by KSL and the *Salt Lake Tribune*. We did the show coincidentally with local celebrations throughout the Inner Mountain Empire; we dramatized the founding and cultural and industrial development of those towns. We did quite a bit of remote work; we covered an awful lot of special events there."

Networks and advertisers realized that there were things they could learn from some of these local stations. Folksy fifteen-minute shows like *Facts About Fido* tried to bring that small-town feeling to a nationwide audience. In the mid-1930s, Captain Tim Healy convened the *Ivory Stamp Club* every Monday, Wednesday, and Friday afternoon at 5:45 (Eastern) on NBC. As a magazine article described it: " 'And so, good night, boys and girls from eight to eighty. Next Wednesday night I will bring you another fascinating story behind the stamp.' Thus does Captain Tim Healy, world traveler and lecturer, and one of the leading authorities on stamp collecting, bid adieu to the fastest growing club in existence, a club whose membership increases by thousands every week, every single member newly captivated by what Captain Tim terms the 'fascinating story behind the stamp.' " With an estimated nine million stamp collectors across the country, NBC knew that the potential audience for this show was as great as that for any music or comedy outing.

And even though the novelty aspect of radio had all but worn away, there were still occasions when the sheer adventure of broadcasting still held sway. *Radio Guide* described how 1936 coverage of a total eclipse would be handled: "Doctor Donald Menzel, director of the Harvard-MIT Eclipse Expedition, and other leading scientists from all over the world, will describe for NBC listeners the preparations that have been made for observing the total eclipse of the sun in far-off Siberia to take place on June 28. The broadcast will originate at Akbulak, Siberia, and will be heard at 3:30 P.M. EDT. On Thursday at 11:35 EST Doctor Donald Menzel and other members of the expedition will describe the solar eclipse. The program will then be switched several hundred miles farther along the path of the eclipse to Kustanai, where scientists from Georgetown University and the National Geographic Society will describe the phenomenon."

No local station could hope to achieve this level of excitement; this was where the networks had a definite advantage over the small-town folks.*

⟜

At one time, if one wanted to move up in the radio industry, there were several destinations from which to choose. Chicago became a national center of broadcasting, in part because it was home to so many large companies (read: sponsors) and advertising agencies. Chicago and Detroit were, in fact, the only Midwestern towns to infiltrate the network airwaves and establish national prominence. Chicago was the more influential of the two, and it remained for years a mecca for aspiring radio careerists.

But by the mid-1930s, change was in the air; or rather, the need for change. In January of 1934, Julie Shawell wrote in a *Radio Mirror* editorial, "What was wide-eyed wondering over an almost magic phenomenon a dozen years ago became a complacency of familiarity that with some set owners was later succeeded by a

---

*Humorist H. Allen Smith recalled, in *A Short History of Fingers*, the time in 1936 when NBC sent a crew to record the swallows leaving Capistrano. All the equipment was set up, the nation waited with collective breath held to hear the sound of millions of whirring wings, and nothing happened. The swallows had left a day early.

hypercritical attitude.... They soon weary of anything. They want tricks—a rabbit out of a hat, only not the same rabbit and not the same hat—every night."

Another complaint was voiced in *Radio Daily* on April 6, 1937: "Protests of increasing number and loudness are being heard from listeners against the very disconcerting situation of two or three programs (meaning chiefly similar type programs), all of which they want to hear, being on the air at the same time.

A young Chicago actor strikes a pose at the NBC microphone, for the benefit of a publicity photographer in 1931. His name is Don Ameche, and he is the juvenile lead of *Empire Builders.*

"Some nights, notably Monday when a lot of folks stay at home, there rarely are more than two or three outstanding shows on the air in the whole evening.

"But Saturday and Sunday nights, the very days when many persons go out, and on various other evenings during the week, there are batches of fine programs in conflict with each other.

"Regardless of the problems involved in trying to eliminate this confusion, sponsors will find it worth tackling for a very definite business reason.

"The reason is that, when listeners find two or more of their favorite shows on the air at one time, they try to get the most of the entertainment portions from each one by tuning out the commercials in each case."

Complaints, complaints! In an editorial of August 10, 1935, *Radio Guide* declared, "Radio is exhausting its supply of stars. The screen, stage, and opera are being hard pushed to supply the famished appetite of radio for more great artists.

"The public demand for sensational programs is placing a big burden on broadcasters. It is one that no amount of money can help. Silent Hollywood borrowed from the stage. The talkies borrow from stage, concert and opera, and radio has gobbled them all up and nearly digested them.

"With sponsors matching dollars for the top-notchers and the public demanding more and more from each broadcast the supply is well nigh exhausted.

Hollywood can only produce about sixty film personalities that are acceptable to the unseen audience.... If the demand keeps up new stars will be as rare and widely sought as a Kohinoor diamond and just about as expensive."

In short, the radio audience was becoming saturated, if not downright bored, with the regular fare the networks had to offer. It was no longer content with anything that simply happened to fill the time. It was the quest for fresh ideas—and new, more promotable programs—that led network radio to Hollywood. Up until this time, Los Angeles had been just another local market, although it had served as the linchpin for some West Coast mini-networks. Now, major advertising agencies looked to Hollywood to give radio a badly needed dose of adrenaline.

For the actors already working in Los Angeles, this meant a great deal: more money, more prestige, more work. John McIntire recalled that the very notion of a coast-to-coast hookup was cause for excitement. "There was an awful lot of wonderment about whether it was going to work, and the difference in time. It was a very momentous thing when they had the hookups."

His wife, Jeanette Nolan, recalls, "I was on the first transcontinental from here: *Omar Khayam*, which was produced at KHJ. Raymond Paige had the orchestra, and Stuart Buchanan announced it. I was playing one of the Hindu girls. We rehearsed it for ten days . . . and then the excitement of that moment, when we knew that we were going to go across the earth. . . . Here we were going to be going through the sky as far as the air would carry us. It was just overwhelming for one to be connected with that.

"My darling brother Phil had sent me a telegram from Wisconsin: 'Your lines so clear for the world to hear.' I was ecstatic. All my acting joys became a mural, a heavenly mirage in the center of which was this glorious new honor for the West. Knowing that we were part of New York City, at that moment, *that* was the apex. Hosanna in the highest. I was living in a dream. And when I went to pick up my check, it was an astonishing $7.50. That did it. That meant that I had truly arrived."

So, it seems, had Hollywood as a radio capital. Louella Parsons' *Hollywood Hotel* was the first major network show to emanate from Los Angeles, in 1934. To produce it, the sponsor had to pay a reported $1,000 an hour for use of telephone lines; anyone using the lines West-to-East had to endure such charges, while the reverse direction was much more nominal. (When Burns and Allen headed West to make a movie in 1934, their contract with the New York–based Guy Lombardo show required them to bear the considerable expense of cross-country phone lines so they could continue to appear "live" on the program. According to Burns, "We lost $200 a week every week we were on the radio; the phone call was that much more than what we were getting.")

A sure sign of prestige for Los Angeles's KFI: an appearance by John Barrymore.

In 1935 the heavy tariff was modified, and Los Angeles became a more feasible location for radio. *Lux Radio Theatre* had begun in 1934 in New York; less than two years later, it was reinvented in Hollywood. In its June 20, 1936, issue, *Radio Guide* awarded its Medal of Merit to *Lux Radio Theatre*, and its editor wrote, "I didn't see what they could do to improve the fine, rich fare of drama they had presented from Manhattan. Now I know. . . . Personally, listening to those famous actors under the direction of Cecil B. DeMille, all of them broadcasting from their own front yards, gave me a new thrill. Already, interested listeners have written to *Radio Guide* that this Hollywood program is exactly to their taste, and that it gives new significance to the frequent appearance of guest stars from the film colony. Already, they have said, Monday evening has become a more important spot on their radio calendar."

The migration West was not immediate or all-encompassing. Some shows remained firmly anchored in New York, Chicago, and Detroit. At this stage of the game, ad agencies had to determine whether they could justify the expense of a repeat broadcast for each coast-to-coast program. Remember, a show that aired in New York at 8:00 P.M. was being heard in California at 5:00. Given that the bulk of the nation's population resided in the Eastern sector, that was acceptable for some sponsors and network executives. (To this day, scheduling of events ranging from the Academy Awards and the Super Bowl to the President's State of the Union address are geared for prime time on the East Coast.)

Now, with shows moving to Los Angeles, the question was whether or not to broadcast live to the East at 5:00 or 6:00, or bear the expense of two separate performances, so both Eastern and Pacific time zones would hear the show at 8:00 or 9:00. The bigger, more successful shows did double duty. The smaller, or unsponsored, shows went one time only.

That is why, even into the network era, there was still an unusually active West Coast radio scene, in both Los Angeles and San Francisco. A number of slots during West Coast prime time were vacant (because there were no rebroadcasts from New York) and had to be filled.

Still, there was an undeniable excitement connected with a coast-to-coast hookup. Los Angeles–based actors coveted jobs on a "t.c." (transcontinental) show. But George Burns, for one, remained pragmatic. He recalled, "This woman said to me, 'I heard your show on Monday night here in New York, and my sister who lives in St. Louis, she heard the same show I did at the same time.' " Burns' reaction was not as wide-eyed as his listener's. "You see," he concluded, "the machine was the star."

Not quite. Now, in addition to hometown, homegrown talent, and feed and grain reports, and ethnic entertainment for an immigrant community, and religious services, radio was providing a national continuity for Americans: nightly news reported and observed by Elmer W. Davis, Lowell Thomas, and Gabriel Heatter . . . dramatizations of current events from *The March of Time* . . . relief from daily chores with the soap-opera sagas of *Our Gal Sunday*, *Ma Perkins*, *John's Other Wife*, *Myrt and Marge*, and *The Goldbergs* . . . after-school adventures with *Jack Armstrong, the All-American Boy*, *Little Orphan Annie*, *Superman*, *The Green Hornet*, and *The Lone Ranger* . . . a daily dose of *Amos 'n' Andy* . . . a weekly update of the pop music scene on *Your Hit Parade* . . . classical music on weekends with Arturo Toscanini . . . surefire laughs on Sunday nights with Jack Benny and Edgar Bergen.

Radio made this country smaller, and smarter. It brought the finest dramatic and musical performers to the farmhouses of Iowa and the Kansas plains. The cornfed comedy of *Lum 'n' Abner* had its audience, and so did the egghead-oriented *Information Please*. There was variety, and there was choice.

Advertising tainted the airwaves to some degree, but there was also a healthy amount of unsponsored programming that maintained standards of excellence in music, drama, and discussion. Only *some* of radio played to the lowest common denominator.

Within a decade of its widespread introduction to the public, radio became indispensable. And what is more remarkable, in its tireless efforts to fill air-time seven days a week, three hundred and sixty-five days a year, much of radio became memorable as well.

2

Writing for Radio

"A Boy In Kaki and A Girl In Lace"

"Kate Smith Program"

June 12, 1942

Re-recording

PART ___ OF ___

MADE IN U.S.A.

Jerome Lawrence is best known as the coauthor (with Robert E. Lee) of such Broadway plays as *Inherit the Wind* and *Auntie Mame*. Many playwrights of his generation, including Arthur Miller, Robert Anderson, John Patrick, and Arthur Laurents, cut their teeth in radio, but, Lawrence says, "when it came to putting it in their *Playbill* [biographies], they didn't do it for years and years, because if you said you were a radio writer, people thought you wrote soap operas."

Lawrence never felt embarrassed about his radio work; he is proud of the medium and his work in it. In the introduction to his 1944 book *Off Mike*, he wrote, "Radio has wings. It has no stage to keep it within the limits of a proscenium arch, no camera to confine to things that may be seen. The imagination of the listener is our most ardent and helpful collaborator."

"It was theater of endless possibilities," he said in an interview years later. "When we did *Lost Horizon* on radio, you heard a high, thin wind, some flute music, and you're there! You don't have to have all that heavy scenery."

Robert E. Lee, Lawrence's longtime partner, put it this way: "The thing that you were able to achieve in radio was involvement. Participation. Because you didn't have all the pieces to the puzzle. The person coming to the radio set had to bring some of the pieces and fill in. Even if there were forty people working in the studio, they were all concentrating on one ear."

No one knew this better than Arch Oboler. A feisty, iconoclastic, and reflective man, he wrote all sorts of radio plays (and even penned the notorious "Adam and Eve" comedy sketch for Mae West, Don Ameche, and Charlie McCarthy that got West banned from the airwaves in 1938), but his stock in trade was mystery and Grand Guignol. Oboler didn't indulge in cheap thrills; there was a point to every story, and his best work made particular use of radio's ability to fire a listener's imagination.

An especially potent episode of his famous anthology series *Lights Out* focused on a quarreling couple who suddenly found a hideous monster sitting in their apartment. Paralyzed with fear, unable to take their eyes off the creature, they are forced to stop arguing. During the course of a long night, they start to talk calmly to one another, and begin to understand the source of their mutual bitterness. As their voices, and their attitudes, soften, the monster disappears; he was simply a personification of the hatred that had grown within them both.

This half-hour drama is still gripping and effective today, but if it were "literalized" on television—if you could actually see the monster—it would lose all its power. It was *designed* to work in concert with the listener's imagination: a perfect radio play.

"It was a very intimate medium," Oboler explained. "I needed no special effects department, other than the imagery. I discovered that I could with a word, a strain of music, a bit of sound, make the terror and horror pictures look as true as a Model T Ford against a Ferrari."

But not even a talent as great as Oboler could hit a home run once a week—or once a day. The demands of commercial radio were daunting, to say the least. In his contribution to Jerome Lawrence's *Off Mike*, Oboler wrote in 1944, "The medium is a quicksand into which millions of words disappear without a trace. All the stories printed monthly in magazines, if assembled into one script, would not be sufficient to keep a network's monitor loudspeakers chattering for a week." He referred to the bulk of radio material as hamburger writing: "The writer's creativity is thrown into one end of the machine and it comes out neatly packed, with the advertiser's labels at the front and the back and in the middle.

"Fortunately," he added, "radio's need of material is so great that even the good writer gets a chance once in a while."

While drama quickly became a staple of radio programming in the 1920s, it took time for anyone to recognize the special needs and requirements—let alone potential—of the medium. One of radio's most prolific writers, Carlton E. Morse, who created and scripted two memorable shows, *One Man's Family* and *I Love a Mystery*, recalled, "When I first started to write, which was back in 1929, nobody knew how to write for radio, for the air. They were taking old movies and old stage shows and trying to create something for the air, but it was never quite right. And so from 1929 to 1932, I was being paid to learn to write for radio." The main lesson he learned? "My shows were always built of relationships between people. A plot came out of the relationships; the plot was secondary to the relationships. That is where you get the warmth and the colorfulness of personality."

It was, coincidentally, in 1932 that a booklet called *Radio Playwrighting* was published which addressed the issue of radio's uniqueness. Author Jane Sloan wrote, "One of the fundamental requirements in radio dramatization is simplicity. A complicated plot, innumerable characters, varied locales, while permissible in a novel or even on the screen, are prohibited by the limitations of radio presentation. C. L. Meuser in an interview published in the *Radio Digest* puts it very concisely when he says: 'A good radio play must have two things—an elemental dramatic situation and structural simplicity.' "

Over a decade later, True Boardman, the principal writer for the popular *Silver Theatre* program, told aspiring radio authors that crafting the introductory scene of a radio drama was the toughest challenge of all: "Your audience must be told where this story is happening, to what kind of people it is happening, and what the chances are that it will happen interestingly enough to keep him from tuning over right now to Frank Sinatra or The Quiz Kids. That first scene sets everything: locale, mood, tempo, and, to a large degree, audience. You will rewrite it oftener than anything else in the script, and with better cause. It has to be good."

He also offered this advice: "Instead of filling your every available second with plot, give yourself room. Let your yarn have and retain a natural richness and flavor. Let your characters talk a little longer about a little less. We'll know them better, like them better, and perhaps even come to feel they bear some resemblance to real people . . ."

E. Jack Neuman put it another way: he felt his mission as a working radio writer was "to be brief, to be concise, and to get an opening line that knocked them on their ass."

Radio drama presented special challenges to any writer accustomed to the conventions of the stage, or even the printed page. There was, for instance, a chilling moment in the third act of the stage play *Libel* in which a man was presented in the courtroom as a "human exhibit." Unable to see or hear, his face gnarled and immobile, he was alive only in the dictionary sense of the word. "When he was wheeled on stage," recalled radio writer George Wells, "the audience froze in sheer horror."

It was Wells' job to adapt that play for *Lux Radio Theatre*, and preserving the impact of this scene was his greatest challenge.

"The solution," he later wrote, "was simple. Before the exhibit's entrance his appearance was described by a doctor on the witness stand, going into far more detail than did the stage play, but without picturing the creature exactly. The impression left with the audience was chiefly that the man was a horrible spectacle. After a proper buildup the judge ordered the exhibit brought into court. As the door opened to admit him there was a dead pause. Then a woman spectator gave a piercing shriek of pure terror and had to be led from the court.

"We had accomplished our objective. The radio listeners pictured the man through the woman's fear and built their own mental image of the creature, making it as horrible as they could or dared. A new device? No. Effective radio? We thought so, judging by the comments received."

In a 1932 essay entitled "What Constitutes a Good Radio Mystery," Charles H. Gabriel Jr. outlined for aspiring radio scribes the essential difference between writing for the eye and writing for the ear: "The radio audience for detective and mystery fiction wants stories dramatized—not read, to them. Therefore, you have to translate thinking into action. Instead of the hero's figuring out in thought without action, that the villain must have leaped to the window, tore open the window and dropped to the ground, you have to have the hero suddenly leap from his chair, rush to the window, see the scratches of the villain's hob-nailed boots, peer out into the wild night and see the heavy imprint of the man's feet on the ground below while the wind (sound effects) snarls and whistles about his head. Again, the narrator can continue only so long before his talk must be turned into action . . ."

Ah, but how to weave narration into a storyline without overreliance on a third-person narrator? Robert E. Lee disdained a narrator as a "lame gimmick . . . it's too easy." But some shows seemed to lend themselves to conventional narration; it's hard to think of *Sergeant Preston*, *The Lone Ranger*, or other formulaic adventure series without it. ("A fraction of a second after the first wild burst of gunfire from Webb Kramer and Mex, The Lone Ranger and Tonto slipped from their mounts and ducked behind a nearby rock. Then the masked man's guns went into action. [gunshots] Marjorie Holmes and Rusty were caught in the cross-fire; they were confused and too frightened to move, until The Lone Ranger shouted at them." *The Lone Ranger*, "Honest Debts," May 10, 1946)

Many programs turned to first-person narrative as an alternative, which made great sense in radio terms and personalized each story. Orson Welles took credit for developing the technique in the late 1930s; in fact, the original title of his Mercury series was *First Person Singular*. Later, *Dragnet*, *The Adventures of Sam Spade*, and a spate of other mystery/detective programs made excellent use of it before it threatened to become a cliché. ("Mamie led me to a large Cadillac parked in the no-parking zone. She tore the ticket up and ate it. . . . Pretty soon we were winding up a private road to a fine old colonial mansion. Two or three private patrolmen were guarding the entrance; they all needed shaves. They kind of nodded as we went up to the front door. Naturally enough, it didn't open, but a peep shutter did." *Sam Spade*, "Tears of the Night Caper," July 24, 1949)

One writer hit on another way of dealing with the problem in the outstanding wartime series *The Man Behind the Gun*. In *Off Mike*, Ranald MacDougall recalled, "Quite by accident, during the writing of the third program, the 'you' technique was discovered. Instead of the conventional narration to the effect that 'the radio man listens on his earphones, waiting for a report from the scouting force,' it was found that a more personalized narration was incredibly more dramatic and inter-esting. Thus, 'You're sitting there, with the earphones digging into your skull, waiting and listening . . . listening for the sound of a circuit key being opened somewhere in the thousands of miles of sky all around you . . . waiting for the sound of static . . . the sound of the scouting force calling you. And the sweat drips down your forehead and into your eyes, and the earphones weigh a ton and are digging into your skull an inch at a time, and still no sound. No sound anywhere.' "

As written by MacDougall, directed by William N. Robson, and read by Jackson Beck, the impact of this script, and the many that followed, was tremendous.

There was another pitfall good writers tried to avoid, which George Wells called the "look-see" system, "a form of allegedly dramatic conversation in which a character carefully describes all visual incidents to a companion, or stooge. This treatment is supposed to make everything clear to the radio audience and usually does, including a vivid impression that the character regards his companion as four years old or totally blind. 'Look!' says the character. 'That car at the curb! A blue sedan with white sidewalls!' "

Juvenile adventure shows could be forgiven for dependence on look-see dialogue ("I'll just open this window and see if anyone's outside . . ."); more sophisticated programs, aimed at adults, strove to avoid it.

Radio writers also had to become conversant with a tool that didn't exist in other forms of writing: sound effects.

In his 1932 essay, Charles Gabriel instructed novice writers, "If you go beyond a half page without something to break the strain you've gone too far. The sound effect is a priceless thing but it's got to be done right. So many would-be radio writers bring in impossible effects, such as a door swinging *quietly* on its hinges. Try to do that! Or there is the '*inaudible* breathing of the criminal,' 'the *silent* footsteps,' or 'the *soundless* slither of the snake's body across the cabin floor.' Be reasonable. Your sound effects must mean something. However, you've got to tell the audience what sound you're trying to imitate. He may have a 1923 Umpty-ump set and the sound effects may be static to him. Therefore, always put in someone's mouth the description of what is taking place."

Most radio writers indicated sound effects as part of their script, but not every writer understood sound as well as Irving Reis. A young engineer for CBS in New York, he had dramatic aspirations, and wrote several scripts ("Meridian 7-1212," "The Half Pint Flask," "St. Louis Blues") which impressed his superiors at the network. When program chief William B. Lewis decided to inaugurate *Columbia Workshop* in July of 1936, to encourage experimentation in both writing and production of radio plays, he appointed Reis director of the ambitious project, and encouraged him to broadcast the pieces he'd already written. "Meridian 7-1212" was a perfect example of a play that used both sound and the inherent immediacy of radio to build a suspenseful situation. The title of the play refers to the telephone number New Yorkers could call in those days to get the correct time, provided not by a machine but by a human being—a seemingly passionless one.

Reis's script indicates exactly how dialogue, music, and sound effects are to be orchestrated for dramatic effect. It opens:

OPERATOR: (*On filter mike*) When you hear the signal the time will be eleven thirty and one quarter. (*Tone*) When you hear the signal the time will be eleven thirty and one half. (*Tone; cross-fade into music*) When you hear the signal the time will be eleven thirty and three quarters. (*Tone. Music, in a highly stylized arrangement sneaks in as voice fades, then comes up full, punctuated every four beats with oscillator tone; then dissolves into the sound of typewriter tapping speedily. It stops suddenly on cue, and dialogue begins*)

WATKINS: (*Hardly articulate*) Damn! (*Rips paper from machine and crumples it*) Why can't I get . . . (*Puts another piece of paper in machine, starts typing again; then door opens*). Oh! Hello, Jim. I didn't know you were here.

The constant, unerring drone of time announcements continues throughout the half-hour, first as counterpoint to the action and then as a passive participant in it. Watkins is a writer for *Manhattanite Magazine* who comes up with the idea of doing a story about the telephone time service: who calls in, how the "girls" who run it do their job, etc. Meanwhile, we learn that one of those operators is functioning under a terrible cloud: her brother is going to be executed for a crime he didn't commit . . . at midnight. The magazine writer tries to learn what kind of people phone in for the time. Rather than have a third party explain the answer, Reis provides a series of unrelated vignettes to show us: a married man whose insurance policy runs out at midnight, and decides to kill himself . . . two drunks in London who try to circumvent a liquor curfew by proving that it's still evening in New York . . . a naive sailor on leave whose latest "girlfriend" gave Meridian 7-1212 as her telephone number.

Finally, we go to the office of Hyland, a lawyer who defended the innocent man, where he is holding the shady witness who lied in court. The lawyer's young associate, Neil, finally starts torturing the defiant tough guy, who blurts out the truth—that he was paid to lie.

NEIL: All right, rat. (*Sock. Body crumples*) There; now he'll be quiet for a minute.

HYLAND: My God, we've got it! We've got it!

NEIL: We'll have to move fast. What time is it?

HYLAND: Quarter to twelve.

NEIL: But you said it was quarter to twelve last time I asked.

HYLAND: Good Lord! My watch stopped . . . I'll get it. (*Picks up phone. Dials ME 7-1212*)

OPERATOR: (*On filter*) When you hear the signal the time will be eleven fifty-nine. (*Tone: Phone drops to floor*)

HYLAND: An innocent boy is going to die in one minute.

OPERATOR: (*Distant at first, as if coming through receiver on floor*) When you hear the signal the time will be eleven fifty-nine and one quarter. (*Tone. Dissolve next speech from filter to clear*) When you hear the signal the time will be eleven fifty-nine and one half. (*Tone*) (*Her voice starts to break*) When you hear the tone the time will be eleven fifty-nine and three quarters. (*Tone*) (*The sob is audible now*) When you hear the signal the time will be . . . (*Pause*) twelve o'clock. (*Tone*) (*A high-pitched oscillator whine starts low behind the last call, then is brought up as the full resonance of the Hammond organ and low-frequency oscillator are added. It builds to a crescendo as she screams: 'Tommie! Tommie!' then cuts suddenly into a body fall. Music full, then down and out*)

Douglas Coulter (assistant director of broadcasts at CBS in the late 1930s) wrote in his introduction to a published version of "Meridian 7-1212" that the play offers "a significant demonstration of the latitude that radio offers to the writer who has complete mastery of the technical opportunities offered by engineering setup sound effects, and other physical equipment . . . Reis's understanding of the potentials of radio technique and his manipulation of the materials of radio have produced a dramatic result that would be impossible in any other medium."

Some years later, Reis and Robert E. Lee collaborated on a *Suspense* script in which, Lee recalled, "we drove a guy out of his mind by—and this goes to Irving's interest and my interest in mechanics and electronics—by just gradually amplifying the sound of a drip of water. Now, this was something that was fabulously effective on radio, because first of all, you just heard this little tinkle—plink, plink—and then it got to a point where it was thundering, it was shaking the loudspeaker, this drop of water. It was called 'Fury and Sound.' "

One of the most chilling sound-effects sequences ever heard in a radio play occurred in "The Hitchhiker," another memorable episode of *Suspense*. Near the end of the show, a half-crazed man driving cross-country from New York to California, who's been haunted by a recurring vision of a hitchhiker, pulls up to a pay telephone to call home and see if everything is all right—and if he's lost his mind. As the dispassionate, nasal-voiced operator tells him to deposit $3.85 into the coin box—$1.50 at a time—we hear the man drop one quarter after another (almost reflexively counting them as they pa-*ching* into the metal receptacle) until he's finished, and then wait for the outcome of the call. It will be, in fact, the conclusion of the show. In this case the sound was not simply a vivid re-creation of a real-life sound everyone in the audience could recognize; it was a brilliant dramatic device to forestall the poor man's crucial call.

"The Hitchhiker" and another *Suspense* classic, "Sorry, Wrong Number"—without question two of the most famous shows in radio history—were written by Lucille Fletcher, who to this day extolls the virtues of radio drama. "The suggestions you could make just by a note, by a sound, by the handling of the material . . . the swiftness of it . . . and you had such a short time, twenty-two minutes. The audience provided a good part of it; if you could excite their own imagination, they filled in the rest, so that the sparseness of the medium was to its advantage."

Fletcher was a Vassar graduate who, during the Depression, was happy to land a job as a clerk-typist at CBS in New York for $15 a week—typing *other* people's scripts. She had already seen some of her short-short stories published in the *Detroit Free Press*, but a steady paycheck was not to be disdained. "I got the idea of writing for radio," she says, "because one of my 'short shorts' was done by Fred Allen. When I saw how they did it, how Fred Allen's scriptwriters turned that little story into a radio show, I realized that I might be able to do the same thing and earn more money." She built up her nerve and submitted her first script "on spec," encouraged by her then-boyfriend, CBS conductor-composer Bernard Herrmann (whom she later married).

Lucille Fletcher has the distinction of having written two of the most famous radio plays of all time, "The Hitchhiker" and "Sorry, Wrong Number." Working at CBS in New York also enabled her to meet her first husband, composer-conductor Bernard Herrmann.

She was also encouraged by the atmosphere around her. "It was a lot of young people who had found a new way of expressing themselves that was so satisfactory and so exciting; they were all aflame with ideas. CBS was an exciting place to work, and we were given, in a way, free rein. You could do almost anything.

"When I got into movies I was depressed by the enormous amount of people that all had something to say about a script. There was too much money at stake. There was no money particularly at stake in these sustaining programs." (Sustaining programs—shows that filled airtime but had no sponsor—were the spawning ground for talent of all kinds, including writers like Fletcher.)

Another busy radio writer started his professional life as a pharmacist; in fact, the first play he sold was about a pharmacist, an effective one-act called "One Special for Doc." His name was Milton Geiger, and he broke into radio at a time when a number of hour-long variety programs (Rudy Vallee, Kate Smith, etc.) included ten-to-fifteen-minute playlets every week. Some of them were so well received that Geiger was able to resell them every few years to other shows looking for dramatic fodder to showcase big-name guest stars. "One Special for Doc," about a pharmacist with horse sense who talks a young man out of suicide, was first performed by Henry Hull on *The Rudy Vallee Show*; in later years it served Walter Huston, Parker Fennelly, Guy Kibbee, Ray Collins, Don Ameche, Joseph Cotten, and Ezra Stone equally well.

Obviously, a medium so hungry for material couldn't count on original stories day after day; adaptations of popular and classic novels, short stories, plays, and movies took up a great deal of the slack.

When Orson Welles won his summer series berth at CBS for the *Mercury Theatre*—in the midst of an already hectic schedule—he and his producing partner John Houseman scrambled at the last minute to reduce Bram Stoker's *Dracula* to size for their debut production. As Houseman later recalled for Karen Latham Everson and Annabelle Sheehan, "We wrote the script together. We had about four days to prepare the whole script. We did spend one extraordinary night; we had dinner together and started work at Reuben's, which was an all-night, very famous restaurant/delicatessen, and we started at dinner time and worked all through dinner, all through the night and through the early morning. I remember we had at least three meals, including breakfast; theoretically Reuben's stayed open all the time, but in fact they liked to wash up the floor, but we stayed nevertheless and they washed the floor under our feet. About 9:00 in the morning we had finished with paste-pot, glue, scissors and all kinds of ways to make a short version—because we only had fifty-five minutes—of Bram Stoker's *Dracula*. And it was a book Orson had always had a passion for, so it was all very exciting."

Once the Mercury was a going concern on radio, they hired a young writer named Howard Koch to adapt books and plays for them. He summed up this period of his career by saying, "The best way to learn anything is by experience. I learned by working with John and Orson. I learned a lot of my profession; I was still in a way an amateur, and that experience professionalized me. Good training. I would listen to the broadcast and ask myself how I could have gotten more visual effect than I had. I learned by doing."

Some adaptations came with specific challenges beyond the expected. Producer-director Fletcher Markle thought of Hemingway's *A Farewell to Arms* as "a dream to adapt," since it was already written in the first person. But when he tried to arrange for radio rights, permission came with an unexpected hitch: "The deal we made with Hemingway's then-agent was that, yes, he would agree to the fee, but the adaptation could not have any non-Hemingway words in it. And he had to approve it before we could broadcast. So I did that adaptation myself, not wanting to have somebody else have to be paid off and told, 'Sorry, the Great Man won't have anything to do with it.' I even wrote the descriptions of the music cues in Hemingway vocabulary, putting in quotes what the music was intended to communicate. And it was sent off to the Cinco Baheya in Havana, and came back ten days later A-OK."

Some may have chafed at the idea of reducing an epic-length novel to radio-show length, but Robert E. Lee defended radio adaptations (though he hated that term)—and put them into context as well.

"We did *David Copperfield* in half an hour," he said with modest pride, explaining that demands on authors of an earlier day were different. "Lots of times people spun these things out because they had a contract to write fifty episodes. Trollope in particular—a marvelous example—didn't have the slightest idea how he was going to end when he started it. But lots of times you could distill. Wouldn't you rather have a very good jigger of the very best liquor than to have a gallon of grocery store wine?

"Plays used to be five acts long. *Cyrano de Bergerac* was a five-act play. Much of the reason for this was so that people could go out during four intermissions and parade around and show off their clothes and talk with their friends. And the tempo of life was different. The tempo of life today is much swifter; it's a *Reader's Digest* tempo.

"What you would try to do is put yourself into the frame of mind of the author and say, 'What is most essential in *David Copperfield* to get across in thirty minutes?' That's a constructive attitude. Now it's a different work; it is a new work based on an old work."

Lee met his lifelong partner Jerome Lawrence when both were working in New York in 1942. They took to one another immediately, and over dinner on the balcony at Howard Johnson's, they decided to collaborate on a script. In fact, they wrote their first script together there, on yellow writing pads. Lawrence's roving assignment at CBS allowed him to do outside work, but Lee's contract with advertising agency Young and Rubicam did not, so at first he had to use

Jerome Lawrence and Robert E. Lee worked as partners for more than fifty years. Long before *Inherit the Wind* and *Auntie Mame* made their reputations on Broadway, they were prolific radio writers and directors.

a pseudonym: Ulysses S. Grant! Their first script was quickly sold to *Columbia Workshop*.

Then, Lawrence recalls, "In the course of about a month and a half, we wrote eight scripts, and by a fluke, the eight scripts we sold all got on the air in the same week—two of them on the same night, on different networks. Shows like *Lincoln Highway*, *First Nighter*, *Manhattan at Midnight*." Lee realized that he could make more money as a full-time freelance scriptwriter than he could under contract, and quit his job. During the war, the twosome became founding fathers of Armed Forces Radio Service, where they worked on hundreds of shows. They also had the distinction of contributing an original half-hour to Norman Corwin's series *Columbia Presents Corwin*, titled "A Pitch to Reluctant Buyers," in 1944. (Corwin returned the favor by agreeing to narrate their D-Day program, *Lord Haw-Haw Will Not Be Heard Tonight*.) Later, they produced, directed, and wrote a very successful syndicated series, *Favorite Story*, hosted by Ronald Colman, and worked as writers-for-hire on such popular programs as *Request Performance*, *Young Love*, and *The Railroad Hour*.

Lawrence and Lee were nothing if not versatile, but that was the calling card for most professional radio writers. Professionals knew how to write long or short, satisfy a sponsor who didn't want certain taboo subject matter addressed, and cater to a star who wanted key scenes from a movie retained in the radio version. Most of all, they knew how to write to a deadline. It required discipline and resilience. A working knowledge of the classics was also an asset to any writer hard up for storylines. As True Boardman put it, "To date, I have written *Hamlet* twice, *King Lear* once, *Julius Caesar* four times and *Romeo and Juliet* oftener than I should confess. *Faust*, too, has done yeoman work on occasion, as well as the *Odyssey* and the *Iliad*. The same people in the same basic situation with clothes of a different age and dialogue to suit. It's almost always a sure way out."

⟶

Radio writers may not have had the prestige of playwrights (or the luxury of time afforded those men of the theater) but they did have one advantage over them: a camaraderie with their acting and directing colleagues. Unlike stage plays, where so much was riding on opening night reviews, radio plays were an everyday occurrence; when a performance was finished, everyone breathed a collective sigh and moved on to the next show.

"We were all very close," recalls E. Jack Neuman. "It was a lot closer than a [movie] soundstage. We'd all work like hell for seven or eight hours and then we'd go out and get some food and get drunk and chase girls and stuff like that."

No one ever recorded whether Carlton E. Morse got drunk or chased girls, but he did enjoy his actors' company, and got more out of it than good fellowship: he fashioned characters for his long-running daytime drama *One Man's Family* based on the individual personalities—and strengths—of the actors in his troupe.

As he later explained, "I had worked with the group of players I finally selected for several years before the *Family* came into being. Therefore, I had the opportunity of creating characters in my mind and selecting the actors to play the roles before a line of dialogue was written. Then, with each character clearly in mind, and a mental picture before me of the actor who would play the role, I began to write. Actually, not only was I writing fictional characters but I was also writing something of each of the actors into the part."

Morse was a phenomenon among radio writers. A prodigious, hard-working man with strong moral fiber and a gentle sense of humor, he arose at 4:00 every morning for the better part of three decades to write *One Man's Family* (first for radio, later for television), which he also directed. *One Man's Family* was the quintessential soap opera, a multigenerational story that enabled listeners of all ages to find someone with whom to identify—from the patriarchal Henry Barbour (often referred to as Father Barbour), who was given to sermonizing on a variety of topics, to the series' "young people," the five Barbour children (and then grandchildren) who were susceptible to all the pitfalls of life and love, marriage and family.

As radio historian John Dunning wrote in his book *Tune In Yesterday* (1976), "Taken singly, the chapters of *One Man's Family* are dull and occasionally over-sentimental. The problem is that no one can pick up a novel, turn to the middle, and expect to be carried along instantly. Taken in vast units of entire serials [which Morse identified on the air as Book 21, Chapter 3, etc.], the underlying characterizations go to work, the family becomes as real as the old friends halfway up the next block. . . . *One Man's Family* was simply the most addictive show of its time."

The show offered a continuity unrivaled in radio history. Listeners followed the story of the Barbours for twenty-seven years! Younger characters grew up on the air, along with the actors portraying them. The Barbours persevered through the Great Depression and World War Two, just like families who were listening to them on the air. As Morse fashioned a special bond with his acting troupe, he forged a unique partnership with his audience.

Carlton E. Morse obliges the publicity cameraman as Chicago's Myrt and Marge (real-life mother and daughter Myrtle Vail and Donna Dameral) visit San Francisco in 1935.

Then in 1939 he created the inventive, outlandish, larger-than-life *I Love a Mystery*, charting the far-flung adventures of three soldiers of fortune named Jack Packard, Doc Long, and Reggie Yorke. It was as different from *Family* as any show on the air, yet just as distinctive. These were full-blooded, pulp magazine–style yarns, offering the three jaunty proprietors of the A-1 Detective Agency a globe-trotting menu of adventures, from investigating reports of werewolves to trying to solve a series of grisly slasher murders in a creepy old mansion. Morse knew how to pepper each script with vivid detail, yet strike a balance between plot exposition and personality-driven dialogue. These stories wouldn't have been the same without the rich—and contrasting—characterizations of Jack, Doc, and Reggie. If audiences couldn't predict what would happen next, that was understandable: Morse didn't know either! He usually allotted three to four weeks for each story, but he never outlined his serpentine plots ahead of time. This was perhaps the most amazing adventure of all. What's more, for much of the show's run, it appeared in fifteen-minute installments, every day.

As Morse later recalled, "I had to write fifteen pages a day for the *I Love a Mystery* story, five days a week, and I had to write *One Man's Family*, a half-hour show (once a week), so I was working seven days a week writing fifteen pages a day, plus doing all the direction and production of the radio shows, so I had no time for anything else."

Taking on a cowriter, or even an apprentice, was anathema to Morse, who mother-henned every single script. And yet, he said happily in later years, he never felt the pressure of a deadline. "I get more pleasure than anybody else I know, doing what I'm doing."

Raised on a farm, he was accustomed to rising early and doing

A 1945 trade advertisement for one of the few radio writers whose name was recognized by the listening public.

chores, so starting out at 4:00 A.M. seemed perfectly natural, especially as it enabled him to work uninterrupted for several hours. "It got to the point where I would just sit down to the typewriter with a blank page and sit there for a few minutes, and then start to write, and the minute I started to write, I was lost to the world, for as much as two and a half hours." Later, when he would rehearse with his cast, he sometimes marveled at what he had written—unable to explain where it had come from, other than his formidably fertile mind.

*Morse was not the only prolific radio writer, although he was certainly one of the best. In its June 1935 issue, *Radio Stars* magazine detailed the output of Bob Andrews, a former reporter who was now responsible for the popular daytime drama *Betty and Bob*: "He turns out a *Betty and Bob* episode every day. Plenty of radio writers would call that a fair-sized job. But in addition he writes alone all the episodes of *The Romance of Helen Trent*, *Judy and Jane*, *Just Plain Bill*, *Skippy* and others—thirty-five installments a week all told, five episodes every day, even if he works Saturdays and Sundays!"

⟿

While Morse gave endless pleasure to fans of domestic drama and high adventure of the pulp variety, Norman Corwin dazzled discerning audiences at night with his stunningly original radio plays. Like Morse, he lived to write, and from the late 1930s through the end of the next decade, he had the opportunity to do so for a nationwide audience with almost complete—and unprecedented—autonomy.

The price he paid for this freedom was an unforgiving deadline. CBS offered him an opportunity to fill a half-hour of airtime every week, and to produce and direct his own scripts, in the series *26 by Corwin* (1941), *This Is War!* (1942), *An American in England* (1942), *Columbia Presents Corwin* (1944–45), and *One World Flight* (1947). It was a dream come true for any writer . . . but the dream had nightmarish qualities, as well. In 1944 Corwin wrote, "When I was writing and producing a script a week I would spend my first day thinking, my second in despair, my third working on the early pages, my fourth revising what I had written in the first three, my fifth racing the clock to finish the script in time for the mimeographers, my sixth casting and conferring, my seventh rehearsing and broadcasting. Sometimes the conception, the basic idea, even the subject itself, did not occur on the first day, or else I might make a false start. Sometimes I was into my fourth day before an idea or an approach would take shape. In such a case I would practically have to turn

Norman Corwin, in a pensive moment posed for the CBS photographer.

out the script overnight—and that can be real hell. My first drafts have almost always had to be my last drafts."

Not every Corwin script was a gem, but each one was unique. CBS boasted in an ad for *26 by Corwin*, "The only consistency in this series is its inconsistency!" One week, the listener might hear a lighthearted meditation in rhyme called "The Undecided Molecule," with Groucho Marx in the lead. Another week, a murderer's first-person diary of his crime, taken verbatim from British police records ("The Moat Farm Murder," with Charles Laughton). "Daybreak" was a journey in music and words around the circumference of the globe. "Descent of the Gods" was a parable about Greek gods visiting our twentieth-century planet. There were original operas and stories from the Bible. And one week, when money was getting tight for production of the series, Corwin dealt with that crisis—and his potential writer's block—by presenting, tongue in cheek, "A Soliloquy to Balance the Budget."

Corwin could be puckish, satiric, or solemn. He attracted some of the finest actors and composers on both coasts to work with him in the rarefied atmosphere of his CBS berth. And if he regretted the inability to polish his scripts through additional drafts, he certainly gave his "first drafts" some pretty polished productions.

He earned the sobriquet "radio's poet laureate." The title was never challenged.

Corwin started out as a journalist; in fact, he went directly from high school to a position on a local newspaper. In his late teens he was the radio editor of the *Springfield Republican*, which led to his first job on the air when the local Westinghouse station asked the newspaper to provide a nightly fifteen-minute newscast.

As he later wrote, "I worked as a reporter on my radio routine in the afternoon, got to work at two in the afternoon, then after dinner I prepared AP and UP and INS copy which came in over the printers that was not suitable for broadcast. It was a different rhythm, a different approach between the eye and the ear; I innately was aware of that, so I would rewrite these things, and at 10:45 went over to that studio and broadcast."

Reading his own copy over the air sharpened Corwin's awareness of writing for the ear—and also drove home the impact of the medium. "I was conscious of the fact that I was talking to a great many people, talking to them in their homes; it was at once public and yet private, which is a phenomenon of broadcasting."

Corwin had no background in theater, but traces his involvement in drama to a lifelong love of poetry. "At the same time I was doing the newscast I interested the manager of the Westinghouse station in a program called *Rhymes and Cadences*, and I took the poetry of others and spoke it; I was pretty good at that."

When he later moved to New York, and got a job writing radio copy for the publicity department of 20th Century-Fox, he became a loyal listener of W2XR (later WQXR), a station that specialized in classical music and news. "They did all kinds of news, including commentary on ballet and opera, and I wrote them a letter saying that I was a fan and I enjoyed their programming, but the most ancient of the arts was not represented. And that is poetry. I had an idea for a program, and they responded and said come over and audition for us."

It was as simple as that. Corwin was hired—at no pay—to read poetry once a week on W2XR. Growing ambition inspired him to adapt the *Spoon River Anthology* for the air one week, and that show got him hired by CBS—not as a writer, but as a director. Apparently, it was the presentation that impressed his new employers.

In due course, Corwin approached William Lewis, vice president of programming at CBS, and got the go-ahead not only to produce a Sunday afternoon poetry series, but the direction to call it *Norman Corwin's Words Without Music*. The proprietary title was something "you don't dare ask for until you've been in the business for twenty years and you've established big hits, or you're like Coppola or Lucas and you do it with a hundred-million-dollar profit," says Corwin today. "But with that largesse I certainly wasn't going to say, 'Hey, I don't like that title at all, Boss.' "

The show went on the air in the fall, but as Christmas approached, Corwin realized he hadn't planned a seasonal program and, on the spur of the moment, concocted a title, *The Plot to Overthrow Christmas*. He then composed a whimsical, rhyming play to match the title, which earned him a favorable "buzz" around the CBS offices. (The play has been revived since then, often with stellar actors in the leading roles.) Two months later, he wrote a serious parable about Italy's bombing of civilians in Ethiopia called *They Fly Through the Air*. This time the buzz went beyond the office hallways.

"It was a powerful piece, apparently, because I found, to my astonishment, about eight days later, my picture in *Time* magazine and a column about my play. Then the *New York World-Telegram* sent a reporter over and they took my picture and on and on. . . . And it won the award for the Best Dramatic piece of the year from the Ohio Institute of Radio (this is in the days before the Peabody Award). It made a big difference in my life."

Corwin wrote prose that read like poetry—heightened language, if you will. No wonder actors like Fredric March and Charles Laughton were happy to participate in Corwin's productions along with such radio stalwarts as Everett Sloane and Ray Collins. March starred in one of the author's most daring and impassioned broadcasts, *Untitled*. Picture yourself listening to the radio in April of 1944, in the midst of daily news bulletins about Americans—loved ones—mired in combat thousands of miles overseas. At the movies, you might have seen *The Sullivans*, a sincere, tear-stained Hollywood tribute to the all-American family whose five sons died together at sea. In wartime movies, there were only good guys (Us) and bad guys (Them), and not much room for questioning of motives on either side.

Imagine, then, tuning in to CBS and hearing Fredric March say, with matter-of-fact solemnity, "With, uh, reference to Hank Peters, he is dead. That much is certain." The play goes on to explore the life of this young American who has died in combat, through the words of his family, his friends, his fellow soldiers, the doctor who brought him into the world, even the German soldier who killed him. Along the way, their thoughts are held in counterpoint to the observations of the narrator, who holds the world at large accountable for the war which has taken Hank's life.

After his fiancée speaks of him, and the memories she cherishes, the narrator says, "In your picture album, have you not left out the gallery of senators who voted down the League of Nations? . . . Tonight, your arms lie empty of your lover because it was assumed in local legislative circles after one such war as this the world was none of our concern. The empty pillow beside your own is stained with oil we sold the enemy."

Corwin with actress Irene Tedrow. As both writer and director, Corwin had a close relationship with many of his actors.

A local newspaper editor then rails against young Hank for a letter he sent, accusing the paper of taking an anti-war and Fascist stance, just because its editorials opposed "the excesses of labor, and warned the public not to encourage racial equality . . . It was typical of letters we received from numerous victims of propaganda, and so naturally we didn't print it."

The narrator defends Hank's earnest beliefs, and concludes, "On the day he died, reconnaissance had told them that the foe lay straight ahead, but Pete knew very well, some of the enemy was back at home, publishing . . . daily and Sunday."

At the end of the half-hour, we learn that the narrator is Hank Peters himself, and that his surviving thoughts are focused on the point and purpose of his death. "I am dead from the mistakes of old men, and I lie fermenting in the earth," he says, warning that he will be listening to the ceremonial pronouncements that will surely follow this war. But idle words will not satisfy him: only justice, justice for the little man and the oppressed. "I shall wait and I shall wait in a long and long suspense for the password that the Peace is setting solidly," he says. "On that day, will you please let my mother know why it had to happen to her boy?"

This was what Corwin was capable of, a level of drama—personal, politicized, doggedly American—that few, if any, radio writers could equal. Network officials couldn't censor Corwin's words because the first time they heard them was when they were broadcast over the airwaves. Rarely has such trust been placed in a creative individual. (Not that Corwin wasn't also a good showman, as he proved when he occasionally directed other people's scripts, or when he decided to open some of his shows with dialogue before the "main title" was announced—an innovative scheme that served as an effective audience-grabber.)

It was Corwin's CBS benefactor, Bill Lewis, who proposed that he write a show to commemorate the 150th anniversary of the Bill of Rights, to be broadcast on December 15, 1941. Neither of them could have known then that a week before air date the country would be plunged into war. When the show, titled *We Hold These Truths*, did air—with an all-star cast led by Orson Welles and James Stewart, and a closing speech by President Roosevelt—it was heard on all four networks and reached what was arguably the largest radio audience in the history of the medium.

Like all of Corwin's best work, it was built on a foundation of genuine curiosity and the quest for knowledge—about the nature of the Bill of Rights, how it came about, and how it affected people. Corwin was never one to take the easy or obvious road, nor was he given to cheap sentiment. He celebrated what was best about America by showing its flaws as well as its strengths, by refusing to duck issues and controversies that had always surrounded the amendments to the Constitution.

But this unprecedented broadcast was just a warm-up for the writer-director's greatest achievement: a program designed to celebrate V-E Day that would air on May 8, 1945, with the title *On a Note of Triumph*. If Orson Welles' *War of the Worlds* was the most notorious radio broadcast of all time, this was surely the most celebrated. And again, it was pure Corwin.

At a moment in history when anyone would have forgiven—or even expected—bombastic, jingoistic hosannahs to victory and promises of a bright future, Corwin went in another direction entirely. He opened his show with cheers—"Take a bow, G.I.; take a bow, Little Guy"—and revelry (a pseudo folk song, "Round and round Hitler's grave, round and round we go . . .")—but then he paused, and asked Americans to think. To reflect. To ask themselves a handful of crucial questions: Whom did we beat? How much did it cost to beat him? What have we learned? What do we do now? And is it all going to happen again? In answering these questions, he hoped to acknowledge and confront Americans' collective fears, as well as their hopes for the future.

In this unique and extraordinary program, Corwin not only spoke to the nation; he spoke *for* the nation. There was nothing highfalutin about his script, nor did it talk down to any "common denominator" in the audience; it spoke to the listener with clarity and eloquence. (The man doing much of the speaking was narrator Martin Gabel, who gave a superb reading of the script.)

The show was a tremendous success, on every level. Says Corwin, "I got letters that were more beautifully written than the program. One man wrote that it left him so charged that he couldn't sleep. He was a pianist, and he had to come downstairs and resolve something on the piano. A woman wrote saying she was not in a mood to rejoice, even though it was a happy moment for the country; she had lost her brother. I think there was that element of, 'I didn't expect THIS so soon.' Instead of a news broadcast [they got] a rounded, poetical, political, historical work. It operated on many levels, but the thing about it is that none of this was calculated. You write it the best you know how; you write it from your gut and from your head, and if it turns out that it satisfies those needs and enacts those roles, fine. You can't rely on it and you can't schedule it. It's unpremeditated, and it's spontaneous, really."

The show was repeated in a second live broadcast days later, and that version was also released as a 78 rpm record album. A copy of the script was published by Simon and Schuster and headed to the top of the best-seller list. No less a personage than Carl Sandburg called it "one of the all-time great American poems."

Another of the medium's great individualists, Arch Oboler, later said, "There was only one writer in all the history of radio that I considered a fine writer. That was Norman Corwin, and he was a poet. I was a melodramatist, he was a poet."

Arch Oboler, unlike Corwin, started out to be a playwright. With his sights set on a life in the theater, he entered the world of radio in the hope of making a living. "I spent a great deal of my time seated on the area that one sits on at NBC in Chicago, trying to get the vice president in charge to read my plays. I remember very well what I was told, that radio was not ready for ideas; it was pure entertainment, and if I would write something funny they would read it. That was my first experience.

"When they told me how much I was going to be paid, I lost some of my enthusiasm, because I was to be paid $75 for the hour and it had taken me three months to write that play. And there was no such thing as ownership in those days; when you sold it to the network, it belonged to them." This was in the 1930s.

"I was terribly hungry and I discovered that if I managed to finagle a part in a play I would earn $21 more, so I talked my way into having a line or two." Thus an auspicious career began on a humble note.

Then an opportunity presented itself. "A man named Bill [Willis] Cooper had been doing a midnight program called *Lights Out*—horror stories. He wore out quickly because you have to be slightly insane to write the kind of plays that Bill Cooper felt was good radio,* and which I quickly discovered was the only radio I wanted to ever write . . . and that was the intimate, in-the-mind sort of radio. I realized quickly that people in charge of radio didn't listen after 11:00, and I realized further that it would be fun to experiment. So I took the job and had a lot of fun. I learned to write for a medium which, up to that time, dramatically, at least, had been badly bastardized as a combination of the theater and motion pictures. I [also] quickly discovered that in order to protect myself I had to be the writer and had to be the director. There's no middle ground."

Lights Out has sometimes been described as a horror show, which is not quite right. As Oboler put it, "I didn't write about little men arriving from another planet, monsters with dripping talons and grotesque faces from the special effects department walking down streets and looking for prey. I wrote about the terror we each have in us. The woman who let us down, the man who left us, the boss we

---

* When Willis Cooper returned to radio in 1947 after a spell in Hollywood, he created another eerily effective series called *Quiet, Please*, which produced at least one genuine classic of terror, "The Thing on the Fourble Board," and another imaginative episode, "Bring Me to Life," which was based on a radio contributor's battle with writer's block.

hated, the opportunity that we missed, all the terrors, the monsters within each of us. That's what I wrote about. And those things don't change."

Oboler's best shows cut through the air like a knife. "My very first broadcast on *Lights Out* caused too much feedback. I had decided that I was going to use a stream of consciousness technique, and I wrote a play called 'Burial Services.' It was a simple play. A sixteen-year-old girl was being buried; she had died suddenly, and around her grave stands the family. The open grave. Just before the final moment of the clods being thrown on in, I go to the mind of the father, the mother, the sister, the brother, the boy who thought he was madly in love with her, and so on. The point of my story was that I was showing—in a sort of *Rashomon* manner, and this was long before *Rashomon*, come to think of it—the disparity of what people thought, what they said openly and what they were really thinking. And then I went to the grave, and the girl was not dead; she couldn't open her eyes, she could hear, but she couldn't speak. And the play ends with the clods falling in the grave.

"That broadcast taught me two things: the tremendous impact of radio—because of its intimacy, an impact far greater than any other medium we've ever had and ever will have—and the responsibility of the people doing radio. I had forgotten that in that tremendous audience there were many people who buried their children. I remember one letter in particular; over all these years I remember it. It was written on a ragged piece of paper, a woman's handwriting. It said 'I buried my sixteen-year-old last week. Remember that, Arch Oboler.

Arch Oboler, director, protecting the work of Arch Oboler, writer, by guiding it onto the air.

Don't forget.' I've never forgotten; it stayed with me all the years.

"I could frighten an audience without tearing into the consciousness of a woman, the memories of a woman who has buried her child. I could have made, for example, that child so special a child that it couldn't possibly have reawakened the memory to anyone of their children. That is such a simple thing for a playwright to do. But to make it Every Child in that grave, that's wrong. That's wrong."

Like Corwin, Oboler found tremendous freedom within his arena. "I had no censorship. I did a play about abortion, but I did [it] by indirection, so I had no problem. I never had anybody say to me, 'You cannot write this,' because I always approached the subject obliquely. I did a play called 'Profits Unlimited' in which I point the finger at the profit system. Now, to do that back then was like calling your mother bad names in public. As long as I left the sponsors alone, that was it."

Giants like Oboler and Corwin were given enormous respect in their day. Their plays were anthologized and published, made available in playscript form, and widely praised and discussed. They stood out from the crowd, and deserved to. But, with certain exceptions, they did not command the audience that some of their more commercial-minded colleagues did.

Writer True Boardman, whose bread-and-butter job was writing scripts for the Hollywood anthology series *Silver Theatre*, addressed the disparity between the two breeds of writers in a 1945 essay: "There is—and who of us shall deny it?—a faint, and not always that, aura of disgrace about being a radio writer who consistently and determinedly writes for those anomalous creatures known as sponsors. It's seldom anything spoken. But the radio-workshop boys have that look in their eyes when they meet us that seems to say, 'For money! You should be ashamed. There are words for that sort of thing.' And so there are.

"More or less seriously, the simple fact is that if you really intend to write commercially for radio, you must accept, as a prerequisite, the necessity to compromise ... You write—when you write radio for the long green stuff—in a prison. The thickness of the walls and the strength of the bars vary with different sponsors, but four walls are always there. This theme is taboo; that narrative device is against policy; you can't deal with such-and-such a type of character."

Jerome Lawrence once wrote a series for CBS in Los Angeles called *Portraits of Life*, which was sponsored by the celebrated cemetery Forest Lawn. Lawrence recalls, "Their commercial—which made us throw up in the control room—was always a little girl saying, 'My grandma lives in Forest Lawn.' And then Art Baker, with this syrupy voice, would say, 'Yes, your loved ones will live forever at Forest Lawn.'" In keeping with that thought, in spite of the fact that the shows were all biographical pieces, no one was allowed to die—not even Abraham Lincoln! What's more, Lawrence was given a list of words he could not use, among them "stiff," "cold," and, of course, "dead."

The Whistler, sponsored by Signal Oil, didn't think automobile accidents were good for business, so car crashes were banned from all scripts on that series.

And, long before comedian George Carlin developed his "seven words you can't say on television" routine in the 1970s, there were other words—none of them blasphemous, most of them relating to bodily functions—which were considered verboten on 1930s radio, according to an article in the January 1935 issue of *Radio Stars*. Among them: *belly, diarrhea, pimples, pregnancy, belching, phlegm, blood, pus, colon, vomit,* and *eruptions*. (*Eruptions?*)

Networks and ad agencies were sensitive about discussing censorship at that time; many of them denied that it even existed, beyond a kind of self-censorship based on good taste and public acceptance. (The general manager of New York's WOR claimed there were only three words that were taboo on his station: *hell, damn,* and *nigger.*) That, of course, was nonsense. Scripts were "sanitized" on a regular basis, to such a degree that writers Jerome Lawrence and Robert E. Lee finally vented some of their anger at NBC censor Wendell Williams by writing a scene where a ship called S.S. *Wendell Williams* was torpedoed!

⌒

"Radio writing is the literature of today," says a pompous soap-opera producer in Joseph L. Mankiewicz's movie *A Letter to Three Wives*, "The literature of the masses."

"Then heaven help the masses!" replies Kirk Douglas, as an English professor. "The purpose of radio writing, so far as I can see, is to prove to the masses that a deodorant can bring happiness, a mouthwash guarantee success, and a laxative attract romance."

Indeed, anyone looking to attack radio during the 1930s and '40s wouldn't have to look far. There *was* a lot of bilge, especially during the daylight hours. Consider the opening summary of a 1939 episode of *Pretty Kitty Kelly*:

"Michael Conway, Kitty's former sweetheart, now her lawyer, is working with might and main to prove Kitty innocent of the murder of Mademoiselle Dupain. It is Michael's theory that the two foreign agents, Colonel Orisini and Aristide Leon, are the real culprits, that the murder was only another of their schemes to prevent ratification of the treaty between the United States and the Argentine, which Kitty's fiancé brought to America. Meanwhile, the success or failure of Kitty's defense seems to hinge on the gun with which Mlle. Dupain was shot. The police have traced it to a gangster, Fred Lutman, but through Lutman's sweetheart Irene Egan, Kitty and Michael have learned that Lutman sold the gun through a Sixth Avenue pawnbroker named Henry Glicker. Exactly what use Michael will make of the information is yet to be learned."

Whew!

Still, the better radio writers did more than merely fill up time between commercials. They created vivid word-pictures for millions of listeners, and even managed to say something worthwhile now and then.

On January 24, 1945, a *Variety* story was headlined, " 'Mr. D.A.'s B.O. Smash Proves That Right Treatment Will Sell 'Realism.' " The story: " 'Social Significance' and 'propaganda,' instead of being the commercial poison often represented in the past, are responsible for one of the great program success stories of recent years. This is the interpretation many in the trade are placing on the recent attainment of the number four niche in the Hooper popularity survey by the Jerry Devine-managed 'Mr. District Attorney' on NBC.* This show is now almost exclusively a reflection of current events, controversy and ideological matters.

"Those who have long contended that broadcasters and advertisers were seeing hobgoblins in closets that held none are pointing to 'D.A.' in proof that all the industry palaver about not 'shocking' listeners with realism, not upsetting them with ideas, etc., is sheer misreading of the evidence.

"The point made by trade observers is that Devine has built up the know-how for handling hot subjects and has turned so-called 'dangerous themes' into big audience, big rating, big payoff for Bristol-Myers, his sponsor."

⌒

There was no rule that said commercial writing couldn't be good. Nor was there a tenet that good, commercial writing couldn't be done fast. E. Jack Neuman and his partner, John Michael Hayes, had their routine down to a science, when their careers were humming in 1940s Hollywood. "We lived in the same building," he recalls, "and the way we'd work was meet every morning at ten o'clock for coffee, and we would plot whatever we were gonna write that day.

*Devine carried on a tradition that had been established by the show's original producer, Ed Byron, and chief writer, Robert Shaw.

Then we would flip a coin to see who took the first act, who took the last act. And we would set it very carefully. Then we would meet again at 5:30 or 6:00 for a drink; I'd read his, he'd read mine, we'd correct, then we'd call in the secretary, who happened to be his girlfriend—and eventually became his wife. She typed it up, and we'd go out and get drunk and eat, or he would cook.

"We'd do four or five a week, and take on all comers. We had a card printed once that said, NEUMAN AND HAYES: WHOLESALE AND RETAIL WRITING. MYS-TERIES, WESTERNS, ADVENTURES. FAST BUT GOOD.

"We were always in there on rehearsals and everything else. We serviced the scripts; we always promised that, too. We'd go to CBS and sit in on the first reading and right after that, the director would say to the cast, 'Everybody take five, unless anybody's got anything to say.' Somebody would add this, that or the other thing, then John and I would go in the booth and he'd say, 'I think we're about two and a half minutes over; have you marked anything?' And we'd both marked possible cuts, and some changes. You'd always find words somewhere that are awkward to some people. Then we'd wait until they got with the sound and music for the dress rehearsal, and see if they were on time. In the meantime, we'd be upstairs discussing another show with somebody else, and getting our next day's work straight and ready.

"It was probably the greatest learning ground I could ever get into. I didn't really know beans about structure or writing until I was forced into it every week. And it was hard labor, but it taught me the discipline of writing; other guys have said the same thing."

It also paid very well. Said Neuman, "I found I couldn't really afford to do pictures because I was getting so good at radio I could write one a day, and they were paying me anywhere from $500 to $600 a script, to $750, maybe $1,000 a script. I could make $4,000 or $5,000 a week in radio and [in] the movies, I was lucky to get $500 a week on a term contract.

"One time [producer-director] Bill Spier came to us and said he had a won-derful idea. They were all going to take a three-month vacation in Europe. So they wanted to know if we could write thirteen episodes ahead of time, and we did. We made the deadline. Then they all left, and we were stuck for the money." John Michael Hayes bummed an airplane ride to New York to get their money by confronting the co-owner of the producing company at his son's college graduation!

Still, it's understandable why some radio writers were sought after by the stu-dios. John Michael Hayes went on to write the memorable screenplays for Alfred Hitchcock's *Rear Window* and *To Catch a Thief.* George Wells was signed by

MGM after a nine-year stint on *Lux Radio Theatre*, where he adapted the works of authors as diverse as James Hilton and Ernest Hemingway. He remained with MGM as writer (and later producer) for more than a decade, and wrote (or cowrote) such films as *Angels in the Outfield* and *Designing Woman*, which won him an Oscar.

Some writers worked in radio simply because it was there. For budding playwrights, from Arthur Miller (who wrote for *Cavalcade of America*) to Paddy Chayefsky (who sold scripts to *Theatre Guild of the Air* in the early 1950s), radio helped pay the rent while they were trying to establish themselves. Miller wrote in his autobiography, *Timebends*, "It was an easy dollar and allowed me to continue working at plays and stories and took less time than teaching or some other job."

Cavalcade's producer-director Homer Fickett looked upon Miller as "his utility man, whom he could phone in an emergency for a half-hour script to be conceived and finished in a day. Two or three times a year he would find himself rehearsing a script too substandard to be broadcast on *Cavalcade*, radio's class act, but these alarming revelations often came to him only two or three days before the broadcast date. There would then be a desperate phone call, and on my agreeing to pitch in he would messenger a book about some incident in American history, and I would read it by Wednesday evening, cook up a half-hour script on Thursday, and get it to him on Madison Avenue by Friday morning . . . For this I received five hundred dollars, a good solid piece of money at a time when my used Nash-Lafayette had cost me two fifty and my Grace Court house came to twenty-eight thousand." Miller's most impassioned play was a portrait of Mexican leader Juarez that paralleled his life and career to Abraham Lincoln; it was brought to life on *Cavalcade* by no less than Orson Welles.

Former movie actor Blake Edwards had written a pair of low-budget Westerns, but got his first real opportunity to write scripts on a regular basis on such late 1940s/early 1950s radio shows as *The Lineup*, *Yours Truly, Johnny Dollar*, *Suspense*, and especially *Richard Diamond*, whose star, Dick Powell, took a liking to him and enabled him to direct his first filmed television shows. (Powell also liked Edwards' penchant for inside jokes. On the *Richard Diamond* episode from July 23, 1949, the detective read aloud the names on some apartment building mailboxes, including Lillian McEdwards, Blake's mother, and Mrs. Mike, the title of Powell's next movie.)

Lifelong radio fanatic Ray Bradbury worked up the courage to send one of his early short stories, published in *Weird Tales*, to William Spier at *Suspense*. The suave producer-director invited young Bradbury to his office, then asked him to his house. "I'd sit there with him and [his wife] Kay Thompson and we'd talk about stories, and finally they began to broadcast them. It was glorious, because those were dream times; I'd have cocktails with Orson Welles and Ava Gardner—they were going together at the time—and Agnes Moorehead. So it was the first time I really felt accepted around Hollywood."

Adapting to the medium of radio was no effort for Bradbury whatsoever, because "I grew up on radio and it was in my blood." In fact, the teenaged Bradbury used to haunt the Hollywood radio studios in the

A fourteen-year-old Ray Bradbury poses with George Burns in 1935. Says Bradbury, "He was incredibly kind to me, read my dreadful Burns and Allen scripts, said they were great, said I was a born writer."

1930s, coaxing his way into broadcasts on a regular basis. "When I was fourteen, in the summer of 1934, I saw George Burns out in front of the Figueroa Street Playhouse, which is now the Variety Arts Club, and I asked George if he'd take me into the broadcast with a friend of mine. He said yes, and the curtain went up and Burns and Allen did their radio show for the two of us. They started using audiences six or seven weeks later. I began to write scripts for George and Gracie, and every Wednesday night, I'd turn in a new script to them. I would type them in the typing class at Berendo Junior School behind my teacher's back, so she wouldn't know what I was doing. And of course they were lousy, but George pretended they were okay. He was very kind. They actually used one of my routines, I think it was February of 1935.

"About 1982, I went to an awards ceremony at the Cocoanut Grove to give an award to Steven Spielberg and in the middle of the awards, I looked over in the corner and here's George Burns; I haven't seen him in thirty years, forty years or so. And I told the story, and when it was all over, George rushed over to me and said, 'Was that you? Was that you? I remember you!' "

The doors weren't open quite as wide to other, less ambitious newcomers, but neither were they shut tight. One program, the long-running *Dr. Christian* series, actually solicited scripts from its listeners and put them on the air. Actress Lurene Tuttle remembered, "The real writers on the show had to fix them quite often a lot, because they were really quite amateurish. But they had nice thoughts, they had nice plots. They just needed fixing; the dialogue didn't work too well." (One fledgling professional who freelanced for *Dr. Christian* was Rod Serling.)

There were other amateurs within the radio industry itself. Actors, sound effects men, and others with a creative bent found producers and directors perfectly amenable to looking at their writing efforts, and putting them on the air. Busy actor Vic Perrin wrote a wonderful *Gunsmoke* script—with a good part for himself, naturally. That same show aired episodes written by its soundmen Ray Kemper and Tom Hanley and even its star, William Conrad. (Kemper had also contributed scripts to the *Count of Monte Cristo* series, on which he did sound effects.) *Gunsmoke* regulars Parley Baer and Harry Bartell collaborated on a *Suspense* episode; actors John Dehner, Sheldon Leonard, and Jerry Hausner also sold scripts to "radio's outstanding theater of thrills." The fourth episode of *The Whistler* back in 1942 was a mystery penned by ubiquitous radio actor Joseph Kearns. And after playing Johnny Dollar for a while, Bob Bailey thought he could try his hand at a script; director Jack Johnstone liked it and put it on the air.

CBS sound-effects man Ross Murray, who moonlighted as a scriptwriter in the 1950s.

Soundman Ross Murray, who worked at CBS in Hollywood, had been a pilot in the Air Force during World War Two. One day he hatched a story idea involving airplanes and pitched it to a woman who was writing supervisor on *The*

Whistler. She said she'd be willing to read it if he wrote it up; he did, and some weeks later she bought it. His first sale netted him $250, at a time when he was making $65 a week doing sound effects.

"A couple of months later, I decided to try it again. I always felt anybody can write one script. I think everybody has one script in them; it's the second one that's the toughest." So he set his sights on *Suspense*, since it paid twice as much as *The Whistler*.

One day he went to see the show's producer-director, Elliott Lewis, and asked, "How come you've never bought a script from a soundman?" Lewis replied, "Well, I guess if I got one . . ." Murray asked if he would think of it as a script by a writer, or a script by a soundman, "because the poor benighted soundman has to write a script twice as good as the average writer to get it bought." "No," Lewis replied, "I'd give it an honest shot."

At that, Murray pulled the script out of his inside pocket. Lewis called him the next day and said, "Come sign a contract." The next time he pitched an idea to Lewis on the phone, the producer asked how soon he could have it. "Tomorrow," said Murray.

"Don't you ever do that to me again," Lewis scolded. "Don't you ever tell me you can bring me a script in one day, because some directors will say it's got to be a piece of shit if you can write it in one day."

Nevertheless, that's exactly how Murray worked—although he learned not to admit it to his employers. "I used to write 'em in one day. I'd come home from work and it was sandwiches and my typewriter. I'd write all night, when the house was quiet and the kids were asleep. I had already plotted the damn thing for a week or two, driving to and from work. So I knew where I was going, and dialogue came relatively easily."

Murray eventually wrote some fifty scripts for CBS during the 1950s, while continuing his regular work as soundman; he even did sound effects for some of his own scripts, though not the first one, because, he says, he was too nervous.

⟜

Significantly, three of radio's greatest writers—Corwin, Oboler, Morse—consistently directed their own work. They seemed to know (or if they didn't, they learned) that seeing their scripts through production onto the air was the only way to complete this form of expression with total satisfaction.

It is worth noting, then, that some of the medium's best directors also wrote.

William N. Robson, one of the finest director-producers in radio history, also wrote many excellent scripts—from the landmark "An Open Letter on Race Hatred," an eloquent and dramatic response to Detroit's terrifying race riots of 1943, to the playful "An Interview with Shakespeare" for *CBS Workshop* in 1956. Irving Reis, Robson's contemporary and compatriot, was another director who also wrote top-notch radio plays. And Elliott Lewis, who wore every hat imaginable—actor, producer, and director—also penned a good number of scripts for series he supervised, including *Suspense*.

Writer-director William N. Robson *(left)* goes over a script for *Hawk Larrabee* with Elliott Lewis and Barton Yarborough. Lewis, like Robson, functioned as both writer and director at times, but also enjoyed a thriving career as a top radio actor.

As network radio headed into its final decade, the caliber of writing not only got sharper, and bolder, but in many ways more adult. Some of this is attributable to the fact that the big guns—sponsors, ad agencies, and the networks themselves—were more concerned with television, and left radio to its own devices. The medium also seemed to draw on the same inspiration as movies of that era; as Westerns grew more mature in the postwar years, so did radio "oaters." *Gunsmoke* debuted on the air the same year that *High Noon* was released in theaters. Science fiction was as popular on radio as it was on screen; in fact, it can be argued that shows like *X Minus One* and *Dimension X*, which adapted the stories of leading writers like Ray Bradbury and Robert Heinlein, provided more consistently intelligent science fiction than Hollywood movies did.

And as private eyes grew increasingly hard-boiled in movies, so it was on the air (although there was never a gumshoe as insouciant as Howard Duff's Sam Spade on film, more's the pity).

Paul Dudley and Gil Doud wrote the pilot script for *Yours Truly, Johnny Dollar* in 1948 and offered as much snappy, "hard-boiled" dialogue as one might find in a handful of movies: "That kid's liquor sure can hold him . . . Everything about her kept flagging down my train of thought . . . Just the right amount of size 12 in a dress that looked like a well-tailored fig leaf ... When she was through looking you over you felt like the Sunday supplement."

Even contemporary issues and concerns found their way into radio scripts from time to time. *Gunsmoke* dealt with a formidable array of human concerns during its nine-year run. William N. Robson contributed an effective anti-racist script, titled "Never the Twain," to the short-lived Western series *Fort Laramie* in 1956. Top writers like Gil Doud and Bob Tallman, Morton Fine and David Friedkin, Antony Ellis, and Les Crutchfield were amazingly prolific and remarkably consistent in the quality of their scripts.

But good writing couldn't keep radio alive against the tremendous competition of television, and so a dramatic medium that had achieved a kind of perfection was allowed to die. Some writers easily found work writing TV scripts; others never achieved the same success in other forms that they had enjoyed on radio. All of them missed the fun, and the relative freedom, that radio offered. (E. Jack Neuman, already busy in television, agreed to write scripts for *Yours Truly, Johnny Dollar*, under a pseudonym, because he enjoyed doing it.)

It was, for all involved, a special time, and for creative writers, a wonderful outlet. And if recognition was sporadic, there were moments that made it all worthwhile. Frank Sinatra took a special liking to Jerome Lawrence and Robert E. Lee when they wrote his *Songs by Sinatra* series in 1947, and as part of his studio-audience warm-up, he'd insist they leave the control room to take a bow, saying, "I want you to meet the guys who made this show good."

3

Directors

To the vast listening audience, the most prominent director in radio was undoubtedly Cecil B. DeMille. This stentorian-voiced theater veteran and movie kingpin introduced the *Lux Radio Theatre* every week for nine years, from "Holly-wood." Officially introduced as "your producer," there could have been little doubt in listeners' minds that he masterminded every show.

In truth, DeMille was merely an actor on *Lux*. No one played the part of moviemaker-cum-rajah quite so well (including his successors on the series, William Keighley and Irving Cummings), but the fact remains that DeMille never directed a line of that show; he didn't even attend rehearsals. The real director, who slaved an entire week to put the prestigious production on the air, was never credited. During the show's long Hollywood run, it was in fact directed by Frank Woodruff, Sandy Barnett, Fred MacKaye, and Earl Ebi.

In contrast, the live studio production of *Philip Morris Playhouse* was directed in New York by Charles Martin, who behaved like a Hollywood version of a Director with a capital D. Announcer Ken Roberts recalls, "Charlie gloated in being in the studio where everybody could see him, including the audience, and he would go mad, crazy, directing actors as if he were a symphony conductor." Radio may not have produced an equivalent to movies' DeMille, but it did breed a number of talented, often innovative directors who came to know their medium and its capabilities at least as well as DeMille knew his.

One of the first "star" directors in radio—a man whose name was attached to his shows, creating a public awareness rare for any director—was Phillips H. Lord. An actor and born entrepreneur, he gained fame in the role of Seth Parker, the elderly, cracker-barrel philosopher on a show that attracted a huge weekend audience beginning in 1929. No one could have predicted that the man who played this hymn-singing New Englander would branch out into blood-and-thunder crime drama, but

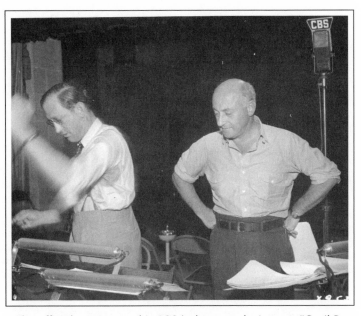

The official caption on this 1936 photo reads, in part, "Cecil B. DeMille, director of the CBS Lux Radio Theatre, at work developing a musical background for one of his famous radio plays . . . with the musical director, Louis Silvers." In truth, the first time DeMille heard Silvers' music was when it was played on the air, but no one played the *role* of director better than DeMille.

that's exactly what happened when Lord sold NBC his idea for *G-Men* in 1935. The program evolved into the more fully developed *Gang Busters* the following year on CBS, a true-crime saga loosely based on actual FBI cases, and broadcast with the blessing of Bureau director J. Edgar Hoover. Lord emphasized his involvement with the series by acting as its host during the first few seasons, interviewing a local law enforcement official (played by an actor) to lead into each week's story.

Lord's approach to the material was hard-hitting, and his approach to radio drama unsubtle. He grabbed the radio listener with *Gang Busters'* powerful opening sequence, mixing police sirens, machine guns, and various sounds of mayhem and activity. In its heyday, the show was said to have employed the largest "army" of sound effects men—and equipment and turntables—in radio, all under Lord's watchful eye . . . and ear.

Lord eased from the director's post to the producer's after several years, and relinquished his role as host to Col. H. Norman Schwarzkopf (father of the latter-day military hero and a celebrated figure in his own right as the head of the New

Jersey State Police, who played a major role in the Lindbergh kidnaping case). He went on to launch other programs (notably *Mr. District Attorney*) and follow other pursuits. At one point, when he was living comfortably on an island off the coast of Maine, he arranged to have a transcription disc of each week's *Gang Busters* rehearsal sent to him to critique before the program aired a few days later. He may not have been an active, hands-on director after a certain point on any of his shows, but he left his mark on them just the same.

"The great wonder of radio," said writer-director Arch Oboler, "was that . . . the good director had the opportunity of holding all the strings of the puppets in his hand, for that short period of time when [a show] was on the air. To rehearse the actors properly, and the music, to interweave those with the sound effects people, so that at the given moment it would happen—and happen right—that was a great excitement."

In fact, radio directors often had more control, and more freedom, than movie directors. They had more responsibility than many stage directors, since they frequently functioned as their own producer and casting director. And they had to do what film or theater directors did—create a *show*, from scratch—in a fraction of the time. But, unlike directors in any medium since silent film, they were able to direct their actors *while the show was being performed*, using an elaborate series of hand gestures. (During final rehearsals, the director communicated with the actors, sound effects men, and musicians from his glassed-in control booth over a P.A. system by pressing the "talk-back" button.)

What really set radio directors apart from their colleagues in other media was a unique challenge: to conceptualize their programs for listeners—not viewers.

One of the best, Fletcher Markle, explained, "You simply have to be aware that it's for your audience's ear only—that's all you have to go on—and make a clarity coming into the ear that you can 'see.' I think the next thing a radio director has to think about is tempo, and not to let any kind of accidental monotony occur. Whereas in any visual medium there are all kinds of things you can do to accentuate or illustrate or divert, you cannot do [that on radio] because you're only coming into the ear."

Or, as the prolific Himan Brown puts it, "I've got to make you believe that what you're hearing is *real*. And dammit, we did."

⤳

Some "prestige" directors enjoyed the luxury of directing one show a week. But a typical staff director was busy from morning till night, as he juggled a variety of chores for a number of different shows—including preparation of scripts, auditioning and casting actors, presiding over rehearsals and dress rehearsals, and putting shows on the air.

Jack Johnstone looked back on the 1930s and 40s and remarked, "Those were busy days. I left the house right after breakfast, got home between midnight and 1:00." Hi Brown recalls, "I used to do four or five shows a day. I got up in the morning and did *David Harum*, then I did *John's Other Wife*, then *Dick Tracy* and *Terry and the Pirates*; at the same time I was doing [such nighttime shows as] *Bulldog Drummond* and *Grand Central Station*. I always had a Sunday show; Sunday was a great day for drama."

Said writer-director Carlton E. Morse, "I was just thinking of what a loose life we were living. Getting up at four o'clock in the morning, writing until 6:30 or 7:00, going out and getting the coffee, coming back and casting shows and taking care of all the business end of things. Then going down into rehearsal . . . The first rehearsal was for cutting and that was pretty good—it hit pretty close and the second rehearsal we got down to words and phrases and then we usually had to break. Then one final rehearsal just touching the highlights before we went on the air. It got so [on] *One Man's Family*, especially after twenty years, people knew their characters so well and the tempo and the texture of the script so well that one run-through was about all

Anton M. (Tony) Leader directs Gene Kelly and Ethel Barrymore during an on-mike rehearsal for a 1948 episode of *Suspense*, "To Find Help."

that was needed, just for timing and technical difficulties. So that became easier and easier as the years went on."

Dresser Dahlstead, who worked with Morse during the Hollywood run of *I Love a Mystery*, confirms, "We rehearsed very religiously, we really did. We did it right—well, with Carlton in the booth there wasn't anything else you could do. You *had* to be right."

Familiarity was a cornerstone of radio and the way it worked. Unlike the theatrical world, or the operation of a movie studio, radio functioned 365 days a year. Maintaining a constant output—let alone some degree of quality—was largely dependent on the fact that directors worked with the same staff and the same group of actors all the time. They came to know and rely upon one another.

When an actor arrived as a newcomer with a working troupe on any given show, he had to catch on fast. Peggy Webber remembers that when she first got the chance to work with Morse, "You were so in awe, so impressed with the style of what he was already doing, you wanted to fit into that mold, so you were very sensitive to how his thinking already was. He never said very much; he would press the talk-back and clear his throat, and say what page he was concerned about, and your name, and that would be it. And then you'd sit there and say, 'Ah yes, yes, I know what you mean!' And that was about the way he directed."

Actor Howard Duff elaborated, "You didn't have much time to direct in radio; that's why casting is so important. You've got to get people for whatever part you think you need, and you've got to get them to do it right away, because you never had time to f—— around. So I don't remember a hell of a lot of direction. If someone was wrong, he would just be replaced."

Occasionally, there were other forces at work in casting. Sound effects man Terry Ross recalls with amusement that when Bill Sweets was directing *Gang Busters*, he drew on a stock company of performers every week as most directors did. "But the other prerequisite was that they had to be able to play poker, because in those days we had to do two shows, one for here [in New York] and the second show a couple hours later for the West Coast, so you had to fill in that time between, and that was always a poker game."

William Spier, one of radio's preeminent (and better-publicized) directors, confers with a receptive-looking Orson Welles, who acted on a number of Spier's *Suspense* broadcasts in the 1940s.

William Spier was one of radio's top directors; actor John McIntire, who worked with him often, felt that one of Spier's strengths was that he "was so perceptive as to the capabilities of each individual. He might say, 'Listen, John or Jeanette, why don't you try this?' And it was right. That was one good reason for having stock companies; the directors knew the capabilities [of their actors] and knew how to make you as good as you should be, or to help you. That was very important."

All of this had to be done in shorthand style. There wasn't much "direction" per se. But directors still set the style, and tone, and standard, for every show. Writers came to recognize this as well as actors, and tailored their scripts to the demands and expectations of each individual "boss." William Spier was sophisticated and intelligent, and those qualities characterized his work on *Suspense* and *The Adventures of Sam Spade*. E. Jack Neuman, one of his top writers, says, "He had a great sense of how to use humor. He'd take a script that was pretty good and when he got done with it it would have that something extra."

Jeanette Nolan (Mrs. John McIntire) says of her many directors, "Every single one of them had something, some personal expression that was magnetic. Their faces were so eloquent when you were working. If you happened to look and you would see them with you, loving it, you knew that you were doing what the script demanded . . . and woe be unto you if you could feel that there was lethargy anywhere. You were ready to go and take poison.

"Sometimes Arthur Pryor [director of *The March of Time*] would come out and say, 'I don't want to say much, kids, but the most important thing is to read *all* of the script.' Zoink! As though you were being stabbed; that was just the beginning and the end; that was all he needed to say, and everybody went into his own separate horror house and reviewed his brain and wondered what he'd been doing . . ."

"Some [directors] had more subtlety than others," observes actor and narrator Jackson Beck. "Some blended subtlety and brass like an orchestra leader knows when to bring in the brass after the fiddles, knows when to take the brass, fade it out and bring the fiddles back with the cellos or the saxophones. What makes a great musical director made a great radio director because the whole thing was music in their ears."

Beck worked for Norman Corwin, William N. Robson, and Brewster Morgan—among the best directors in the medium. He believes that they were good "because they were radio, they weren't mucked up by the theater. They weren't confused by movies. They had a vehicle that was on its own and they knew how to shape it. Robson had an unerring ear for what was right and what was wrong. These guys knew what the hell they were dealing with: they were dealing with . . . a completely distinct and different art form, like nothing else."

Indeed, few radio directors came from theatrical backgrounds. Jack Johnstone was destined to become one of the busiest directors in the business; in New York he directed such long-running shows as *Buck Rogers* and *Superman*, before moving to Hollywood and helming *Orson Welles' Almanac*, *Richard Diamond*, *Hollywood Star Theater*, *The Six Shooter*, and *Yours Truly, Johnny Dollar*. He, like so many others, became a director by chance. He was working at an advertising agency, earning $32 a week, when one of his colleagues was assigned to write the daily daytime adventure serial *Buck Rogers*. After a while, his friend asked if Jack would like to take a crack at it, and he did; before long he was sharing scriptwriting chores on a regular basis. Then one morning the show's director, Carlo D'Angelo, called to say he couldn't make it in time for rehearsal and asked if Jack would run through the show with the actors. He did, and before long D'Angelo recommended that he be promoted to the director's post full-time.

"Later," Johnstone recalled, "when Kellogg's canceled the series, a friend of mine was a salesman for CBS and I told him that I could write and direct—the whole schmear—if he could sell it. And he did. A few weeks later I started doing the whole job on it, and my take-home pay was not $32 a week but $300 a week." What's more, after Johnstone filled in for a missing announcer one day, his boss suggested he continue doing *that* job as well!

⌐

Himan Brown was a born entrepreneur who got the radio bug early on. While still in college, he negotiated for the radio rights to the hugely popular comic strip *Dick Tracy* and put that show on the air.

Flush with success, he then snagged rights to another long-running comic, *The Gumps*, for $250 a week. "Now, *The Gumps* were *All in the Family* in 1933," he explains, "a little vignette that ran every day: ten and a half minutes of Andy and Min Gump, and Chester Gump, the family. And I needed a writer. So I was at Brooklyn College and I turned to the guy in my English class, who did very well; he wrote good short stories and he got an A, and he was on the football team. I said, 'You're going to write good Gumps for me, aren't you?' He didn't know what I was talking about, but we worked together because I didn't know what I was talking about either; his name was Irwin Shaw." Another early "discovery" of Brown's was future Broadway composer-lyricist Frank Loesser.

Hiring and working with writers was a major part of a director's job. Says

Brown, "People could get to me, but the stuff that came in over the transom was never very good. Occasionally I picked up a writer because he had credits from Chicago, or from the Coast, [or] he came to New York and was doing a play. Otherwise, you cultivated your own writers, and you developed them, and they got to know what pleased me. I'd get an outline from my author which on three, four, five pages says what we're going to do; I'd talk it over with the author, then he goes and embellishes the outline and gives me a little longer outline, then he writes the script."

Brown continued to function as his own producer for years to come, and he gained a reputation for being unusually economical. He boasts, "I did *Grand Central Station*, and I did the entire show—five actors, six actors, music, sound effects, announcer, the works—with me as producer, or whatever you want to call it—for $750." (As a point of comparison, *Lux Radio Theatre* at the same time was costing upwards of $20,000 per hour-long episode.)

One of his coups was putting *The Thin Man* on the air in 1941, which came about by a series of happy accidents. "MGM really screwed itself," he recounts. "Somehow they bought all the rights to Dashiell Hammett's *The Thin Man* except the radio rights! 'Cause in the middle 1930s, their lawyers didn't think anything of radio. All of a sudden, his agent Leland Hayward woke up and said, 'Hey! We own the radio rights.' And I was searching around for a series for Woodbury Soap, and I was able to make contact with him. I paid a lot of money for *The Thin Man*; I paid $750 a week just for the rights, that was a lot." Hammett even dropped in on the broadcasts from time to time, with Lillian Hellman in tow. "Listen," says Brown, "he wouldn't let me go on the air and destroy his characters."

If all this sounds like Himan Brown was more of a producer than a director— in the conventional, accepted sense of the term—then consider his working credo: "If you've got the right words and you've got the kind of actors that I've always used, the best thing the director can do is keep his mouth shut. Sure, I had to time the shows, I had to be sure that things came in on cue."

More important, he had to have an ear; a finely tuned ear. As he says, "*Contrast* is terrifically important. You could never do four women on radio; their voices would all sound the same. The contrast has to come not only in voice and manner but it comes also in the content of what you're doing."

⌒

Content was the primary concern of William N. Robson, one of the giants of radio. Educated at Yale, he found himself working in radio in Los Angeles in the mid-1930s, piloting a popular crime show heard only on the West Coast. "I was the writer-producer of *Calling All Cars*," he told Karen Everson and Annabelle Sheehan. "I was home in my apartment writing the show for the following week, and at 2:30 in the afternoon a phone call came from the secretary of the head of the studio. Dick Wiley came on and said, 'Bill, a big story just broke: four members of the board of governors of San Quentin prison have just been kidnaped and taken by their kidnapers out of the prison, and are being followed somewhere in Marin County. Can you do a dramatization for it?' 'Well, I'll do it for this week's show on Friday. That will give me three days.' He said, 'Bill, we have an open half-hour at 5:00.' I said, 'You've got to be kidding!' He said, 'Look, could you do a dramatization? We've got actors here, there's an orchestra rehearsing, the actors that you use are rehearsing another show.' I said, 'Well, all right, if you're crazy enough to want to do it, I'll do it, or I'll try.' "

He began typing a script immediately, using his imagination—and his knowledge of the crime milieu—then went to the studio, where information was coming over the teletype machines. "I had my friend and assistant Sam Pierce standing by, and as I'd write a character I'd say, 'I want David Brand to do so-and-so,' so he's casting and getting the script as it came out of the typewriter, getting it mimeographed and distributed to the cast, and the musical director-conductor. And so it went for the next hour or so. There was about a minute to go when we heard, 'They've got 'em! They captured them.' Where? 'In Petaluma, in front of a creamery.'

William N. Robson gets ready to throw a cue from the control room. This is how actors and sound-effects men (like the one wearing headsets in the foreground) saw their director during an actual broadcast.

"I actually threw the opening cue as I walked in the door [of the studio]. When we walked out of the place, everybody was just exhausted. We walk out and I hear Dave Wiley call down the hallway, 'Hey Bill, don't let anybody go home . . . the network wants it at 8:00.' Then, leaving the building, I heard the newsboys calling 'Extra! Extra! San Quentin prison break.' I had scooped the newspapers!"

That remarkable show, and Robson's overall work on the series, became his ticket to New York. "My best friend in radio was a fellow named Irving Reis. We first got acquainted when he was the engineer on the first big entertainment/musical show to come out of Hollywood, *Hollywood Hotel*. And I was doing things on *Calling All Cars* that attracted Irving, because he had an idea about an experimental radio program that he wanted to sell to CBS. We became fast friends on that basis: experimental radio.

"He went back to New York and sold this idea to Bill Lewis, who was one of the seminal agents in radio broadcasting, the head of programming for CBS. He knew talent when he saw it and gave it the opportunity. He was responsible for the tremendous ferment that happened at CBS during the early years of experimental broadcasting, broadcasting that was done without sponsorship. We were permitted to examine problems and solve or not solve them publicly."

There was an inborn excitement in the air; it was the excitement of discovery and experimentation. The *Columbia Workshop* fostered that feeling, and it spread to other broadcasts as well. As a staff director, Robson worked on all kinds of shows, but his primary energy was directed at programs that worked at stretching radio's boundaries. "We were in the business of selling ideas, not soap," he said proudly in later years.

"We were celebrated for the fact that we had an L.T. rating. L.T. you can translate as 'less than a trace.' We never had a large audience on the *Columbia Workshop*, but we were a succès d'estime. We were an influence. And we never had a sponsor; we were never presented for sale. This was truly a laboratory for ideas."

It might seem in this case that Robson was more a writer and thinker than a director—in the accepted sense of that term—but in fact he was keenly aware of sound and its impact. When he directed Archibald MacLeish's verse play *Air Raid* for *Columbia Workshop*, "We had a situation of the German fighter bombers coming in from a great distance over a small town in northeastern Spain . . . I wanted the effect of planes [coming] before you see them, before you really hear them. There's this kind of strange sound that develops into the sound of an airplane. So I said to the sound-effects man, 'I want this effect of these planes coming in to start under sixteen cycles per second.' The guy looked at me and said, 'You're crazy! That's the threshold of hearing.' I said, 'Yeah, I want it to start at twelve.' He said, 'But nobody will hear it.' But by God, it started from nowhere."

Robson was a perfectionist who drove his writers and sound effects men as much as he drove himself. But it was that quest for quality that created such shows as the remarkable—and unparalleled—wartime series *The Man Behind the Gun.*

Director William N. Robson reviews a script for his extraordinary wartime series *The Man Behind the Gun,* with musical director Nathan Van Cleave and actor Frank Lovejoy.

Every week, Robson brought listeners to the front lines in a series of highly pitched stories that put a human face on the nuts-and-bolts of war. From the canine corps to the invasion of Sicily, this weekly program transmitted vivid sound portraits to the living rooms of America, and won a Peabody Award in the process. Writers included Alan Sloane, Ranald MacDougall (who went on to a successful screenwriting career), and Arthur Laurents (who became a preeminent playwright).

Jackson Beck, who narrated *The Man Behind the Gun,* calls Robson "the best director I ever worked for. The word 'bravura' was invented for Robson: rough, tough, broad, expansive, a guy who knew what the hell he wanted and knew how to get it. He had a feel and a touch for production, for character. In actors, he hired the best." Robson remained a "radio man" for the rest of his life, moving back to Los Angeles in the late 1940s, and staying with CBS well into the 1950s producing, directing, and sometimes writing such shows as *Escape, Suspense,* and the final incarnation of the *Columbia Workshop* in 1956. He spent the remainder of his working life plying his craft in a different arena, at the Voice of America.

Robson came of age at CBS at the same time as another remarkable "creature of radio," Norman Corwin. Though celebrated primarily as a writer, Corwin started at the network as a staff director, and then directed every one of his own celebrated scripts. Like most of his colleagues, he had no prior experience as a director in the theater.

"I had good advice by a friend who was working for NBC," he recalls. "He told me never to acknowledge that I didn't know what I was doing, to forget all my previous contexts at work, and realize that I was in charge, that I was the director, and that I was in a hiring position.

"I looked upon my actors and musicians and my soundmen and my engineers as collaborators, which indeed they were. And the better they were, the better I was. So my productions were happy productions. They didn't have strain, they didn't have intrigue. That was the nature of radio, too. When you're doing a play, you can get little cliques and you get some kind of intrigue going in the company against the director or against the star or against the leading lady, or the producer, or any number of combinations for trouble. You have actors who are insecure because they're not quick studies and they're down on their lines and they flop. There are all kinds of irritations. But in a radio studio, even the most complicated shows are rehearsed and on the air within twelve hours, and there wasn't time for that, nor occasion for that."

As a gentleman—and a humanist, to use a more contemporary word—Corwin treated his actors with grace and courtesy, beginning with the audition meeting. "Having been a poor kid, lower middle class, a job holder and seeker, my empathy was always with the applicant," he explains. "And so when some scared actor or actress came to see me, they were a little nervous, this was their living, I would not sit behind my desk. It was a small office and it had a desk with a couple of chairs, and I would go over to them just to equalize the space between us. I would talk to them about themselves, again, very casually. I

Norman Corwin, bringing a show to fruition from inside a control room.

Corwin *(center)* in active rehearsal with Charles Laughton, unidentified man, and musical director Bernard Herrmann. Corwin attracted the best talent on both coasts for his CBS anthologies.

didn't start, 'What have you done?' I didn't like that approach. I enjoy acting. I found out they really liked that. It disarmed them and they felt at ease."

This continued throughout the rehearsal process. "I never, never once even approached embarrassing or humiliating an actor or actress. I never lost my cool; if there was something wrong, I would take them aside. I would never, never attack the dignity of an artist when it was simply a matter of interpretation or making myself understood. If they couldn't do it, and it happened now and then where an actor just wasn't up to it, I sometimes had to relieve that actor. But I took very great pains to explain that this was my responsibility, that I had made an unfair demand on that actor, so that the ego of that actor was protected."

At the same time, Corwin the director was ever mindful of the sanctity of his script. One of his actors, Peggy Webber, recalls, "He didn't let anybody skip a comma or a breath or anything. It all had to be worked out to the utmost detail, almost to the point where you used to wonder if there'd be any spontaneity left in the performance because he worked so diligently with everyone. He got what he wanted. He was a perfectionist, and particularly with timing and sound effects, things like that. He didn't leave anything to chance."

Corwin had no independent knowledge of the technical workings of radio, but like everyone who got caught up in the creative process, he became interested in how sound could enhance the words in his scripts. "Engineers were routinely assigned to me," he recalls. "Usually they were good people, and there were one or two who were below my expectations or requirements, and again, in a way that protected their dignity, I managed to see that their schedules could be changed without them ever knowing it." He found that even engineers could be creative partners, not merely technicians. "And when they're treated that way, as equals, not as underlings, they respond. . . . They never say to you, 'Gee, I don't think that should be done,' but 'Let's see, maybe it can be, let's try it.' "

Most radio directors appreciated everyone's contributions; some showed their gratitude in more tangible ways than others. Fletcher Markle admitted that when his *Studio One* became *The Ford Theater*, and he suddenly had a lavish budget (thanks to his new sponsor, the Ford Motor Co.), "I actually spent much more time on an hour radio show than I should have, but I wanted the actors, the working actors, to get a decent check. So I did things like having a dress rehearsal the day before the broadcast. That extended the check for the actors."

Having that session recorded on acetate discs had another valuable benefit. "Particularly with guest stars who hadn't had a great deal of radio experience, it was an ear-opener for them to hear, with the orchestra, the dress rehearsal. It saved me an awful lot of explanation and cousining and taking them up tenderly when they could hear the boo-boo they had made."

The one thing Markle found it difficult to do was to direct himself and the rest of the cast at the same time. A former

Fletcher Markle discusses script changes with cast members Louis Quinn, Madeleine Carroll, and Everett Sloane for a *Studio One* broadcast, of "A Farewell to Arms," while his assistant (holding pencil and stopwatch) makes notes.

actor, he enjoyed working on-mike from time to time, but found it frustrating. Once, Walter Huston requested that he play opposite him, and Markle happily obliged. The first reading went well, but then, he recalled, "Away from the table, and up at the microphone, I realized that I couldn't get everything properly stitched together, and apologized to Walter but said, 'It won't be fair to you.' "

It was inevitably the guest stars who needed extra attention from directors.

Working radio actors received virtually no direction at all; they were hired because the directors knew they could and would deliver. William Conrad echoed the response of countless other radio veterans when he said, "I never had anyone give me a line reading in my life."

Writer-director Jerome Lawrence recalls, "It was very tough to direct directors, especially Orson. We had a technique; we would go into the studio and say, 'Orson, Friday night, when you whispered that line, we all got goosebumps in the control room.' We called that 'The way you did it Friday night' technique of directing directors."

Welles' stubbornness took many forms. Elliott Lewis recalls a time when assistant director Sterling Tracy—who was known for his punctiliousness regarding the precise timing of shows—was sent out on stage during a live audience show to get Welles to speed up his performance. "So Tracy, in front of the audience, goes over to Orson and he makes a big circle, holding his index finger out, meaning Orson should go faster, and Orson pays no attention to him. Orson just grabbed his finger and kept on going, and held him there in front of the audience, because he was gonna finish the way he was gonna finish. Let him get the time somewhere else!"

There were other show business figures who were virtually undirectable, chief among them the legendary Al Jolson. Jack Johnstone remembered an incident involving his friend and mentor, Carlo D'Angelo. "They finished a skit and Carlo punched the talk-back and said, 'Al.' And Jolson said, 'Yeah, whaddaya want?' He said, 'Al, I think if you accent the word *groom* in that last gag, it might get a bigger laugh.' Jolson said, 'Who the hell do you think you are, you little dago son of a bitch, telling Jolson how to read his lines? Look, Buster, I've been in show business too many years; I know all about it. And I've got seven million bucks to prove it. What have you got?'

" 'Friends, Al.' "

⌐

As one of the busiest—and best—radio actors in Los Angeles, Elliott Lewis had worked with all the top directors in the business. But radio acting never satisfied him, and in the early 1940s he started writing scripts.

"The director of *The Whistler* was a man named J. Donald Wilson, and he would buy scripts," Lewis recalled. "If I had an idea, I'd tell him about the idea and then I'd go home and write it. Sometimes I'd have written in a part for myself, sometimes not. My first jobs on *Suspense* were acting on that show. Then

I'd sit there with Bill Spier when the script was ten minutes long and suggest cuts and changes, because it was something I'd been doing. So then when he would get scripts that needed work, he would give me 350 bucks to rewrite a script—meaning cut it, boost it up a little bit, whatever. Then when I had a notion for a good *Suspense* story I would tell him and I was suddenly writing *Suspense*."

Spier respected Lewis's work, and even let him direct from time to time. Spier lived in Malibu, and Lewis got the impression that when the director knew he had a bad script, or a sticky situation, he would phone in sick and suggest that Elliott fill in for him. "I would be faced with something that I was supposed to direct, all cast, with an unhappy star because the script was twelve minutes long, and [composer] Lud Gluskin was already screaming on the phone, saying, 'I can't write music to this goddamn thing—you're not gonna broadcast all of it.' "

Just the same, it gave Lewis his baptism of fire as a radio director, and after World War Two, he tried to ease out of acting and onto the other side of the control-room window. On the terrific late-1940s high-adventure series *The Voyage of the Scarlet Queen* he held down both jobs simultaneously, as director and star. Then in the early 1950s he was producing and directing three shows that aired *in succession* on CBS on Sunday evenings: *Broadway's My Beat*, *On Stage* (in which he also starred with then-wife Cathy Lewis), and *Crime Classics*. "Directing and producing all three, performing in one of them and writing openings and occasional scripts for whichever. And it was marvelous," he recalled more than thirty years later. Just how did he keep track of what he was doing? "You keep it straight because you don't think about it until you pick it up. When you pick it up and look at it, then you say, 'Which one is this? Oh yeah, I remember. Okay. Now I've got a fix on this. Good.' "

Obviously, Lewis leaned on a strong assistant who would keep tabs on a script's timing, not only page by page but line by line. "He knew the first rehearsal, the first mike reading, the dress rehearsal, the first broadcast and the repeat broadcast. And he'd keep track of those so he would tell you at any time in the booth exactly where you were." When Lewis would be performing at the mike, he would keep eye contact as much as possible with his assistant, Kenny McManus. "Every time I looked up he had to give me exactly where I was, so I could adjust my performance, and I could, without changing the performance noticeably, pick up or slow down fifteen or twenty seconds on a page."

McManus also helped with a timely nudge when Lewis "lost it" one day in the midst of his three-show-a-day marathon. "I must have been very tired. I was sitting in the booth, and the engineer said, 'Go ahead, please.' And I knew it was me, and I forgot what I was supposed to do. And Kenny was sitting here and he

The caption for this CBS publicity photo referred to Elliott Lewis as "Mr. Radio," and that was as good a description as any. As actor, writer, and director, he embodied the best the medium had to offer.

nudged me and I leaned into the mike and said, 'Music, Lud.' It seemed to me that that was about three minutes; when the smoke cleared and we were off the air I said, 'I just couldn't think of that word.' Kenny said it was less than a second; it just seemed ... everything gets into slow motion."

As an actor, Lewis had railed at what he felt were inefficiencies in the production of many shows—particularly the big, prestige programs that took days to prepare. As a director and producer, he practiced economy without sacrificing quality. Here is his breakdown of how a typical half-hour show might come together:

"Let's say the cast call is 10:00 this morning, which is first reading around the table. Coffee, scripts, everybody says hello as they're marking their scripts. 'Leonard, you're going to play Arthur, Mary Jane, you're going to play so-and-so.' Kenny has his watch, and his pencil, and we go. Now, you wait for sound effects; everybody knows that. You say, 'Just a minute, who's that coming?' In my mind, I'm doing a car driving up, making the sound, door closes, starts to walk toward the house, now you'd read the next line. It's like conducting a piece of music; each time you do it, it's going to come out without deliberately going 'one, two, three.' You know how it comes out; that's a clock you have [inside]."

At the end of the first reading, "We would sit there and we'd make any obvious changes that I'd want to make. Then I'd say, 'Okay, let's put it on mike.' Now I'd go up in the booth. The sound effects people have brought up from their room all the equipment they will need for this show. They're all in there, in the corner; they put their headphones on: one earphone is the show, the other earphone is me, in the booth, on my mike. When I press the button on my mike I cut off the whole system and everybody can hear me. The actors get to the microphone; now we do it that way, with starts and stops. 'No, that's not gonna work;

let's try this.' And when we're done, 'Can we run that sound pattern? The soundman has to go get something? All right, have a cup of coffee.' And so on and so forth. It would take an hour or so, hour-and-a-half.

"By now it's well after 12:00, 12:30 let's say; break the cast and sound effects until 2:00. Get the script ready with the changes we have just made for Lud Gluskin, or Sandy Courage or whoever's doing the music on that show. He comes in at 1:00; the musicians start drifting in, they get set up, tuned up. He rehearses them on each cue, according to the corrected pages he has, and if it's a show with narratives or sequences that he has to underscore, the A.D. [assistant director] has a timing for it. So the conductor takes his clock and conducts, so he sets [the timing] in his head—because he's not working from a click track [as in movie scoring], he's working from the people. Now he's marked his script that when the car starts he should be at bar B, or when the narrator says 'What the hell do you mean?' he should be at two bars before D.

"Then the musicians break for five minutes, then everybody comes back together, ready, and you can do a rough dress rehearsal. At 3:30 or 4:00 you do your dress rehearsal; you're gonna be finished then at 4:15 or 4:30. You now have a half an hour, because 5:00 is when you go on—in the East 8:00—so you have a half an hour to tighten, to make your final changes, do all of this stuff.

" 'Everybody ready, clear your throat, go to the bathroom ...' The last thing everybody does is go through the script and make sure their pages are in order. Because the terrible thing that would always happen is that in all of this mess, somehow page 19 got where page 6 is. And then it's

```
#19   Monday, February 9, 1953                          (REVISED)


                    AUTO - LITE Presents


                        "SUSPENSE"


                         Starring

                    MR. WILLIAM POWELL

                           in

                  "The Man Who Cried Wolf"

                         CAST

        MEROS.............WILLIAM POWELL

        LILJA.............LILLIAN BUYEFF

        CARDOZAS..........JACK KRUSCHEN

        SENOR
        VOICE I...........STEVE ROBERTS

        EDITOR.............JOHN DEHNER

        PEPE...............BYRON KANE

        VOICE II
        ZAPATIN............JOE KEARNS


 Dir...........Lewis        REHEARSAL:   Studio 1
 Sec'y.........Curcio
 A.D...........McManus      cast:   10:30 - 1:30
 Eng...........Carr                  3:00 - 5:00
 Sound.........Bayz
               Murray       orch:   2:00 - 5:00
 Annor.........Wilcox
 Comm'l..                   comm'l: 3:00 - 5:00
 Narr..........Thor
 Music.....Gluskin/8        AIR:    5:00 - 5:29:30
                                    (local: 9:00 - 9:30)
```

This cover page for a 1953 *Suspense* script indicates the director's timetable for the day of broadcast, and how many people he had in his troupe, both on-mike and off.

madness. Although by that time, everybody kind of knows the show. Then at 5:00 I'm in the booth; cast is ready, music is ready, sound effects are ready. Stan, or Pat, or whoever the engineer is, looks at his big clock and his lights; he gets a signal from Max to control and he says, 'Go ahead, please.' You say, 'Music live; fade the music. Announcer, you're on.' And that excitement, it's just great."

Jack Johnstone refused to be confined to a glassed-in booth; he stood right next to his actors, as indicated here, with Bette Davis rehearsing for a 1949 episode of *Family Hour of Stars*.

Although the director was able to talk to his sound effects men and music conductor over headsets, he had to rely on pantomime to communicate with his actors while a show was on the air. A series of hand gestures came into common usage: a finger pointed at an actor indicated his cue to begin, a slash across the throat a signal to cut off, a hand drawn toward the face meant the actor should move closer to the mike, etc. (One fellow threw cues so violently that he repeatedly broke his finger on the control room glass!)

Jack Johnstone adopted a different technique. "Most directors directed from the control room," he explained. "I directed in the studio, wearing a pair of earphones with heavy muffs on them so that I couldn't hear any sounds directly. I'm thoroughly convinced it's the only way to direct a radio program, for several reasons: it gave you much better control over the whole show. If the show began to run a little slowly, a guy would stand in the control room and wave his arms frantically until some actor looked up, or maybe all of them, then they'd all stare up. Whereas, in the studio, right next to the actors, I could tell one actor to speed up just a little bit and another one, perhaps even to slow down. If an actor was too close to the mike I could push him back gently, or move him in. Sound effects cues were never missed when I was in the studio."

Jerry Devine liked the idea, too, and used the same technique when directing *Mr. District Attorney* and *This Is Your F.B.I.* Not every actor appreciated having a director exhorting him to perform at such close quarters, but as a former actor himself, Devine gave his performers a sense of being "with" them all the way. He also began every rehearsal session with a kind of locker-room pep talk.

Two other former actors found considerable success as radio directors; what made the transition unusual is that both of them were *actresses.* Although many facets of radio production were male-dominated, both Edna Best and Helen Mack rose to the top of their profession in Hollywood radio circles. Best, a British leading lady who came to America with her husband, actor Herbert Marshall, numbered among her credits the *Sherlock Holmes* series with Basil Rathbone and Nigel Bruce. Mack, perhaps best remembered as the leading lady in 1933's *The Son of Kong*, helmed such popular series as *A Date with Judy*. "They taught you so much, just in little subtle ways," recalls Peggy Webber, who is certain that their experiences as actors helped them immeasurably in their new positions. "Oh, absolutely, because later I worked for a couple of women who had never done this before, had never acted and there was no comparison. They did their job with the stopwatch but they had nothing really to contribute, but Edna Best and Helen Mack were both very relaxed and full of fun, and their instincts were so right. They were a delight to be with, and they made it all a joyous occasion."

Like Jack Johnstone and Jerry Devine, Orson Welles directed his shows from a perch in the studio, not from the booth, but that's where the resemblance ended. Welles was unlike anyone else in radio—or in the whole of the theatrical world, for that matter. Arthur Anderson, a Mercury actor, told Karen Everson and Annabelle Sheehan, "I have a picture of Orson on a podium about a foot high, with a music stand [for the script], and earphones, so that he could hear the effects and other things, with his faithful assistant Bill Alland, whom he referred to as Vakhtangov, with a container of pineapple juice, and with his pipe in his hand. He could give hand signals with the hand that had the pipe, or the other hand, it didn't matter which, and Orson was in control, in command, and he loved this."

"That's why the similarity between a conductor and Orson always struck me," said sound effects man Cliff Thorsness to documentarian Frank Beacham. "He

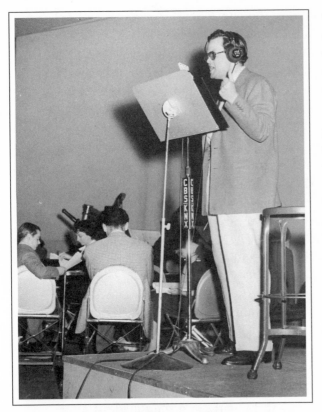

Orson Welles directs from his podium at CBS in Los Angeles, his headphones serving as his link to the control room.

was really conducting the ingredients of his radio show at the same time he was acting. To my knowledge I never was aware of him giving anyone a wrong cue.

"He knit these ingredients together like nobody else did. He had a strong, charismatic force, if I can use that expression, that I think was contagious to his actors, his people he worked with." Orson Welles was, of course, the wunderkind of the Broadway theater at the time that he made his radio debut as an impresario with *The Mercury Theatre* on CBS in 1938. He had spent several years gaining experience as a radio actor, on *The March of Time* and a number of other prestigious shows, and in the starring role of Lamont Cranston, aka *The Shadow*, while continuing his pursuits in the theater. When it came time to direct a radio production—as well as star in it—he brought startling and exciting new ideas to the process. But he also faced a challenge: how to maintain a full slate of Mercury productions on stage and radio at the same time, as both actor and director.

His solution was to rely on some trusted associates, including his producing partner, John Houseman, an eager assistant named Richard Wilson, and the man who gave him his start in radio, actor Paul Stewart. It was Stewart who in fact would cast, direct, and rehearse Welles' radio plays. William Alland, another Mercury stalwart, would usually perform Welles' part for these preliminary sessions. Then, on rehearsal/broadcast day, Welles would leave his theatrical chores behind and focus on the radio play at hand. Richard Wilson explained, "There was the period in which Orson listened to what Paul or I had done and how the show was put together, and make some comments, change things, transpose scenes. 'That stinks, that's wonderful, that's no good, the music is terrible there—got anything else, Benny?—and can't it extend into here? Or can't it stop there?' " Then there would be a dress rehearsal in which those suggestions would be incorporated.

John Houseman elaborated in an interview with Karen Everson and Annabelle Sheehan. "It would be very difficult for an associate producer-director to stage a show and then come in at the last moment and pump energy into it, but not in radio. It was very easy, really, for Orson with all his great brilliance to come in at the last two rehearsals—which he normally did—and make the show his own."

Welles' last-minute arrival on the scene extended even to his most famous radio production, *The War of the Worlds*. Houseman recalled, "He didn't touch it, he didn't go near it until the day of the performance, but what he gave it was audacity, tremendous courage. The reason that show worked as well as it did was . . . nerve . . . the slowness of the show in the beginning. Those credible pauses were maintained, and Orson really stretched those. The reason the show works as it does is that the acceleration is very carefully calculated and is quite extraordinary; that is why by the time you are twenty minutes into the show you are moving hours at a time . . . and no one even noticed." That sense of timing and tempo was Welles' specialty as a director.

There were times that Orson's associates fretted because he wasn't concentrating on his radio work at all until the last minute, but he almost always managed to pull a proverbial rabbit out of his hat. And he did it week after week, in a way he was never able to duplicate, either in the theater or film, for a very specific reason. Richard Wilson explained to Frank Beacham, "Radio was the only medium that imposed a discipline that Orson would recognize, and that was the clock. When it came time for Mercury to go on the air, there was no denying it. I can't think of one theater production . . . that was not postponed, but [in] radio, he knew every week that clock was ticking, that red light [would come] on and say 'On the Air.' And good or bad, right or wrong, boy, that was it. It was the only discipline Orson was able ever to accept."

Peggy Webber, who worked with Orson later on, in Hollywood, told Beacham that this feeling of urgency became infectious. "The one show that stands out so strongly in my mind that I did with him on radio, he had to cut about twenty minutes from the show, and he didn't come to us until five minutes to air time with all of these tremendous cuts—pages, handfuls to be torn out of the script. I think all of this was part of the adrenalin rise that he used; it helped him, and gave an urgency and a poignancy to his performance, and to everyone else. He gave you this feeling: the deadline is here, you're going to rise to the occasion or else! And you did, because he inspired you so with the bravura, the way he took it himself."

It must be stressed that Welles was not careless nor uncaring about radio; quite the contrary. He loved and respected the medium. But he was a law unto himself.

Writer E. Jack Neuman recalls, "He would say, 'My dear boy, this is the best script you will ever write . . . *but* . . .' and you'd end up rewriting the entire thing. And he didn't care whether you got any sleep. But he drove himself just as hard. Everything he did was great. He had such great ideas."

Said Richard Wilson, "He asked of the audience just a little bit more than others were asking in terms of a theater of the imagination: a little more demanding of them that they listen and imagine and set a stage and enter a world, which he then better than anybody else could fill out with his ear, with his ability to cast, and the tastefulness of his choice of material."

But Welles' approach went beyond generalities. "Things that we take for granted really were big developments," Wilson recalled, "in terms of rhythms, and total rhythms of the program, scenic rhythms, climaxing of rhythms within a scene and things like that. It's like choreography in dance, and it comes on the beat.

"So the rehearsals would not be like other rehearsals which concerned themselves mainly with the sense of the scene, or the reality of the acting, of any of those components. A lot of our rehearsals were spent in—'Now you come in on the last syllable of . . .' and 'You chime in on the third syllable of his saying, How do you do?' And so forth. The same way he cut in film."

Welles also liked to establish a tapestry of sound, not just a series of isolated sound effects. This became the norm on the better radio shows from the late 1940s onward, but Welles put it into practice a decade earlier. His production of "Algiers" on *The Campbell Playhouse* was much talked about from an aural point of view—even by his sponsor, who wrote a letter after the broadcast asking why the background sounds were so loud. Welles' reply: "Who told you it was the background?"

He could terrorize his associates and his technicians, reaching for precisely the effect he wanted, but he never abused his actors. He held them in the highest regard, especially the troupers who formed the nucleus of the Mercury players, many of whom he'd met while breaking into radio on *The March of Time*. One such colleague was Richard Wilson, who soon became a jack-of-all-trades associate. "He and I would talk about the casting," Wilson recalled, "and in the earlier days of radio the big proportion of our radio work, the heart of the castings stayed within *The March of Time*, so it became a problem of, 'Well, what will Marty play this week?' or 'George Coulouris would be wonderful for that' or 'Let's use Edgar Barrier because his voice is sort of high and it will contrast . . .' "

When Welles moved to Hollywood and made his legendary film debut with *Citizen Kane*, he not only took his Mercury actors along—Joseph Cotten, Agnes Moorehead, Ray Collins, Everett Sloane, Paul Stewart, George Coulouris—but he carried with him the tenets of pacing and juxtaposition of sounds that had characterized his radio plays. And while it is true that Welles became a supreme visual stylist, he never forgot—or forsook—his radio roots.

One wouldn't expect to hear the names Orson Welles and Jack Webb mentioned in the same breath, but when Webb got the opportunity to create his own brand of radio plays, he brought a spark, and a unique approach, to the medium that recalled Welles at his best.

Webb had been a busy, working radio actor in San Francisco in the 1940s. He tried a little bit of everything, even a self-named comedy show at one point. (As surviving tapes attest, *The Jack Webb Show* was fairly clever.) He finally hit pay dirt with a moody, West Coast private-eye series called *Pat Novak for Hire*. Written by longtime colleague Richard Breen, it was Webb's ticket to Hollywood. Because ABC had replaced him as Pat Novak, Webb at first starred in soundalike shows such as *Johnny Madero* and *Jeff Regan, Investigator* before resuming the role of Novak on the full ABC network.

Although technically an actor playing a role, Webb already had definite ideas about radio drama and how it should be approached. E. Jack Neuman, who first worked with him on *Jeff Regan*, recalled, "He's the one who told me, 'You've got to climb the mountain and plant a flag in every scene. Every scene can be like the ending of an act.' He tried to hit a home run every time he came to bat, and he did it almost every time. And he was a very hard taskmaster. But he created the idea of dramatizing reality, and the film and television industry owes him a lot."

Webb continued to work as an actor-for-hire in Hollywood, and began getting roles in movies as well, but his brass ring came along when he mapped out a police show called *Dragnet* and persuaded NBC to let him make an audition recording in 1949. The network liked it enough to put it on the air without a sponsor. An experienced director, Bill Rousseau, was supposedly in charge, but the actors knew whose "baby" it really was. Peggy Webber remembers going home one night and telling her mother, " 'I don't know why he even keeps

Jack Webb rehearses a *Dragnet* episode with costar Vic Perrin; sound-effects men Wayne Kenworthy and Bud Tollefson are in the background. Right now, all eyes are apparently on the control room. Incidentally, this photo was taken by busy radio actor Harry Bartell.

another person there as a director; he doesn't let the fellow do anything.' Shortly thereafter, he dismissed Bill, and he took over the reins."

For the actors, working on *Dragnet* was an experience like no other in radio. Says Webber, "He told me I should understate everything, underplay it all, speak everything as if you're not acting. Then they developed over a period of time a style where you didn't get close to the microphone at all but stood back away from the microphone. This was Jack's idea that he'd get a more natural performance if you weren't speaking directly into a microphone. And it of course was correct.

"For years he wouldn't use Bill Conrad; he used to give us speeches about how he wouldn't use a guy who was a voice actor. He used to say, 'I wouldn't use one of those voice actors listening to themselves. I don't want those rounded mellifluous tones. I want people who sound like *people*.' He was adamant about this. He developed a little stock company of about eight of us, and we did most of the shows for the first three years."

One of his original group, Herb Ellis, didn't understand the point—or the purpose—of the *Dragnet* monotone. "He was so vertical in the way he wanted everybody to play, that I felt there was no humanness, because we all talked the same way. Why it struck America and struck a chord, I don't know, but it did. But to my mind, everybody talked robotically. Once I ventured to say, 'Can we just do a . . .' 'NO! This is the way I want it.' Fine. And he was right."

Webb was so wrapped up in *Dragnet* that nothing else mattered to him, including his relations with fellow actors. He was loyal to most of them, and continued to employ many of his radio colleagues for decades to come on television, but he was just as quick to lash out with verbal abuse. Some of them knew how to take it; others did not. He was just as demanding of his engineer, Raoul Murphy, and his soundmen, Bud Tollefson and Wayne Kenworthy, but they found his insistence on capturing exactly the right sound stimulating, not defeating. *Dragnet* boasted of the most sophisticated and believable sound patterns on the air, and Webb's matter-of-fact approach to police work was a startling contrast to the *Gang Busters* school of drama.

Flush with *Dragnet*'s success, he and Richard Breen concocted a second series, *Pete Kelly's Blues,* about a trouble-prone cornet player in a 1920s New Orleans speakeasy. It was a pet project of Webb's, incorporating his love of jazz, but it was short-lived, serving only as a summer replacement series in 1951. (Webb later revived it as a feature film in 1955, and a TV series in 1959.)

Webb was an innovator, and it was an unfortunate bit of timing that television stole him away. He decided to direct the TV version of *Dragnet* himself, as well as the 1954 theatrical feature of the same name, and that left no time to devote to the ongoing radio series beyond turning up for recording sessions.

⌒

Jack Webb was one of the few radio directors to make a successful transition to television, but that had more to do with his ownership of *Dragnet* than his arresting visual style. As with writers, dramatic television tended not to draw on proven radio talent, but to develop its own new breed of craftsmen (with a handful of exceptions, including Fletcher Markle).

The cream of radio directors continued, instead, to do what they did best, remaining active in radio right through the 1950s, even as the ship was sinking. It's hard to believe that such popular series as *Gunsmoke, Suspense,* and *Yours Truly, Johnny Dollar* would have survived into the early 1960s if they hadn't been under the command of such experienced men as Elliott Lewis, William N. Robson, Jack

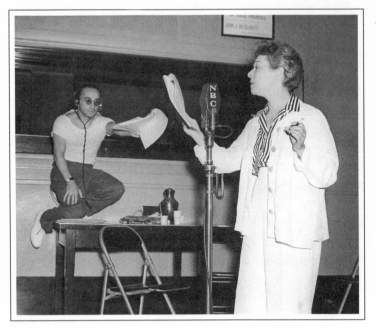

Arch Oboler obviously enjoys the immediacy of being in the studio with his actors.

Johnstone, and Norman MacDonnell. And if some of them never found another arena that offered the same creative freedom, they all had cause to look back on their radio work with great satisfaction.

The emotions felt by a director are perhaps best summed up by Arch Oboler, who remembered one broadcast in particular. "I did an hour play, the first hour original play that NBC had ever done coast to coast, called *Miss Lonely Heart.* It was the story of Madame Tchaikowsky, and the star was the international actress Nazimova, who was toward the end of her life; she had never done radio before. So there she was in front of a microphone with a cast of my best radio people, and off in the distance was, so help me, the Toscanini symphony orchestra, and beyond that, a few feet further were three or four sound effects men with their consoles, and my hand went up and I pointed at the glass and they started. When that hour was over, something inside of me said, 'It'll never be better.' It couldn't be."

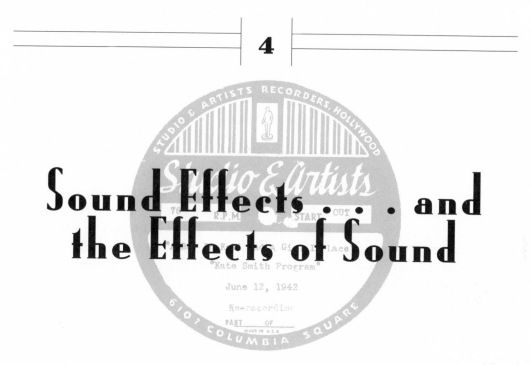

4

Sound Effects . . . and the Effects of Sound

Jack Benny and his troupe arrive in New York by train for their weekly broadcast, and are greeted by a porter who dutifully brushes off their coats. He greets Jack, and we hear the sound of the whiskbroom (*whisk-whisk, whisk-whisk*). He greets Mary Livingstone, and again we hear the sound (*whisk-whisk, whisk-whisk*). Then he greets Don Wilson, and we hear: *whisk-whisk, whisk-whisk, whisk-whisk, whisk-whisk, whisk-whisk, whisk-whisk, whisk-whisk* . . .

Benny's was the most popular show on radio. Everyone knew Don Wilson was fat, and Benny knew that everyone knew it. This gag drew a bigger, more sustained laugh than any line of dialogue possibly could, because it grew in intensity as the audience caught on. It also required the audience to use its imagination, triggered by a particular, recognizable sound. That was radio.

It isn't clear who developed or used the first sound effects in radio dramatizations, but in a medium bursting with discovery it couldn't have taken long for someone to realize that sound enhancement of some sort was necessary to produce the illusion of reality.

By the 1930s the medium was developing specialists who did nothing *but* create and execute sound effects. Like announcers, they mostly wandered (or stumbled) into the job, there being no known precedent for this kind of work.

And like many announcers, these sound effects men were often performers who simply found a new and different vehicle for expressing themselves.

In fact, one must disabuse oneself of the notion that sound effects men were technicians. Some of them were, but many—or perhaps we should say, the *good* ones—were performers first and foremost. This was no work for a robot; it required a definite sense of timing and dramatic emphasis, which the best men had, or developed.

And yes, it required ingenuity, too.

Creating a presence of sound on a dramatic show required fledgling soundmen all over the country to make much the same discoveries in radio's early years: a portable door was necessary, for comings and goings; hoofbeats had to be simulated for western stories, and coconut shells would approximate that sound (though some found that beating on their chest, close to the mike, got much the same result); special boards would have to be installed so footsteps could be easily enacted and clearly heard.

As radio developed, more realistic sounds were sought: hoofbeats would sound different on snow than they would on dried ground . . . a lady's footsteps were different from a man's . . . and some doors creaked, especially in eerie mystery stories.

Some of this advancement came about because of ambitious and dedicated soundmen; some of it came about because of exacting directors and producers.

Orson Welles saw sound as his artist's canvas. He wanted layers of sound—and was one of the first radio men to create such a tapestry. In the opening moments of his production of *Algiers*, we hear the many sounds of the Casbah, that bustling marketplace, interacting and overlapping. John Houseman remembers the Mercury troupe spending endless hours searching for just the right sound to simulate a head falling from a guillotine blade in *A Tale of Two Cities*. Finally, they decided that cleaving a head of lettuce in half did the job. In another stroke of inspiration, they agreed that the caverns of Paris that Victor Hugo described in *Les Misèrables* would be well imitated by the reverberating sound of their studio men's room!

It was, indeed, a time of discovery. When asked how the incredible sound of Buck Rogers' rocket ship was created on that famous 1930s radio serial, director Jack Johnstone smiled and recalled, "CBS New York had an excellent air conditioning system at that time. There were huge grates, perhaps four by four, for exhaust and intake; the sound effects man took a spare script and plastered pages over the whole thing, which stuck because of the draw of the air, except for a small spot in the middle of it, out of which he placed a microphone. The air conditioning system provided the sound for the rocket. Where we had Killer Kane flying a different ship and needed a rocket background for his, the engineer sent it through a filter, to give a little different sound."

Arch Oboler's most famous sound effect on the creepy series *Lights Out* was the sound of a man being turned inside out! It was accomplished, rather simply, by soaking a rubber glove in water and turning it inside out while a berry basket was crushed.

Said Oboler, of his experiments with sound, "I quickly found out that if you chopped a watermelon for the sound of a skull being cleaved, that was it, no more. I never used it again. That was the ultimate orgasm."

⟜

Some elementary sound effects were used in theatrical productions, notably a "thunder sheet," which consisted of a piece of sheet metal suspended from a rack; when struck with a hammer, it produced a loud thunder crack. When tugged back and forth, it created a wonderful rumbling sound. Stage plays also required doorbells, telephone rings, and other such simple sounds, which were equally simple to perform offstage.

The real predecessor of the radio soundman was the drummer in a vaudeville orchestra pit, who was called upon to provide percussive emphasis and punctuation for comedy and novelty acts using wood blocks, cowbells, ratchets, and other paraphernalia that was part of most drum kits. It was, in fact, a former drummer who may lay claim to the title of radio's first sound effects person.

His name was Arthur W. Nichols, and he decided to invent a sound effects machine, intending it for use in theaters to accompany silent movies. Nichols had first performed effects when he toured the country with Lyman Howe, a pioneering producer of travelogues, in the early part of the twentieth century. Then, after twenty years of vaudeville drumming, he set himself to the task of creating a permanent sound effects contraption.

As reported in *Popular Mechanics*, "Scores of different sounds are accurately reproduced on an electronically operated noise maker to be used with motion pictures. Small electric motors, controlled by push buttons, actuate most of the sound units which can be combined and altered to produce fading, distant and other effects. The entire outfit is compactly constructed in a single cabinet or table, about five feet high and less than two feet deep, and is intended to be operated by the drummer. The sound of falling trees, crashing glass, trolley cars, doors slamming, handsaw and acetylene torch are a few of the unusual noises that this unit successfully imitates. How the sound of the trolley car was produced gives an idea of the elaborate care the inventor took in constructing the apparatus. He first studied the noise carefully and then made repeated experiments at duplication, finally succeeding in imitating the sway of the tracks, the hum of the motor, the bell, air brakes and other parts. The wheels of six pairs of roller skates, numerous gears and pulleys, two motors and compressed air were finally arranged to make all the usual noises for an electric car in motion, and in starting and stopping."

Nichols told an interviewer, "It was a tough job, much tougher than it might have been for some people. For I had no mechanical background on which to rely. All my life I have spent making noises in the theater. But I set up a microphone in the kitchen, so I could listen and tell what the sounds should be. And then I set to work. In the kitchen, I built this machine."

While Nichols was slaving over his invention, working ten to fourteen hours a day for nearly a year, talking pictures came along and all but rendered his creation obsolete—for theater use. The handwriting was on the wall: his future, and his invention's, was in radio. To that end, he began listening to see how his artificial sounds reproduced through a speaker.

"There were no engineering principles upon which I could rely. All I could do was experiment in the kitchen, checking up on the microphone until the radio sound was accurate. Many, of course, reproduce exactly—a duck quack is very good. But a pistol shot, for example, is difficult. A real shot would tear the microphone to pieces. So we have to strike a pillow with a stick. It may not seem possible, but that sounds exactly like a shot over the air."

Nichols' machine was formidable, enabling the operator to imitate an airplane (using a fan with strips of cardboard or leather attached) or the sound of the sea (utilizing a perforated wheel rubbing against a thick canvas filled with peas). Before long, Nichols and his wife, who served as his assistant, were under contract to the Judson Radio Program Corporation in New York City to provide effects for all of its programs; a short time later they moved to the CBS station, WABC.

Then, in 1931, the unthinkable occurred: Arthur Nichols died of a heart attack. His widow, Ora, had worked side by side with him for several years, but at first the management at WABC doubted whether she could actually fill his shoes. It didn't take them long to find out.

In the December 1934 issue of *Radio Stars*, Ora Nichols was named one of the "Nine Greatest Women in Radio," alongside Mrs. Franklin D. Roosevelt, Gracie Allen, Gertrude Berg, Jessica Dragonette, and Kate Smith. "Her name . . . meant nothing to me," admitted the author of the featured article, "yet all executives immediately placed her among the first nine. I investigated and discovered that Ora Nichols is the most important of any one on that list. Radio could have progressed without a Kate Smith, without a Dragonette, without the others, but without Ora Nichols I doubt if it would be in such an advanced stage. She is head of Columbia's sound department. Six men work for her, take her orders. Since she has been with Columbia, Ora D. Nichols has invented 1,000 sounds.

"It was Ora who discovered that an egg beater whirring close to a microphone sounds like a lawn mower. The sounds she invents are kept in little black

Ora and Arthur W. Nichols pose with their paraphernalia at CBS, circa 1930. Together they blazed a trail for others to follow.

wooden boxes. These boxes even astonish NBC's sound department. Sometimes their members go over to Columbia just to look and marvel, for the NBC sounds are encased in heavy unwieldy contraptions, while Ora's can be carried by a woman."

Nichols was a simple, modest woman who enjoyed her work, and took it seriously. "You can wreck a whole program by missing one sound cue," she told a reporter in 1932.

On January 24, 1933, C. M. Underhill of the advertising agency BBDO wrote to Mrs. Nichols that for an upcoming broadcast of the *Socony-Vacuum Show* they would need the following: record of crowd cheering; crack of baseball bat on wall; record of crowd murmurs, talking; sounds of plates, glasses, tableware; table glass; telegraph instrument; door, opening and closing.

In another letter, he added, "The 5th show in the series, February 24th, will feature Amelia Earhart. On that date we will have to have every conceivable airplane effect, inside, outside, throttling down, engine exhaust, etc. I just thought I would let you know about this in advance because these sound effects alone will make or break the show."

Producers, directors, and executives came to rely on her, and she never let them down. After the "War of the Worlds" broadcast, Orson Welles sent her a handwritten note which read, "Dearest Ora: Thanks for the best job anybody could ever do for anybody. All my love, Orson."

⟜

Ora Nichols had the benefit of learning her trade from someone who had made a careful study of sound effects. Most other soundmen in radio's heyday backed into this field of endeavor, usually from some other area of show business.

Ray Erlenborn became one of the best soundmen in radio and television, and is still plying his trade in the 1990s; typically enough, he came to it by accident, in the mid-1930s. "When you worked in a radio studio in the early days, they were liable to stop you in the hall and say, 'Come in and do something.' Well, at 10th and Hope in the Acker Building [in Los Angeles] was an early radio station. You'd go up in the car elevator, up to the top floor, and they had a little radio studio there. I was doing a program of my own where I sang and played the ukulele; I had done this in vaudeville and I was now doing it on radio. So I walked in one day and the guy grabbed me and said, 'We need you to help with sound effects.' They were doing a show called *Penzoil News Review*, which was a magazine of the week type show.

"They had two sound effects men there, Charlie Forsyth and Len Wright. Charlie Forsyth later built a lot of big equipment, like a great big drum twelve feet wide; he did *Lux Radio Theatre* all the years that they were doing it, as a freelance sound effects man. Len Wright was a pit drummer from the Orpheum Theatre, and of course, pit drummers catch cues all the time; they're practically sound effects men when they play for vaudeville acts.

"They had a big pipe organ in the studio, and they wanted me to do the airplane effects. To do an airplane effect on the pipe organ in those days you just leaned your whole arm on a keyboard, and fade 'em in and fade 'em across; the planes would be passing overhead miraculously with all these *vroom* kind of sounds, from the low end of the keyboard."

A gregarious man and a natural performer, Erlenborn was making $25 a week as a master of ceremonies on a juvenile show that moved from KFWB to KNX. Things were hopping at that CBS station in 1938, as more and more network shows were moving out from New York. There were only two soundmen on staff at the time, Clark Casey and Cliff Thorsness; when management offered him $25 more a week to go on staff as a soundman, he didn't hesitate. His comic abilities made him less a sound technician than a featured performer on *Al Pearce and His Gang* (where he worked for ten years), *The Joe Penner Show*, and *The Joe E. Brown Show* in the late 1930s. "I got a lot of appreciation for creating things for comedy shows, where on a dramatic show they sort of took you for granted," he recalls.

Manufacturing the sound effects in those days required a certain mechanical know-how. Every network and studio of any size had a shop where the soundmen could experiment and build equipment they needed for a particular effect. Of course, no two worked alike.

Says Erlenborn, "At NBC, their house doors were like you were walking into a castle somewhere. They were eight feet tall, and they would build them with a sound baffle in the back that was about fourteen, sixteen inches wide. They were big, heavy doors. We built ours economically, on two-by-fours, and I really don't think the sound was that much different. At NBC they had splash tanks that were twelve feet by twelve feet. They'd move them into the studio, and it took up the whole corner of the studio for the splash tanks, but they felt like more water meant a better water effect. Our splash tanks were about fourteen inches square on a rolling tub

Ray Erlenborn hams it up for the camera, but don't be fooled: there actually might be a moment when he would have had to fire a gunshot and play a slide whistle at the same time!

that we could just roll in real easily to any studio; we had paddles on a crank handle which revolved inside of the tank to give us splashes."

There was a lot of physical labor involved in doing sound; not only did the soundmen help construct a lot of their apparatus, but they had to physically move it in and out of the studio for each program. When the show was done at an outside theater, that was even more of a trial.

"I did things like *Big Town*, with Edward G. Robinson and Claire Trevor," says Erlenborn. "That was an audience show, and we did it at the Wilshire Ebell

Sound-effects man Keene Crockett keeps one eye on the script as he prepares to fire a gun and manipulate a turntable effect. It looks like this was an especially busy broadcast.

Theatre, which was a long ways away; we had to truck all of our equipment over there from KNX, and truck it back and set it up, and [then] strike it. In New York the sound guys had helpers that were just set-up-and-strike guys; they didn't even touch the stuff. We did all our lifting and carrying."

Having a set-up staff was indeed a luxury, but it was not without its peril. New York soundman Terry Ross remembers a fateful evening when he got a surprise from one of these young men: "We had a set-up department; these were the boys who were more or less hopeful of becoming sound effects men sometime in the future, but whose responsibility was to push the equipment into the studio and place it in position for us to use.

"We had a door that we used for *Inner Sanctum* with squeaky hinges. We got the hinges and buried them in the dirt out back and watered them down like plants for a couple of weeks or so, till they got nice and rusty, then brought them out and mounted them on the door a little bit askew, so they would squeak. So I was doing *Inner Sanctum* and one of the set-up boys came to me and said, 'Terry, I fixed the door for you.' I said, 'What do you mean?' He said, 'I oiled the hinges on the squeaky door.' This was just before showtime. What the hell do you do when the signature of the show was a squeaky door?" What indeed. Ross faced the situation as any good soundman would have: he imitated the sound of the door with his voice.

Soundmen performed quite a lot of sounds vocally, and were expected to imitate a variety of household pets whenever the script called for it. Actress Lurene Tuttle recalled at least one occasion when the professional on the scene was upstaged, however. "One time on the *Hollywood Hotel* show," she told radio historian Chuck Schaden, "the soundman was supposed to do a little yipping, yappy dog, like a terrier. He sounded like a Newfoundland dog or something, and the director kept saying, 'That won't do.' So Olivia de Havilland was sitting next to me and she says, 'I can do a very good dog.' And I said, 'Well, I don't think they'll let you do a dog, this is an audience show; you're a star, you can't do a dog.' And she says, 'I'm going to do it.' So she went over to the director, went in the booth and said, 'I'd like to try doing this dog for you.' So they put her behind the screen and she went on the show and did that yipping dog."

That upstaged soundman may have been chagrined, but in all likelihood he took it in stride. Because of the quantity of work demanded of each person on staff, and the daily grind, there was no room for specialists: every soundman had to be able to "do it all." One show might require an exhausting half-hour of hoofbeats, while another would only require a fire-alarm bell to be rung on cue for a live commercial.

"If you count every single little dinky show, starting with the news at 7:00 or 7:15 in the morning and ending up with *The Richfield News* at 10:00 at night, you could do four or five shows a day," recalls Hollywood soundman Bud Tollefson. "Then again, you'd have a day where you might have nothing but maintenance in the room, cleaning guns, things like that. I can't tell you how many times I had to work Sundays and all I did was *One Man's Family*, and all the sound effect that was on that show was a clink of two glasses at the end of the show!"

A sound-effects man's work was never dull: this unnamed artist is crushing berry boxes while apparently closing a door with his foot!

There were two kinds of sound effects in radio: live and recorded. From the earliest days, it was apparent that some sounds couldn't be imitated in the studio and had to be played on records. These were mostly "sustained" sounds: an automobile, airplane, or train, the whooshing of wind or the rushing of a river.

It might seem, at first blush, that this made the soundman's job easier, but that was not the case. Manipulating turntables was as precise a job as performing live effects. Those recordings only lasted several minutes apiece, so for a show that required a background sound for the entire half-hour, the soundman would have to repeatedly move from one disc to another.

"We had four arms for three turntables," explains Ray Erlenborn, "so that we could bring one arm over and set it down and start the grooves, and then as it started to run out, set another arm down and cross-fade so that we could keep continuing an airplane in midair or a car running along the road, or rain, for that matter."

Some recorded effects were not sustained, but specific sounds, and these had to be cued to perfection. Terry Ross explains how it was done: "The recordings, when we used them, were 78s, and if you had to cue up something like a gunshot, you would put the needle down on the record until it came to the gunshot, which you could hear by putting your ear close to the record, and then back the record off a half-turn or so, depending on the torque of the platter. Then on cue you'd release the record with the volume turned up. If you had timed it properly, the gunshot would go off at the right time. From there, we went into tape, which was easier to handle because you could cue that up visually with a cue mark on it. Now we're using cartridges and all you have to do is put the cartridge in and press the button and the effect happens."

Sound effects men would have appreciated cartridges back in the 1930s and '40s; not only are they efficient and reliable, but they don't wear out, as acetate discs did. The 78 rpm effects library had to be rerecorded on a periodic basis because the records became too scratchy.

On complicated shows, there might be two soundmen at work, one doing manual effects, the other working the turntable, but in many instances both men would be doing several things at once.

Most soundmen preferred doing live effects whenever possible because it gave them a greater degree of control, and enabled them to coordinate their work more smoothly with the actors in the studio. But even here, things could go wrong. Says longtime CBS soundman Ray Kemper, "There were many times when a gun would jam and nothing would happen. That's the reason that as a soundman, if you used guns, you would always have two—one in each hand, and they were both cocked. If one didn't go off, you shot the other one.

"When we had [the sound of] a knife going into wood—somebody throwing a knife and it'd go zing-*conk*—what you would do is you would take a knife and you'd have a big block of wood and you'd stick it into a block of wood. One guy [on the staff], for some reason or other, liked to take a little block of wood, hold it in his hand, and go *wham!* And we used to say, 'Please, Jack, don't do that—you're gonna miss one day,' and sure enough, on the air one day, he missed and hit his hand with the knife. Well, blood goes all over the place, he passes out, it was terrible."

Accidents were rare; innovations were commonplace. A staff soundman would work several shows a day—or more—and be expected to come to each broadcast fully prepared. As often as not, he would be assigned to the same show every week, or every day, and as a regular he would get to know the program's general needs. (Remember, a "stock" opening or even a commercial in those live-radio days that might involve sound effects was done afresh *every single time*.) Even so, there was no telling what a scriptwriter might dream up that wouldn't be sitting on the sound department shelf ready to go.

Nila Mack, the creator and director of the beloved children's program *Let's Pretend*, wrote in the 1944 book *Off Mike*, "One of the most interesting and hard-working days I've spent at CBS was creating unusual sound effects. Walter Pierson, head of our Sound Department, is a most cooperative fellow. I told him a few of my sound problems. Fortunately for me, he is an imagina-

How to break glass without risk of injury: this was a specially constructed cabinet with levers designed to break glass safely—but loudly.

tive person, for when I spoke of needing the effect of 'moonbeams shimmering,' a 'flying trunk,' a 'magic carpet,' he didn't blink an eye. He only asked what day it would be convenient, set up the studio equipment, and when I arrived, there were ten sound men and Pierson ready to go.

"All day we worked. We blended music with manual apparatus. Two or three recordings were mixed into one. The Hammond organ came in for a severe workout. But at the end of the day when we finished, I had a lovely path of moonbeams on which the Princess of the Moon descended to visit her earth parents. I had a flying trunk (on the secondhand side) that flew and zoomed, and when it finally landed and bumped its way to a stop, it made the audience laugh. I even had a believable, charming sound to use when the Emperor in the story of the Chinese Nightingale tied silver bells on every flower in the fabulous garden."

Experiments took place on a daily basis. Director Elliott Lewis recalled, "To change the sound, they would put certain sound effects or certain actors in the airlock between the hallway, the studio, and the control room. There was an airlock so people walking in and out weren't letting in outside sounds. If we had a good rain effect, there was a rain machine and you could change the sound of it by what the water was hitting (brush, or tin or whatever) and it would be put in the airlock, turned on before the show went on—as we wanted the background of the rain for this particular sequence."

Writer Ranald MacDougall remembered some of the work that went into creating specific and convincing sound effects for the dramatic World War Two series *The Man Behind the Gun*: "In one case, for example, the sound of a destroyer dropping depth charges was created by playing the record of a cement mixing machine at $33\frac{1}{3}$ revolutions instead of the usual 78 of the ordinary phonograph. On one occasion, too, it took several hours of experimentation to discover that the nearest approximation to the noise of a parachute snapping open was a piece of silk being snapped in front of the microphone."

The show's innovative director, William N. Robson, had another idea that would make his combat series sound like no other. As he told radio historian John Hickman, "[There is a phenomenon known as] the threshold of sound. You're in a quiet room, you talk quietly; if you're in a crowded room, at a cocktail party and everybody is talking and the music is going loudly, you can talk louder and everybody else talks louder and the threshold of sound goes up. Now, in order to create this situation with my actors, I produced this show with two 24-inch speakers on . . . the dead sides of the dynamic [non-directional] mike, pouring the sound effects into both ears of the actors in front of that mike. And when those guns went off and when the PT boats' motors went all full, those fellows had to shout to hear themselves, and therefore, you had [a] little trick of authenticity. The reaction that used to please me was the reaction of the military men, who would say, 'Well, you must have flown the plane, you must have been down in a submarine . . .'"

Every director had his own approach to sound effects and the use of sound. Some used very little—to save time and money. Their shows were dramatically sound, but spare on sound effects. Others had distinctive techniques.

Ray Erlenborn recalls, "There were a lot of directors—Dave Owen was one, on *Scattergood Baines*—who made . . . the whole cast work on one mike. The sound effects man would walk up to the mike and do things, then walk away, because one mike in the studio was a lot cleaner than having six mikes open all the time. Lum and Abner used to do their show that way, too: one microphone. You would place your door a little away so that it was a little bit off the mike, then you'd do your door and your footsteps there with no footstep mike.

"You had to understand the director you were working with, because you do it the way *they* want it, not the way *you* do, unless they give you a free hand, like so many of them did." Talk to any veteran sound effects man and you'll get an earful about dealing with these creative gentlemen.

"You used different psychology with different directors," says Ray Kemper. "Bill Robson was a stickler for perfection; if the script called for the rattle of onion-skin paper, you better damn well have onion-skin paper there. We had a show once that called for ten thousand drunk chickens. Bill James and I were doing the sound. Now, how the hell are we going to do ten thousand drunk chickens? Particularly with Robson directing this thing, because we know what he's

Bob Prescott at work, possibly making the sound of metal scraping against metal. In the 1960s Prescott did a record album based on sound effects called *Cartoons in Hi-Fi* (aka *Cartoons in Stereo*).

gonna do. So we thought and thought, and what we did was this. We went into the recording booth, and we recorded a bunch of records of chickens clucking and crowing and stuff like that. We played that record, and superimposed over it Bill and I vocally chicken-hiccuping and clucking and hiccuping. We overdubbed and overdubbed, and when we finished, it sounded pretty darn funny, pretty darn good. I mean, what does a drunk chicken sound like? Then Bill says, 'He's never gonna believe this,' and I said, 'I've got an idea.' So we took this tape and we went into the studio where they cut discs in the same building, and we asked a friend of ours who ran this thing to transfer this to disc, which he did, put it on a big twelve-inch disc. It looked very professional; we got a very professional looking label and labeled it '10,000 Drunk Chickens.'

"So now we go to the show, and sure enough, it comes up to this thing, we play this disc, and Bill hits the talk-back button and says, 'What the hell are you guys doing? That's not ten thousand drunk chickens!' I knew he was going to say it, so I didn't say a word. I took the record off the turntable, walked over to the booth, held it up against the glass so he could see the label. He looked at it and said, 'Well, I'll be damned.' And he never said another word."

Orson Welles was also known to be demanding of his soundmen. Says Terry

Ross, "I remember we were doing one show he was directing and he wanted the sound of a pregnant woman walking across the room. Several of the guys did the footsteps and he said, 'No, that's not it! That's not it, doesn't sound right, doesn't sound right . . .' So finally we got one of the guys to come down who was a little bit effeminate, and he minced his way across and Orson said, 'That's it, that's exactly what I want to hear.' "

Bud Tollefson worked at NBC for several decades, but he never knew a perfectionist to rival Jack Webb on *Dragnet*. "Jack was a very fanatic guy about realism. He spent a lot of time—in those days, it wasn't a lot of money—to perfect these various backgrounds for all of his shows. I spent hours, literally hours, recording outdoor backgrounds for this man. And if the scene took place at 2:30 in the morning on Los Feliz Boulevard, at the intersection of Commonwealth, he wanted a background that was 2:30 in the morning at Los Feliz and Commonwealth. I would go out and record this stuff for him and then come back and transfer it to acetate discs and use it on the program."

Once, Tollefson and his partner Wayne Kenworthy found themselves performing sound effects on the roof of the NBC building at Sunset and Vine—while the show was being broadcast—because the scene in question was set on a rooftop, and doing it "for real" gave them both authentic background noise and the sound of granulated asphalt on the rooftop.

A good director wasn't satisfied until the sound was just right, and there was good cause for this concern. Artificial-sounding effects could weaken the dramatic impact of any scene. For a segment of *Columbia Presents Corwin* titled "El Capitan and the Corporal," Norman Corwin wrote a scene in which a couple scramble madly down a flight of steps to catch a train—talking all the way. As R. LeRoy Bannerman related in his book *Norman Corwin and Radio: The Golden Years* (1986), "In rehearsal, Corwin was not content with the synchronization of the soundmen's footsteps, and he chose to have his actors create their own by dashing up and down steps in a stairwell adjoining the studio. It was quite an accomplishment, considering the broadcast was live and the action continuous. With no break in the dialogue, Joe Julian was handed a portable mike as he and Katherine Locke left the standing mike to walk through the studio exit into the stairwell. There, he was relieved of the hand mike and, together, he and Kate ran up and down the steps, the sound being picked up by microphones strategically placed at the top and bottom of the stairs. The ensuing action not only provided realism in running footsteps but the accuracy of a breathless performance as well."

Lesser directors made a show of casting about for *le son juste*, but their associates recognized this display for what it was. Says CBS soundman Ross Murray,

"There are directors who just point the finger and have nothing to add, except ego, and a person like that was easily fooled by a good soundman. You'd take the record off, put it in the drawer, futz around a little bit, take the record out again, change the EQ, change the speed—'cause our turntables were variable speed turntables—and he'd say, 'That's the one I wanted!' "

Terry Ross describes one director of *The March of Time* as "a visual director. We had a scene that was taking place in the wintertime, and this fellow said, 'I want to hear the snow falling.' Well, of course, snow falling doesn't make any sound. So I told the engineer, 'When I give you the high sign, kill all the microphones in the studio.' He said Okay, so I went out and got some white paper and tore it up into small bits, came back into the studio and said to the director, 'I think this is what you're looking for.' I walked over to the mike, held up a pane of glass, gave a nod to the engineer, who killed all the mikes, and I took the broken pieces of paper and let them fall onto the pane of glass. The director said, 'Oh, that's just what I wanted.' Of course, he heard nothing, but he *saw* what he thought was the snow falling."

The job of a soundman, of course, was just the opposite: to read words on a page and think in terms of sound. Says Ross, for example, "A ferry boat coming into a dock: we would stop and think how many different sounds you might hear on that. You'd hear the water lapping, the sound of the engine, the sound of the crowd milling around, cars starting up, there's a lot of effects you could put in. The major things were usually indicated by the writer, then you could dress it up a little bit. If it said the scene is taking place at night, what do you do? Do you put in hoot owls or crickets or nightbirds or wolves or what? You read the story and see what is supposed to happen and then add these various effects to it, because sound is the window of the mind."

"This is the mark of a good soundman," agrees Ross Murray, "bringing up other possibilities. The script would come in, you would read the show, and say, 'Wait a minute, if he's gonna be on a roof in New York, maybe there's some guy training pigeons nearby.' You bring up things to enhance the theme."

It all started with the script. Most radio writers indicated on the printed page the sounds to be heard in every scene, although some were more explicit than others. It was the job of the soundman assigned to each show to read through that script and then prepare his effects for the day of dress rehearsal and broadcast.

In the heyday of network radio, scripts were generally distributed a week ahead of time, and the diligent soundman learned to read his copy as soon as possible, in case that particular show required constructing (or recording) something new.

At the first reading on show day, the soundman would indicate most effects vocally, just to give the actors and the director an idea of what to expect, and how much time to allow. There were times when after the first read the soundman would have to go to the storeroom and work under deadline pressure, because the director had come up with a new idea, or wasn't happy with the effect that was planned. Even after the first on-mike rehearsal there might be revisions that would involve hatching a brand-new effect from scratch.

Veteran soundman Robert L. Mott, in his book *Sound Effects: Radio, TV and Film* (1990), recounted a story, perhaps apocryphal but certainly on-target, about a woman at CBS named Margo Phelps who joined the sound department in a secretarial position. Early on, she delivered a message to one of the staff.

MARGO: Oh Bill, there's an added effect on your new show. They want the sound of a train.

BILL: What kind of train?

MARGO: They just said a train.

BILL: Running or standing still?

MARGO: . . . a train . . .

BILL: Express or freight?

MARGO: . . . all they said was . . .

BILL: Fast or slow?

MARGO: I'll call them back.

After checking with the proper parties, she called back the sound effects man and reported, "It's a long freight train . . . running on a level track for ten pages. It then climbs a long hill for fifteen pages and then comes to a stop in a station. It stays there for three pages and pulls out . . . and, oh yes . . . there are four train whistles . . . two on level track, one going up the hill, and one when it pulls out of the station." She paused, then asked if there was anything else the man needed to know.

BILL: Steam or diesel?

A good soundman took pride in knowing these specifics and serving the show as well as he could. A good director valued that quality and encouraged it. The knock on a door could indicate a great deal: was it the rapping of an anxious policeman, or the tentative approach of a teenager about to pick up his first date?

When footsteps were called for, the soundman had to know not only who was walking, but why and how. Was it a man, or a woman? Fat or skinny? Were they eager, frightened, furtive, joyful? So much could be conveyed in just the sound of those steps.

After the umpteenth re-creation of the *Suspense* classic "Sorry, Wrong Number," its star, Agnes Moorehead, was interviewed for the September 12, 1952, issue of *TV Radio Life* magazine, and declared, "The sound man is extremely important. A mood can be projected expertly, you know, in the mere dialing of a telephone."

An indication of horse's hooves seems fairly straightforward, but here again the soundman had much to question: was the horse ambling or galloping? And what kind of surface was the horse traversing—grass, mud, snow, a dusty Western street?

Soundman Berne Surrey is performing not only in tandem with—but in sync with—Agnes Moorehead in this performance of the famous tour de force *Suspense* show "Sorry, Wrong Number"

A card file in a typical radio sound department would include such listings as: felling tree with axe; felling tree with saw; monks chanting; football crowds; horse and wagon in snow; horse and wagon on gravel road; cavalry: horses passing at trot; horses passing at gallop.

What kind of car, what caliber of gun, what season of year? A pattern of convincing sound effects depended on detailed answers to all those questions, and more.

⌐

Sound effects began to be called "sound patterns" in the late 1940s and early 1950s, when the art of sound reached its peak on network radio.

One show that featured sophisticated sound patterns was *The Voyage of the Scarlet Queen*, a wonderful high-adventure series starring and directed by Elliott

Lewis. This series presented a veritable symphony of sound to the listener, opening with a whoosh of wind, colorful seagoing music, a crash of cymbals, a man in the distance shouting, "Stand by to make sail!" then the creak of a cabin, and the commanding voice of Elliott Lewis saying, "Log entry: The ketch *Scarlet Queen*, Philip Carney, Master." In these seafaring sagas, there would scarcely be a scene that didn't feature layers of effects. In fact, soundman Ray Kemper recalls that the series' chief writers, Gil Doud and Bob Tallman, "would write a complete cue that would take a third of a page just for sound effects, and *then* get to the dialogue!

"It was quite a procedure just preparing for that show, because you didn't have a whole lot of time; we would work at it, get everything prepared, bring it up there and then, boy, it was just gung-ho, you were going from that moment on and it never stopped, but it was a great show, I did enjoy doing it."

Kemper's partner on the series was Bill James, but sometimes the requirements of the script were so extensive that they would request a third man to help out. They often had all three turntables going at once, on top of the live effects being produced on the spot.

"I never worked so hard in my life," says Kemper. He and James "would have as many as four or five records on each turntable, sequenced, so that you could take them off and get to the next one as quickly as possible to your cue mark. We would have perhaps one cue standing by and the other two would be running; you got so adept at that, you could cue up a record and drop the other arms on other records. This guy working the turntable was as busy as a one-armed paperhanger, but the other guy, the second man is so busy doing manual sound effects, that every time Bill and I finished a show, we were exhausted."

One distinctive sound on that series was the sound of the ship creaking at sea. Kemper explains how it was done: "We had a box about twelve inches long, about four inches wide, with a cotton rope tied at one end. It went through there, looped around about a half-inch dowel pin, and then was attached to a strong spring; this spring was then attached to the back of the box. On the outside of the box was a handle attached to the dowel pin so that you could turn that dowel; we put a lot of beeswax on it so that when you moved the handle, it would creak back and forth. You could go fast and you could slow it down, you could do anything you wanted with [that creak]. That sound effect was subsequently used in many, many things."

It wasn't just the sound effects that made *Scarlet Queen* so good; it was a perfect orchestration of story, character, music, and sound.

The intelligent and creative use of sound effects was also a major ingredient in the success of *Gunsmoke*. Soundman Kemper, who worked in tandem with Tom Hanley, believes that much of the credit for that belongs to the series' director, Norman MacDonnell, who never liked to "cheat" on sound.

Cheat? Kemper explains, "If you walk from Point A to Point B and then you have to return, you should walk the same amount of steps. Most directors simply wouldn't allow it. They would say, 'Turn around and walk back,' and you'd go two steps and that's it, they're into the script again. And you couldn't convince them it was important to return the same amount of steps. Norm MacDonnell, if you had a particular distance to walk, gave you the time to walk back again. Once in a great while we'd cheat if we were hurting for time, but most of the time, he gave us all the time we needed.

"Another form of cheating would be a fight. A lot of directors just wanted to hear a bunch of scuffling and some swats on a hand, and that was it. Not Norm MacDonnell, no sir. When we did a fight between Matt Dillon and a baddie, you stood there toe to toe and you painted a picture. There's nothing but sound effects and grunts from the actors and when you heard this, your mind conjured a picture, saw a picture of two large men just beating the hell out of one another. Big, heavy blows: one in the gut, one in the chin, stagger back and so forth, and when they'd fall, they'd take time for a stagger and a fall. You'd come out of there sometimes with bruised elbows from doing body falls, and bruised hands doing fights, but you always felt a great sense of accomplishment on that show. It was always greatly appreciated."

Because *Gunsmoke* set such a high standard, Kemper and Hanley were particularly unhappy with the sound of gunshots on the air. The engineering system at CBS had an automatic "limiter" which protected the machinery—and the listeners' ears—from anything too loud. It was there for a good purpose, but it defeated the reproduction of realistic gunshots. Kemper and Hanley decided to do something about it.

First, they gathered an arsenal of guns—all kinds, because being good soundmen, they knew that a .45 sounded different from a rifle. Then they tried recording them in a remote location, only to wind up "of all places, at Bill Conrad's Laurel Canyon home in the Hollywood Hills . . . He was at a dead end street, and he was surrounded; it was almost a natural amphitheater, and it was just ideal. We knew this would probably shake the neighbors up a little bit, so I called the police department, and they said OK but go around and tell the neighbors, which we did. We recorded a tremendous amount of gunshots, then we went back to the studio with this and we were ecstatic with the results. They sounded for the first time, like what we wanted. So we edited all those gunshots onto a master reel, and each week, we would go through [the script] and see just what sequence of shots we had to have, and edit onto a cartridge.

"The first time we used them, we took the output of our tape machines and went directly into the line, bypassing the speakers, and by going directly into the line, we could bypass the limiter. The shot would be very loud and realistic, and if we had to have the ricochet, we had an extra amount of ricochets separate that we recorded; we would edit those onto the tail ends of the shots and have these all ready. Norm said, 'For the first time, gunshots sound like gunshots.' [Director] Jaime Del Valle heard them and he said, 'I will never do a show without those gunshots,' and he didn't. They subsequently were used on *Have Gun, Will Travel*, *Johnny Dollar*, and a lot of shows."

The coming of tape was a boon to all soundmen, because it simplified the Rube Goldberg–like operation of turntables, and enabled them to prerecord realistic sounds on natural locations for use in the studio. At first, those recorded sounds had to be transferred to disc for use on the air, because the networks still forbade use of tape for broadcast. By the 1950s that rule was gone, and soundmen took a giant leap forward.

When Jack Webb learned about the development of tape, he jumped at the chance to use it on *Dragnet*. Soundman Bud Tollefson recalls, "He bought us one of the very first tape recorders at the time, a Magnacord, and it was awkward because it was AC-operated." Before long, however, NBC acquired one of the first battery-operated portable recorders for its sound department. "The reason it could stay at speed is because it had an outside attachable flywheel," Tollefson explains. "I'd record the stuff on that, come back and transfer it over to the AC one in the studio, and then edit that before I'd have it transferred to disc."

Dragnet was unexcelled in its realistic use of sound. Bud Tollefson put in a great deal of his own time to record effects for the groundbreaking police series. "We always started because one certain show needed it, but we always tried to get extra stuff for future shows. When we did City Hall, we just did every single room down there. Plus we had access to Lincoln Heights Jail, we had access to the police cars . . . I don't know if I should tell anybody this, but the L.A.P.D., when Parker was the Chief, gave me a police car and let me drive it. Wayne [Kenworthy] and I took it out in the Mojave Desert, near Palmdale someplace, and recorded the daylights out of it: pass-by, sirens, inside radio calls, you name it; we worked a full day up there.

"We had a *Dragnet* sound effects library, but the only way I could get away with that was to say that the other people in the sound department could use it. It had to be stored there for their use, but very few times any other show wanted stuff like that, so it was almost a private collection for Jack Webb."

Few directors were as fussy about details, but the results were there for all to hear: in one show, when Sergeants Friday and Romero are chasing a suspect through an underground walkway joining buildings in downtown Los Angeles, the sound of footsteps is heard on a concrete floor, until a door is flung open. The chase is still on, but now it's going up a flight of steel stairs—with a slight echo in the hallway!

Tollefson and Kenworthy only got approval for a third soundman "when it took more than two hands and four feet. However, Wayne and I taught ourselves how to walk double, so we could walk for four instead of two; that wasn't a big problem, but when a sound effect had to be way off mike—when we were doing other things *on* mike—we'd need that third body over in the corner."

Being a soundman was never dull. As Terry Ross says, "There was nothing rote about it, or routine. Every show was different. You had certain standard effects, of course, which occurred on every show. On *Superman*, you always had the same effect when he was flying, or landing,

Actor Harry Bartell took this revealing overhead shot of a *Dragnet* show in progress, with Jack Webb and Vic Perrin at the mikes, soundman Wayne Kenworthy working the turntables, and his colleague Bud Tollefson performing footsteps on mike.

or taking off. We developed a sound of wind and transferred it to an acetate record, so that we could cue it up for the takeoff. Then we had another platter on which we had his continuous flight, and we'd run that until it was time for him to land, and we'd go into record number three which was the sound effect of landing."

But what if a *Superman* script called for the sound of a heartbeat? Ross discarded the idea of using a real heartbeat, because it couldn't be controlled. "You couldn't speed it up or slow it down on cue. So we used to take a piece of sponge rubber and put it on the turntable and stop the revolving, then place the stylus—the needle—on the rubber and tap the turntable lightly. That was then amplified through the regular amplification system on the playback turntable and that gave you a lovely thump-thump which you could regulate."

Every script brought with it specific needs. "Gus Bayz and I were doing *Suspense*," Ross Murray recalls, "and we got a script that had a basketball game. We looked, and didn't have a basketball game, so we took a tape recorder, went to the YMCA in Hollywood with our sneakers and asked if we could use their basketball court when nobody was using it. We set up the machine with the microphone, then Gus and I ran back and forth, squeaking our sneakers and making little guttural sounds from time to time. The echo was perfect, because the place was empty. That was a perfect basketball game, with no crowd. That means you can do anything you want with that: you can make it outdoors, you can make it with a tournament."

But Murray reached his pinnacle as a sound effects artist when he and his colleagues worked on a now-classic episode of *Escape* called "Three Skeleton Key." It's the story of three men, loners by nature who work at a remote island lighthouse. One night they watch, helplessly, as a ship runs aground near them, and then realize that the strange "moving curtain" on its deck is a blanket of rats! With mounting horror, they watch the rats invade their island, then desperately try to protect themselves from invasion inside the lighthouse.

So. How do you simulate the sound of thousands upon thousands of rats? "We did it with berry baskets: chewing berry baskets, crunching berry baskets, and using cork on glass. A wet cork on glass rubbed back and forth quickly makes the squeak of a mouse. By doing many of them and rerecording and rerecording, you had thousands. That was a three-man show, with all the mice, and the running up and down the steel stairs, and the light in the lighthouse."

Wait a minute: the sound of a light in a lighthouse? "We created the sound of that light going around and around; there really is no sound, but you gotta hear something," says Murray. This addresses an intriguing aspect of sound effects: when is "real" not realistic?

Says Ross Murray, "Sometimes the sound effects that the listener expects to hear—the sound in his imagination—is the best one, and the real thing is no good." A modern automobile doesn't make much of a racket when starting, as older cars did, nor can you hear obvious shifting sounds when it goes from one gear to another, but Murray says that wouldn't make for good radio drama. "So you have to fool 'em a little bit. Anytime you have urgency in an automobile takeoff you slip in a little brake squeal. It's called enhancement."

Nowhere were sound effects "enhanced" more than on comedy shows. The single most famous recurring sound effect in radio was the clatter of junk cascading out of Fibber McGee's closet. The key to this running gag's success was that the falling junk made noise *in a funny way* . . . with an inevitable "punctuation" sound after the tremendous splatter had died down.

Similarly, Jack Benny's soundmen over the years made a point of creating new and funny ways to devise the sound of Jack's ancient car, the Maxwell. Mel Blanc imitated the wheezing automobile at one mike while other sounds were blended into the mix. "We even had a thing with a bunch of syrup jars that were put in a circle with a fulcrum and an arm coming out that would hit the cap on the syrup jar so as it went around it hit these six things and go bububububu; that would be part of the car sound," says Ray Erlenborn.

Jack Benny and his writers didn't stop there: they actually included Jack's longtime soundmen in their scripts, and made their supposed foul-ups and insubordination part of their behind-the-curtain-of-show-business atmosphere. In fact, the voices of Virgil Reimer and Gene Twombley were never heard on the air; it was usually Frank Nelson or Mel Blanc portraying these good-natured (and hard-working) colleagues.

(Years later, when Stan Freberg got his own comedy show on CBS—the last live, big-scale show of its kind to air on network radio—he was thrilled to find that he had "inherited" Benny's legendary sound effects man, Gene Twombley. Freberg boasts that he can still perform the trick of sounding like two people walking at the same time, a feat taught to him by one of the Old Masters.)

Jack Benny's Maxwell became one of the most familiar, and laugh-provoking, sounds on radio . . . but it wasn't just the sound effects that made the Maxwell funny: it was the *performance* of those sounds. A sound effects man had to acquire a comic sense as keen as that of a seasoned comedian.

Ray Erlenborn explains. "If there's going to be a laugh line, you don't slam a door on that laugh line; you wait until the laugh is over and then slam it. Or if there's a cue coming up that calls for a phone to ring, you wait for the laugh to dwindle down before you ring that phone bell. All these things you learn to time yourself with an audience when you're doing a comedy show, and that's what I loved to do. And that's why I did so many comedy shows."

In fact, Erlenborn developed a hilarious demonstration of sound effects which he performed as part of the CBS Tour for many years, and as an audience warm-up on a number of shows. But when he was onstage, he was too canny—and too professional—to try and compete with the stars at the mike.

Some audience shows hid their soundmen behind screens, lest the spectators be distracted from the stars at the mike. On dramatic shows, there was the risk of audiences laughing at the sound effects performance during a dramatic scene. Many comedy shows did just the opposite, figuring that any laugh was a good laugh.

Indeed, listening to comedy shows, one often hears a double laugh for a single gag: the first laugh is in response to the gag, while the second responds to the sound effect, and the sound-man's performance of it.

There's that word again: *performance.*

Cliff Thorsness, one of the top soundmen on the West Coast, says definitively, "We were actors; we *became* actors. We had to work with the people, and their mood and delivery and their timing particularly, so that we had to be a part of them." Performing those effects "live" was part of the process, he feels. "It's a little difficult to throw a cassette in of the knock on a door and time it with an actor so an actor feels it and we feel it. The live sound effects always were more effective in creating a picture."

Lux Radio Theatre's longtime soundman, Charlie Forsyth, shows some of the tricks of his trade to guest star Virginia Mayo.

William Conrad confirmed this view. "They're artists," he declared, adding that he was working in concert with soundmen "every moment of the way. You don't even look at anybody; you turn your back to the director . . . and you narrate watching what they're doing, and you're synched."

Ray Kemper, who worked on *Gunsmoke* for ten years, developed a rapport with Conrad and the other actors in that ensemble that affected his performance—and theirs. "If Bill Conrad reacted in a certain way, Tommy [Hanley] and I would pick up on that and react, so it would enhance what he was doing . . . and he knew we would do that. We came to trust one another very much that way."

When television came along, the need for sound effects was diminished considerably. There was no cause to gently rattle a cup and saucer to establish a kitchen scene when a viewer's eyes identified the setting instantaneously. Offstage sounds were still required from time to time, and comedy/variety shows still used comic sound effects to get laughs. In fact, some of the same men who worked for Jack Benny in the 1940s and early '50s were providing sound effects for Red Skelton and Carol Burnett on television in the 1960s and '70s.

But the art of creating sound patterns for the mind's eye remained the exclusive domain of radio. Even today's movie sound-effects experts, who piece together soundtracks inch by inch on what is called a "foley" stage, sound by sound, stand apart from the artists of radio's golden age, for two key reasons: they can record their sounds over and over again until they're satisfied (unlike the radio men, who had one shot over the air—and no room for mistakes), and, just as important, they perform their sound effects disembodied from the actors on-screen (unlike the radio artists, who had to work in complete harmony with the actors—becoming, in effect, extensions of those actors).

Even in the halcyon days of radio, sound effects men often moonlighted to do movie work; it brought in extra money, but it wasn't as satisfying or enjoyable as working in radio. For one thing, there simply wasn't the same camaraderie.

Carlton E. Morse, creator and director of the legendary programs *One Man's Family* and *I Love a Mystery*, recalled, "Our sound effects man became a member of the cast, just like a talking person, and the result was that we had some of the greatest sound effects in the country."

Asked what he liked best about radio, ace soundman Cliff Thorsness replied, "The great fellowship and the great closeness of people who worked in radio."

Like actors, writers, and other performers, sound-effects artists bathed in a warm glow of friendship, good times, and pride in their work. For them, as much as any other contributors to that era, radio's heyday was indeed a golden time.

5

A Skill and an Art: Radio Acting

One morning in 1988, I was privileged to sit in on a reading and rehearsal for one of Peggy Webber's productions for CART (California Artists Radio Theatre). The assembled group of actors were there to flex their acting muscles in the unique discipline of radio acting. This particular production was a re-creation of Norman Corwin's "Ann Rutledge," which was first heard on the *Cavalcade of America* in 1943. The star, portraying Abraham Lincoln's first love, was Jeanette Nolan, who had played the same part forty-six years earlier.

Miss Nolan, then seventy-seven years old, had a deeply lined face, but when she started reading her part as Ann Rutledge, a small miracle occurred: by means of some incredible alchemy, and through the use of her voice alone, she *became* an eighteen-year-old girl. There was no evidence of "acting" at all.

I thought perhaps my reaction was intense because I wasn't used to being in the company of such professionals, but when I later spoke to some of Nolan's colleagues, I learned that they, too, were awed by her great artistry.

Artistry is not a word one often hears with regard to radio acting, yet that is precisely what it was. What's more, the medium was blessed with an extraordinary number of performers who understood that art and took it to the highest level of expression.

Jeanette Nolan and husband, John McIntire, in Hollywood in 1943 to appear on *Suspense* for William Spier, who had directed them both in *The March of Time* in New York. They were among the cream of the crop, and Spier knew it.

Said Sheldon Leonard, "I've been in most aspects of the entertainment industry—legitimate theater, radio, motion pictures, television—but of all these areas of the entertainment business, the highest level of professionalism was to be found on radio."

Jeanette Nolan is as eloquent as any of them in assessing her fellow actors. Watching her colleagues perform in other CART productions, she says, "I was mesmerized. Here's Lou Krugman, who is a great actor; he can play anything you ask him to. When we did *Treasure Island* I looked and I saw Vic Perrin, all of these people who can immediately go so far beyond what you thought was the potential, and excite you with a whole new character that you've never heard of in your life. Nothing to do with looks, all to do with imagination and a deep creative germ that you're born with."

Radio actors learned to delineate the many facets of a character that were normally conveyed through facial expression, makeup, or costumes. Says Rosemary DeCamp, "You could almost flesh out the person—where he fit in the social scheme of things, where he came from, the climate he was living in, what his job was—all those things can be conveyed with the voice."

Singling out just a handful of actors among the very best isn't easy, because there were so many top-flight professionals. But ask most radio veterans whom they considered the best and a few names constantly recur. From those who worked in Chicago and New York, one often hears the name of Raymond Edward Johnson mentioned, along with those of Everett Sloane and Bill Johnstone. Among Hollywood people the one name mentioned more often than any other is Elliott Lewis.

"Elliott Lewis was the greatest actor of them all," says veteran radio writer

E. Jack Neuman. "He could break your heart with a word; his timing was impeccable."

Lewis had little if any formal training as an actor; he was bitten by the bug while attending high school in Los Angeles, and broke into radio in his teens. He was, in other words, a natural. Listen to his performance as the poet and loner who enters the twilight world of a department store at night in *Escape*'s "Evening Primrose," and hear the longing and tenderness of his character. Listen then to his own remarkable production of "Othello" on *Suspense* (with his then-wife Cathy Lewis as Desdemona, Richard Widmark as Iago, and Joseph Kearns as Cassio) and hear how vital and immediate he made Shakespeare's speeches—authoritative, believable but conversational at the same time. This is the same Elliott Lewis who spent nine years playing Phil Harris's smart-alecky sidekick Frankie Remley on *The Phil Harris–Alice Faye Show*!

Lewis had the ability to make you believe whatever he said. Cast as the skipper on the high-adventure series *The Voyage of the Scarlet Queen*, he was completely convincing as seagoing ship's master Philip Carney—never corny or overblown.

And yet, said Lewis, "I never enjoyed acting. I was able to do it, because . . . it's a trick, and it's a trick that somehow I knew how to do, without any training. Somebody—True Boardman—called me and I walked into the studio and he handed me a script and I gave a performance. And he said, 'Well, do you want to work next week?' and fine, I was off and running. I didn't know what I'd done. I thought I wasn't that good." Others disagreed.

Talk to any West Coast actor about radio and it won't take long for the name of Hans Conried to come up. One of the most prolific performers in the medium, he mastered a dazzling range of dialects and tackled both serious and comic parts with enthusiasm. Indeed, he never met a part he didn't like. Or, as his colleague Gale Gordon put it, "He was an actor-holic. I'm sure that Hans' idea of heaven would be to do a play that had thirty characters, men and women, and that he would do them all."

Conried did in fact take on a number of unusual jobs during his long career. In the early 1940s he was paid to stand by for John Barrymore in case the alcoholic actor couldn't pull himself together for his weekly appearances on *The Rudy Vallee Show*. Later in that decade, when the comedy series *My Friend Irma* was transferred to movies, his running part of the aged Professor Kropotkin was played by the much older character actor Felix Bressart. But when Bressart died during production, Conried was hired to take his place—and, in garish makeup, match the long shots which had already been filmed with the other actor!

Three revealing snapshots of Hans
Conried taken by youthful actor
Conrad Binyon in the late 1940s.

Writer-director Arch Oboler
worked with both men, and
admired them greatly. "The
difference between Elliott and Hans," he said, "is that Elliott hated acting and
Hans loved it. Elliott thought it was beneath him. Amazing. Not in the early days,
but as he went along; he felt he was in the wrong place, there was something
wrong with being an actor, which of course is nonsense."

Most likely Lewis' disdain for acting grew from the fact that it came so easily
to him. His ambitions lay elsewhere, in writing, directing, and producing, and he
got to realize those ambitions in radio as well as television.

❧

So how exactly did these actors do what they did? What enabled them to read
words off a page and create a picture in the listeners' minds? The best of them—
like Lewis—could achieve this even in their first glance at a script. Elliott Lewis
explained, without false modesty, that even at a cold reading, "You're not only
reading and giving a performance that could have gone on the air, but as you're
giving a performance here, you're reading about it on the page. It's like the oboe

player that, as he's blowing out, he's sucking in more air so that he can be continuous. It's the same thing."

Experienced radio actors got so good at cold readings that some of them disdained too much rehearsal. At a radio re-creation for SPERDVAC (The Society for the Preservation and Encouragement of Radio Drama Variety and Comedy) in the 1990s, actor Lawrence Dobkin, after giving a superb performance, said—only half-jokingly—"You spoil a script by understanding it."

John Astin, best remembered for his television work on series like *The Addams Family*, got a foothold in radio when he came to New York in the 1950s, and still speaks glowingly of John Larkin, who, he recalls, "was 'off the page' in the first reading."

William Conrad made the same boast as many other longtime professionals: "I used to be able to pick up an absolutely cold script and go on the air with it and never make a mistake. Just tell me what the character is, or what's he called, and roughly what it's about . . . and that's all I need."

It wasn't just that Conrad could read without stumbling; he used his imagination to disappear into the character. "I had a picture [in my mind], but I was never consciously referring to it. When I was rehearsing I got the pictures, but by the time we got on the air, I was playing—it was happening. *The scene was really happening*."

Theater people were extremely wary of radio actors' ability to do so well in cold readings. Paul Stewart told researcher Anthony Tollin, "I remember my own experiences as a Broadway actor; I would go and read for a part, and they'd say, 'Well, you probably won't get any better,' because I was reading at performance pitch. In one instance they brought me back two or three times because they were not sure of me."

Was this superficial acting, then? Not on your life. Said John McIntire, "I think it was just because there were such goddamn good actors."

And, as every radio professional will attest, no one ever took their job lightly; they were steeped in a tradition that demanded them to give one hundred percent effort to every performance. Said Lurene Tuttle, "There are very clever people in the business now who are just voice characters, who . . . turn on Voice 36 or Voice 9 or Voice 12 or something. But we always worked from the full person, at least I did, and I know that all of us tried to work that way because that's the only honest way to do it. You have to have a person who lives and breathes and walks and is alive, rather than just turning on a voice. You could conjure up, through imagination, anything you wanted to be."

Howard Duff, who costarred with Tuttle on *The Adventures of Sam Spade*,

The versatile (some might say indispensable) Lurene Tuttle with Vincent Price at a table reading for an episode of *The Saint* in the late 1940s.

among other shows, said, "She could just take hold of a part and do something with it. As I said at her eulogy, I think she never met a part she didn't like. She just loved to work; she loved to act. She's a woman who was born to do what she was doing, and loved every minute of it, I guess."

That kind of commitment wasn't unique; it's precisely what distinguished the great radio actors and set them apart from the crowd. And woe to the actor who tried to get away with a perfunctory read. As the prolific writer-director Carlton E. Morse wrote in *Off Mike*, "There is nothing that will kill a serial faster than indifference on the part of actors. If the actors become bored with the job they're doing, so does the writer, and the show is dead. And actors and writer know the show is dead long, long before the public does or the Crossley rating registers the fact."*

Don Ameche had his own formula for success in radio. Said the actor, "I could always envision where I was. If I was in a car, it was easy for me to talk a little louder over the motor—you know, that kind of thing. It got to be second nature." When he was playing an intimate scene with an actress he tried to look at the actress as much as possible across the mike, and only glancingly refer to his script. "It was as real . . . as I could possibly make it. One of the reasons I think I was as effective in pictures as I was is that I kept a lot of that naturalism from radio. I could see that on the screen, and that pleased me."

Ask experienced actors if they think radio acting was glib, and just watch them bristle. Says Parley Baer, "I think the only time an actor was glib was when the

*Crossley and Hooper ratings were the forerunners of today's Nielsens.

part called for a glib character. Actors gave their all in their performance, and the tears were just as real as they would be on the stage."

Echoed William Conrad, "There were a lot of actors who were glib and superficial no matter what they did, but the good [radio] actors were just as good as any actors in any medium."

In fact, said Kenneth Roberts, "Many great stage actors would come to radio and they'd be awful, because they were used to many weeks of rehearsal to prepare, and they couldn't accommodate the speed that was required in radio."

Jackson Beck agrees. "There were any number of stars, and I mean really big people, who could not read off a piece of paper and make it sound real. They knew it and wouldn't take a radio job for any amount of money because they knew they were gonna stink it up. There were lots of stars who were so trained to memorize that they couldn't come in at one o'clock in the afternoon and go on at eight o'clock at night because in that time they couldn't memorize thirty-five pages of script. These people got the script one week ahead of time and tried their damnedest, but in radio you cut and you edit; you don't do that in the theater."

The credo of most working radio actors is well articulated by Parley Baer, who says, "I don't know of a radio actor who, at the first reading or whatever, could not see the character he was playing. Maybe the actor didn't see him as you did, but that was the beautiful part of radio. If there were five million people listening, you were giving five million different perfor-

John Barrymore is sometimes credited with the invention of this device, meant to keep histrionic actors like himself from moving too close or too far from the microphone in the heat of a performance. More likely it was a desperate measure on the part of the engineer or director to keep their sound levels on an even keel! True radio professionals would have disdained such a prop. Barrymore and then-wife Elaine Barrie are seen here performing "streamlined Shakespeare" on NBC in 1937.

mances. If there was a word of technique involved in that sort of thing it would be *belief*. You had to believe what you were saying; you had to be just as concerned with what you were saying even though some people said you only had to read it. That's why actors used to hyperventilate sometimes when they were climbing mountains that weren't there."

He adds, laughing, "You also had to keep your pages from rattling."

How to handle a script was, indeed, one of the mundane but crucial skills a radio actor had to acquire. Adele Ronson recalls, "You had to be very careful. A lot of people dropped the pages on the floor as they finished. I didn't like doing that, so I just put it underneath, but I was very quiet about it."

Parley Baer, radio actor extraordinaire, with James Stewart, one of the best of the Hollywood stars who moonlighted on radio.

Then there was "mike" technique. Actors had to learn how to sound as if they were walking into (or out of) a room without actually doing so. Elliott Lewis explained, "The actor worked on either side of the ribbon mike; the flat sides were absolutely 'dead.' On a long, long fade-in, the actor stood right as close to it as he could get, and then he turned and made a big circle to make his entrance."

Says Parley Baer, "The ability to fade in, fade out, or drop the voice was tantamount to an entrance or exit [on the stage]. Shadings and colorings were our makeup, they were our wardrobe in many instances. It's much like a musician modulating and modifying tones. People like Bill Conrad and some of those stentorian people could crack a roof, but a lot of them had built-in techniques of never using the entire force of their volume. You got the feeling that Bill, no matter how tough he got, he could be twice that tough, or happy, or sad."

That control came not from formal training, but from experience. Like most of the radio actors with great voices, Conrad did what he did instinctively. Of his booming voice, he said, "There was always a danger thing in my voice.

Now, I don't know how that got there, but I covered everything with a black drape . . . I never took a drama lesson in my life, I never even thought about what it is to be an actor. All I thought about was the money that it was possible to make, maybe. And it turned out to be possible. I was just f——ing lucky to have a voice that fascinated people."

Conrad and Baer costarred in the long-running *Gunsmoke* series in the 1950s, and with their fellow actors—who represented the cream of the Hollywood talent pool—created unusually rich radio drama. One of the hallmarks of the show was its sense of quiet, of underplaying. Says Baer of their Old West setting, "It was a time of shooting and fighting . . . but conversations were not like that at that time. You figure that everything was quietly conceived and modulated out of an office or around the campfire. People lose sight of the fact that in those times, quiet was their safety, really, because even the rustle of clothing could be detected in the quiet prairie by sharp ears. That was one of the things that I think

Art Van Harvey and Bill Idelson seem to be enjoying themselves while performing as Vic and Rush Gook, respectively; that's exactly the feeling a listener had tuning in to *Vic and Sade*.

we tried to portray, that it was a time of underplay. I think we maybe overdid it at times, because it was a technique that worked."

Another asset afforded the *Gunsmoke* cast was a familiarity among the players that enhanced the ensemble work. This was true on many shows, of course, where after months or years of working together the performers seemed to almost breathe in unison. The precision of their verbal byplay, including interrupted sentences and half-finished thoughts, on the daily *Vic and Sade* broadcast wouldn't have been possible if Art Van Harvey, Bernardine Flynn, Billy Idelson, and Clarence Hartzell hadn't worked together for such a long, long time. (In fact, Peggy Webber characterizes their work as "the finest radio acting I ever heard.")

On the other hand, Orson Welles had an unwitting formula for spontaneity that kept his fellow actors alert, during the heyday of the *Mercury Theatre* period in New York. Because he was busy with theater projects during the course of the week, he didn't attend rehearsals in his guise as actor or director. One of his troupe, the wonderful Alice Frost, recalled, "Many times he had someone standing in for him at our dress rehearsal, and I used to be so angry about it at the time; he would come on and it would be a different performance, naturally, than the one that—I think it was Ev Sloane sometime, and Paul Stewart—[gave]. They were excellent actors . . ." But, on reflection, "I always thought after, It's good—it keeps you on your toes: you have to listen and react."

Having an interesting voice was, of course, a tremendous asset, but working actors had to be able to adapt their voices to suit any situation. Some actors had a facility for dialects and foreign accents; others had to learn.

Says Rosemary DeCamp, "All you had to do really was to give an accent that approximated what the listener expected you to sound like. That was about all it was, about that accurate."

Parley Baer observes, "[Doing] dialects is like the ability to play music. A dialect is not just a question of misplaced consonants or something like that; it's a melody. There are a lot of dialects I can't do, and accents as well, but if you hear the melody, if you hear the tune, it's just like playing music."

A favorite anecdote is told about Hans Conried and a fellow actor standing outside the CBS studio on Sunset Boulevard one day when the beautiful film star Linda Darnell walked by. The actor admired Miss Darnell, but Conried dismissed her by saying, "I'll bet she can't do one dialect!"

Bear in mind that radio actors not only had to give a full-bodied performance, but also had to be able to concentrate. Said Elliott Lewis, "Twenty minutes before airtime, when you've finished your dress rehearsal, and you have three minutes to cut, people better have a sharp pencil and pay attention because they're crossing things out and then you've got to add others, and it's easy to get lost, and people would get lost."

While on the air, they had to keep one eye cocked toward the control room, to see if the director was issuing instructions to slow down or speed up. One ear had to be listening to the sound effects, to make sure the actor and effects man were in perfect sync. There was movement from one mike to another, and script pages to keep in order. It was no mean feat.

Performing before a live audience gave radio actors a different set of challenges. Some directors would actually employ dramatic lighting on stage to help the actors set a mood, which was often an effective tool. On at least one occasion, however, a blue gel in the spotlight completely blanked out the blue mimeograph ink of the scripts, rendering them invisible to the bewildered cast!

Other producers required cast members to dress formally for evening performances. Announcer Dresser Dahlstead recalls, "Don Gilman, who was the vice president of NBC on the Coast, was a fine gentleman, and at 6:00 every night, everybody had to get in formal attire, tuxedos and long dresses. This is radio, but he felt it lent something to the prestige of the people, that they would perform better. It made you feel kind of elegant, I think, and it was nice watching all these people wandering around, the girls in their pretty dresses . . ."

One of the challenges of doing a dramatic program for a live audience was the need to work the microphone and ignore the people in the theater. Says Raymond Edward Johnson, "You weren't playing for them; you were onstage but you were there for the audience 'out there.' It was kind of a bastard thing; you can't be true to two masters at one time."

Sometimes the logistics of a broadcast aided a performer. Lurene Tuttle played twins (one good, one evil) on an episode of *The Whistler*, and found that using two microphones helped her to stay in character. "I had the time to physically become the other person as I moved from microphone to microphone," she explained, adding, "My imagination has always been strong, from the time I was able to talk."

The lifeblood of each performance—with or without an audience—was adrenaline, and it started to flow when the red light went on and the director threw the first cue. Jackson Beck recalls it vividly: "You were up. You were up and you were ready to go. This is it and there's no going back. If it happened to be a very good show, as soon as the light went off, we'd all congratulate each other because we knew we'd done it. You know, we crossed the finish line first.

"You got inured to it after a while, but don't tell me that it didn't happen—because you could look around and see it in their faces, and you could feel it, the vibes. You knew damn well you'd done a good job. The beauty of it was working with another actor—two, three actors working together on a scene and if one of them started to go, the other guys pulled him back and pulled him up, ad-libbed around him or supported him.

"We supported each other not only for the sake of the show, but on a personal level, because we all had our weak moments and we all knew one of these days we're gonna bomb, and we wouldn't let each other bomb. You were off in this spaceship all by yourself for fifteen minutes or a half an hour and you've got to get back to land safely. There was a sense of support; you might hate the guy, he might hate you, but it was there."

Mutual support was crucial to every show. If, in a scene between two actors, one finished first and had no further lines—but was still supposed to be there listening—it was considered good form for the second actor to remain at the mike, as a courtesy. Some actors betrayed this trust, and according to Parley Baer, "You could almost tell if an actor had walked away, because there was some intonation—I don't know what it was—but there would be a drop in temperature."

The adrenaline rush was not limited to live broadcasts, either. Hans Conried recalled what it was like working for early transcription services which recorded fifteen-minute and half-hour syndicated programs. This was in the days before tape, when the ability to edit was unheard-of. "I used to work for C. P. McGregor," he told an audience of his peers at Pacific Pioneer Broadcasters. "They paid $3.50 or $5.00 for the show, and we would have to stand by. God forbid the announcer would make a fluff on the end of a fifteen-minute platter; we all had to do it all over again. It was impressed upon us that since we were being paid $3.50, to peel the wax cost 75 cents and if you were responsible for such a peeling two or three times in your experience with that employer, you were looking for another job."

On a 1940s series version of *The Count of Monte Cristo*, actors had to sweat out the times—more than once—when the script was still being completed while the show was on the air! Carbon-copy script pages were handed to the cast in midstream and, says Parley Baer, "God help the fellow who got the fifth copy." Carbon paper smudges were one by-product of the broadcast, but that was nothing compared to the panic when the director realized that the script was too short. "Then, of course, you got a signal to slow down, when you had a minute and a half to go, and about a third of a page to do it in," Baer recalls. "Boy, some of those finales were done in slow-motion."

Actors developed an innate sense of timing, as well as performance level, but they were only human, and subject to human frailties. Norman Corwin gathered a stellar cast, headed by James Stewart, Orson Welles, and Lionel Barrymore, for his 1941 broadcast on the Bill of Rights, *We Hold These Truths*. Stewart and

Welles each narrated large portions of the script, with Welles taking the powerful, hour-long show to its conclusion. At dress rehearsal, Welles built his performance in intensity, measure by measure, to a thrilling climax, and when it was over, the cast spontaneously burst into applause. Welles was pleased with the response, but Corwin feared that it might somehow go to his head. And it did. When, several hours later, the show was actually broadcast, Welles started out at the fever pitch at which he'd concluded the rehearsal—and then had nowhere to go, vocally or emotionally. The show is still impressive today, but Welles' narration sounds overwrought.

The greatest hurdle facing any radio actor was tripping on his own tongue—and, if he did, finding a way to regain his composure. Microphone veterans have dozens of stories about on-air flubs and the tumult that often followed.

Jackson Beck recalls one children's show for which the commercial copy, promoting Kellogg's Pep, was written in a form of double entendre about putting buttons on your beanie. "It struck everybody and we fell on the floor; we started laughing. That was in rehearsal. Then we went on the air and Dan McCullough broke up while he was doing it. We were dying in that studio . . . we were writhing on the floor. You had to get up, go pick up your cue, and go on with the scenes and it was an absolute disaster, and at the end of this thing, we were in hysterics. One of the guys had a habit of fluffing anyway, and he got mixed up on a word and started to fluff all over the place, mispronouncing the words, which made it even worse, and then he'd mispronounce it another way and he tried to recover and recover, till somebody stepped up and interjected a line and took the scene away from him for a minute till he could recover himself. You just kept on going."

To keep on going was the thing; how to do it was the problem. "One time on *Red Ryder*," Parley Baer recalls, "Bill [Willis] Bouchey, who had a magnificent voice, was leading a bunch of us after Red Ryder, intent upon doing him a bit of no-good, and he did one of those stage whispers which shook the rafters. He said, 'Keep your tinger on the frigger.' Well, we exploded and poor Bill knew he had said something wrong; in the booth, everybody's collapsed, and those who didn't have scenes with him are rushing to the sides to stuff velour in our mouths. Bill went on with his lines, but he was mouthing the words 'What did I say? What did I say?' "

Another flub became famous, with several actors claiming to have spoken the misbegotten speech. William Conrad said it was his goof, during a movie adaptation in which he was playing Loretta Young's husband. "Just before the end of the first act, we were playing a love scene and I had asked her to marry me and she said, 'I can't tell you now.' And I said, 'All right, in that case, I'll be up for your answer in the morning.' Music, commercial. On the air comes the time, the show is going fine and I say, 'All right, in that case I'll be up your ass in the morning.' Well, the audience went, the orchestra went, the conductor went . . . everybody went. It was hysterical. The musicians were making mistakes all over the place . . . It was the worst thing I ever did in my life, and it just came out."*

Such stories are always good for a laugh, but in the context of radio history it's important to point out that flubs like that were remarkably rare. Radio actors achieved a level of perfection that was simply amazing, considering the way shows were ground out day after day, and considering that they were often rushing from one show directly to another.

Jeanette Nolan remembers the night that John McIntire was to play George Washington on an episode of *Cavalcade of America* to be broadcast from the 46th Street Playhouse. McIntire was also announcing Raymond Gram Swing's nightly newscast, which immediately preceded the prime-time drama. Like any seasoned radio pro, McIntire not only knew how to get from one location to another in moments, but how to switch mental gears. For him, it was just another day of work. For the audience, it was one more example of radio acting at its finest.

Nolan's memory of the evening is vivid and detailed. "We had an ambulance standing by to bring him . . . to the theater. He had the first line in the script; he left the air [on the Raymond Gram Swing program] at twenty-eight minutes after, or whatever, and had to be on [the next show] at thirty-one and a half past. And I'm telling you, the audience was in the house, the curtain went up, and there was the *Cavalcade of America* music, and here comes Ted Jewett doing the introduction to Mount Vernon and so forth. We're all sitting out there in our costumes, Agnes [Moorehead] sitting next to me, I'm pregnant with Holly, and we're watching and holding on to each other. Finally the dear little black man who's been in that theater his whole life looks on and signals to me that John has come through the door, and here he is walking out in his tails and he walks up to the microphone, on his cue, and says the first line that he had, and you heard in his

---

*In the interest of accuracy, but not wanting to spoil a wonderful story, it should be said that other radio actors, including Elliott Lewis and Lurene Tuttle, told this same story as having happened to *them*.

speech the wooden teeth of George Washington. And he had established that character."

What enabled him to do that? One might say equal doses of preparation, concentration, and talent . . . the qualities that distinguished all the best radio performances.

Says Nolan, "It was pure magnificence, that's all."

6

Your Announcer . . .

n the 1932 film *State's Attorney*, John Barrymore turns off a radio and says disdainfully, "I wonder what radio announcers tell their mothers they do for a living."

Sarcasm aside, Barrymore's wisecrack does raise an interesting question: How, and why, would anyone have decided to make radio announcing a career? The answer is simple: in the early days of radio, almost no one did. A later generation may have looked to famous and prosperous announcers as role models, but at the outset of commercial radio, virtually everyone who became an announcer did so by accident, misdirection, or default.

And yet, these dulcet-voiced gentlemen established a presence as potent as that of any so-called stars. Indeed, many of the best announcers became well-recognized personalities, and active participants in the shows they announced. Think of Don Wilson and *The Jack Benny Show*: that association that spanned four decades, well into the television era. His name became synonymous with the comedian; when Benny took his show on the road, he made every effort to bring Wilson along. The show wasn't the same without him. Bing Crosby felt the same about Ken Carpenter. Sponsors were no less concerned about any change in the status quo; when Fibber McGee and Molly took their summer vacation, announcer Harlow Wilcox was obliged to stay behind and extoll the virtues of Johnson's Wax on the company's summer replacement shows.

Some, like John Conte, Marvin Miller, Bill Goodwin, Harry Von Zell, and Art Baker, were able to launch successful careers in the movies from the springboard of radio announcing. Goodwin fared rather well, winning prominent supporting parts in *The Jolson Story* and *So This Is New York*, among others; Von Zell got decent character parts in films like *Till the End of Time* and *The Saxon Charm*. The most successful—and complete—transition from the airwaves was made by Paul Douglas. Douglas was on the CBS staff for many years, though

```
NOTE TO ANNOUNCER:    Make local announcements every fifteen minutes
                      except on dramatic programs which depend on a
                      succession of thought.

                      "There will now be a brief pause in the
                      Fleischmann Program for station announce-
                      ments. This is WEAF, New York City."

                      TIME: (     :    )

                      FLEISCHMANN RADIO HOUR

(    )(    )
8:00 - 9:00 P.M.         OCTOBER 24, 1929              THURSDAY

1.(DOWN THE ROAD TO SUNSHINE) - (RUDY VALLEE AND HIS CONNECTICUT YANKEES)
  RUDY VALLEE:

            Heigh-ho everybody!  This is Rudy Vallee broadcasting
  the Fleischmann's Yeast Hour.  We're now playing "Down the Road
  to Sunshine," the song which will introduce our program at this
  time every Thursday night.
  (Music comes up, Vallee sings chorus, and music ends . . piece
   should take 1:15 to 1:30 according to tempo)
  GRAHAM McNAMEE: (No Music)

            Good evening, ladies and gentlemen of the radio
  audience.  This is Graham McNamee announcing the program sent you
  by the makers of Fleischmann's Yeast.  Tonight we want you to
  picture a quiet, luxurious supper club, where soft, mellow blue
  lights cast their shadows over white linen and sparkling glass
  and silver . . waiters hurrying to and fro. . palms all around . .
  clear-eyed, clean-cut young men dancing with beautiful girls in
  lovely gowns.  And up here on a little stage at one end of the
  room Rudy Vallee and his Connecticut Yankees providing that
  wonderful music of theirs.  Everybody is looking his best and
  feeling his best tonight.

            All the girls seem to have smiling lips and sparkling
  eyes and lovely complexions.
```

his bombastic personality never won him any popularity contests among his colleagues. An introduction to playwright-director Garson Kanin led to his casting in the Broadway comedy *Born Yesterday*, in which he played the rough-hewn, self-made business tycoon Harry Brock. It was a tailor-made part, and the play's huge success led Douglas to Hollywood and a long starring career in such movies as *A Letter to Three Wives*, *Angels in the Outfield*, and *Executive Suite*. He never gave radio a backward glance.

Announcers were radio's jacks-of-all-trades, expected to be able to handle everything from calling the plays at a football game to accurately pronouncing the names of foreign-born composers on a classical music program. At different times they wore the cloak of salesman, when doing commercial pitches, and distinguished observer, when introducing special guests in the studio or at public events. They had to be articulate, intelligent, and fast on their feet. A good voice was just part of the job requirement.

"It is no mere coincidence that the top-ranking announcers are, almost without exception, also college men," wrote Art Gilmore and Glenn Y. Middleton in their 1940s training manual *Radio Announcing*. "Higher education sharpens the alertness of young men and women and provides them with knowledge of the bases of our society and its mores. . . . In a fast-changing world, knowing how to make adjustments, or choosing for one's self the course of action best suited to the situation, is the keynote of success."

In 1933, a 10-cent newsstand booklet profiled leading announcers of the day. Here is the capsulized biography of Graham McNamee, arguably the first announcer superstar, that appeared in that publication:

Graham McNamee today is conceded one of America's best known radio announcers, and the dean of his profession. But if you ask McNamee what it takes to become popular before the gilded 'mike'—and be able to call notables by their first name—he will shake his head in despair. McNamee went into radio as a temporary occupation until he could obtain sufficient bookings as a concert artist to keep the wolf from the door. He has traveled across the continent to spend two hours describing a college football game. He once came near exhaustion keeping America's radio audience informed as to the doings of their delegates at the drawn-out Democratic National Convention of 1924. Each time the NBC has broadcast the running of the Kentucky Derby—Graham has been at the microphone. It was his voice that described Lindbergh's triumphant return from Paris after his trans-Atlantic flight. Again all America listened to the

Graham McNamee parlayed his radio popularity into a syndicated newspaper column, as advertised on this poster.

versatile announcer as Richard E. Byrd returned to New York after his Antarctica expedition. Stay-at-homes welcomed his description of the inauguration of President Hoover. During his eleven years of broadcasting, McNamee estimates he has used more than seven times the maximum number of words in the dictionary. And seldom has his pronounciation been challenged. During his talks with kings, queens, cardinals, football captains, presidents, prize-fighters, and what-have-you, it is estimated that more persons have heard his voice than of any other man alive.

McNamee made his first 'broadcast' from a Washington, D.C. hospital on July 10, 1889. Boyhood found him in a choir, and with such promise he continued his study of voice past the amateur stage. Concert artists were not so much in demand, so Graham obtained a job as a salesman. He soon found himself in New York, not too well supplied with money. Then he took up jury service at $3 a day. One day during the court's noon recess he chanced to pass the old studios of WEAF at 195 Broadway. He decided to save 50 cents which he would spend at lunch and look over a broadcasting studio. It was then that one of the world's greatest radio personalities started on the proverbial ladder to success.

The top radio announcers *were* successful; they enjoyed prestige, popularity, and handsome salaries. They also made what they did look easy.

The contemporary public's image of an old-time announcer was cemented in the late 1960s by latter-day radio personality Gary Owens, who introduced each segment of the popular TV series *Rowan and Martin's Laugh-In* in an announcer's booth, standing next to a vintage microphone, script in hand and hand cupped to his ear.

The colorful hand gesture was not a comic invention, according to veteran announcer Andre Baruch. "That was a fact, and there was a reason for it," he explained. "Today we use cans—headsets—but if there's a big orchestra in back of you, like on *Your Hit Parade*, you can't hear what you're saying. So if you put your hand to your ear you can at least hear yourself. Some fellows held onto their ties; the reverberation would come from your necktie if it was tight enough."

⌒

Announcers lived a peripatetic life in radio's heyday; broadcasting from a studio was just part of their job. In the pioneering days, many so-called announcers at local stations around the country also unlocked the door in the morning and fired up the transmitter. But there was a certain quaintness even in a network job.

"A typical day was when you came in at 6:00 or 6:30 and you signed the station on," recalls Kenneth Roberts of his earliest days on staff at CBS in New York. "Then you spent perhaps a few hours in what was known as Little Siberia, which was an announce booth where you did nothing but every fifteen minutes or half-hour be expected to say 'This is WABC New York.' That's what CBS was called in those days." Then there would be a series of soap operas and musical programs—often fifteen minutes in length—before taking off for other musical locations around Manhattan. Roberts' favorite daytime remote was the Ritz-Carlton Hotel, "which was a plum because you always were treated to lunch."

Hotels were among the more genteel surroundings for broadcasts in those days. Jimmy Wallington used to do special events with John Hix, of the "Strange as It Seems" newspaper feature. Among his milestones: the first ship-to-ship broadcast in history, the world's first broadcast from a submerged submarine, and the first broadcast from an underwater diving bell in use at sea. In that still-primitive era, announcers took microphones aloft in hot-air balloons, underground in caves, and anywhere else that might make for a colorful broadcast.

⌒

What motivated a young man to become an announcer? As noted before, few of them set out on that path. Don Wilson and Harry Von Zell were singers; most other famous voice-men had acting ambitions. For Kenneth Roberts, the Depression put an end to that career, and caused him to think about radio as a means of making a living. "I decided to try it, and I laid out a campaign for myself: I was going to attack every borough in New York. There were many radio stations in the city at that time, and Brooklyn had four stations, all of which shared the same wavelength, but they were four independent stations. I resolved that on Monday I would do Brooklyn, on Tuesday I would do the Bronx, and so on. My first day, on Monday, I went down to Brooklyn and the first station I walked into was WLTH, 'the Voice of Brooklyn.' And the man said, 'What do you do?' I said, 'Well, I'm an actor, really, but I was interested in trying my hand at this new profession.' He said, 'You walked in at a lucky moment. My announcer just left—he got a job at CBS—so I guess I'll hire you.' I said, 'No audition?' He said, 'No, you don't have to audition.' And I got the job. And that was the end of my searching. It was 1930, and I got $30 a week, which was considered tremendous money at that time. I stayed there for six months, doing many different things in addition to announcing: I answered the telephone, I swept the office, I tried to sell time on the telephone (we had a sales talk which was written out), I arranged the programs, I read poetry, I played the piano. It was great experience. We were only on the air four hours a day, but during those four hours I did an awful lot."

Howard Duff started as a staff announcer in Seattle. He'd acted at the Seattle Repertory Playhouse, but "I realized that I wasn't going to get paid for acting. What voice training I had was self-imposed. I used to practice reading copy all the time—anything with a lot of words to it. I'd go through a magazine and read all the advertising out loud. And, of course, I did Shakespeare. When I was in the broadcast booth at KOMO in Seattle, I'd turn off the lights and do whatever I could remember—*Richard III*, I guess, because I was in that production. I guess I got lucky, and this was during the Depression, so any job you had you didn't want to lose." He was barely twenty years old at the time.

A young Kenneth Roberts (center), in formal dress, banters with the popular comedy stars Colonel Stoopnagle and Budd in the early 1930s.

Mel Allen, later to gain immortality as the voice of the New York Yankees, was just out of law school in Alabama, and visiting a radio broadcast in New York during the late 1930s when he was invited to audition—and then offered a CBS staff announcer's job. He had no previous radio experience, "outside of doing some football games on a local station in Birmingham. But in retrospect, I had done a lot of things outside the classroom—sports editor of the school paper, student manager of athletics, on the debating team, and all that kind of stuff. So taking an audition was like reading for a part in a play in the dramatic society, I would suppose. Anyway, one thing led to another and I won a couple of auditions for commercial shows and I was suddenly making a hundred dollars a week and I was just out of college. I never thought I was going to stay with it, but I thought, well, I'll just stay a little bit longer; you can always start to practice at law." Allen roomed for a while with two fellow CBS staffers, Andre Baruch and Ralph Edwards. They all prospered, and while Allen never got to hang out his shingle as an attorney, it's clear that his intelligence (and education) stood him in good stead as both announcer and sportscaster.

George Ansbro's inspiration to become an announcer was being in the company of—other announcers. His first brush with radio was as a boy soprano on Milton Cross's Sunday morning show on WJZ, but his youthful singing career came to an end when his voice changed. At sixteen he found employment (by boosting his age by two years) as an NBC page; the year was 1931, and the salary was $15 a week. It was in this role—as a glorified, if uniformed, gofer—that he got to observe the comings and goings of men like Graham McNamee, John S. Young, and Jimmy Wallington. They seemed glamorous figures to him, so he cast them as his role models. When, a short time later, NBC announced auditions for the position of "junior announcer," he applied, and won the job. He was still announcing fifty-eight years later when he retired from ABC Television. (Ansbro never really changed employers: he started with NBC, which had two separate services, the Red and Blue Networks. The Blue was spun off into a separate entity known as ABC in the 1940s, and Ansbro remained there until his retirement in 1990.) Turned down for war service, he worked continuously all those years, and could boast that he was the only announcing voice heard on *Young Widder Brown* from its debut in September 1938 to its demise in June 1956, eighteen years later!

⌐

It might seem incredible that the men who bore such distinctive voices had no formal speech training, but that was often the case. Most of the greats were naturals—or self-taught, like Jackson Beck. "Announcers always went for the middle-American hard 'r,' " he recalled. "It took me years to learn it, and when I did I got more work. When I was a child and grew up in New York, I didn't know 'r' was in the alphabet. I called my mother 'mutha' because that's the way my family spoke. And when I found it was necessary to roll your r's, or hit the r accent, emphasize the r, that's when I started to make a buck."

One of the first nationally known names, Ted Husing, decided to give mother nature a helping hand: he had his nose broken and reset to change the tone of his voice! His boss at CBS "had consulted with some of our acoustic engineers, and they believed that my voice would have more resonance if my antrums were widened . . . The following day, a small mallet expertly shattered my nose—and I had my antrums widened. My voice sounded better, and my nose didn't lose its sensitivity," he confessed in his 1959 autobiography, *My Eyes Are in My Heart*. He also claimed that such seemingly drastic measures weren't uncommon back then.

In the 1930s, radio announcers were expected to have sonorous voices and to speak in a formal manner. (Some grumbled that NBC head announcer Pat Kelly simply wanted everyone under his supervision to sound the way he did.) The American Academy of Arts and Letters gave a medal every year called the Diction Award, which became the mark of prestige for such winning announcers as Milton Cross, Alwyn Bach, John Wesley Holbrook, Alois Havrilla, Frank Knight, James Wallington, and David Ross, though radio pundit Robert J. Landry later wrote, "To have the American Academy think one pure of tone and orthodox of pronunciation was to stand accused of elocution and vocal primness. An-

Ted Husing, the most popular sports announcer of his time, actually had his nose broken under a doctor's supervision—to enhance his vocal reproduction!

nouncers cherished instead the backslap of the mob. It was better to win a cup for being popular with the homefolks, like Graham McNamee and Pat Barnes, than to be acclaimed by the tutors of speech." Not everyone agreed with Landry; prestige for prestige's sake, especially in a young medium like radio, was nothing to sneeze at.

"David Ross was the senior announcer at CBS," recalled Andre Baruch. "He was a short man with red hair, and a voice like an organ—it was just beautiful. I don't know anybody on the air today who has better diction, or a better sounding voice. He would do a program called *Poet's Gold*—'O wilderness of drifting sands, o desert caravans, the desert's heart is set apart unknown to any man . . .' It would flow out, and everybody loved his voice." But Ross was not without his puckish side, according to Baruch: "He and a few other fellas at CBS used to do Shakespeare in Yiddish in the lobby at 485 Madison Avenue."

The NBC Announcer's Audition—full of tongue-twisting phrases and formidable names of Russian composers—became the stuff of legend in the radio business. If you could pass that test, you could do anything on the air. Dresser Dahlstead recalled a "cattle call" audition at NBC in San Francisco to find two new staff announcers. "They did everything that you can imagine to throw you.

They gave you a whole list of names of composers—foreign names—titles of songs that you had to go through. They'd stand you in a studio and say, 'OK, describe the studio.' It was really something. I think it took a week of weeding out and weeding out and it finally wound up that I was one of the two."

Andre Baruch remembered, "NBC had a phrase they used: 'the seething sea ceased to see, then thus sufficeth thus,' which was rather silly, but they used it to see if your diction was perfect. Of course, in the early days of radio, the pronunciation, the diction, the phraseology, the grammar, were most important. Today it's entirely different. But as the years went on, it wasn't what you said so much as the way you said it."

Even NBC's speech specialist, Vida Ravenscroft Sutton, who hosted a program called *The Magic of Speech*, was willing to concede this point. When Jimmy Wallington won the American Academy medal, she commented, "His diction is far from perfect. But he has a dramatic style. A great enthusiasm. He brings to his reading a gusto and a sincerity which outweigh the technical defects of his speech."

(To answer an obvious question from a 1990s perspective, I will quote from a *Radio Stars* article of January 1935 about Miss Sutton: "Always truthful, Miss Sutton does not encourage young women to strive for jobs as radio announcers. In the entire country, there are less than a dozen and these for local stations. For the networks there is only one, Claudine MacDonald, and she is much more the hostess and mistress of ceremonies.

"Opportunities for women, however, are as broad as radio even if the announcing field seems temporarily closed. In the dramatic field, the need for good interesting voices is constantly growing. There is also an opportunity of even larger proportions in the writing, producing, and executive field.")

◠

As radio developed, personality became the key to successful announcing—more than a man's vocal timbre or oratorical qualities. "A natural metamorphosis took place because people suddenly viewed announcers not so much as . . . presenters, but more as human beings," said Andre Baruch. "They started listening more and they became more familiar with them. The voices were very distinctive. You're not going to mix up Harry Von Zell with Andre Baruch or Ted Husing or Ralph Edwards. We started to loosen up."

Some announcers had fought the stentorian approach. Harry Von Zell told radio historian Chuck Schaden, "An advertiser in radio would give me copy, orating and pounding and shouting his wares, and I simply couldn't do it. I said I will not holler at people in their own houses. You must speak to them as if you are sitting there with them in their home and appreciate if they keep that dial tuned to where you are. You owe them a great debt of thanks for allowing you in and letting you stay. But they never got it!"

It was Ralph Edwards' friendly, warm, personal approach to commercials on daytime soap operas that all but revolutionized announcing in the late 1930s. Rather than reading the advertising copy strictly as written, he would ad lib and embellish, injecting conversational punctuation along the way, as if speaking casually—and personally—to each female listener. At the end of a fifteen-minute soap opera, it would be time to wrap things up and lead to a closing commercial. Edwards did it beautifully. "You know," he began, "when you listen to *Life Can Be Beautiful*, you get the feeling that Chi Chi and Papa David and all the others are sort of like old friends— don't you think that's the way it is?— friends that you look forward to visiting with every day. Now, I never heard of anybody looking forward to dishwashing but [chuckle] just the same, I know a lot of you feel friendly to the soap that helps your hands look nice and gives you speedy suds at the same time. Yes, ma'am, I mean good old Ivory Flakes . . ." Reproduction on paper of this September 21, 1939, broadcast can only hint at the brilliance of Edwards' approach. Dick Tufeld, then a drama student at Northwestern University, and later to become a top-flight network radio and TV announcer, remembers being wowed by Edwards' unique approach and adopting him as a role model. (Incidentally, Edwards' canniness was not limited to

Jimmy Wallington, one of the first wave of popular announcers, is seen here with Judy Canova and the omnipresent studio clock.

announcing; he later became producer as well as host of such wildly successful shows as *Truth or Consequences* and *This Is Your Life*. Announcer Ed Herlihy later recalled that when Edwards gave up his incredible announcing schedule—some eighteen shows a week, mostly for Procter and Gamble—to do *T or C*, he, Jay Stewart, and Mel Allen gleefully divvied up the spoils.)

When popular Ken Niles was asked for advice to beginners in the mid-1940s, he wrote, "Voice quality is important, technique is a must, but above all, be natural, sincere and friendly." In their instructional book, Art Gilmore and Glenn Y. Middleton wrote, "The very foundation of good radio speech is natural-ness." Not that Gilmore and Middleton didn't believe in fundamentals as well: "The primary step in achieving naturalness is the improvement of voice and dic-tion by constant practice, making sure you read all exercises ALOUD! . . . Among the most common mistakes to overcome are (a) the omission of the final 'g' in words ending in 'ing,' (b) the failure to give full value to the vowel tones of the diphthongs 'ou' and 'ow,' and (c) the hissing of the letter 's.' . . . The announcer must [also] work to eliminate the monotonous effect caused by sameness of inflec-tion and tempo. Finally, excellence of speech depends, in addition to these other elements, upon proper breath control."

When all was said and done, announcing meant more than merely reading. As Jackson Beck put it, "Anybody can get up in front of a mike and say 'Come to Jones Department Store.' But to say it and make 'em come there . . . that's where your acting comes in." Small wonder that so many of the best announcers were also actors.

Beck, so well remembered for his opening "It's Superman!" send-off on radio (and still heard on a flurry of TV commercials in the 1990s), decided to suppress his acting ambition in favor of announcing. "I found out that the character man comes and goes, but the announcer is there every day. And I figured, what am I fooling around with all this [acting] stuff? Everybody knows I can do it, and if they want me to do it, I'll do it—but I want to be there every damn day. It's a steady job, and I can get better money for that than I can for playing an Irish cop or a Spanish conquistador or whatever. I made the switch. I started insinuating myself into announcing situations and auditioning for them."

Amusingly enough, *Superman*'s star was doing the same thing in reverse. Clayton "Bud" Collyer was primarily an announcer, working on everything from daytime soaps to such prominent nighttime programs as *Cavalcade of America*. A legion of younger listeners, however, knew him only as the Man of Steel, who had the uncanny ability of lowering the pitch of his voice from that of Clark Kent whenever he declared, "This looks like a job . . . for Superman!"

A number of performers managed to lead "double lives," acting on some shows and announcing on others—among them John McIntire, Marvin Miller, Ernest Chappell, Kenny Delmar (who in the late 1940s did double-duty by announcing Fred Allen's show and portraying blustery Senator Claghorn), Larry Thor, William Conrad, and Paul Frees. Truth be told, there was barely an announcer in the business who wouldn't drop every-thing for an acting part. When he was making top dollar as a "name" announcer in Hollywood, Hy Aver-back gladly worked for scale in the supporting cast of *The Lineup*. Art Gilmore was grateful for occasional parts on *Lux Radio Theatre*. Wendell Niles (Ken's brother) was ready to sacrifice a portion of his lucrative an-nouncing career to star in the adven-

Jackson Beck, whose thundering voice announced such shows as *Superman*, moved up to first-banana position as the star of *The Cisco Kid*.

ture serial *The Adventures of the Scarlet Cloak* in 1950, but an audition episode never yielded a sponsor.

Fred Foy became a top announcer at Detroit's WXYZ in the 1940s, and in 1948 won the prestige assignment of speaking the unmistakable words that her-alded the arrival of *The Lone Ranger*—"A fiery horse with the speed of light, a cloud of dust and a hearty hi-yo, Silver!"—three nights a week. Eventually he was selected as understudy for the show's star, Brace Beemer, but he never got to go on—until one evening when the actor showed up with an acute case of laryngitis. Foy was pressed into service as the Masked Man on the evening of March 29, 1954, and as a surviving recording attests, he not only sounded remarkably like Beemer, but acquitted himself quite well in the part. A man who simply "read words" couldn't have pulled that off.

But even a professional as solid as Foy admits that his greatest challenge was not playing a part or meeting his responsibilities on a national show. It was,

rather, trying not to break up on the air. Foy and his WXYZ colleagues—
Bob Henry, Bill Morgan, Hal Neal, and Norm Lenhardt—found that the best

way to relieve the monotony of their day-to-day schedule as staff announcers was to do their best to crack each other up on-mike. Foy admits that he was an easy mark. One day, shortly after he had begun a live fifteen-minute newscast, one of his colleagues crept into the studio. Foy heard what sounded like rain on a tin roof; it was one of his colleagues, urinating into a metal wastebasket. "I was finished!" he

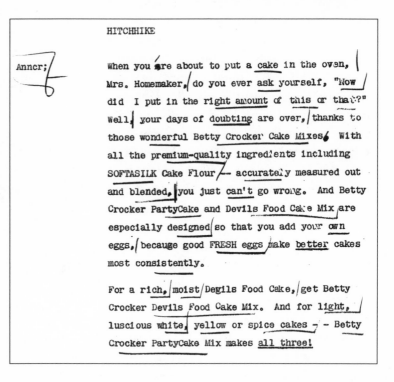

Fred Foy, announcer on *The Lone Ranger* in the late 1940s and early '50s, marked his pages, as many announcers did, to indicate which words to emphasize . . . especially for those all-important commercials!

later wrote. "Convulsed with laughter, I quickly cut off the mike and did the only thing possible to fill in the silence. I grabbed a record and in panic spun the turntable. Even to this day I remember the wild coincidence. The record I had so hurriedly picked up was 'April Showers.' "

Despite these shenanigans, Foy did take his job seriously, as indicated by some of his surviving script pages. Like many announcers, he would mark his copy, underlining words deserving special emphasis, and indicating breaks or pauses in each sentence. Kenneth Roberts recalls, "I had all my own secret hieroglyphic signs about where my voice would go up and where it should go down. I prepared very carefully, and it helped me, especially when you did commercials which made no sense anyway. One sentence did not follow another in any logical reason at all, and to make it sound intelligible, it really required work on my part."

But there were no rules about this. Art Gilmore recalls, "A lot of guys would make marks; they'd go in a corner and work on it. I found the more I worked on it, the worse I became. There was a certain spontaneity that's lost when you overrehearse."

⤳

Announcers had to be able to think on their feet; most of them had the experience of presiding over live events where timing was vague and anything could happen. If covering a parade where a delay caused the procession to march in place for five minutes, they had to call on their gift of gab and make sure there was no dead air. They had to learn how to "stretch" and ad-lib when something went wrong on a performance show. They had to learn how to keep calm when announcing late-breaking news.

Gabriel Heatter catapulted to fame, according to radio historian Robert J. Landry, "on his *tour de théâtre* the night Hauptmann, the murderer of the Lindbergh baby, was electrocuted. Because of a time mix-up Heatter had to fill some forty-five minutes. He went through this ordeal by verbiage without dropping a syllable or sounding an unprofessional 'er' or 'uh.' Nothing like it had been witnessed since Lillian Leitzel did 102 consecutive one-arm somersaults over her own shoulder on a trapeze in Ringling Brothers-Barnum and Bailey Circus."

In short, announcers had to know how to handle themselves in any situation. That, along with acting experience, made many of them excellent straight men for radio comedians. Perhaps the first man to be identified with that role was Graham McNamee, who played straight for Ed Wynn as *The Fire Chief* in the early 1930s. If listeners hadn't paid attention to his name at the beginning of the show, they certainly knew it by the end, because Wynn fell into the habit of mentioning his name in every single line of his routine. ("It seems that the man she's going to marry, Graham, is a professional; he's a professional tattooer, and he has designs on her.") McNamee, for his part, would address Wynn as "Chief" in every response or straight line.

Harry Von Zell had been announcing a variety of shows, including the super-serious *The March of Time*, when he joined Fred Allen's *Town Hall Tonight* in 1935. One week, a member of Allen's stock company, Teddy Bergman (later known as Alan Reed), was unable to perform and Von Zell was recruited to take his place. Allen liked what he heard and put the announcer into more comic situations in the weeks that followed.

By the time Von Zell left Allen to join Eddie Cantor, he was no longer merely an announcer; Cantor made him a virtual costar of the show. When Cantor learned that Von Zell's wife was expecting a baby, he immediately saw comic possibilities, and turned the pregnancy into a long-running gag, with the announcer eventually naming his child—on the air, that is—Eddie Cantor Von Zell Jr. By the 1940s, Von Zell was so closely associated with comedy that he even starred in his own series of comic two-reelers, produced by the same division of Columbia Pictures that made the Three Stooges shorts. And, of course, he enjoyed a long run as announcer and foil for Burns and Allen on television.

In time, virtually every radio comic adopted the idea of using the announcer for something more than just reading announcements. Some took to it more gracefully than others.

Hy Averback, who spent a number of years on the air with Bob Hope, feels that the secret to being a good straight man is "paying attention. It's not going into business for yourself; you know you're there to feed that person. As a matter of fact, I would advise actors coming onto the Hope show that if he's going to milk [a laugh], you just stare at him; don't you turn to the audience. Just let him do it, let him milk it. And if it really gets to an exhausting point, he'll almost let you know that you can break out of character."

The one arena in which announcers could break out for themselves was during the audience warm-up. This ritual, which has remained essentially unchanged for sixty years, is a means of welcoming a studio audience, getting them used to the trappings of a studio and the upcoming broadcast, and making sure they're in a good mood so they will laugh loudly and applaud with fervor.

Many announcers relished the opportunity to take the spotlight immediately prior to the show itself; it was their chance to be top banana, if only for a little while.

Andre Baruch recalled, "I would explain about applause and how good it is for you, because when you bring your hands together the blood comes rushing up through your arms and you feel better. Suddenly, in the middle of it I'd stop and say, 'First, I want to introduce in the audience one of the top wrestling champions of the world, Strangler Lewis.' And of course everybody would turn around to look, and I would

Two of the best-known announcers in radio, and two of the funniest, Harry Von Zell and Don Wilson.

point and say, 'Oh, pardon me, madam.' That gag is still being used. I told a lot of jokes, did a lot of funny stuff, even did magic tricks." Corniness was never out of fashion in the warm-up.

Harry Von Zell blazed another trail for his colleagues, without setting out to do so. In 1935 he was wooed from his comfortable CBS staff position by the Young and Rubicam advertising agency. He then became "their man," and was assigned to various shows they packaged on both CBS and NBC. Other announcers began to feel that doing commercial pitches, especially on highly rated nighttime shows, was worth more than their standard weekly stipend. Bolstered by the recent passage of the Wagner Labor Act, CBS network announcers banded together in 1936 and formed AGRAP, the American Guild of Radio Announcers and Producers, heralded as the first union in broadcasting. They fought for, and won, a five-day, forty-hour week (down from six days, with twelve-hour shifts) and accepted no increase in salary in lieu of $5 per commercial.

"There was one thing we wanted which we couldn't get without great difficulty and that was a union shop," recalls Kenneth Roberts. "And we struggled over that for weeks. The company was adamant; they would not grant us the union shop. Eventually, Mr. Paley appeared on the scene; he had not been part of negotiations until then, but he appeared this one afternoon and said, 'Now what is this all about? You seem to want something that I'm against; what is it?' I proceeded to explain that the union shop is not a closed shop; it did not preclude him hiring whomever he wanted, it's just that whomever he hired would become a member of the union. And after I got through explaining it to him, he looked at me and said, 'I travel in very fancy circles in this city, and I'm looked upon by my elegant friends as somewhat of a left-wing rebel. And you make me feel like a conservative. And I don't like it. You can have your union shop.' "

Announcers were widely regarded as radio's ultimate professionals, but they were only human, and even the best of them had to fight boredom at times. Andre Baruch recalled his early network days when "I ended up in a little studio on the 23rd floor of the CBS building, a little two-by-four studio with a control panel. All I had to do was wait until somebody said, 'This is the Columbia Broadcasting System.' I would wait fifteen seconds, punch a button and say, 'This is WABC, New York.' In those days, the local station was WABC because the original owners were the Atlantic Broadcasting Company.

"Anyway, it's very dull sitting in a studio with nothing to do, just waiting for your fifteen seconds to say, 'WABC, New York.' So I would fall asleep. Once I was caught sleeping and the engineer came in and tapped me on the shoulder. I right away punched down the button and said 'WABC, New York' and got it just in time. The next time I was drowsing, halfway through the H. V. Kaltenborn show, the engineer came in to see if I was awake. He tapped me on the shoulder, and just as Kaltenborn was saying, 'And the trouble with the U.S.S.R. is . . .' I punched the button and said 'WABC, New York.' "

Jackson Beck explained that when an announcer dons a pair of headphones, "One phone is you, the other phone is the show, but the director can cut in on the 'you' phone, so that he could say 'Slow it down, speed it up, do this, do that.' You in the meantime are thinking about something completely away from what you're doing. I'm thinking about playing golf. You have no idea how your mind works, you're off in all directions . . . I'm worried about can I get a cab out of here to get to where I'm going from here, shall I have dinner with whom, all this stuff . . ."

Art Gilmore was drifting into the doldrums during a broadcast of *Dr. Christian* one day when "I heard this snapping of fingers, and I looked over. Jean Hersholt was at a table—later on in the series, he sat at a table rather than be at the same mike with the rest of the cast—and he snapped his fingers. I thought, 'What the heck is going on?' I went over; he had left the last seven pages of his script in the dressing room upstairs. Now, we're on live, coast to coast. Well, talk about luck; normally I'd read my commercial and then I'd turn to the back page and sit there. And fight sleep. Five-thirty in the afternoon is a dull time; you're kind of ready for dinner and you need a little pep. That one particular night, I was following along with him and when I heard the snapping I was able to give him my script."

This was not the first time, nor the last, that an announcer rode to the rescue of a broadcast. It was, however, typical of the breed whom so many people considered the bedrock of radio.

Many top announcers made a smooth transition to television, including Don Wilson, Harry Von Zell, Andre Baruch, Kenneth Roberts, and Groucho Marx's favorite straight man, George Fenneman (whose claim to fame in radio was being one of the two sober-voiced announcers on *Dragnet*). For the most part, they continued to serve much the same function as they did on radio—performing warm-ups, billboarding the show, reading commercials. Some veterans were usurped by younger "pretty-boy" types whose good looks made them prime TV material, but the radio veterans continued to thrive doing voice-only work.

A contemplative portrait of Andre Baruch.

Television expanded the notion of announcer as sidekick, which reached its zenith with the long-running collaboration between Johnny Carson and Ed McMahon. They met when Carson became master of ceremonies for the daytime quiz show *Who Do You Trust?* and McMahon was the announcer. During Carson's long reign as host of *The Tonight Show*, McMahon evolved into an all-purpose

A young Art Gilmore poses in Hollywood with actress Lurene Tuttle.

second banana whose popularity exceeded that of any "mere" announcer on the air. However, two long-running late-night shows made more traditional use of announcers, in an interesting throwback to radio's way of thinking. When *Saturday Night Live* debuted in 1975, producer Lorne Michaels made the unusual choice of NBC veteran Don Pardo to introduce the show. His old-fashioned, hard-sell approach was in sharp contrast to the hip, young feel of the comedy program, yet it seemed to work for the show. Similarly, David Letterman chose booming veteran Bill Wendell (a onetime colleague of his hero, Ernie Kovacs) to introduce *Late Night with David Letterman*, and its CBS successor, *The Late Show with David Letterman*.

Both Pardo and Wendell functioned exactly as radio announcers would in the old days: they rarely if ever appeared on camera, yet their voice and delivery set the tone for their shows, and became indelibly identified with them. (So much so that when Wendell left Letterman in 1995, the producers hired a soundalike to replace him.)

Need I add that both men started their careers in radio?

7

And Now, a Word About Sponsors

SYDNEY GREENSTREET: Gaze into my eyes. You are in my power. You will do my bidding. You will fulfill my slightest wish. You will obey my every whim.

BOB HOPE: This guy's crazy—he thinks he's my sponsor!

(from a 1940s Bob Hope broadcast)

It might be hard for a modern-day television executive to grasp, but in the heyday of commercial radio, sponsors (not networks) controlled the medium and the shows they bankrolled. Networks were merely the facilities through which programs were broadcast. Thus, Bob Hope's wisecrack was a matter of kidding on the square: When the sponsor talked, everyone listened, even if they grumbled under their breath.

Radio shows were not only owned by the sponsors, they were *identified* with them. Jack Benny's greeting of "Jell-O again" became a national catchphrase. Fred Allen was sponsored by Ipana toothpaste every Tuesday, and after appearing with Benny one Sunday night, Portland Allen remarked (on the subsequent Allen broadcast) that his turning up on a different night of the week was causing listeners great confusion. It got so bad, she said, that their neighbor upstairs started brushing his teeth with Jell-O.

Modern-day radio and television bombard us with a blur of commercials, but way back when, a single sponsor controlled an entire show. Products were

Jack Benny and Mary Livingstone say "Jell-O again" to their millions of fans in this promotional photo. Jack and Jell-O were virtually synonymous for years.

even part of the programs' names: *Kraft Music Hall*, *Lux Radio Theatre*, *Fitch Bandwagon*, *Camel Caravan*, etc. In the earliest days of commercial radio, the sponsors even appropriated the names of the performers: The Interwoven Pair [formerly The Happiness Boys], The A&P Gypsies, The Cliquot Club Eskimos, et al.

Some of those associations were contrived, but others were felicitous. On his debut program as host of *Lux Radio Theatre*, producer-director Cecil B. DeMille good-humoredly remarked, "Is it possible that the manufacturers of Lux Soap asked me to produce this series of programs because of all the deluxe bathtubs that have been seen in my pictures? They *should* have a soft spot in their hearts for me.

"But," he continued, "I think the real reason goes back far beyond the recollection of any of us. When William the Conqueror whipped the Saxons at the Battle of Hastings in 1066 the Blount DeMille family crest was born. The motto on that crest is 'Thy Light, My Life,' which is of course in Latin, and reads *Lux Tua Vita Mere*. So you see, Lux has been a household word in the DeMille family for 870 years."

Not every association was so harmonious, but that didn't stop ad agencies from trying to make them seem that way in their sign-on slogans:

"Pabst Blue Ribbon's thirty-three fine brews blended into one great beer presents thirty-three fine talents blended into one great comedian—Danny Kaye."

Or, "The greatest name in rubber, Goodyear, invites you to meet America's greatest western star, Roy Rogers."

Worse yet, Abbott and Costello's 1940s radio show, which featured Marilyn Maxwell and Skinnay Ennis and His Orchestra, opened with a flourish from the orchestra and the bold announcement, "C for Comedy, A for Abbott, M for Maxwell, E for Ennis, and L for Lou Costello . . . put them all together, they spell Camel!"

An incongruous mix of sponsor and show never stopped a copywriter from forging ahead. In the midst of a very tense adaptation of Alfred Hitchcock's

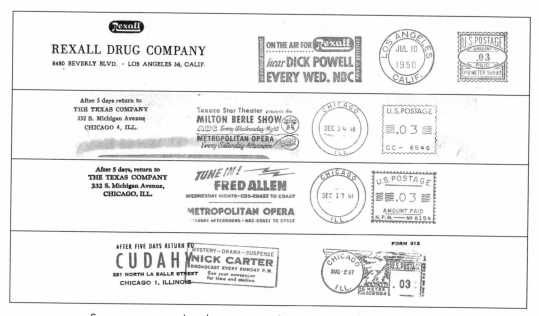

Sponsors never missed an opportunity to promote their radio shows, as these postage-meter cancellations confirm.

thriller *Suspicion* on *Academy Award*, a buoyant announcer interrupted the dire doings with this segue: "When things around *you* seem strange, you need a bright smile." His mission: to sell toothpaste.

No one seemed to think it odd that during a broadcast of *Kraft Music Hall* in which host Al Jolson performed a plethora of Jewish dialect material, the follow-up commercial suggested Kraft meals for "your Lenten menu."

Slogans were one hallmark of radio commercials, and constant repetition imbedded them in the national consciousness: "Good health to all from Rexall" . . . "Ipana for the smile of beauty, Sal Hepatica for the smile of health" . . . "Quaker Puffed Wheat—shot from guns" . . . and of course, "L.S.M.F.T." (for the uninitiated, "Lucky Strike Means Fine Tobacco").

"Serutan is Natures spelled backwards" prompted Milton Berle to crack that when he was sponsored by that company, his program aired from 9:30 P.M. to 9:00. Peg Lynch was forever fond of a local shoe company that implored listeners,

"Don't spend your life two feet away from happiness." *Fibber McGee and Molly*'s Don Quinn once devised a gag product called Capistrano Root Beer—"where the swallows come back." Some trademarks were sound-oriented, as in the chirpy rendition of "Rinso-*White*, Rinso-*White*," or the memorable foghorn bellow of "Beee-Ooooo" to encourage listeners to avoid body odor by using Lifebuoy soap ("Why be half-safe?").

One catchphrase that never made it on the air is vividly recounted by several colleagues who remember the copywriter for Sealtest in the early 1940s. Says writer Larry Gelbart, "He used to hang around the Brown Derby, and prided himself . . . that he always had the latest jargon. At one of these dry-runs in front of an audience, the announcer comes out and says, 'I'm the schmuck who drives the truck for Sealtest' and then does his copy. Well, we fell down in the booth, and we said afterwards, 'What do you mean, "I'm the schmuck who drives the truck for Sealtest?"' He said, 'Well, I hear everybody at the Brown Derby calling guys schmucks . . .' I said, 'That means prick, you dumbbell,' so he took it out."

Looking back on commercials from the vantage point of the 1990s, one sees the origin of names now so familiar that their actual meanings have faded away: Palmolive was pronounced Palm-Olive, to indicate the oils used in their soaps. Vintage commercials also point out the vast changes in our daily lives since the 1930s and '40s: Kraft Miracle Whip was touted as an improvement over homemade "boiled" salad dressings. *The Shadow*'s longtime sponsor Blue Coal encouraged listeners to "order a trial ton today."

But Blue Coal was a northeastern company, and *The Shadow* had a national audience. So entrepreneur Charles Michelson devised a solution. "We sold the show to Grove's Four-Way Cold Tablets in the Mid-East and Pacific Coast, and the Carrie Salt Company in the Midwest," he told a meeting of SPERDVAC in 1992. The challenge was to convey the proper commercials to the appropriate regions of the country. "I'm no engineer, but I figured this out," Michelson boasted. "The program originated from the Empire Theater in New York. . . . On the center stage was the announcer and on the left stage we had a 'telephone booth' for one of the other announcers and on the right stage we had a 'telephone booth' for the Carrie Salt announcer. The job was to coincide the commercials for all three so they went in and out at the same time."

There were many longtime marriages between product and show: Johnson's Wax and Fibber McGee and Molly, Pepsodent and Bob Hope, Ralston and Tom Mix, Ovaltine and Little Orphan Annie, to name just a few. Many of those sponsorships were the result *not* of market testing, field surveys, or advertising agency pressure: they were personal choices of the company chiefs. In the modern era of demographic research and conglomerate ownership, the idea sounds almost quaint, but those were simpler times. Many of America's corporate giants were still under the firm control of their founders (much like the radio networks themselves). Those men expressed their personal taste through their choice of programs to sponsor.

Orson Welles believed that to be one of the greatest distinctions between vintage radio and modern television. "There were all kinds of sponsors," he remarked. "Nutty ones, rightists, leftists, idiots, very bright people—and as a result, you had a big variety of shows, because they were expressions of different kinds of people . . . not only the artists who made them, but the people who paid for them. And now, whatever you can do on television is a reflection of the three people [at the networks] who control what television is, all of which are looking with beady eyes on each other, which is rather cannibalistic, isn't it?"

⌐

In radio's earliest days, there was heated debate about the wisdom of commercializing the medium; it was anathema to many people. In 1924, Secretary of Commerce Herbert Hoover said in an address to the National Association of Broadcasters, "I believe the quickest way to kill broadcasting would be to use it for direct advertising. The reader of a newspaper has an option whether he will read an ad or not, but if a speech by the President is to be used as the meat in a sandwich of two patent medicine advertisements, there will be no radio left. To what extent it may be employed for what we now call indirect advertising I do not know, and only experience with the reactions of listeners can tell. The listeners will finally decide in any event."

This would not be the only time Mr. Hoover's crystal ball was cloudy, but he wasn't alone in his beliefs. A full decade later, after commercials had become a mainstay of broadcasting, theatrical impresario and radio host S. L. "Roxy" Rothafel wrote in the January 1934 issue of *Radio Mirror*, "As a direct sales agency radio is a flop. And the sooner the sponsors realize it the sooner they'll eliminate the plethora of commercial advertising that is stuffed into the ears of potential patrons. *Radio is the greatest builder of goodwill.* But that good will may be destroyed by irritating interruptions of a program to plug a product. The very purpose of the broadcast may be thwarted by a lack of discernment, lack of showmanship.

"If I were a merchant I would advertise my wares through a combination of radio and newspaper advertising. I'd build good will on the air, and I'd tell 'em what I had to sell in the advertising columns."

Many advertisers tried to turn their theme songs or jingles into popular songs, and even published sheet music to that end.

Few sponsors heeded Roxy's advice, though a handful of companies took the high road, on "classy" shows like *The Voice of Firestone*, *The Bell Telephone Hour*, and *Hallmark Hall of Fame*, which promoted the companies' images more than specific products.

In the 1930s, the networks made a show of taking a position on what constituted inappropriate or undignified advertising. The mention of a product's price was considered crass, for instance, on network radio. According to radio historian Robert J. Landry, NBC had a list of some eighty words that were forbidden in commercial copy, including stomach, pregnancy, blood, phlegm, hawk, infection, and retch.

CBS' William S. Paley scored a public relations coup in the early 1930s by announcing that he would henceforth refuse all advertising for laxatives, depilatories, and deodorants, as well as censoring programs involving "unpleasant discussions of bodily functions, bodily symptoms or other matters which similarly infringe on good taste." In point of fact, as Sally Bedell Smith pointed out in her biography of Paley, *In All His Glory* (1990), this was merely a grandstand play; he forbade *new* accounts to sign on with CBS, but had no intention of shooing away sponsors who were already in the fold. (Remember, Paley started out as a sponsor; it was the success of commercials for his La Palina cigars that first interested him in radio.)

⟿

Nothing better illustrates the sponsor-show relationship than the story of *Lum 'n' Abner*, as researched by Tim Hollis for *The Jot 'Em Down Journal*, official publication of The National Lum 'n' Abner Society. Chester Lauck and Norris Goff were struggling cornpone comedy performers who were beginning to establish themselves in Hot Springs, Arkansas. Their station manager recommended that they go to Chicago to seek sponsorship for the show. Goff's father urged them to visit the Quaker Oats people there, but for an entirely different reason: he was in the wholesale grocery business, and wanted to know if Quaker would provide him with a private label of oats for his company. During a meeting on that subject, Goff and Lauck mentioned their real reason for coming to Chicago, and the company representative agreed to let them audition.

Goff explained what happened in a 1966 interview: "They were having a Board of Directors meeting and all these old gray-haired men were sitting there in these tremendous big chairs. So we told them, 'We don't need a mike . . . we'll put the show on here.' So we asked them to turn their backs to us. And I never will forget all these old men getting up and lifting these heavy chairs, and turning them around. When all that would have been necessary was for Chet and I to spin around and turn our backs to them. But they bought the show that day!"

Days later, Quaker's advertising agency, Lord and Thomas, called to inquire what kind of show their client had committed to . . . and no one at Quaker could quite describe it! Nevertheless, the company arranged for *Lum 'n' Abner* to make their network debut on July 27, 1931, on NBC.

In February 1932 Quaker, feeling the pinch of the Depression, dropped its radio sponsorship across the board. *Lum 'n' Abner* was off the air for a while, but then the entrepreneurial duo had an idea: they printed a hardcover book called *Lum and Abner and Their Friends from Pine Ridge*, and convinced WBAP Fort Worth to allow them to go on the air on a sustaining basis, so they could sell copies of the book. In short, they became their own sponsor.

In 1934 the show, growing in popularity, acquired another full-time sponsor:

Horlick's Malted Milk. It was apparently the first show ever sponsored by the company (which had been around since 1883), and Horlick took it on for one simple reason: company founder/president William Horlick liked *Lum 'n' Abner*. He personally renewed their contract in 1936, and posed for pictures with "his" comedy stars.

That association was more personal than Lauck and Goff may have realized. Just weeks after that contract renewal, Mr. Horlick died at the age of ninety. When the agreement expired in 1938, the company withdrew its support. In losing a fan, *Lum 'n' Abner* had also lost a sponsor.

By that time, however, *Lum 'n' Abner* was a radio institution, and they flourished, with a variety of sponsors, for many years to come.

⟿

A sponsor's word was law; a manufacturer or its ad agency often overrode the network in terms of policy and decision making. Smart sponsors put a lot of faith in their advertising agencies, and thus it was major firms like J. Walter Thompson, Young and Rubicam, BBD&O, McCann Erickson, and Foote Cone and Belding that really ruled the airwaves.

For some sponsors—and agencies—a show's producer or director was just another hired hand. Elliott Lewis remembered that when he worked on the popular Sunday matinee series *Silver Theatre* in Los Angeles, "We not only did a transcription disc on Friday night, we shipped the disc to the advertising agency nabobs and the sponsor in New York. They would listen to it and call the agency guys that were sitting in the office waiting for their comments on Saturday, and they would discuss what we had been rehearsing and what they heard on the disc."

Many companies felt that when they sponsored a show, they not only owned the program, they owned the language being spoken on it. Any inadvertent references to rival products (or soundalike words that might remind listeners of those products) were forbidden. Announcer Art Gilmore recalls that early in his career, he couldn't work on certain shows because his last name was the same as a popular brand-new gasoline of the time. "They would never let me use my name, and they were quite narrow," he says. In a football game, "if somebody had a 76 on their jersey, they wouldn't let them say that, because that was Union Oil."

Fellow announcer Hy Averback remembers that while it wasn't always graceful to substitute the word "fortunate" for "lucky," that change was required on any show sponsored by a cigarette other than Lucky Strike. Andre Baruch once worked a show sponsored by Chevrolet where the characters were forbidden to "ford" a stream.

Those same announcers had to toe the line for their commercial bosses. Kenneth Roberts once won the Ex-Lax account, but with it came the curse of having to please its president. "The factory was out in Brooklyn, I remember. I used to have to ride to Brooklyn and go to his office, where he would hand me the copy and send me into an adjoining room and he would set up a microphone and had a loudspeaker in his office. He would ask me to read the commercial that was to be released the following day, which I did. Then he would coach me on how he wanted it done, and I would listen to his direction and attempt to do the program as he wished; that went on every week. He would then come to the

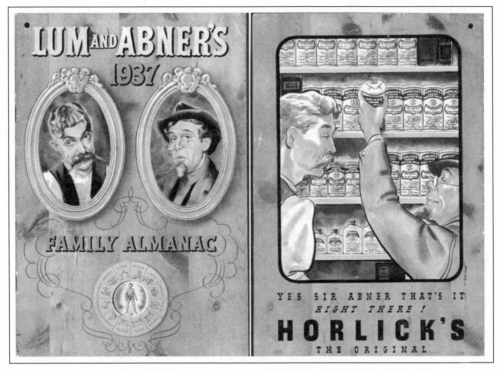

In 1936 and '37, thousands of listeners sent in for *Lum and Abner's Family Almanac,* an elaborate publication that also extolled the virtues of Horlick's Malted Milk.

studio, and after we had gotten off the air, he would grab me and say, 'Kenneth, that was just the way I wanted it. It was absolutely perfect.' I said, 'Thank you, I appreciate that,' and the next morning he'd call me and say, 'Kenneth, would you mind coming out to the office again today?' And I'd come out and he'd say,

'You know, there was one point in the commercial, where, I don't know, it just wasn't . . .'

"This went on for many, many weeks and finally I said to him, 'Sidney, what is happening here? You tell me how to do the commercial and I do it your way; I get off the air and you say it was wonderful, that it was perfect, exactly as you wanted, and the next morning you're always finding fault. I can't go on like this.' He said, 'Well, I'll tell you the truth, Kenneth, I liked it very much, but when I get home, my mother says, "You know, Sidney, when you say Ex-Lax I believe you, but when that announcer says it, I don't believe him." ' " Roberts quit on the spot.

Such whimsical behavior became notorious in radio, where sponsors' wives were often as formidable as the clients themselves. Vocalist Bea Wain was under contract to Bristol-Myers, and once appeared on a show hosted by film star Fredric March. "It was an audience show," she recalls, "and up in the side is what they call the client's booth. That's where the sponsors or their friends or relatives would sit during the show and rehearsal. When I sang my rhythm song I moved, not intentionally, but obviously my body moves. I keep time with my body, and my back was turned to the sponsor's wife. And at the end of the show the sponsor's wife told the agency people to fire me. Fredric March was standing there and he said, 'If this girl goes off the show I am off the show.' " March saved not only her job, but her dignity.

The mercurial behavior of commercial sponsors became so widely known that it was satirized in scores of Hollywood movies with radio backdrops, as early as 1932's *Blessed Event* (in which Mr. Shapiro of Shapiro's Shoes, replete with Old World accent, insists on having his say on the air) and continuing through such delightful parodies as the 1942 Mickey Mouse cartoon *Symphony Hour*, in which Peg-Leg Pete, playing cigar-smoking big-shot Sylvester Macaroni, watches his highbrow music program turn into a Spike Jones–like shambles.

Murray Bolen, a top radio producer for the Young and Rubicam agency who rode herd over *The Jack Benny Show* during its Jell-O days, remembered, "General Foods had a distributor out here [in Los Angeles] and I had to furnish him with a few tickets so he could be a big man and get people into the audience. He used to come to the show and I had to throw him out of the control room; I made it a fast rule, and put him in the upstairs one where he couldn't come [near us]."

As for the association between the ad agency and the client, Bolen said in his experience—which, admittedly, was with one of the top agencies in the country— the sponsors left them to do their job. "They gave us credit for knowing what we were doing, for doing our best; when we didn't do it right, we heard from headquarters." Bolen said his job was mainly a diplomatic assignment where the challenge was to keep everyone happy: the star, the sponsor, and the network.

⟜

Some relationships between sponsor and star or producer were cordial, marked by mutual respect. Some were edgy at best, a battleground at worst. Fred Allen suffered sponsors as testily as he did network censors, and was always ready to fight for words and lines that lesser minds objected to.

As corporate America grew, some of the personal contact of the early days was lost. But not completely.

Himan Brown was producing and directing *Grand Central Station* in the 1940s; the sponsor was Listerine. It turned out that the president of Carter's Little Liver Pills played golf on a regular basis with the president of Lambert Pharmaceuticals, which made Listerine. One day Brown got a phone call from the Carter executive, saying that his friend had suggested he call. "I want to do a show for Carter's Little Liver Pills. I know what they're paying you; can you do a show for me for the same money?" Brown recalls him asking. There was just one hitch: NBC wouldn't accept a laxative as a sponsor. Fortunately, the newly formed Blue Network was not nearly as fussy. A friendly former NBC executive told Brown, "I've got a new network; I'll take any sponsor." And that's how *Inner Sanctum* was born.

Decision-making clout rested elsewhere when James Stewart, at the peak of his popularity in the 1950s, decided to do a radio series, *The Six Shooter*. The show's producer-director, Jack Johnstone, recalled, "Chesterfield begged and begged and begged for months trying to get sponsorship, but Jim didn't feel that because of his screen image that it would be fair . . . for him to be sponsored by a cigarette. There was another advertiser who wanted very much to sponsor the show, but again Jim, and MCA, which owned the show, said no."

CBS, looking for a new dramatic anthology series in the late 1940s, commissioned director-producer Fletcher Markle to create *Studio One*, which like the *Mercury Theatre* a decade earlier used a repertory cast to dramatize classic novels and plays. Midway through its second season the show acquired a sponsor, Ford Motor Company, and with it a brand-new name: *The Ford Theater*. Along with the name came its namesakes: the two Ford brothers (Henry's sons), who were eager to have hands-on participation in the show.

Sponsorship, Markle recalls, meant "an awful lot more money." But he also recalls with a grin, that "the Ford brothers lusted for stars. And when we ran out of them in New York, we had to move in 1948 to Hollywood, for thirteen weeks, to get all the biggies." Ford wasn't as interested in the classics as it was in adapting popular movies, a la *Lux*.

The brothers were often in attendance for the Friday-night broadcasts, but one night, a particular guest star decided to have some fun at their expense. Bob Hope was being featured in an adaptation of the movie comedy *The Awful Truth*. After dress rehearsal, Markle stopped by Hope's dressing room, where the comedian was surrounded by his writers. Hope asked Markle if the Ford brothers would be sitting in the client's booth that night, and when he was told they would, he suggested an idea to "shake them up." The show usually opened with a tease or blurb from the play, followed by a music cue by the orchestra and the name of the program. Hope proposed that after Markle announced, "This is the Ford Theater," the music be stretched out as he cracked, "Isn't that where they shot Lincoln?"

The comedian quickly added that he would take full responsibility for the line, and Markle went along with the gag. When Hope made the crack on the air, it got the big laugh he expected . . . and when the broadcast was over, the Ford brothers walked to the stage, just as he expected. Benson Ford wasted no time in telling Hope, "That took us by surprise, Bob . . ." but Hope caught him up short by replying, "No problem, at least it's another product." When the brothers realized that Hope had in fact mentioned the name of their other line of cars—Lincoln—they were completely disarmed, and happily joined the comic in his dressing room for a drink.

One man who refused to relinquish control—or contact—with his programming was the legendary George Washington Hill, president of American Tobacco Company. Although he never deigned to show himself in person, everyone who worked on Lucky Strike's *Your Hit Parade* knew that Mr. Hill was listening in his office—and, according to some stories, dancing to the week's hit songs with his secretary! (His preferred tempo was referred to around the show as "the businessman's bounce.") Hill was a notorious despot who was broadly caricatured by Sydney Greenstreet in the movie *The Hucksters* (based on the novel by former ad man Fredric Wakeman). He was the kind of boss who demanded that employees sign loyalty oaths; if there was anything that displeased him on a Lucky Strike–sponsored show, a telephone call was sure to follow.

Soft-sell was not in Hill's vocabulary. Commercials for American Tobacco products hit listeners hard and often with their slogans. "Lucky Strike Green Has Gone To War" and the oft-repeated "L.S.M.F.T." were familiar to every radio listener not only because the company advertised on popular shows, but because the phrases were repeated as many as four times in a single commercial!

Hill insisted that announcers who read his commercials be familiar with his company. Andre Baruch, longtime announcer for *Your Hit Parade*, spent considerable time touring American Tobacco factories, and even attending tobacco auctions. "Hill's dictum [was that] you've got to learn the business so when you get up before the microphone, you're not just reading words," Baruch recalled.

But that wasn't Hill's only dictum. In 1948, Jack Benny found himself in an embarrassing—and potentially provocative—situation when a longtime supporter, columnist Walter Winchell, asked him to help promote Winchell's pet charity project, the Damon Runyon Cancer Fund, on one of his broadcasts. Benny didn't, and Winchell was miffed, so the comedian immediately sent a

"Your LUCKY STRIKE Hit Parade"		
Presented for your pleasure by the manufacturers of		
Luckies - a light smoke		
OF RICH, RIPE-BODIED TOBACCO — "IT'S TOASTED"		
WEEK BEGINNING MONDAY, JULY 13, 1936		

Position This Week	SONG	Position Last Week	Position 2 Weeks Ago
1	Take My Heart	4	7
2	These Foolish Things Remind Me Of You	3	6
3	You Can't Pull The Wool Over My Eyes	10	10
4	Is It True What They Say About Dixie	1	2
5	The Glory Of Love	7	1
6	It's A Sin To Tell A Lie	8	8
7	Would You	2	5
8	There's A Small Hotel	5	4
9	Robins And Roses	6	3
10	On The Beach At Bali-Bali	13	*
11	Stompin' At The Savoy	12	*
12	Let's Sing Again	*	12
13	No Regrets	*	*
14	Cross Patch	*	15
15	She Shall Have Music	9	11

* Did not win a position in "YOUR HIT PARADE" for that week.
Copyright 1936, The American Tobacco Company, Inc.

THE phrase "The cream of the crop" is not an advertising phrase—it is not originally even a creation of our organization. This phrase was first used by the farmers to describe the kind of tobacco our buyers bought for LUCKY STRIKE Cigarettes. It is in fact an unsolicited testimonial to the basic quality of a great brand.

George W. Hill
PRESIDENT

Luckies - a light smoke
OF RICH, RIPE-BODIED TOBACCO — "IT'S TOASTED"
Copyright 1936, The American Tobacco Company

Lucky Strike created an indelible association with *Your Hit Parade*. This was part of a sweepstakes mailing from 1936.

telegram, explaining that he would definitely support the charity's upcoming fund-raiser, but couldn't plug it on the air: "Because I am sponsored by a cigarette program we are not permitted at any time to mention the word cancer," Benny wrote, adding, "Please keep this confidential for my sake."

Although sponsors bought and packaged shows, and negotiated for the most favorable time slots, it was still the responsibility of the network to fill its schedule full-time. When a sponsor couldn't be found for a particular show, or time period, the network had to fill that time itself. The resulting shows came to be known as sustaining programs.

Shortly before he died, Orson Welles recalled, "The reason that radio was often very good, and better than television is, is because there were many sustaining shows. That meant shows without sponsors, paid for by the networks, and given prime time. There is no such equivalent in television."

Rather than take the attitude that unsponsored time should be dealt with as easily and cheaply as possible, radio networks often used that time to present programs of quality and even daring.

Producer-director William N. Robson declared, "The commercial purveyors were in the business of selling soap. We were in the business of selling ideas."

Norman Corwin admits, "Three out of four times I figure, were I sponsored, the sponsor would have said, 'Gee, are they going to get this in Topeka?' No commercial program would have given me the kind of freedom I had as a sustaining show on CBS. That was the kind of radio that was made in heaven."

Corwin's often-cerebral plays were too high-toned for many radio listeners, which is precisely why CBS scheduled them opposite Bob Hope's program on NBC, figuring to attract the kind of people who *wouldn't* be tuned in to mainstream comedy. Nevertheless, Corwin wanted an audience, too, and found himself in a position of "hoping against Hope," as he wryly put it.

It isn't known what hopes CBS held for Orson Welles' *Mercury Theatre on the Air*, but it began its radio life as a sustaining show, scheduled opposite the enormously popular *Chase and Sanborn Hour* with Edgar Bergen and Charlie McCarthy on Sunday evenings. The budget, as Welles' producing partner, John Houseman, recalled, was $5,000 a week, which had to cover everything (story rights, scripting, actors' fees) except the use of the CBS engineering staff and orchestra. The program remained unsponsored until the fateful night of the "War of the Worlds" broadcast in 1938, which generated more publicity and attention than any show in the history of the medium. Within weeks, the name of the program was changed to *The Campbell Playhouse*, because, as Houseman said, "I guess they figured if Orson could make 'War of the Worlds' and the Martians credible then he could make Campbell's chicken soup credible.

"Suddenly there was much more money," said Houseman, "but there were also conditions: more contemporary novels, more 'names.' Well, of course since they gave us the money to buy the names we were able to buy the names. . . . It became a much more conventional show, although Orson maintained a strong independence." Though *The Campbell Playhouse* did more movie adaptations and fewer literary classics, it was still head and shoulders above radio's run of the mill. As Welles declared on its inaugural broadcast, ". . . The makers of Campbell's Soup don't believe in all this talk about the radio audience having the average mentality of an eight-year-old child. They think the radio listeners are the same people that go to the pictures and the theaters and read books. They reason that even the most popular radio entertainment should be addressed to the adult citizenry of America. I can only hope that what I do with *The Campbell Playhouse* will prove how much they mean it and how right they are."

Welles did not become a huckster for Campbell's; he left that to announcer Ernest Chappell. But other shows cleverly integrated their commercials into the scripts, often in a humorous way, so the advertisements became part of the program itself.

On *The Fibber McGee and Molly Show*, announcer Harlow Wilcox would suddenly—and peremptorily—appear in the midst of the week's story, and though he was not a character in the town of Wistful Vista, Fibber or Molly would engage him in conversation that would lead to a message for Johnson's Wax. Obviously, writer-director Don Quinn felt the audience would accept the banter between the fictitious Fibber and Molly and the very real Wilcox, understanding full well that it was simply a device to make the commercial as painless as possible.

That very device even became fodder for jokes. When the announcer turned up one night, Fibber queried impatiently, "What do you want, Wilcox? Though as the guy said when he sat on the bee, I have a deep-seated suspicion."

(Quinn had no compunction about kidding his sponsor, but he felt there were definite limits. "Whatever is being sold must never, never be held up to ridicule," he wrote in 1944. "The circumstances under which the subject is introduced, the person who introduces it, everything surrounding it may be made the butt of devastating wit if available, but the product—ahhh, the product! It's our bread and butter, kids; let's keep it right side up.")

No one pulled this off better than Jack Benny, whose writers wove commercials into the fabric of the show so neatly that they often got big laughs while still selling the product. But only Jack Benny could have fashioned an entire half-hour script out of his *change* in sponsors. After many years with Jell-O, Jack had a falling-out with his advertising agency, and parted company with them and their product. Fully aware of the strong association he and Jell-O had established with the audience, Jack decided, with his writers, to turn a potential liability into an asset.

The show that aired on October 1, 1944, dealt with Jack's nervousness about pleasing his new sponsor, Lucky Strike cigarettes. He even reminded announcer Don Wilson that Luckies didn't come in six delicious flavors!

The premise of the half-hour show was a meeting Jack was going to attend later that day with the new sponsor's representative, a Mr. Riggio. After his usual preliminaries with his cast of regulars, Jack leaves for the meeting. When he arrives at the sponsor's office, he's told to wait, as the gentleman is in conference. Over an intercom, we hear the secretary informing Riggio that Jack Benny is in his outer office. Riggio thanks her, turns off the intercom, and says, "I'm sorry for the interruption—now what were you saying?" And in response, we hear the unmistakable voice of Fred Allen saying, "You're making a big mistake in hiring Benny."

The laugh that follows is tremendous—and richly deserved. There are many reasons Jack Benny ruled the airwaves—and concocting a scheme like that one is just one.

As late as 1951 Benny was still able to pull off a gag based on his Jell-O association. In a medical skit, Frank Nelson plays a doctor who gives Jack an X ray. Wondering aloud at what he finds in Jack's stomach, he mutters, "Strawberry, raspberry, cherry, orange, lemon, and lime . . . Haven't you eaten since then?"

Shamelessness reached its zenith on the adventure shows for children that aired in the afternoons and early evenings. Here, impressionable listeners were wheedled, cajoled, and bamboozled into buying Ovaltine, Quaker's Puffed Wheat, Hot Ralston cereal, and other products because (a) they were enthusiastically endorsed by the show's dashing hero and (b) it was necessary to buy the stuff in order to send away for some swell premium. (Nor was hero worship limited to youngsters. The *Tom Mix Ralston Straight Shooters* was a pet project of "Old Man" Danforth, founder and president of Ralston, who'd been a Tom Mix fan when he was a kid.)

The *Dick Tracy* serial featured a Dick Tracy Jr. character whose main purpose was to appear in the commercials, encourage the listeners to become Dick Tracy Junior Detectives (by sending in a box-top from Quaker Puffed Wheat or Puffed Rice), and read message in code for the boys and girls to decipher at home; his involvement in the actual stories was minimal. During one multi-part story in 1938, about a quest for The Ring of Ocillis, Junior appears in the story just long enough to admire the amazing ring Dick acquires as part of the case. The ring has a secret compartment, which is supposed to protect its owner through its magical powers. Junior makes a big fuss over the ring, more than once, mentioning it again when the show's announcer talks to Junior at the end of the program. This gee-whiz conversation continues the next day.

The stars of *Can You Top This?* (Senator Ford, Joe Laurie Jr., and Harry Hershfield) had to vie for audience attention with a billboard-scaled sign proclaiming the name of their sponsor. Most studio-audience shows featured the sponsor's name prominently on the stage.

By now the bait is on the hook. The show lures its young listeners along, promising a special announcement in a day or two "that you won't want to miss," without actually saying that they're going to offer that very ring as a premium. All they're doing is setting the stage and whetting the appetite.

Imagine the effect this must have had on youngsters who, like Dick Jr., were entranced by the idea of a magical ring. After three days they must have been drooling! No wonder mail-in premium offers on these juvenile shows were so successful throughout radio history.

One of the most famous was Little Orphan Annie's message decoder ring, immortalized by humorist Jean Shepherd in his 1983 movie *A Christmas Story*, where the eagerly anticipated message the young boy deciphers turns out to be "Be sure to drink your Ovaltine."

According to Jack Benny's longtime writer Milt Josefsberg, when the comedian signed with American Tobacco in 1944 he took the precaution of writing into the multi-million-dollar contract a separate clause that permitted his wife,

Mary Livingstone, to smoke any brand of cigarette she pleased . . . because Jack knew she preferred Parliament, which wasn't one of George Washington Hill's products!

Companies took this kind of thing quite seriously. Actor-announcer Jackson Beck recalls, "Philip Morris had a client representative who went around and if he saw you smoking, he came over and investigated as to whether you were smoking Philip Morris cigarettes. If you weren't smoking Philip Morris cigarettes and you were taking their money, you were fired. We would take an empty Philip Morris pack and put Lucky Strikes into it, then we'd light the cigarette at the end where the name of the cigarette was printed so if he looked at what I had in my mouth he couldn't see a name. He even went into your pocket and pulled out the pack."

To encourage this kind of loyalty, most sponsors sent packages of their products to the stars of their shows on a regular basis. Ruth Henning recalls that when her husband Paul worked for Burns and Allen, "Swan Soap was a sponsor of Burns and Allen, and they used to send us lots of Swan Soap. Our girl was just little then; she played with them like blocks and built houses out of Swan Soap."

Sponsors were also well known for sending freebies when a comedian happened to plug the product on their show, even if it was a casual mention in the course of a joke. Sometimes this wasn't quite so innocent or spontaneous, and there were professional product pluggers who worked hard to get their clients' brand names mentioned on the air, however fleetingly.

Hans Conried recalled this practice before an audience of colleagues at the Pacific Pioneer Broadcasters. "The payoff was not in cash, as I recall, but anything from whiskey to services; all sorts of products were available, and it became so prolific and so available that a canny writer would appeal to one agent and say, 'What will you pay me for a Hudson mention?' And he would tell him. Then he would call the other and say, 'What will you pay me for an automobile that you are handling?' And he would compare the value of it.

"We [the actors] did not resent it so much unless the joke was a bad one; now, the good writers gave you good jokes and it didn't hurt your laugh as an actor. The fact that we were seldom afforded even a whiff of a bottle of Calvert Whiskey . . ."

He also told the story of one writer who "received so much merchandise that he was obliged to fill his garage with cases of goods and remove his joke file. Then an unseasonable rain struck, and there was never a funny show written by this man again."

The 1950s brought many changes to radio, as it did to American life in general. Writer-director William N. Robson was working on an espionage series for CBS during the witch-hunt era, and had an almost surreal conversation with a network executive, who told him to tone down anti-Commie propaganda in his scripts. "We're against Communists," he intoned, "but remember, Communists buy products, too."

It was a radio veteran—and a former ad agency executive—Sylvester "Pat" Weaver who, as head of programming at NBC, led the nascent television industry away from sponsor control in the early 1950s, and put the networks in the driver's seat. As television exploded during that decade, sponsorship of network radio programs declined, and a growing number of still-popular shows found themselves on the air on a sustaining basis. Unwilling to allow a half-hour drama to unfold uninterrupted, CBS insisted on at least one interruption in shows like *Gunsmoke*, *Suspense*, and *Have Gun, Will Travel*, then twiddled away the time with silly and often sanctimonious public service announcements: Mail early in the day for better postal service, Don't lose your head behind the wheel of a car, etc.

It was almost enough to make a listener nostalgic for "real" commercials!

8

But Seriously, Folks . . .

The story is told of a famous comedy writer who took an airplane trip cross-country in the 1940s, when trains were still the preferred mode of travel. The plane developed engine trouble and was forced to land in the first convenient clearing, which seemed to be in the middle of nowhere. The passengers and crew were fearful at first, but then heard the sounds of men approaching. They were Indians, who informed the stranded group that they had landed on a reservation. The Native Americans took them in and offered food and shelter for the night.

There, in the wilderness, miles away from any form of modern civilization, the passengers sat around a campfire with their hosts. When one of the Indians inquired what this particular fellow did for a living, he replied, "I write for a radio comedian named Fred Allen."

The Indian snorted. "Huh! Everyone know Fred Allen write his own material."

Such was the writer's fate in the heyday of radio. Comedy writers were particularly slighted, even by the men who employed them. Humorist Max Shulman once remarked that he'd never pursued a job in radio because he always heard comedians referring to "my writers" the way they would say "my neckties."

Comedy veteran Paul Henning agrees with Shulman. "Everyone who has been a writer for any time at all has felt like a tie or a shirt."

Leonard Stern ruefully recalls, "For six years I was called Neighbor and Toots, nothing else. It got so I once introduced my wife as Mrs. Toots." It seems that Stern's bosses, Abbott and Costello, addressed *everyone* they met as Neighbor and Toots.

Writing teams were invariably referred to as "the boys." Sol Saks says, "Sometimes the director would come in, who was five years younger and made half as much money as I did, and say, 'Get the boys in to fix this.'"

Still, says Saks, "The good, intelligent performers always valued writers; they may have mistreated them, but they valued them."

Some performers—legendarily, Fred Allen and Jack Benny—even became allies. As Allen once said, when a producer came in to complain about something, "Where the hell were you when the paper was blank?"

⌐

Comedy writing broke down into three fairly distinct types during the golden age of radio: joke writing for joke-telling comics; continuity writing for the "character" comedians or leading players of situation comedies; and the quieter, more observational humor of such shows as *Vic and Sade* and *Ethel and Albert.*

Jokes—or gags, if you will—became the stock-in-trade of vaudeville comics during the first few decades of the twentieth century. When vaudeville headliners wound up in radio, they faced the awesome challenge of having to create and perform brand-new material every week.

George Burns explained why this came as such a shock. "In vaudeville, if you had seventeen good minutes, and if you played every theater in the United States, big time and small time, you could play for eight or nine years without repeating one theater. So you never had to change. To show you how important minutes were, we had one lousy joke. (The joke was this: I said to Gracie, 'A funny thing happened to my mother in Cleveland,' and she said, 'I thought you were born in Buffalo.' That's the joke.) Now, we were going to put that joke in our act; we booked three days out of town *to break in that one joke*! And here on radio you did new stuff all the time."

Or, as Fred Allen once remarked to Clifton Fadiman, "In one season of radio, 39 weeks, we would tell more jokes than Weber and Fields probably told in ten years."

One of the first people to recognize this challenge and devise a method for meeting it head-on was the legendary David Freedman. As his colleague Carroll Carroll wrote in his book *None of Your Business,* "David, a real scholar and onetime short-story writer for *The Saturday Evening Post,* wrote material for Eddie Cantor (for more money than he could make any other way) to finance his addiction to slow horses in fast company. A compulsive gambler, David was forced to make millions to feed his habit. So he organized the world's first gag factory . . .

"Freedman's atelier of puns, quips, funny sayings, and vaudeville yocks occupied walls of files in his three-story Central Park West penthouse apartment, where he had a corps of young men combing periodicals. Although other gagsters followed David into the radio joke-writing business and compiled gag files, none of them had any idea of how to use them with the same skill and efficiency that came naturally to David."

Freedman's genius was in knowing how to "switch" an old joke into a new one, by simply changing a word or two to make it seem like a comment on a current fad or folly.

Is it any wonder that so much comedy writing became formulaic? Tried-and-true situations, catchphrases, running gags, and supporting characters with their own unvarying "shtick" were part and parcel of radio comedy.

In 1945, Sherwood Schwartz, then a staff writer for Bob Hope (who went on to create and produce such TV series as *Gilligan's Island* and *The Brady Bunch*), compiled a list of practically surefire gag topics as part of an essay on comedy writing for the book *Off Mike.*

"There are always a whole variety of timely references which make a happy joking ground for the comedy writer," he stated. "These include personalities in the news, like Frank Sinatra, Mrs. Eleanor Roosevelt and Henry J. Kaiser; events in the news, like the shortage of Scotch and Kleenex; song titles of the day; various advertising slogans like 'L.S.M.F.T.' and other popular phrases like 'basic seven'; a whole host of military expressions like 'Sad Sack,' 'out on maneuvers,' and 'G.I.'; and several hundred more reflections of everyday life, reflections which constantly change from day to day, as the events themselves change. Oh, yes. And thank God for Superman and Mr. Anthony."

If many of those references seem antiquated or even arcane today, consider what a reader fifty years hence might make of a Jay Leno or David Letterman monologue drawn from the day's news headlines.

At a time when there were dozens of gag-oriented shows on the air, the quest for surefire punchlines bordered on desperation, and certain catchphrases and references became commonplace. One could never hope to count the number of references to the La Brea Tar Pits uttered during the heyday of radio comedy. Groucho Marx wrote to his daughter Miriam in 1945, "I don't care about jokes on Glendale and other surrounding territory. However, the temptation to insert these in a script is always overpowering to a radio writer for he knows that they are sure laughs in the immediate theatre where we're playing and, apparently, he doesn't give a damn about people in Vermont or even in New Hampshire."

Risqué jokes held out a certain temptation for comedy writers, as well. *Radio Stars* magazine reported in January of 1935, "Fred Allen went on the air with some gags about 'The Full Moon Nudist Colony.' Gracie Allen (no relation) has also quipped about 'nudism helping a girl get a lot of things off her chest.' Eddie Cantor has had nudist wisecracks. But those days are gone forever. The moguls have ruled that there shall be no more jokes about nudism." Network censorship, which grew more pervasive (and absurd) with each passing year, was the bane of every radio writer and comedian.

No one told more jokes—or better ones—than Bob Hope, an exceptional performer who gathered around him an extraordinary team of writers. Many of them went on to distinguished careers in films and television; one such veteran, Melville Shavelson, remembers what it was like at the beginning of Hope's long-running show in the late 1930s.

"The turnover there was pretty rapid; Mr. Hope was a tough taskmaster. At the end of the first thirteen weeks there were eight of us that had been brought out from New York; five were fired. He hired five new guys, but he had to give the writers he fired two weeks notice, so for two weeks there were thirteen writers writing the show."

Hope demanded a lot of his writers; each one (or each team, as some worked in pairs) was required to write his own version of the show, top to bottom. Then, at a weekly meeting at Hope's home, everyone would read his material and be judged. Only the cream of each contributor's work was folded into the final script.

Says Shavelson, "You'd sit around all night and you would read your material, and if you could make the other writers laugh—and their jobs depended on their *not* laughing—the joke would be checked and it went in the show. And that's where I developed my first ulcer. Milt Josefsberg was my partner at the time, and he was very angry because Norman Panama could get laughs with Mel Frank's material because Norman could do a Groucho Marx. So if you wanted Hope to hire you, you should have teamed up with a performer, not a writer."

The situation was much the same when Larry Gelbart joined the staff a decade later. "We would meet at his house in North Hollywood, and he would read the jokes. He would put a check mark next to any joke he liked the first time through. Then he would read them again and if that joke still held up, he'd put a line through the check. Then he'd read it a third time and if the joke still held up he'd put a circle around it. Now someone, I don't remember who, would cut out

Bob Hope and his writers in the 1940s. Judging from the smiles, Bob must have liked the latest gag in the script. *Left to right:* Sherwood Schwartz, Mel Shavelson, Hope, Al Schwartz, Jack Rose, Milt Josefsberg, and Norman Sullivan.

all the check/circle/cross jokes and make a routine of those jokes. Then he might say, 'No, let's put this one here and that one there,' and then he'd have his monologue.

"There was no laugh machine; there was no sweetening. He really had to earn his laughs out there, and the jokes had to earn their laughs."

What made the job even tougher was the lack of context or continuity; Hope's brash-young-man image was all the writers had to work with, both in the monologues and in the sketches. Says Norman Panama, another charter member of the Hope radio team, "He never really developed a character. The closest thing to a character was a joke formula called 'arr.' Somebody once wrote a joke that said the room was so small the mice crawled in on their hands and knees. Arr. And that sort of became a vogue in radio in those days. You fasten onto these cliché situations, so you can do them week after week. He didn't have any really developed persona except that he was very facile and a great joke-teller."

Shavelson remembers another running punchline that ran out of steam. "We had a signature for the show, which was 'Give me a drag on that before you throw it away.' When anybody said anything, we'd say, 'Give me a drag on that before you throw it away.' And finally somebody told [Bob] what it meant. We were doing that with Judy Garland, who was fourteen years old at the time, and MGM took her off the show because of it. And the network cracked down."

Early on, it was decided to audition the entire show for a studio audience on Sunday night, then refine the material for its Tuesday broadcast. It was a sound idea which was later adapted by others, for a simple reason: Hope soared to the top of the ratings during his very first season on the air. But this gave the writing team two deadlines a week, instead of one. First they would gather and read their material for Hope on Saturday; this often ran into the wee hours, because the finished, collated script had to be submitted to NBC before 10:00 Sunday morning in order to be mimeographed.

Then there was a huddle after the Sunday night tryout, to assess which material worked and which didn't. This meant more rewrite assignments over the next two days. (Hope never mimeoed his opening monologue, for fear that someone might steal the jokes between Sunday and Tuesday.) Then came the broadcast itself. But even the ON AIR sign in the studio didn't mean the job was finished.

Mel Shavelson recalls, "On one show, we went on the air, and Hope didn't like the blackout for the sketch; we were on the air and he still didn't like it. We were writing, and writing, and he kept throwing them out; he finally agreed on a joke just about thirty seconds before it went into the sketch and it laid a big egg. But that's how immediate it was."

The learning process continued as Hope performed his program twice, once for the East Coast and once for the West. Says Shavelson, "You'd do exactly the same show and one show would play and one wouldn't, and you'd have to figure out why that was. One little incident could change the whole feeling of an audience, so it was the greatest training ground for a comedy writer there could be. It doesn't exist anymore, because the laugh machine covers all faults; you're writing for machinery now, not for human beings. You're not out in front of an audience, live in front of a national hookup—with millions of people listening, and if somebody makes a boo-boo or if a joke falls on its face there's no possible way to cut it."

No one outside of the writing staff had any appreciation or understanding of the work that went into those laughs. Norman Panama lamentingly recalls the reaction of the studio audience: "You'd hear the comments of people walking out: 'Well, you know, he writes all his own stuff' . . . 'Isn't he funny?' Well, of course, he *was* funny, and he had a great memory; he's a great comedian. And it was marvelous for us."

George Burns had a completely different approach to crafting the weekly Burns and Allen show. He didn't want the job to encroach upon his private life, or his writers'.

"Nobody brought in anything on paper," he recalled. "We wrote it in the office. We'd sit here, like I'm talking to you, and we'd think of an idea. You see, if the writers have to write at home, they write at night. When they come in in the

George works with longtime writers John P. Medbury, Harvey Helm, and Willy Burns (George's brother) as Gracie gags it up for the camera, in this 1938 shot.

morning they're tired, they can't think of anything. Like this, they come in; they can go out with their wives, they do anything they want, come in fresh in the morning. We get an idea and if it sparks us we stay with it, if not we get another idea. We sit here until it works; that's the way I work.

"At one time I had four writers in one room getting $250 apiece, and four writers in the other room getting $75 apiece—young writers. And when they got good, we put them in the other room."

The audience never knew— or suspected, most likely—that George was "the brains of the outfit," that he was more than simply a great straight man. (When Paul Henning wrote to his mother and said he was going to write for George Burns, she replied, "Congratulations, that's wonderful, but who writes for Gracie? *She's* the one who says the funny things.")

"I used to be in the [writers'] room all the time," George explained. "I never took billing as a writer, but I know what made Gracie and myself a really good team was that I had a talent off the stage, and Gracie had it on the stage. I was able to think of it and Gracie was able to do it. And that's what made us a good team."

One of Burns' staff writers was his brother, who bore the brunt of George's occasional bursts of temper. Longtime associate Paul Henning recalls, "If he had to let off steam, he'd let off steam to Willy; he'd just give him hell, blame him for anything. One day Willy said, 'Listen, George, I don't have to take this from you. I can go back to Brooklyn and do what I was doing before I came out here.' And George—brought up short—said, 'What was that?' And Willy said, 'I was sitting at home and you were sending me $50 a week.' "

Willy was in fact a valued member of the team. And George was a respected boss. Years of experience in vaudeville had given him tremendous comedy know-how. For one thing, he was smart enough to realize when it was time for a change.

"We were in radio for I would say, maybe ten years, and our rating kept dropping. See, if your rating drops five points, that's not too bad—there's something great against you that night. But when you start to drop a half a point and a point, and a half a point, then a point, then another half, you're losing your audience. And we started dropping that way.

"I'm in bed one night, two in the morning, and it finally hit me: I said, we are too old for the jokes we're doing. We were married, and on the air we were single. Gracie was flirting with the announcer, Bill Goodwin. So I woke up Gracie. I says, 'Kid, I got it. I know why we're losing our ratings.' She says, 'You do?' 'Yeah,' I says, 'our jokes are too young for us. We're married, you know.' The next week I went on the air, I said, 'Ladies and gentlemen, Gracie and I have been married for a lot of years; we've got two children, and so from now on we're Burns and Allen, a married couple.' And you tell different jokes when you're married."

That's what kept Burns and Allen on the air—and on top—for so many years.

The hours and the rewards of writing for a continuity show may have been similar to writing for a star comic like Bob Hope, but the methodology was somewhat different.

Abe Burrows (later to become one of the leading lights of Broadway musical comedy as both writer and director) described the routine of writing *Duffy's Tavern* for, and with, its star Ed Gardner, in the book *Off Mike*: "The first thing that happens is a little guy calls you up and says: 'Fred Allen is going to be your guest next week.' The little guy who tells you this is now through for the week. He doesn't have to do anything until the following week when he calls you up and says: 'Your guest next week will be Cary Grant.' . . .

". . . *Duffy's Tavern*, let us remind you, is a story show. That is, we get one basic plot, and stick to it all the way through . . .

"So we call a conference to get a story-line for Fred Allen's appearance. We look under the rugs. No story-line. We look out the windows. No story-line. We go out to lunch. No story-line. But finally somebody remembers that St. Patrick's Day is coming, and on St. Patrick's day, Duffy, the unseen proprietor of the Tavern, always holds what he calls his 'Spring Semi-Annual St. Patrick's Day Musicale and Pig Roast.' So we say, why not let Archie try to hire Fred Allen as the M.C. for the Pig Roast? Then Duffy won't want Fred, and Fred will have to audition for him. This will give us a splendid opportunity to louse up Allen and have a lot of fun while Duffy is insulting him.

"Okay. We have our premise, our springboard, our basic situation. We then lay out a three-page synopsis describing what everybody does and when: Archie, Eddie Green, Finnegan, Miss Duffy. We also decide where to place the commercials (without these, it's futile work) and the musical numbers."

The chore of writing the show was divided among the staff writers, who then gathered with Ed Gardner to go over the material. Larry Gelbart, who joined the staff when he was just a teenager, remembers, "Ed did a lot of drinking and he might read the first ten pages of what you'd written and then think that page eleven sounded familiar and in fact it was, because he was going back to page one again."

But, says onetime staffer Sol Saks, "Ed's standards and taste were very important in that show, [even though he did not] do the nitty-gritty work." Saks also remembers what the weekly grind was like: "We worked all night until airtime to get that script mimeographed, hurried over to the studio where the actors would read it over once, broadcast it, drop the scripts into the wastebasket and go home, and we would go back to work. So it was an eighty-five-hour week, because the last session was twenty-four to twenty-eight hours, always one session.

"I started at $200 a week. Once I said to Ed in exasperation, 'Well, I can't make that funny; I'm no genius.' And he said, 'Then what am I paying you all this money for?' "

꩜

The notion of a writing staff was a radio innovation. Vaudeville acts were generally written by individuals (with or without the participation of the performer); plays were often written by collaborators. But the idea of a roomful of writers participating in the creation of a single script was new . . . and, given the deadlines and workload, necessary. There were no "mid-season reruns" in those days of live broadcasts and thirty-nine-week seasons.

Most staffs were compartmentalized into specialists. On the Hope show, it was Norman Panama and Melvin Frank who wrote the guest-star sketches, which those aspiring playwrights saw as mini-playlets with a beginning, a middle, and an end. (As it turns out, they went on to write many screenplays and Broadway shows, so the experience was useful.) Other staffs pegged which writers were best with topical jokes, which fared better with character material, etc.

Jack Benny's writing team had a stenographer whose sixth sense about comedy made her a valuable participant. As George Balzer recalls, "Periodically either I or someone else would say, 'Jeanette, read us back what you've got.' And she'd go back to the beginning and start reading, and invariably, the lines that she picked out of all the conversation and kept were the lines that we wanted. All the other stuff was just passed over."

Each staff had its own way of working. Paul Henning recalls, "On *The Rudy Vallee Show* we used to meet, discuss an idea briefly, and we'd all go to the beach. We worked in Manny Manhoff's apartment, at the El Jardin, and there was a switchboard and an operator. The operator had instructions that if the producer called she was to say, 'Oh, the boys just went out for coffee, and I'll have them call you when they come back.' Then she would call us at a secret number at the beach. We'd be surfing, playing volleyball, or lying in the sun."

On the other hand, Don Quinn,

```
WEAF                    RUDY VALLEE SEALTEST PROGRAM
                  #26      New York       (13)
10:00-10:30 P.M.
AUGUST 29, 1940            "BURNS"                  BROADCAST
- - - - - - - - - - - - - - - - - - - - - - - - - - - -
RUDY VALLEE    C P DICKSON      PAUL HENNING      BUD WEBBER
ED GARDNER     EDGAR FAIRCHILD  CHARLIE ISAACS    E G FILE (5)
FORD BOND      SIDNEY FIELDS    BENNY KREUGER     SOUND (2)
ABE BURROWS    KEITH FOWLER     McKEE & ALBRIGHT (10)  ALAN REED
W K CROCKET    MELVIN FRANK     NORMAN PANAMA     PEG LA CENTRA
ELIOT DANIEL   FRANK GALEN      HOWARD WILEY      BETTY GARDE
                                                  BEATRICE KAY
                                                  IRENE HUBBARD
- - - - - - - - - - - - - - - - - - - - - - - - - - - -

                    MUSIC ROUTINE
         PAGE              SELECTION
          1        "MY TIME IS YOUR TIME"
          4        "LOCH LOMOND"   (JEANNIE)
          2        "OH, CHI CHORNIA"

          5        "ROAMIN' IN THE GLOAMIN'"  (VALLEE)
          8        "MY HEART'S IN THE HIGHLANDS"  (VALLEE)
          8        "JEANNIE"  (VALLEE)
         10        "FLOW GENTLY, SWEET AFTON"  (VALLEE)
         14        "COMIN' THRU THE RYE"  (DUET)
         16        "MY LOVE IS LIKE A RED, RED ROSE"
         19        "AULD LANG SYNE"   (PRODUCTION NUMBER)
                   "MY TIME IS YOUR TIME"
```

Look at the roster of writers for this 1940 *Rudy Vallee Show*: among them are some of the future bright lights of Broadway, movies, and television.

the man behind the beloved, long-running series *Fibber McGee and Molly*, was compulsive. "Don was an absolute genius, but he committed suicide, really; he killed himself by his work habits," Henning reports. "Don would postpone and procrastinate until the very last minute. Then he would get a big pot of coffee and two cartons of cigarettes and he'd sit up all night. All night. And I admired him so much that I began to think that that was the way to write, so I tried it, but I couldn't." Quinn also had a hard time delegating any of the writing to someone else. He hired young Henning but couldn't relinquish control of his "baby." Still, Henning describes his onetime mentor as a "wonderful, brilliant man; never went beyond high school, he just read constantly, widely." The result was a great love of puns and wordplay.

Most successful shows had a guiding light. Sometimes it was the creator, in other cases the head writer, and in certain instances it was the star. Occasionally all three were one in the same.

Ed Gardner, for instance, was the heart and soul of *Duffy's Tavern*, but Sol

Saks observes, "After the show was off, we found out he was a terrible, terrible writer on his own. Ozzie Nelson was the same way. On his own show, he was a good editor. He could not write when he tried to write for anything else."

(It was also Ozzie who objected to giving writers credit on the air, according to Saks. "Ozzie's argument against not giving writers credit was, he said, 'We will lose an illusion; they think we are really making this up as we go along.' " Aside from that, Ozzie earned wide respect for his dedication to the show, and his high standards for the comedy they produced week after week.)

Veteran comedy writer-producer Hal Kanter remembers a time when he was on the staff of the *Amos 'n' Andy* show. One day after rehearsal at CBS, they were all stuck for a blackout line for the second act. "All of us sat there, and there was a considerable staff of writers—some very good writers in that room, in addition to Charles [Correll] and Freeman [Gosden]. And we kept throwing line after line after line, and none of it worked. It was getting late in the evening, and in my naivete, I said to Freeman, 'Supposing the Kingfish were to walk into this room right now, Freeman, and we told him what was going on. What would he say?' Without missing a beat, Freeman immediately shifted his mind into blackface; he became the Kingfish and he said something, I don't know what. Whatever it was, we all fell down, and that was it. Even he was surprised when he realized he knew that character so well; the character possessed him."

It should be noted here that Gosden and Correll wrote *Amos 'n' Andy* for themselves, by themselves, for more than a decade, and provided all the voices heard on the program. They were very private about both their scripts and their performances; during one period they insisted that their announcer and organist broadcast from a separate studio! Throughout the 1930s the show followed a serialized, soap-opera format which galvanized millions of listeners day after day to see what was going to happen to Amos, Andy, the Kingfish, and their cohorts. It was character-driven humor, with few if any "jokes." Then, in 1943, faced with sharply eroding ratings, Gosden and Correll allowed their vulnerable show to undergo a major overhaul. From a nightly fifteen-minute serial broadcast, *Amos 'n' Andy* became a once-weekly half-hour comedy show, replete with gags, supporting actors, a live orchestra, and even a studio audience. At this point its stars and creators put themselves in the capable hands of top comedy writers including Joe Connelly, Bob Mosher, and Bob Ross, who rejuvenated the A&A formula and made it one of the funniest shows on the air. It ran in that format until 1954.

Creating material that was custom-tailored for big-name guest stars was one of the challenges (and for many writers, the perk) of being on staff at a high-profile show. It also had its pitfalls. One time Ed Gardner had a fight with the guest star and fired him, then told the writers to redo the script and find someone else. Hal Kanter remembers his boss on the Bing Crosby show, Bill Morrow, calling late one night to say that character actor Monty Woolley was ill. "We've got a replacement; if you'd come here in the

Hope and Crosby, on Bing's radio show. Some of the ad-libs were scripted ahead of time, some were not.

morning we've got to change a couple of lines," he told Kanter, who replied, "Why, who's the guest star?" "Margaret O'Brien."

By the time Kanter joined the Crosby show in the late 1940s, it was one of the most consistent and entertaining programs on the air, so getting (and dealing with) guest stars was no problem. "Any guest that came on had such respect for Bing; they knew that Bing would not permit or countenance poor material, or bawdy material, or inferior material," he states. "We, fortunately, had established . . . a high level. It was established long before I got there, on *The Kraft Music Hall*. There was a dignity about Crosby and a taste and an intellectual level, or a level of literacy and humor, that was pretty much unapproachable. And nobody ever questioned, 'What am I gonna do?' or 'Show me some material.' Nobody ever said that. They were just delighted to be on the show, to work with the man.

"We used to do jokes about Bing's lack of hair or his quickly receding hairline. Very seldom did Bing ever say anything about a script or ever complain. But we had Fred Astaire as a guest on one show, and we had a joke. Fred said to Bing, 'You used to be taller,' and Bing said, 'Yeah, well, I used to comb mine up.' And Fred evidently didn't care for the joke; he did not want to admit that he wore a piece, whereas [to] Bing it didn't make any difference. But Bing took us aside one day and said, 'Fellas, let's cut down on the bald jokes.' It was the only time I ever heard him complain about anything."

For other stars, complaining was a way of life; some were known to be out-and-out tyrants. Others were woefully insecure. Both types made a writer's existence difficult. Carroll Carroll, longtime staffer on *The Kraft Music Hall*, remembered that Al Jolson's only comments after reading a script were the admonition, written in the margins, "Make better."

Rudy Vallee actually socialized with his staff, and was a gracious host when they were away from the workplace, but his writers learned the hard way that it was unwise to beat him at tennis.

Phil Harris went on hunting and fishing trips with his writers from *The Phil Harris–Alice Faye Show*, but there was never a conflict. Ray Singer, who wrote the show with his longtime partner Dick Chevillat, told a SPERDVAC radio convention gathering, "The six years on *The Phil Harris–Alice Faye Show* were six of the happiest years of my life. They're wonderful people, and it was a writer's paradise, because Phil was the kind of a guy who loved living, and didn't want to be bothered with work or anything else. And he left us alone. We never had to report to him. Dick and I would work out the premise and write the script. Phil and Alice lived in Palm Springs; they'd come in on Friday. And we rehearsed, we'd do a rewriting on Saturday, and do the show Sunday and they'd go back to Palm Springs. He never knew what was gonna happen. And it was left in our hands, which is a wonderful thing to do; and it spoiled us for everybody else."

Gags and sketches filled the airwaves week after week, but it was not the only brand of comedy to be found on radio. In the early 1930s, Kansas City newspaperman Goodman Ace began writing a quiet, subtly hilarious program that he performed with his "awful wedded wife" Jane. *Easy Aces* was a simple, low-key program consisting mainly of conversation between Mr. and Mrs. Before long, it attracted sufficient attention on KMBC in Kansas City to warrant moving to Chicago and the full CBS network. From there the Aces relocated to New York City and continued doing their show, often three evenings a week, until 1945. The show was introduced by the familiar strains of the popular tune "Manhattan Serenade," and an announcer's friendly voice saying simply, "Ladies and gentlemen . . . Easy Aces." Domestic discussions about everything from an out-of-work brother to Jane's purchase of a new dress spurred the scripts. Incidental characters (and a few "regulars") were introduced, but the essence of the show remained the badinage between Ace and Jane, with his frequent response of "Isn't that awful?" becoming a catchphrase. (Ace's curmudgeonliness wasn't entirely a matter of acting. His friend and colleague Hal Kanter says, "He was a wonderfully acerbic, grouchy kind of guy. Even when he was cranky, he was funny. He had a good sense of humor about himself, too.")

Easy Aces was never as wildly popular as Jack Benny or the top situation comedies, but it had a wide and loyal following, because it was so very, very funny.

Jane was Goody's Gracie Allen; she spoke with an amusing twang and specialized in malapropisms, as in "I got up at the crank of dawn." Her "time wounds all heels" became a classic. (On pursuing an acting career, she remarked, "I've always had the smell of goose grease in my blood. I've always dreamed of seeing my name up in tights.") Ace was the Voice of Exasperation, which allowed him to make caustic comments on life in general and

Jane and Goodman Ace, otherwise known as *Easy Aces*. This was comedy sublime.

Jane's antics in particular. (Or as he put it, "a man's best friend is his mutter.") Ace, who wrote the program single-handed, was particularly adept at lacing a script with running gags which would ricochet and reverberate from beginning to end, and draw extra laughs because of their unexpected reappearance.

Eventually, Goodman Ace gave up performing to write for others. His stint with Danny Kaye in 1945 was notoriously unsuccessful for both men, but he found an ideal niche as head writer of NBC's *The Big Show* in the early 1950s. Not only was Tallulah Bankhead's flamboyant personality an inspiration for any writer, but she worked especially well with Ace's great friend Fred Allen, who became a frequent guest. After radio's demise, Ace wrote Perry Como's easygoing TV variety show for many years, before reemerging in the public eye as an essayist for *Saturday Review* magazine and National Public Radio in the 1960s and '70s.

⌒

Goodman Ace, like all connoisseurs of humor, was a fan of *Vic and Sade*. Here was one of radio's highwater marks, a brilliantly eccentric daily fifteen-minute broadcast from Chicago whose characters lived in a world all their own, located in "the small house halfway up in the next block." Victor Gook, a self-amused dreamer, his practical wife Sade (whose only expletive was "Ish!"), their son Rush, a bright adolescent who calls his father Gov, and Sade's charmingly addle-brained Uncle Fletcher, who addresses everyone in the family (male and female) as Honey, were virtually the only characters ever heard on the show during its thirteen-year-run. The program consisted mostly of their conversations, which often ran on completely different trains of thought, only occasionally intersecting. There was little if any "action."

Vic and Sade had many fans, among them actor Walter Huston, who paid a visit to the troupe one day along with poet Edgar Guest *(seated at right)*. That's the show's director, Charles Urquhart, seated just above Paul Rhymer.

The premise for a show might be Sade dragooning her son into cleaning the attic on a Saturday morning—when he'd rather be doing anything else on earth—or Uncle Fletcher reporting on his landlady's brother getting a job at the Ohio State Home for the Agreeable, or Vic proudly preparing lunch and setting the table, in his own idiosyncratic manner ("You'll notice that a symmetry of pattern has been striven for"). In one show, Vic refers to his son at various times as Margaret, Melon Seed, and Harriet—for no particular reason. Sade will come out with the most astonishing and hilarious exclamations ("You could've cut off my nose with a pound of butter," "We're just sitting here with our teeth in our mouth"), but she is never actually trying to be funny. Make no mistake, the Gooks were oddballs of the highest order, but they were also ordinary folks, with traits and habits that made them instantly identifiable (and endearing) to a broad American audience.

It was a low-key program, yet often wildly funny, heard in the midst of daily soap operas which took much of the same raw material seriously. Announcer Bob Brown called it "an island of sheer delight in a sea of tears." Humorist Jean Shepherd has said, "It's as though *Death of a Salesman* or *Our Town* had debuted on a typical Wednesday afternoon between *As the World Turns* and *Against the Storm*, followed by *The Hollywood Squares*."

All the years it was on the air, from 1932 to 1946, *Vic and Sade* was written by one man, an unsung hero of American humor named Paul Rhymer. How he continued to turn out one delightful (and insightful) show after another for so many years, we'll never really know. Suffice it to say that he was inspired. Ray Bradbury has described him as "a junk collector, which is a far step up from garbage. He collected bits and pieces of mediocrity from all our commonplace occupations, all our inane conversations, all our bored afternoons and long evenings when all we could think of to do was trot down to the YMCA to watch the Fat Men Play Handball."

His widow, Mary Frances Rhymer, wrote in 1972, "Often people would ask Paul, in kindness, how he was able to turn out a daily show by himself. He always found the query irritating and answered that he was a writer and so it was his business to write. They probably had their own business which they tended every day? Only once did he seem to admit that all those years of writing against a deadline had been exhausting. It was when he said to me, 'Do you know that I have written more words than Dickens?' (The *Vic and Sade* shows total more than 3,500 scripts.)"

The mention of Dickens was apt, since The Great Storyteller was one of Rhymer's heroes; they shared a delight in crafting odd and onomatopoetic names, from Dr. Whipfang and Mr. Gumpox to Fred and Ruthie Stembottom. In an introduction to a collection of Rhymer scripts, Jean Shepherd noted, "Rhymer has been compared to Harold Pinter by some, Mark Twain by others. Personally, I feel that Rhymer was a complete original . . .

"He never ridiculed or put down people merely because they are what they are. However, he is razor-sharp when it comes to blasting the fraudulent and the inane."

The beauty of *Vic and Sade* was not only in its writing, but in its performance. It would be impossible to think of anyone else in the key roles other than Art Van Harvey (Vic), Bernardine Flynn (Sade), Bill Idelson (Rush), and Clarence Hartzell (Uncle Fletcher). Idelson, by far the youngest of the group, says of the ensemble, "Somebody said it's catching lightning in a bottle. We all came from different

Paul Rhymer examines possible Christmas gifts with his cast, Art Van Harvey, Bernardine Flynn, and Billy Idelson.

worlds, but fate just brought us together. Van was a guy who sold space to the *Hog Breeder's Journal*. He didn't know a damned thing about acting; he was the perfect Vic. He in some strange way understood the character completely, but he didn't understand much else. Bernardine was from high society and was playing this down-home housewife. And I, the son of illiterate immigrant parents from Russia, was playing an alter-ego of Paul Rhymer, probably the most intellectual guy in the world. We just came together and who knows? It's just one of those things. Shouldn't have happened, but it did."

The actors found that Rhymer was not only their author, but their cheerleader. Bernardine Flynn recalled, "Paul Rhymer was our best audience. He said over and over again, 'I thought this script was a bunch of nothing until I heard you people do it.' He gave us full credit when we really didn't deserve it."

Youthful actor Bill Idelson remembers peering over Rhymer's shoulder as he'd bang out a script in his cubbyhole of an office. "I would stand behind him and watch him write the script. He had a lot of unfinished lines; lines with dots, you know, and I would ask him, 'Do you know how that sentence is going to end?' and he'd say, 'No, I don't.' It wouldn't bother him a bit. He almost never went back and rewrote anything; it all just flowed out of him. He'd do a script in about two hours, and we felt his words were sacred; we never (except for timing) tried to do anything with his script."

He used interrupted speech better than anyone in radio, capturing the way real people talked. His characters went off on tangents, often unaware that their conversation partner wasn't traveling along with them. His scripts were dense with layers of dialogue. "Wheels within wheels," he called it.

When, after several fits and starts, *Vic and Sade* left the air in 1945, Paul Rhymer essentially shut down. At one point Bill Idelson, who had resettled in Hollywood, brought Rhymer out to the Coast to meet with someone about writing a movie. "But Paul said to me, 'You know, maybe I've done my work.' He said Shelley did his work by the time he was eighteen or something, and he said, 'Hell, I just might have to face that. I've done my work.' Because he didn't have any feeling for doing anything else after that."

Another daily dose of "recognition humor" was provided by a talented writer-performer named Peg Lynch, the creator and star of *Ethel and Albert*. She started out in radio at KATE, a small station in Albert Lea, Minnesota, where she was an advertising and continuity copywriter. Bored with her routine, and inspired by *Easy Aces*, she decided to try writing a husband-and-wife comedy script—a decade before she got married in real life. The station, happy to have material to fill its airwaves, not only put her show on the air, but pressed her into service as an actress.

"One day I wrote about something that happened at home," she recalls, "the

Peg Lynch and Alan Bunce
as Ethel and Albert, circa 1944.

kind of thing that isn't funny when it happens but makes good dinner table conversation if you want to be amusing. And I got several fan letters; it all went to my head, but also went to my common sense. I realized that I didn't have to sit down and knock myself out every minute to try to think of something funny. All I had to do was look around me.

"You're going to give a party, for example, and you got a script out of who you're going to have, who doesn't get along with who, and what you're going to wear. Then you've also got the party. Something happens at the last minute—something goes wrong with the food—I mean, you can get a week's script out of that."

But Lynch makes light of her considerable comic know-how. It takes a certain gift to recognize the potential humor in a situation, and understand how to build on reality with just enough exaggeration to make it funny. This was her great gift. It was only when she auditioned writers to help shoulder her workload (and read submissions that came in "over the transom") that she realized not everyone could do what she did.

"People seemed to assume because I had little throwaway lines and would write about 'nothing' that the script was about nothing, and they would write four pages of nothing, not realizing that even among those little throwaway lines there was some clue to something else that was going on. It was usually about three things that dovetailed; sort of like doing embroidery." One would-be contributor who submitted an *Ethel and Albert* script treatment was a young John Cheever.

Peg's success in New York came quickly. NBC considered her show, but ultimately turned it down; fortunately, an executive who had just moved to the fledgling ABC decided to pursue her. A recent arrival in wartime Manhattan, Lynch had to use a pay telephone at the corner drugstore to respond to his telegram. ABC liked the show, she was told, because the network's new owner, Life Savers magnate Edward Noble, thought soap operas were trashy, and relished the idea of having a daily series in which each show was complete in itself.

For a long time, Lynch didn't regard her routine as anything out of the ordinary. "I can remember when I got to the network, in 1944, I couldn't believe that's all I had to do was write a fifteen-minute show every day," she says today. Accustomed to rising early, she would approach her typewriter as early as 4:00 and set to work, usually completing her task in two hours—and almost never rewriting or editing. Lynch worked with a two-week lead time, so there were never any deadline anxieties. Her stomach tightened not during the writing process, but when it was time to go on the air: she suffered terribly from mike fright.

When she got married in 1948, in order to take time off for her honeymoon she stockpiled a bunch of shows. "They wouldn't allow me to do repeats. I was writing two a day and recording at night. We went on the *Queen Mary* on our honeymoon, and I slept the whole time."

After five years of daily broadcasts, and a less successful half-hour format program, *Ethel and Albert* was canceled in 1950, but made an immediate transition to television, first in a series of skits on the Kate Smith show, and then as a series of its own. It later made a brief reappearance on radio, and then got one final reprieve in 1958 when CBS expressed interest in a daily fifteen-minute broadcast. Because the name of the show belonged to NBC, this final series with Lynch and Alan Bunce was renamed *The Couple Next Door*, but it was *Ethel and Albert* reincarnate.

Lynch's best scripts ring out with the hilarity born of total audience identification. She knew how to take a simple, believable premise and escalate it to the level of high comedy. It's an art that has since been taken up by such columnists as Art Buchwald, Russell Baker, Erma Bombeck, and Dave Barry.

Radio covered the entire spectrum of humor, from the cornpone antics of *Lum 'n' Abner* and bazooka-playing Bob Burns to the arch irreverence of Henry Morgan, but only a handful of comedians found lasting success. Ed Wynn was one of the first great comedy stars in the medium, but his unvarying and bombastic delivery of jokes, as the Texaco Fire Chief, wore out its welcome with listeners after just a few years. (It must be said, however, that some of those jokes were pretty good. There was the one about his uncle buying a car that died three days later. He went back to the dealer and said, "You said this car would last a lifetime," and the dealer replied, "The way you looked the other day, I thought it would!")

Jack Pearl enjoyed enormous success as Baron Munchausen in the early 1930s, but his dialect humor and catchphrases ("Vass you dere, Sharley?") were too confining to be much more than a fad. Other stars, like Eddie Cantor, found ways to reinvent themselves (as well as their shows) from time to time in order to freshen audience interest.

Don Quinn, the writer who was the heart and soul of *Fibber McGee and Molly* (and later *The Halls of Ivy*), was one of radio's greatest punsters, who loved nothing more than wordplay. ("You're like a boy with a soda, clutching at straws." "I didn't come here to bandy words, bandylegs." "Here's a joke about the Grand Canyon— ah, there's a beautiful crack.") He also created a cavalcade of catchphrases and running gags, including Fibber's cacophonous closet, "T'ain't funny, McGee," the Old

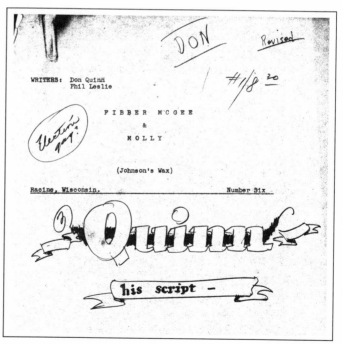

Don Quinn even doodled creatively, as witness this script page from a *Fibber McGee and Molly* broadcast.

Timer's "That ain't the way I heerd it," Teeny's "I betcha," and so many more. But Quinn was canny: he knew not to overuse those surefire laugh-getters, and parceled them out with great judiciousness. He also believed that jokes for jokes' sake caused more than one show to meet an early demise.

"Many radio programs have tremendous audiences, week after week. But they are audiences who would feel no slightest pang of regret, experience no sense of personal loss, if said program were never broadcast again," he wrote in *Off Mike*. "Conversely, the shows which live and build over the years are those for which the listener feels an abiding love and friendship. If you are a star on one of these happy productions, you are, by acclamation, a paid-up life member in good standing of millions of American families.

"They will stay home from bridge parties and movies to tune you in. They will agonize over your misfortunes and gloat over your triumphs. And, what is a far more important thing, they will buy your sponsor's product, whether they need it or not. You'd better mind your p's and q's, too, because you're in their homes on sufferance, though you may stay for years and years if you remain nice people. It is, in this writer's opinion, a burning shame that the sharpest wits of our time (to name one name, Fred Allen, the comedian's comedian and gag-writer's Mahatma) are not using the medium of situation comedy as a base from which to fire their barbs at the fools and fallacies of the time. Should Mr. A ever decide to drop his variety-cum-guest-cum-commentary formula in favor of building himself a radio character, I venture to predict there would be some fast shuffling among the highest-ranking Crossley holders. This gratuitous suggestion is made in the belief that an idea, a gag, a message or a theme gets a warmer reception when delivered by an established fictional character than by a comedian working as a mere comedian. May God forgive me for the 'mere'!"

Quinn may have been right. Fred Allen represented the pinnacle of radio comedy; he was revered by his colleagues, and for an "egghead," he was surprisingly popular with the public as well. "You can count on the thumb of one hand the American who is at once a comedian, a humorist, a wit and a satirist, and his name is Fred Allen," said no less an authority (and admirer) than James Thurber.

Allen started out as a juggler in vaudeville, and from years of experience knew how to play to an audience. "I got into radio the hard way," he once wrote to a reporter. "Back in 1912 I didn't know that radio was going to be invented. I started preparing for the inevitable. I spent twenty years playing in vaudeville and Broadway shows. The inevitable turned out to be radio and when it came I was ready for it."

He had always written his own material, and hated to surrender to the committee system that radio demanded. ("You put your mind on a treadmill in the fall," he wrote to his fellow radio scribe Don Quinn, "and remove it, winded, in June.") His solution was to filter the staff writers' work through his editorial sieve, and embellish their material with his own. According to most eyewitnesses, he wrote the lion's share of each script himself. He drove himself mercilessly, and by the 1940s had to safeguard his health with long periods of rest.

Among the first writers to join Allen's staff in 1936 were a pair of Columbia University graduates, Arnold Auerbach and Herman Wouk, who stayed with the comedian for five years until wartime service intervened. Auerbach later wrote, "Our contributions to his career were small, but we were there. The year Babe Ruth hit 60 homers, even the bat boy must have felt a sense of participation."

Wouk went on to become a prize-winning author and playwright (*The Caine Mutiny Court-Martial, Marjorie Morningstar*); he and Allen remained good friends, and it was Wouk who encouraged Allen to write his autobiographical books toward the end of his life. Wouk later told biographer Robert Taylor that he viewed Allen's knowledge of comedy with awe, remem-

Fred Allen and his beloved Portland, rehearsing on mike in 1937.

bering a time they were talking about a famous incident in which actor Lee Tracy, on location in Mexico, urinated off a balcony onto a Mexican general.

"At the time, the film *The General Died at Dawn* was popular, so I remarked to Fred, 'The General Dodged at Dawn,' and just like that, Fred shot back, 'No, Herman; The General *Dried* at Dawn'—a word's difference, but what a difference."

Listening to Allen's radio shows today, it always seems as if the funniest material is to be found in Fred's ad-libs and comebacks, not in the script itself. In every case, Allen's love of language comes through. He tells guest Billy Rose, "Your activities would cause a thesaurus to slink into a corner and hang its glossary in despair." Then, after Rose's riposte, Allen remarks, "You think I know what a thesaurus is?" in a mild attempt to deflect any charges that he's an intellectual.

Although biographer Robert Taylor insists he was as "plebeian as a potholder," Allen's fascination with the English language was anything but common. Self-educated, he was a voracious reader, and it showed. During a 1941 broadcast, he credited Jack Benny with starting the Chicago fire, explaining that he was so cheap he used to crawl into Mrs. O'Leary's barn as a baby and "have lactic traffic with her cows." No other radio comedian would have—or could have—summoned up that phrase.

Fred Allen gave everything to his show—his time, his energy, his incredible mind, his health—so his never-ending run-ins with small-minded advertising agency reps and network poo-bahs were a source of tremendous irritation. In one notorious incident in the spring of 1947, long after he had established himself as a star and a ratings winner, NBC cut him off the air for defying the network censors by poking fun at a fictitious NBC executive whose sole job was to cut shows off the air when they ran long (as his show had done the week before). The resulting brouhaha in the press caused the network considerable embarrassment, as well it should have.

Allen's remarks to a studio audience one evening have often been quoted, but still bear repeating: "If by chance any of you folks are in the wrong place, you still have ten minutes to get the heck out of here. Heck, incidentally, is a place invented by the National Broadcasting Company. NBC does not recognize hell or the Columbia Broadcasting System. When a bad person working for NBC dies, he goes to Heck, and when a good person dies, he goes to the Rainbow Room. I'll probably have to wait until Resurrection Day and look into the Rainbow Room as I go by."

Allen's long-running "feud" with Jack Benny was one of the richest veins of gag lines in all of radio. The idea came about by chance, and yielded more years of material than either comic could ever have envisioned. It is fitting that this relationship existed between the two men who ranked side by side as the most gifted comedic performers on the air.

⁓

Jack Benny became an American institution. To follow the development of his persona (and with it, the format of his show) from his debut in 1932 to his final shows of the 1950s is like listening to a musician play a piece "cold," with competence but little inspiration, then come to know it better and play with greater warmth and meaning, and finally to know it so well that the interpretation becomes even freer—and richer.

Some of this came from the simple experience of performing for an audience week after week; some of it evolved from a growing relationship among the cast and writers. Much of it was directly attributable to Jack himself, and his burgeoning canniness as an editor of comedy material.

Unlike others who became mini-despots in their fiefdom of a weekly show, Jack never surrendered his fundamental niceness or his generosity of spirit. This is what endeared him to all those who worked for him, including his writers.

Fred Allen with his best audience, Jack Benny, making a stage appearance at New York's Roxy Theater.

The troupe traveled together and virtually invented the working vacation. Benny's longtime head writer, Bill Morrow, later wrote, "We never set out for Palm Springs or any place with a definite idea of what we were going to write. We put down no set ideas to cramp us. We went places, enjoyed ourselves, and *incidentally* wrote something about it. Our good times were reflected in our shows. Our audience, in fancy, traveled with us and had good times with us."

George Balzer came on board in 1943, joining a staff that was already close-knit. He soon learned what the others already knew: that one of the other bonuses of working for Jack was that he was such a great audience. No one broke up more easily.

Balzer remembers an incident early in his tenure with Benny. "Jack comes to this spot in his script . . . and he says, 'Fellas, on page six, I want a new joke.' We don't say anything. He says, 'Something a little stronger.' Silence. 'I want something that kind of buttons up that whole page and pays it off.' Silence. 'I gotta have something better than what we've got there.' And I leaned over and I say, 'Jack, we'll get you a new joke.' He says, 'Oh, you agree with me, huh?' I said, 'No, but it's possible that the four of us could be wrong.' And I'll tell you, he looked at me and literally slid off the chair, sat there in the corner and he's screaming [with laughter]. He was screaming; he got up and said, 'I wouldn't change that joke now for a million dollars.' And he didn't."

Aside from his regular staff, writers and directors who worked with Benny on guest appearances and one-shot programs learned to trust his instincts, and his extraordinary timing. Robert E. Lee had just such an encounter. "I can remember Jack Benny saying to me, give me a 'yes' [in this script]. And I said, 'Why? It's not funny.' He said, 'Of course it's not funny, but it lets me time the laugh.' Because if there's a laugh then the person wouldn't jump at the laugh, they'd have to wait for Jack to say yes. But if it wasn't a big laugh, he could say the yes right away and just throw it away. A superb technician."

The original 1938 NBC caption says it all: "BENNY'S SCRIPT GETS A GOING-OVER. Seated in a circle, NBC's Benny troupe works under Prof. Benny's eagle eye. In the rear are Sound Effectspert Virgil Reimer, and Engineer Murdo MacKenzie. Seated are Don Wilson, Benny, and with his back to the camera is Jack's secretary Harry Baldwin, who is the inevitable messenger boy. Nearly hidden by Baldwin is writer Bill Morrow. Phil Harris, Mary Livingstone, and Kenny Baker round out the circle."

He was also a perfectionist who never let success go to his head. His team of writers would develop their premise for the weekly show on Tuesday, then split up to write half-a-script each over the next few days. "Now we meet with Jack on Friday and we start right from the top," George Balzer recalls. "Jack starts right from the top; he starts reading and when he gets all through, we say, 'Well?' 'Okay, let's go.' Now he goes back to the top, and now we start polishing. This is where we start making the seven words and not the nine; just the right punchline. He may go for several pages and not change anything, or he may reach a spot where he's unhappy, and he says, 'Fellas, this next half-page, I think we can fix it up in here a little, you know?' and then we'd fix it. Then on Saturday we'd go to CBS, to the studio, where everybody comes in and reads their parts. Then when they all go, we sit down and try to cut out the two-and-a-half, three minutes that were too long, and strengthen here and there, wherever it's a little bit weak. That's with Jack. Then on Sunday morning we'd come into the studio about 11:00, something like that, and we'd all read it again, then we'd go on mike."

It was that quest for perfection that made the Benny show so consistently good for so many years.

One week, Jack asked his writers if they would go to Groucho Marx's house to read him the script for his guest appearance. They obliged, but found Marx to be completely unreceptive to their material, and caustic to boot. When they returned to the office and reported this to Benny, he said simply, "Well then, we won't use him." For a comedian to support his writers that way was virtually unheard-of. Several years later, Groucho approached Benny at the Hillcrest Country Club and asked why he never had him on the show. He said, "I'd be happy to have you on my show, but only if you use the script my writers write for you." Groucho agreed and appeared on the show the following week.

Benny and his writers enjoyed one luxury that many other shows never achieved: continuity. George Balzer vividly recalls, "One day he comes into the room and he said, 'Well, that settles that; it's all set. We've signed the deal.' And I said to Jack, 'Well,

Jack Benny confers with writers Edmund Beloin and Bill Morrow in this candid photo from the early 1940s. Mary Livingstone is seated in the foreground, and Dennis Day is partially visible at right.

Jack, I hope you got a good deal.' And he says, 'George, I don't know how good it is; all I know is we'll all be working together for the next seven years.' Now, this comes from a star; you can go home and build a house on that."

Besides job security, the Benny writing staff knew how to mine a joke or series of jokes, not only from week to week but from year to year. Over the course of several decades various gag ideas came in and out of vogue on the program, but some were constant—like Benny's dilapidated Maxwell car. In 1945 the show booked Ronald Colman and his wife Benita Hume as guest stars, and expanded on the notion (often mentioned on the air, but never dramatized) that they lived next door to Jack. It paid off so well, and the Colmans had such a good time, that they became regular guests, several times a season.

One day, in a bull session, the writers hatched an idea about Jack walking to the drug store and stopping to pick up the lid of the Colmans' garbage can to see what was inside. Everyone thought it was a funny idea, but George Balzer said, "Wait a minute, we've got to be realistic; if Jack is heading to the drug store, why would he go back toward the Colman house?" Another writer protested that the

Jack performs with two of his favorite guest stars, Ronald Colman and Benita Hume (Mrs. Colman). Theirs was a mutual admiration society, and the writers seemed to rise to the occasion every time the Colmans were booked on the show.

house would in fact be on the way to Sunset Boulevard, where the drug store would be. After several minutes of arguing, the writers stopped and realized two things: first, this was radio and they could do whatever they pleased; second, they had invented this entire situation in the first place!

Even writers, it seemed, could fall under the persuasive spell of radio.

Some comedy writers became personalities themselves, most prominently Abe Burrows, who gained such notoriety performing song parodies on the "party circuit" in Hollywood that he eventually left *Duffy's Tavern* and headlined his own fifteen-minute show. (Ironically, Ed Gardner had been a producer-director-writer for the J. Walter Thompson agency before his natural comic gifts were utilized "on mike.") After the announcer's introduction, he would say offhandedly, "I'm Burrows, like he said." Taking advantage of radio's invisibility factor, he remarked one evening, "I guess I could tell you exactly what I look like, but that's a lousy thing to say about a guy." Burrows' show was a modest affair, but a funny one, featuring such memorably titled tunes as "The Girl with the Three Blue Eyes" and "You Put a Piece of Carbon Paper Under Your Heart, and Gave Me Just a Copy of Your Love."

Burrows went on to become a popular guest on television talk and panel shows, a path followed by other comedy writers like Jack Douglas and Selma Diamond. Filmmaker Billy Wilder thought so much of Cy Howard, the creator of *My Friend Irma* and *Life with Luigi*, that he cast him in his movie *Stalag 17*, but after several days of filming, Wilder realized that while Howard was naturally funny in person, he was not coming across onscreen. His part was eventually played by Harvey Lembeck.

Professional gag writers even got their own showcase on the short-lived late 1940s program *The Comedy Writers Show*. Here, three comedy pros would parry ideas back and forth in a simple semi-improvisational format; such funnymen as Roger Price, Leonard Stern, Snag Werris, and Sidney Fields plied their trade on this amusing program.

⤵

Some comedy writers grumbled so much about the weekly grind that they became full-time cynics. Others lost their sense of humor except in a professional context; these men were known never to laugh at a funny joke, but only to remark, "That's funny."

But some who came to this medium never lost their sense of wonder or their sense of fun.

For Larry Gelbart, who started as a teenager, "It was wonderful. It was kind of unbelievable, really, that something small and personal and immediate got to be so big and public. It was just kind of a kick to hear somebody read your words, and the magnitude of some of those people was very impressive, that they were reading your words and then an audience was actually laughing at 'em. It was very rewarding."

And while many professional joke-smiths continued writing for comics and comedy shows in the television era, their job was never quite the same again. Says Gelbart, "We didn't realize what we'd lost in a way; we were so pleased to be using this new toy that we forgot the kind of picnic we used to have, where with a word you said you were somewhere. If you said you were somewhere in television, pretty soon you heard people hammering and nailing sets together."

Cy Howard, producer, creator, and head writer of *My Friend Irma*, presides over a script conference with Cathy Lewis and Marie Wilson.

Some of radio's greatest comics, like Fred Allen and Edgar Bergen, never made a successful transition to television. Some, like Jack Benny and Bob Hope, fared quite well indeed, though aficionados still believe they did their best work in radio. A new generation of comedy writers, including Danny and Neil Simon and Woody Allen, sprang up to serve a new generation of television comedians, including Sid Caesar and Jackie Gleason. It wasn't long before radio was being referred to in condescending terms of nostalgia for "the good old days."

But even without rose-colored glasses, it's easy to see that there were peaks of comedy (and its gentler cousin, humor) in radio that were, quite simply, unbeatable in any other medium. And the writers who crafted those gems had much to be proud of.

9

Audiences

A t one time, the idea of an audience attending a radio broadcast and (heaven forfend) applauding or laughing was considered taboo. One can only speculate about the reasons: perhaps it was felt that the audible presence of a crowd would spoil the intimate, one-on-one line of communication between performer and listener.

Whatever the case, when Rudy Vallee made his pioneering broadcasts from the Astor Roof in New York City in 1930, he was so disconcerted by the *absence* of an audience that, in order to accommodate him, a special wall of glass was constructed so people could attend the broadcast and respond—without being heard over the air.

That was soon to change. Eddie Cantor is credited with pioneering the "live audience" broadcast in the early 1930s (though many have questioned since what the alternative to a "live" audience might be—a dead one?). Before long, audiences were a standard fixture of most big-time variety shows, especially those headlined by "name" comedians who depended on immediate response to their jokes. And accordingly, many of the leading broadcasts emanated from theaters, instead of radio studios.

Looking back, George Burns said, "It gave you a live quality that you didn't have on radio. You needed some reaction.

An attentive audience watches a performance of "Michael & Mary" on *The Screen Guild Players* in Hollywood. The sound-effects man is off to the right, as unobtrusive as possible. Ronald Colman, Claudette Colbert, and Donald Woods are seated.

"If there was an audience, you'd play to the audience. You'd play to each other, then look at the audience. But Gracie never did. Gracie never looked at the audience. When Gracie was on the stage she even blocked out the footlights. Very hard to do: To Gracie there was no audience and no footlights, just one on one. Gracie would look at me and tell me and I'd look at the audience, and smoke a cigar."

Audiences added a special dimension to radio; it's hard to think of the Jack Benny or Bob Hope shows without them, and it's clear that lifelong stage performers like Cantor or Ed Wynn would have been lost without those people filling the theater.

At the same time, it's difficult to imagine a cackling audience intruding on the quiet, more intimate humor of, say, *Easy Aces* or *Vic and Sade*. Whoever decided to confine those and other similar shows to a private studio made the right move.

Even on dramatic shows, an audience could play an important role. The listener has no indication that there is a studio audience for Norman Corwin's broadcast *The Lonesome Train*, a deeply moving piece about the train that carried Abraham Lincoln's body, until the end, when the crowd bursts into a huge, sustained ovation, which is allowed to play for a while before the announcer steps in to close the show. And that ovation makes the experience all the more moving and satisfying.

The marriage of broadcast and audience was a bumpy one at first; for one thing, people didn't know how to behave. In May of 1933, *Radio Stars* magazine paid a visit to a small studio upstairs in Carnegie Hall for the *Colonel Stoopnagle and Budd* show. A card placed on each seat read, "It is important that during this half-hour you remain seated so there will be no scraping of chairs and no incidental noise that might interrupt the broadcast . . . the announcer will call for silence just before we take the air. Please cease applause or laughter after any number or skit when the announcer raises his hand."

On the other hand, some shows right through the 1940s had studio audiences in attendance, but instructed them not to applaud! Their laughter was heard at the punchline of jokes, so it was no secret they were there, but nevertheless, Bing Crosby's *Kraft Music Hall*, Frank Sinatra's *Songs by Sinatra*, and the expensive 1939 flop show *The Circle*—with Ronald Colman, Carole Lombard, and Groucho Marx—were among those that tried to stifle audience reaction.

Eddie Cantor and his protégée Dinah Shore perform for the most appreciative audience of all: servicemen.

One clue to the reason for a silent audience may be found in a heated editorial in the March 1934 issue of *Radio Stars*. Editor Curtis Mitchell wrote, "Sunday night after Sunday night I have bent a hopeful ear toward my loudspeaker awaiting [Eddie] Cantor's turn at the mike. It comes, and a storm of laughter invades my ears. Laughter at what? Why is that select studio crowd of 1200 people entitled to laugh at something I cannot see? Eddie races into his script. A line is flung back at him by James Wallington, not very funny, but a tempest of laughs soars into my parlor. It rises like a tide over Cantor's dialogue. His voice is smothered, and so is Wallington's. What is happening?

"Nobody ever bothers to explain. So I never learn. None of us twenty or thirty millions of listeners ever learns. We're just chumps apparently, not worth bothering with.

"Exactly the same thing happens on Ed Wynn's show. On several others, also. It's a vicious custom, one that network officials should not permit ... Ed Wynn and Eddie Cantor should have the decency to realize that the place for them to be funny is in the nation's parlors, not Studio 8H in Radio City."

But just two years later, in December of

Eddie Cantor was liable to do *anything* in front of an audience; one lucky photographer caught him in mid-flight.

1936, that same magazine changed its tune, reporting, "The most conclusive evidence yet offered for the pro-audience side, was at a recent broadcast. The announcer was giving the following week's line-up. At the mention of Robert Taylor a great gasp of delight arose from the audience, followed by a long and wistful sigh. This amazing audience reaction was of such spontaneity that there's hardly a radio audience antagonist left in town."

If anyone was liable to incur the wrath of a listener like magazine editor Mitchell, it would have been Cantor, who was unable to refrain from *performing* for a crowd. His longtime announcer, Harry Von Zell, recalled, "When he worked on radio in front of a microphone, he went through all of the physical motions, the jumping up and down that he became famous for on the stage . . . that little prance that he did, clapping the hands and prancing around. And if there was a passage of music, a segue of some kind, he would literally dance away from the mike, like he was putting on a regular circus performance!"

There was even more to Cantor's physicality. He was known for swatting the derrieres of female guest stars, and even leaping onto the backs of his male colleagues—without warning. "Sometimes," Von Zell recalled, "he would take Dinah Shore, pick her up and start whirling her around his body like an adagio. Nobody ever knew when these things were going to strike him. It was just something that he had to do."

Too bad the audience at home couldn't share some of *that* fun! But Cantor also felt a tremendous loyalty to his fans. A few days before his broadcast of October 23, 1940, he learned that his weekly show would be preempted for a live address by President Franklin D. Roosevelt. Knowing that tickets had already been distributed to hundreds of New Yorkers, he appealed to his sponsor to allow him to put on a show, with his costars and orchestra, even though it would never be broadcast, so those ticket-holders wouldn't go home disappointed! (More than half a century later, Cantor's grandson, Brian Gari, found a transcription disc his grandfather had made of that performance, and released it to the public for the first time.)

Cantor understood that the audience was his *ally*. As writer Larry Gelbart explains, "Audiences are very eager to laugh. You used to wait in line, and you felt very special because there were only a few hundred of you.* I remember going to see Groucho, when he had a radio program with Leo Gorcey and people like that, and it was a great coup to just be in the audience and then see these people live. You were pumped up. You can hear it on sitcom programs today, you can hear somebody getting a scream just saying, 'Honey, I'm home.' The audience is so ready."

Some performers knew how to make the people in the radio studio their partners. Hal Kanter will never forget one night on the Bing Crosby show when Judy Garland was the guest star. "Judy had had a lot of bad publicity and had gone through a rough time. When she finally came out of the hospital and was going to make her first public appearance on the show, at the last minute she got stage fright and got scared to death. She said, 'They're going to hate me; they won't be listening to me, they're going to look for the scars on my wrists . . .' She was an emotional mess, and Bing went in to reassure her. Then when he walked out on stage as usual, he said, 'We have an old friend here tonight. She's been away for a while, but she's come back, and I know that you missed her because we sure did. Give her a nice welcome; make her feel—make her feel *loved*.' Something like that, then 'Ladies and gentlemen, Judy Garland.' She walked out on the stage and that audience just put their arms around her and hugged her and kissed her . . . *relaxed* her. And she did a show that was wonderful. But it was Bing's sensitivity that dictated that. I don't know too many people who would have done that."

Freeman Gosden and Charles Correll didn't want *anyone* in the studio when they performed as Amos 'n' Andy. That was how they'd worked in Chicago, and they maintained the idea after moving west, first to Palm Springs and then to Los

---

*Shows that broadcast from existing theaters had a substantial seating capacity, but studios that were built expressly for radio broadcasts were usually intimate affairs. Elliott Lewis explained, "If you had an auditorium with 300 people or more in it, you had to hire a stagehand, so they built studios that would hold 299 people."

Angeles. Announcer Bill Hay and organist Gaylord Carter were actually situated in a separate studio away from Gosden and Correll, lest the comic actors be distracted by "outsiders." By the 1940s, the show was in need of revitalization, however, and one important ingredient in the new *Amos 'n' Andy* format was a live studio audience. Gosden and Correll had to make an obviously difficult adjustment, but in time they responded to the audience laughter as gratefully as any radio comics.

Most programs welcomed an audience. Producers came to realize the importance of providing a friendly atmosphere for the people who filed in, and made sure they were primed for the actual broadcast. This soon became known as the audience warm-up, and the responsibility for this chore usually fell to the announcer, who developed a regular shtick for getting people in a good mood, and acquainting them with the modus operandi of the show. Some performers also welcomed the opportunity to meet the audience; whenever Chester Morris appeared on the *Lux Radio Theatre*, the actor seized the opportunity to perform magic tricks, a favorite hobby.

On the Bing Crosby show, both the warm-up and the introduction of its star were done in characteristically low-key fashion. Writer Hal Kanter remembers, "Ken [Carpenter, the announcer] usually would walk out and start talking; gracious, no big jokes. He'd introduce John Scott Trotter and the orchestra. There'd be a lot of stuff on the stage—the orchestra, the mikes and all, and Bing would just sort of casually wander around. And usually by design at some point, Ken would do a mock 'take,' and say, 'Why, it's the boss!' And then Bing would say, 'Evening, how are ya?' and the place would come apart. Then he'd say, 'Yeah, Ken, looks like a lively group. We ready to go? How are things in the booth?' Just a little chatting, nothing prepared . . ."

The presence of people who could see what was meant only to be heard provided special challenges. By the time *Amos 'n' Andy* acquired a live audience, most listeners were aware that neither Freeman Gosden nor Charles Correll was black, so that came as a shock only to the most naive and uninformed attendees. But during her tenure in the cast, in the role of Andy's daughter, it was necessary to introduce May Wynn to the audience before the broadcast, so there would be no unintended laughter, or audible ripple of surprise. She was a Chinese-American.

A studio audience had the unique opportunity of watching a white man named Marlon Hurt play the country's best-known black housemaid, Beulah—and then have a conversation with himself when he also took the role of "her" boyfriend Bill. They also enjoyed Marion Jordan magically transforming herself into the wee-voiced Teensy on *Fibber McGee and Molly*.

Gene Autry recalls that a weekly ritual on his *Melody Ranch* broadcast was explaining to the audience that Champion, his fabled horse from the silver screen, would be impersonated for the microphones by a sound-effects man with a pair of coconut shells. He and the soundman would then perform a bit for the crowd, so they could become accustomed to this visual incongruity, and get the laughter out of their system.

Even so, it was hard to stifle a crowd's natural response to patently silly situations—like fistfights in which the actors stood at their microphones, grunting and grimacing while sound effects men huffed and

Gene Autry introduces his world-famous horse, Champion, to Arthur Godfrey's studio audience. On Autry's own weekly show, Champion was played by a sound-effects man!

puffed and hit leather-upholstered pillows. Said director Fletcher Markle, "I simply had to adjust to the fact that this was unalterable, and therefore, we made part of the warm-up to these fifteen to eighteen hundred people [to show] them how sound effects are manufactured, if there was any danger of them being laughed at. We simply demonstrated if horses' hooves were being done with half-coconut shells, or if someone was receiving a lethal blow by a hammer going into a canteloupe, or whatever. It was done for them so they could laugh at it before we went on the air. And if, as occasionally happened, a script fell out of a performer's hand (not the star, one hoped), one doesn't want the audience to break up at this thing, so we used to say that it could happen, and an actor could stand and his whole script would fall—not the one he was going to be working from ten minutes from now. It would be all over the place, and they'd have their giggle over with.

"If we had Charles Laughton in *Payment Deferred*, or any of those extraordinarily suspenseful things . . . Charles was often a comical figure when being his most dramatic. God knows there was never a greater professional than Charles, but I used to ask him to come out in the warm-up and get his round of applause, then say, 'Please show our audience that extraordinary posture you adopt when you are about to put the knife into the man's chest,' or whatever. And Charles would never fail to do this, to protect himself."

Photographic evidence that Red Skelton was constitutionally incapable of limiting his performance to what the audience at home could hear.

On comedy shows, the use of an elaborate sound effect only enhanced the laugh. Actually watching a soundman create the tumult of Fibber McGee's closet, or Mel Blanc imitate the sputtering of Jack Benny's Maxwell was a comic extravaganza in itself. As listeners at home became more sophisticated, they soon came to enjoy the double laugh of the gag itself, and the audience's obvious reaction to what was happening in the studio. (Not every show welcomed this "extra" reaction. Paul Henning recalls that on one comedy show, "We had to screen the sound-effects man from the audience because they would become so fascinated watching him they'd forget to watch the performers!")

The sound-effects men were simply doing their job, but some actors had clever ways of boosting their audience response. Arnold Stang was known to hold a script up to his face, only revealing his distinctive, owlish features when it was time for his entrance. Others mugged shamelessly for the benefit of the "seeing" crowd. Comedy writer and performer Roger Price recalled the first time he saw Hans Conried deliver a punchline that was far from hilarious; the actor came prepared, and milked the laugh by hiking his pants to reveal mismatched socks, one red and one green. It got the intended result, and impressed the young Price, who then devised some tricks of his own. If a line included the phrase "up and down," he made sure to point up on the word "down" and vice versa. The studio audience usually responded.

When an audience *didn't* respond, there was little anyone could do; this was long before the invention of the laugh track, which now enables every utterance on a TV sitcom to be greeted with guffaws. In radio, any joke could lay an egg, and the audience was both judge and jury. A gifted ad-libber like Fred Allen could often recover with a witty response to their lack of enthusiasm, but others, particularly on situation comedies where it would have been damaging for an actor to break character, could only suffer. When Orson Welles hosted a mercifully short-lived comedy program called *Orson Welles' Radio Almanac* in 1944, he stopped after a joke failed to elicit more than a titter and without missing a beat, declared, "I think I ought to explain that this is a comedy program, ladies and gentlemen. Last week we didn't tell the people it was a comedy program. Of course, we told them afterwards and they laughed all the way through Gabriel Heatter."

Welles also did himself in—unwittingly—during the audience warm-up for the *Almanac* series. Director Jack Johnstone ruefully recalled, "Orson decided to do a magic act. He was an amateur magician and a very good one. So the following week—the audience was always called very early—Orson did about ten minutes of magic. Which was great, fine, it got a big hand from the audience, [then] the show went on as usual. The next week he did about twenty minutes. I kid you not. He finally ended up doing a full forty-five minutes, and by that time, the audience was wrung out completely. They couldn't respond if the best comedian in the world was a guest on the show. It just wore them out."

Cary Grant helps Ed ("Archie") Gardner fasten his apron before a *Duffy's Tavern* broadcast. That apron, a sort of good-luck charm, bore the autographs of every *Duffy's Tavern* guest star over the years— a cavalcade of the biggest names in Hollywood.

The most memorable—and consistent—audience reaction in the history of radio was the laugh that opened Ralph Edwards' *Truth or Consequences* every week. The instant the show began, listeners heard an audience issuing gales of laughter, with women shrieking an octave above the merry din. Obviously, these people were watching something funny . . . but what? Ralph Edwards still guards this "trade secret" today, refusing to divulge the answer, since he continues to make use of the gimmick for TV tapings and personal appearances.

Careful investigation has revealed that the secret plan involved staging a stunt as part of the audience warm-up, in which two members of the audience—one male, one female—were challenged to don all the articles of clothing in a suitcase provided them in a certain amount of time, with the winner to receive a cash prize. Through trial and error, Edwards and his staff came to know just how long it would take the average participants to get to the most ludicrous and embarrassing moments of the stunt (the man having to wiggle into a girdle, for instance)—and *that* was the moment the show hit the airwaves. It never failed.

Some performers became experts at "feeling out" an audience. Gale Gordon's sputtering, muttering buildup of exasperation as Mayor LaTrivia on *Fibber McGee and Molly* always wound up with the actor cutting short his own ranting, catching his breath, and after a pregnant pause, snarling, "McGee!" The silence between the climax of his angry tirade and the uttering of "McGee" was as funny as any piece of dialogue.

The actor said he timed those pauses according to the audience sitting in front of him. "I *listened* to the audience, and it occurred to me one day that when there is silence, what is the audience doing? They are thinking about (a) what you might say, (b) *if* you're going to say it, and *when* you're going to say it. There is never a dull moment for them; they're very busy. I used to time those pauses by the audience. I knew just by hearing them when it was time to say 'McGee,' and then it would work.

"Sometimes I'd wait twenty seconds without a breath, sometimes more. I never took a stopwatch and said, 'I'm going to wait twenty seconds.' If I knew they were in a good mood, and receptive, I'd wait longer, and longer, and longer. Jim Jordan used to stand there and start laughing—he couldn't believe that I would wait that long. The people in the booth would say, 'Oh my!' Sometimes they'd wonder whether I'd dropped dead right in front of the mike and hadn't had the sense enough to lie down. But it was the audience; the audience is terribly important to an actor, but so few actors realize it."

⌐⌐

Dramatic shows normally functioned without an audience, but there were exceptions. Edward G. Robinson insisted on having a theater presentation for *The Big Town*, while the *Lux Radio Theatre* and similar movie star vehicles based in Hollywood became popular attractions for visitors and local fans alike.

Elliott Lewis remembered, "If you had guests from out of town, they'd say, 'Can you get me tickets for the Benny show?' It was like getting tickets for the Carson show [years later]." The same was true in New York, as reported by Robert J. Landry in his book *This Fascinating Radio Business*:

"The networks are highly visible and their 'glamor' all-pervading in New York. They occupy some of the choicest playhouses on Broadway. The Theatre Guild itself has turned over the Guild Theatre to the radio showmen, and where once Alfred Lunt and Lynn Fontanne and Earle Larimore held forth on the boards the Mutual network now presents 'Can You Top This?' Everywhere the radio studios and the theatres turned into radio studios remind the public at large and showmen in particular of the importance of the new entertainment-advertising medium. Autograph hunters lurk around the radio halls even as around the Paramount stage door. Approximately 70,000 New Yorkers 'go downtown' to attend free broadcast performances every week. And when the program is especially popular, a Major Bowes, a Clifton Fadiman 'Information Please,' a Phil Baker 'Take It or Leave It,' a Kate Smith, such broadcasts bring out that weirdest kind of bootlegger—the man who in a knowing whisper, eyes averted, offers to sell tickets which have no price but do have value."

On the debut *Martin and Lewis Show*, Jerry Lewis expressed trepidation about facing the radio crowd. Dean Martin tried to assuage his fears, pointing out, "We did all right in nightclubs, didn't we?" "Yeah," said Jerry, "but those people paid ten dollars cover charge, so they had to like us; but at a radio show the audience gets in for free, and at those prices they can afford to hate us!"

Recruiting an audience was not always easy. When Bob Hope did his test-run show on Sunday evenings he hit upon an ingenious scheme: to divert the people who were just leaving the Edgar Bergen–Charlie McCarthy *Chase and Sanborn Hour* at NBC. He figured they were primed and ready. Lesser shows suffered, however, when demand for warm bodies was especially keen. Leonard Stern remembers that when he and his fellow scribes appeared on a low-profile ABC program, *The Comedy Writers Show*, in the late 1940s, they had to keep their wits about them while—on occasion—the entire crowd walked out in the midst of their show to attend a "better" program next door!

Not every star welcomed the presence of a crowd to watch them work. Film actors who'd never been on a stage in their life were often quite rattled by the experience. Joan Crawford once insisted, shortly before a *Lux* show was to go on the air, that the theater be cleared. She wasn't being temperamental; she was simply scared to death.

The fear never left her. Actor Sidney Miller remembers watching her walk away from a microphone during a broadcast and seeing blood spilling from her palm; she'd clenched her fist so tightly that her fingernails had punctured her skin! "She was so nervous and so scared, I helped her back to the table . . . she hated radio."

On the other hand, busy character actress Rosemary DeCamp never minded a full house. "I'm very nearsighted," she explains, "so it didn't confuse me to see the audience; they just looked like a whole lot of pink eggs out there." What *did* concern her was having a wardrobe of evening dresses to rotate week after week for the audience shows.

An audience show often presented logistical problems for the people behind the scenes as well, particularly if the show was performed in a theater instead of a specially designed radio studio. The sound-effects men would have to haul their cumbersome equipment into the theater every week, set it up, and then break it down again at the end of the show. The director often felt isolated from his cast, as some of the control booths were far removed from the center-stage area. But the feeling of broadcasting from a bona fide theater, with a full house in attendance, made up for most of these problems.

⟶

Comedians, as previously noted, thrived on audience feedback. Red Skelton got so fired up for his weekly half-hour show that when it was over, he couldn't bear to stop . . . so he didn't. Every week, fans were treated to an impromptu Skelton "aftershow." "He got steamed up," recalled cast member Lurene Tuttle, "and the half-hour show didn't really satisfy him, so he kept the audience there afterwards. . . . He did at least an hour, sometimes an hour and a half."

Skelton also copied Bob Hope's innovative idea of pretesting his show before a live audience. When Hope went on the air in 1938, he was not yet a nationally known star. His young team of writers was the best in the business, however, and they would prepare a weekly script that was far longer than any broadcast might require. On Sunday night Hope and his cast would perform this lengthy version of the show for a studio audience; then only the good material would be integrated into the Tuesday night show.

"It was the way to go," Hope confirmed years later, "because within three weeks we were number one."

The methodology was far from scientific, however. Melville Shavelson, one of Hope's writers, explains, "We'd do a two-hour show on Sunday before an audience, then we'd check off the biggest jokes and throw out all the small jokes, put the big jokes together, go on the air Tuesday and they'd fall on their face, 'cause he didn't understand that the order of what happened before and what went after had anything to do with why people laughed." Still, a good joke was a good joke, and the audience preview weeded out the absolute bombs.

Hope made some other realizations early in the game. At first he performed his own audience warm-up, using some of his vaudeville act, which was slightly risqué. "It was the dumbest thing in the world," he later admitted, "because then you come out with clean material [on the show] after doing things that were just a little racy, and it didn't play. I couldn't figure that out. Finally somebody said, 'Your warm-up is better than your material.' "

He soon made another discovery: the musicians in the band generally didn't react to his Tuesday-night jokes, because they'd heard them all before. So Hope insisted that the Sunday-night preview be accompanied by two pianos; that way the band would be responsive for the actual broadcast. (At least once, Hope had to rely on the band alone for comfort and laughter; there had been a flood in Los Angeles, and no one else showed up for the broadcast. "So I turned around to the band after my first joke and I said, 'Fellas, help me, huh?' ")

Jack Benny went so far as to have his writers change some jokes between the East Coast and West Coast performances, so the band members would have something new to laugh at. But neither Benny nor anyone else was ever able to understand why, when a cast was obliged to do two performances of the same show the same night, response to the identical script would be different.

Paul Henning recalls that on the Burns and Allen program, "A show we'd do for the East Coast would be comfortably the right length; then the later audience was in a more festive mood and they would laugh longer." That meant the writers had to cut material while the show was on the air in order not to run overtime. Writer Willy Burns, George's brother ("a genius with a stopwatch," according to Henning), would have separate timings for segments, broken down to ten or twenty seconds each, and could figure out which cuts would put them back on time.

But why the longer laughs? Says Henning, "The only thing we could figure was that the later audience was in a more relaxed or festive mood because maybe they had a cocktail before dinner or something."

⌒

As radio matured, measuring "yocks," like measuring the size and demographics of the audience, became more of a science. This didn't sit well with some performers. Stan Freberg remembers that when he was starring on the 1950s series *That's Rich*, CBS executive Guy Della Cioppa would stand in the control room with a "clicker" in his hand, the kind used to tick off the number of people entering an arena. Freberg finally asked Della Cioppa what he was doing, and the exec explained that he was counting the number of audience laughs in the show. "And he says to me, 'Only thirty-seven laughs on the show this week, we've got to do better than that.' He says, 'Benny hits right about sixty.' I said, 'Does he always hit sixty?' 'Well, on the better shows; sometimes it's right round fifty-two to fifty-five.' So I said, 'Look, that thing in your hand doesn't measure chuckles, does it?' He said, 'No, it doesn't measure chuckles.' I said, 'The other thing it doesn't measure is a warm feeling inside a human being who is having a wonderful time listening to this but didn't actually go "ha ha," so you could go "click." ' He didn't understand where I was coming from at all. Now today, they wouldn't need that clicker in television sitcoms because [the laughs] are all laid in. You want sixty-two? Hey, how about seventy-four?"

⌒

Then, as now, there were audience "regulars," and then as now, with so many shows on the air, a shortage of able-bodied seat-fillers would develop from time to time.

Phil Harris remembered looking down from the stage of the Jack Benny show and "the same people would be there every Sunday—not that we didn't love them, and not that they didn't adore the show, but I mean, you're looking in those same faces and they were looking like 'I know what's coming next.' "

Jeanette Nolan got the same feeling when she appeared on *Mr. President* with Edward Arnold. "There was a man who sat in the front row, and when the cast would assemble here he would already be there in his place. We couldn't understand; we thought he was somebody's relative." The show's gimmick was not revealing the identity of the particular president being portrayed that week, until the conclusion of the show, but this loyal attendee was way ahead of the game, or so he thought. "We would hardly announce the first paragraph about the man and he was already knowing."

There were some "professional" audience members who apparently took great delight in developing a loud and distinctive laugh, so they could be heard above the crowd during a broadcast. On a surviving episode of *The Judy Canova Show* there is just such a yowler, and the first time he lets out his unique guffaw, it stops Canova short, just for an instant. For the remainder of the show his repetitive laugh becomes irritating and obnoxious—as it must have been to the performers.

Bing Crosby grew so tired of seeing the same audience members week after week that when he won the right to prerecord his show in the late 1940s, he moved the company lock, stock, and barrel to San Francisco for most of his 1949 radio season.

No one was more contemptuous of his studio audience than Fred Allen. Allen refused to underestimate the intelligence of the listeners at home, but he bemoaned the fact that he had to *play* to the people who showed up at his studio; *their* intelligence he doubted quite seriously. According to Allen scholar Alan Havig, in private correspondence he referred to them as "bums," "yucks," and "morons." He was particularly appalled at the class of people who showed up for the midnight rebroadcast of *Town Hall Tonight* for the West Coast. "Most of them look as though somebody had turned over a pool table and they crept out of the pockets. They will only react to the stupidest material."

Broadcast executive Sylvester "Pat" Weaver was, in the 1930s, an account exec for Young and Rubicam assigned to Allen's *Town Hall Tonight*. He says he'll never forget sitting in the control room, having Allen call him on the inter-studio telephone, while a musical group was performing. "He's glaring out at the audience, and as he tells me this, he glares even more and the audience starts laughing, even though they can't hear him. What he's saying to me is, 'I don't know what you do with the tickets for this show, but I can reach down in my toilet and pull up a better class of people than we've got.' "

Hal Kanter recalls the day that the head usher for *The Bing Crosby Show* approached producer Bill Morrow to tell him that it had started to rain, and ask if he could let the waiting crowd inside fifteen minutes early. "No," Morrow replied, "the band is still rehearsing with Bing, and we're not ready yet."

Fred Allen, that week's guest star, was standing next to Morrow. "Oh, Bill," he said sardonically, "let 'em in. They're bad enough when they're dry."

But in those days before laugh tracks, even the comics who groaned the loudest knew that their success depended in part on the people who stood patiently in line to see their programs in person.

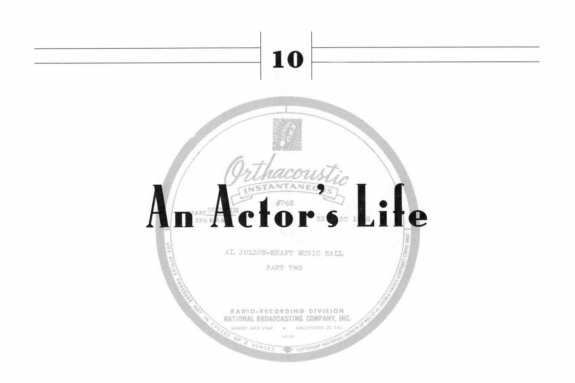

An Actor's Life

Movie actors may have been lured by glamor, fame, or money. Stage actors may have been seeking glory. Radio promised none of these things, but it did offer something the other branches of show business couldn't: steady work.

Even the busiest character actors in movies couldn't be assured of finding work fifty-two weeks a year. Radio actors could.

This was a first in the long and tumultuous history of show business. Les Tremayne (the longtime leading man of *The First Nighter Program*, later star of radio's *The Thin Man*) thinks of the time when actors would be trying to make a living with a touring theatrical troupe, "when the manager would run off with receipts from last week's performance and you're out on the road somewhere, and you had to throw your trunk out of the hotel window and run for your life. That changed when radio came along. Radio was the first time the lay performer ever had the opportunity to work regularly, steadily, stay in one place, raise a family, pay his bills and so on. It was a very unusual situation."

New York actress Alice Frost recalls, "People in the theater sort of stuck up their nose at radio, but it was a very good place to make a little money while you were waiting for a job. I went to New York to be on the stage, not to be in radio, but it began to be a very good way to make a living."

There were other benefits, too. On radio there was no need for makeup or costumes, no traveling to distant locations, no arduous retakes . . . and no lines to memorize. As Hans Conried, one of radio's busiest actors, once explained, "You only had to maintain one or two decent business suits to appear on the audience shows; [there was] no memorization, and no investment other than a red pencil with which to mark the script. It was a very pleasant life in many respects."

Howard Duff, like most actors who started in radio and went on to success in films and television, looked back on his days in radio with nothing but warm feelings. "It's pretty hard to say anything bad about it, because compared to what you go through to make one lousy picture, it's such a snap. Really. We had a lot of fun, most of us. I always did." Others have referred to acting on radio as "a license to steal."

Curtis Arnall and Adele Ronson in full regalia as Buck and Wilma, hoping to please the curious listeners of *Buck Rogers* with a suitable publicity photo. Needless to say, the costumes were never used on the air.

What's more, radio gave actors something unique in their profession: anonymity. The fact that they were heard and not seen had advantages, both practical and fanciful. "No one was worried about getting his nose fixed, nobody was cranky because they were on a diet," says Mercedes McCambridge, later an Oscar-winning film and theater actress, but first and foremost a radio stalwart. The most successful performers never had to worry about being mobbed by fans, or other pitfalls that accompanied screen stardom. That's why successful radio performers were sometimes referred to as "quietly rich."

The only time radio performers had to unmask themselves—other than on live-audience programs—was in the fan magazines, which sprang up alongside the older, more established movie fan periodicals. Photo layouts on popular stars satisfied listeners' curiosity about the way their favorites looked, as well as sounded. Such publicity also forced some actors to don appropriate garb, so as not to disillusion the audience and burst their collective bubble. When *Buck Rogers* became a smash hit in the mid-1930s, its cast was obliged to dress in futuristic costumes for the sake of publicity. "We wore tights and helmets," recalls Adele Ronson, who played Buck's leading lady Wilma, adding with a laugh, "We looked gorgeous!"

But for someone who really loved to act, radio offered the greatest opportunity of all: freedom.

"That was one of the joys of radio," Frank Nelson explained. "It didn't make any difference what you looked like, how old you were, how young you were—whatever you could do vocally, you could do." Nelson was living proof of that. His was the face of a character actor, and once he established himself in comedy parts, especially on the Jack Benny show—he was the man who said "YESSS-S-S-S-S?"—he found it virtually impossible to land a dramatic role on camera. But on radio, he enjoyed the luxury of playing D'Artagnan on *The Three Musketeers*, a variety of American presidents on *Makers of History*, and the central character in *Vendetta*. Even more prominently, as he recalled, "I was the leading man on *Hollywood Hotel*, opposite stars like Jeanette Mac-Donald. For that I got $25—she was getting $5,000, I was getting $25—but I was capable of playing opposite her."

His female counterpart, ubiquitous radio actress Lurene Tuttle, felt the same way. "I could play opposite Jimmy Stewart or Fredric March or Cary Grant or Gary Cooper and Leslie Howard, and on the air I could be the most glamorous, gorgeous, tall, black-haired female you've ever seen in your life. Whatever I wished to be, I could be with my voice, which was the thrilling part to me." What's more, as leading lady to Hollywood's top male actors, Tuttle's parts were meaty and substantial. "It was quite a thrill to play opposite Paul Muni and have a role that was commensurate with his," she said proudly. Ronald Colman signed a picture to her, "Dear Lurene, Thank you for pulling me through so many broadcasts—fondly, Ronnie."

"Not Ronald Colman, but Ronnie," she sighed, years later. "Oh, it touches my heart."

For teenaged actor Elliott Reid, radio became a haven. The stagestruck boy attended Professional Children's School in Manhattan and tried out for one Broadway show after another, but his height proved to be his undoing. At the age of fifteen, he shot up to a full six feet, and he explains, "If you're six feet and you're reading for the part of Fredric March's son and he's five foot seven, you're not going to get it." An audition for radio's *The March of Time* paid off with a part, which soon led to steady casting on that show, and others, where his voice suited a variety of youthful parts—and his height was no hindrance. (Indeed, Reid was one of the few actors who could claim to have gone from radio *to* the Broadway stage, when his fellow *MOT* actor Orson Welles—just a few years older than Reid—invited him to join his brand-new Mercury Theatre.)

At an evening of reminiscence in the early 1970s, Hans Conried said of radio, "We often enhance the memory of an old sweetheart, and since I was virtually a virgin about that time, she still seems very beautiful to me in retrospect."

Even removing the rose-colored glasses of memory, however, radio still seems to have been a dream come true for actors. "Every day was a new day," said Frank Nelson.

Elliott Reid waits for his next cue as June Havoc and John Garfield read their parts in the *Theatre Guild of the Air* production of "They Knew What They Wanted." Gale Gordon is seated at left. Director Homer Fickett cast Reid as a Chinese cook (!) just so he could join the troupe on this field trip to San Francisco. That was the kind of loyalty radio actors cherished.

"Every day was a new challenge, because there were no repeats, no reruns." A working actor might appear on as many as four or five shows a day, playing multiple roles in some productions. The experience was immediate and satisfying, with none of the encumbrances that muddy the waters of show business today.

"It was easier then," says Alice Backes, who started in radio and continues to work today. "In radio you didn't need an agent; you could knock on your own doors. There weren't any casting directors; that's a new bureaucracy."

Ruth Henning went to Chicago in the 1930s to make her way as an actress. "You just tried to get auditions, and they were all cattle calls; for an ingenue, which is what I was, there'd be thirty or forty for every part. It wasn't easy, but I did make a living. You had to have good feet, 'cause you walked all over the near North Side, that area between the Merchandise Mart, where NBC was, and the Wrigley Building, where CBS was, and then all around there were the advertising agencies. We walked that many times a day. Of course, that is when I learned to smoke, because you didn't have anything else to do. You'd sit around waiting for directors to come out of the studios and then you would collar them and say, 'Hello, anything coming up for me?' "

Actor and announcer Jackson Beck amplifies this thought. "You went around, knocked on doors, got your own work. One director would recommend you to another, one actor would recommend you to a producer." It took time and persistence to get to see a busy director, but it could be done.

Radio was accessible; the doors were open. What a glorious time it must have been!

(In contrast, Adele Ronson tells what it's like for an older working actress in the 1990s. "Nowadays, if they're doing a commercial, you get sent by an agent and there may be fifty people [auditioning] to do that one line on the commercial. And the people that are doing it now don't know the old guys at all, or what we've done, so lots of times you don't get the damn thing. Then you always think of the time when you just picked up a telephone and somebody would say to you, 'I have a commercial for you, every day.' They didn't audition you or anything; they just knew they wanted to use you.")

Jeanette Nolan, destined to become one of the greatest performers in radio history, got her first job during the depths of the Great Depression. "I had quit going to Los Angeles Junior College; I didn't have the car fare. Couldn't go to the Pasadena Playhouse. They gave me the lead in a play, and then they offered me a scholarship but I couldn't take it because I didn't have the money for the Red Car. I was working at the Famous [department store] for $2.37 a day.

"True Boardman, whom I'd gone to school at Los Angeles Junior College with, saw me in the Los Angeles library, and said, 'Why aren't you in school?' And I said, 'Well, I can't afford to go, but I'm working at The Famous.' And he said, 'Well, why don't you get in radio?' I said, 'I don't know what you mean.' He said, 'Don't you know about *Chandu the Magician*? Don't you know about *Black and Blue*? Haven't you heard about *Cecil and Sally*?' I had never heard of any of these things. He said, 'I'm going to give you a name and I want you to go to see this man.' So I went to see Cyril Armbrister at Earnshaw Young. He asked me to read. A day after that the neighbor screamed out the door, and I ran like mad; there was a call, and I had a job. I was going to get $7.50, so I went to my boss and said, 'I have to quit.' She said, 'What's the matter?' And I said, 'Well, I have a job and it's going to pay me $7.50.' She said, 'Listen, Sarah Bernhardt, you keep your job; if you get that much work, we'll let you go.' It was just so darling; they kept me on." It wasn't long before Nolan retired from department store clerking and pursued her true calling full-time.

In the early days of radio, getting a job was often as simple as showing up. Hans Conried had just arrived in Los Angeles after a cross-country bus ride with his family. He had performed in a production of *The Tempest* at Columbia University, where he was taking night classes, so when he heard a production of the same play on a newly formed L.A. station, KECA, he went there to present himself as an experienced Shakespearean actor. He was eighteen at the time, and was hired on the spot. He had to do two voices on the first show, and the director, apparently impressed, came to him afterwards and offered him another job. He was rarely idle after that, and delighted to be paid anything more than the 25 cents an hour he'd been earning in a machine shop that manufactured punching bags. On a local Los Angeles show called *It Happened Today* (a blatant carbon copy of *The March of Time*) he was called on to play as many as eighteen characters in a show. The budget for talent was $2.50 a night and

John McIntire and Jeanette Nolan, with Agnes Young (at right) between scenes on *The March of Time* in New York, circa 1935. The MOT gathered some of the finest acting talent in town, and launched many a radio career.

there were five actors, so they got 50 cents apiece. Said the actor, looking back on that experience, "I cannot tell you the enthusiasm and the pleasure we had."

Gale Gordon—indelibly remembered today as foil to Eve Arden and Lucille Ball on television—cut his teeth in radio. He was more experienced than Conried, with a background on the stage, and a number of jobs as "dress extra" in silent movies to his credit. But with the Depression came a certain degree of desperation. "I was between jobs in the theater, and I had long since dropped out of extra work in pictures. I couldn't get onto any lot at all because I didn't know anybody; I didn't have a good agent, or anything else. And somebody said, 'Why don't you try radio? It's new, they'll pay $2.50 for a show, you might as well pick up the money, and it's easy.' "

Gordon found, as others did, that landing a job was simply a matter of waiting in an outer office and getting to see the person in charge. Before long he was a working radio actor, and at one point, according to his recollection, "the highest paid radio artist in Hollywood—$15 a show. And everyone in radio hated my intestines, believe me, because everybody else got $2.50, which was the going rate for a commercial half-hour show. And they could rehearse you as many hours as they wanted, and the station took out 10% for hiring you, because every station was its own agent. So you got a net of $2.25 for a half-hour sponsored show." The program that paid Gordon so well was called *English Coronets*, a West Coast show sponsored by the Barker Brothers furniture store in Los Angeles. The actor's mellifluous voice made him a perfect choice to play a cavalcade of English crowned heads: "I played Charles II, Henry, Richard, Robert Dudley, Earl of Leicester in *The Life of Queen Elizabeth*." Here again was an actor who reveled in the variety that radio offered, though by the 1940s he was pretty well established in comedy roles such as Mayor LaTrivia on *Fibber McGee and Molly*.

Portrait of a youthful Gale Gordon, then one of the busiest actors in radio. NBC was just one stop on his daily rounds.

Enthusiasm and self-satisfaction were important, especially for an actor just starting out, because salaries were modest, especially on a local level where, as Parley Baer put it, "I've done some pretty good acting for a buck and a half."

Credit was largely nonexistent. Even when radio blossomed and the actors became fixtures on network shows, getting credit on the air was unusual. Busy radio actor Jerry Hausner remembered one fellow actor's initiative and cunning. Hanley Stafford had found steady employment as the comically flustered Daddy opposite Fanny Brice's little-girl character Baby Snooks on the weekly *Good News* series. Frustrated because he was given no credit for his work, Stafford seized an opportunity during a lunch break one day. Hausner asked if they might get a sandwich, and Stafford replied, "I want to wait until this place clears out; I have something to do."

"So we waited for the theater to empty," said Hausner, "and Hanley walked over to the piano, and on the piano was [that week's host] Robert Taylor's script, all nicely typed out. On the billboard—the front page—he was to open the show by saying, *'Maxwell House Good News of 1937,'* or whatever it was, 'with Tom Patricola, George Jessel, Sophie Tucker, Frank Morgan, and Fanny Brice as Baby Snooks.' So Hanley walks over to the script, takes his pencil out and writes, after 'Fanny Brice as Baby Snooks,' 'with Hanley Stafford as Daddy.' Now when Robert Taylor came back to the studio after lunch, he picked up the script and he saw things written there. Well, the script girl had made changes so he assumed this was kosher. He got up to the mike and read the billboard '. . . with Hanley Stafford as Daddy,' and nobody made anything of it because everybody assumed that it was supposed to be that way, that somebody had decided it." The billing was repeated the following week and for years to come. Thus, an anonymous actor's name became known to the listening public.

James Stewart tries to make up for a lost meal during rehearsals of the MGM-produced program *Good News*. An actor who was juggling radio and film careers could have an extraordinarily hectic schedule. This picture was taken by MGM director George Sidney.

Others had to fight harder for recognition. Howard Duff had a distinctive voice, and became a busy supporting player in Hollywood during the 1940s (with time out for war service). When producer-director William Spier cast him in the leading role in *The Adventures of Sam Spade*, he became an "overnight" star. The show was a hit, but Duff didn't feel he was sharing the glory.

"I only got mentioned at the last of the show the first two years," he recalled. "So finally I got a big, big, big victory of getting on at the beginning of the show. 'Starring Howard Duff.' Believe me, [Spier] didn't want to do it that way.

"If I just play a part on *Suspense* I don't expect to get anything but credit on the end, but a show that I'm starring in, for Christ's sake, I'm on every goddamn page of the show, so I had reason to believe that part of the popularity of the show was due to what I was doing. I just thought, by God, I'd better get some credit for this."

He and costar Lurene Tuttle were the only ones who did; despite casts filled with the finest radio actors in Hollywood, from Elliott Lewis to William Conrad, no one else was credited on *Sam Spade*. As he had on *Suspense*, producer-director Spier disdained giving actors credit on the air (although he promoted himself generously in the openings of both shows as "radio's master of suspense . . .").

That unfortunate tradition continued when Anton Leader took over the reins on *Suspense* in the late 1940s. Each show finished with the big-name guest star reading a prepared curtain speech. At the end of "Consequence," for instance, on May 5, 1949, James Stewart told his audience, "I want to thank Tony Leader and his great cast of actors for making my *Suspense* visit so pleasant . . ." The names of those actors were not revealed. (The following week, at the end of "The Night Reveals," Fredric March added his own postscript, remarking, "It's been a real pleasure appearing on *Suspense* tonight, and working with this fine cast—especially Jeanette Nolan, who played Marie . . ." One wonders whether that generous mention of Nolan was March's idea.)

Some directors, like Fletcher Markle and Helen Mack, favored the notion of having their actors introduce themselves on-mike, an ear-catching gimmick that enabled listeners to hear the performers out of character, and place some names with voices they'd heard before.

Lux Radio Theatre was an early exception to the no-name rule; at the end of every broadcast, beginning in the 1930s, the roster of supporting players was identified. This likely came about because the show fancied itself a radio equivalent to an evening of theater, and this was the audio version of a cast list in a program book.

That, however, is where generosity ended at *Lux*. Then-actor Elliott Lewis put it bluntly: "*Lux* is the reason we started AFRA [The American Federation of Radio Artists]. Truly. One of the reasons. Your call as an actor for *Lux* was Tuesday morning at no specific time, and the end of your call was 6:00 on the following Monday. There were no times given, nothing. You were doing *Lux* that week. And for this you got $25. When complaints were made to the *Lux* producers, the actors said, 'We have to have a definite call . . .' The producers of course said, 'We can't give you a definite call, because we don't know when we'll need you.' The actors said, 'Well, you'd better figure it out, hadn't you?' Of course, they could and did. And they would break up call, but it still took them a week to put it together."

Jerry Hausner had vivid memories of working on *Big Town*, which put its supporting actors through a similar work week. "We would rehearse from 9:00 in the morning until, I would say, 5:00 in the afternoon, all day long, and while we were rehearsing, Edward G. Robinson [the show's star] had a card table with a type-writer on it. The author of that week's script had to sit there all day long, every day, and rewrite as we went along. He'd read a line and Eddie'd say, 'I don't like that one, cut that out, change this, change that.' He was a stickler for all these things, and that's what made it a good show, but we had to sit there while this was being done. They rewrote and rewrote all week long, and if you were cut out, they waved you good-bye and you didn't get any money at all. You had no protection of any kind. If your part stayed in and it was a minor supporting role, you wound up with $15, $20 for the week, $35 if you had a good part."

These weekly one-hour shows were not low-budget affairs; quite the contrary. On *Lux* and the similar *Hollywood Hotel*, the guest star who headlined each show earned $5,000—movie star money. The rank-and-file radio performers on these same coast-to-coast broadcasts earned $25. One day, Frank Nelson went to his female counterpart on *Hollywood Hotel*, Lurene Tuttle, and announced his intention to get them both a raise—to $35. The producer played tough but finally capitulated. Is it any wonder that Nelson was one of the founders and most active members of AFRA?

(In later years, under AFRA's jurisdiction, the long-running Lux show became a plum for working actors. Gil Stratton Jr. remembers how happy he'd be when he'd get a call for *Lux* in the 1940s, because it meant three days' work and a $133 guarantee.)

Sometimes, actors' ability (and flexibility) was taken for granted. Jeanette Nolan was part of the stock company on Dupont's *Cavalcade of America*, but one week Helen Hayes, who'd been scheduled as guest star, was unable to appear and Jeanette was pressed into service. Needless to say, she was fully up to the task, but when she got her paycheck it was her usual "stock" salary. "I was deeply offended," she recalled. "For a day or two I was depressed, and then I went to BBD&O. I confronted my dearest mentors! I was so gratified when they understood my position; after all, I would be setting a precedent if I were to take my ordinary salary for such a tremendous responsibility as playing the starring role . . . Dear Arthur Pryor of BBD&O agreed."

Elliott Lewis remembered another thorn in his side from the 1940s. "On *The Whistler*, they would record the dress rehearsal and then the cast was ordered—but not paid—to sit there and listen to the dress rehearsal so they could be critical of their performance. I refused to sit there one week because I thought it was ridiculous, and I left. The producer came storming out and he said, 'You're supposed to be in there,' and I was kind of nasty when I was younger, and I said, 'When you pay me to listen, I'll listen. I get paid to perform.'"

Fortunately, most shows weren't as arrogant as that, or as time-consuming as the one-hour "prestige" programs like *Lux*, and most directors were grateful to the cadre of working professionals who populated their casts, week after week. The actors, in turn, may not have been making a great deal of money for each show, but at the end of an average week had accumulated a very healthy sum.

Said Jackson Beck, "When I did *The Cisco Kid* I signed a contract—one show a week, $50, and I thought I was in fat city. My God, fifty bucks for a half-hour, you came in and did two, three hours of rehearsal and you got fifty bucks. Wow, that was a lot." Mercedes McCambridge had no contract for *Inner Sanctum*, but she counted on a weekly call from director Himan Brown and figured that fee as her rent money. One week, "I waited for the call, it didn't come, so I called Hi and said, 'Listen, I didn't get a call for this week's show.' And he said, 'There are no women in it.' And I said, 'That's no excuse, I have to pay my rent! What are you going to do?' so he said, 'Can you play an elevator man?' I said, 'Sure.' I did it and paid my rent. Hi was wonderful."

Howard Duff recalled, "If you did enough shows you could make a living; the more shows you had the better living you made." In order to do so, however, "you were never too far from the phone."

⌐

A radio actor's life was anything but calm. With scores of shows being rehearsed and broadcast every day, and new ones being written, cast, and planned, jobs hatched on an hourly basis—and an unpredictable schedule. As a result, an actor relied on telephone answering services to keep him apprised of the latest "action."

Most of the actors spent their down-time at a series of regular hangouts, like Colby's, a bar and restaurant near CBS in New York. "There was a bar and a balcony where we all played gin rummy—and for high stakes, I might add," recalled Jackson Beck. "And if anybody wanted us, they knew where we were. There was the drugstore at NBC (now a bank). You could sit all day, nobody bothered you; you kept drinking coffee, whatever. There were direct lines where our phone services could reach us, and they'd page us, so it was a great place to hang out; somebody knew where you'd be. And there was a pool room on Sixth Avenue where a lot of us hung out from time to time, but you let your service know where you were and they followed you around."

In Hollywood, "They had Radio Artists Telephone Exchange* [RATE]," explained Parley Baer. "There was one at CBS, one at NBC, one at Mutual, one at ABC and then we had one at the Brown Derby and one at Melrose Grotto, where if you got a message it would click, ring, and then it would write. It looked like a ghost pencil writing your name—'Call so-and-so,' or 'Confirmed,' or something. Those kept you on your toes, but we all kept little notebooks in our pocket."

Peter Lind Hayes, at a 1984 Pacific Pioneer Broadcasters luncheon, recalled his days as one of the "Brittingham Bums," so named for the Hollywood restaurant where actors would hang out, and often be cast in small roles on the spot by production men who'd come there looking to flesh out ensembles on a last-minute basis.

Actors advertised themselves—more literally than usual—in the trade publications, and in annually published casting directories that cited their specialties along with their credits. For the actors in demand, radio could be a seven-day-a-week occupation; trying to balance a career, a home life, and an occasional vacation was no small challenge. Don Ameche, who worked most weekdays on a movie set, recalled having his wife drive his children to the parking lot behind NBC at Sunset and Vine on weekends so he could spend at least a little time with them between rehearsals for the Sunday night *Chase and Sanborn Hour* broadcast!

Still, "it was so civilized," says L.A.-based actor and announcer Hy Averback. "Very seldom would you start work earlier than ten o'clock; you worked in a nice neighborhood. You could walk from studio to studio, you were eating at the Derby every day (or Brittingham's or Nickodell's). And for a young man, it was an exciting time."

CONRIED
YOrk 4433

Hans Conried published this caricature of himself in a 1941 artists' directory, billing himself as "Conried." It didn't stick.

The fact that the bulk of network radio activity was divided between New York and Los Angeles meant something else to the working actor: leading a double life. Giving a great performance "live," with no chance to correct mistakes, is one thing, but in those days before tape (and before the broadcast of transcription discs was permitted on the networks), it was necessary to repeat each major show for "the other Coast" three hours later. In many ways the California actors had it easier, because their first broadcast might be at 5:00, for the East

*Created by Louis Lauria, and later renamed Radio and Television Exchange, for obvious reasons.

Coast; then, they could enjoy a leisurely dinner before returning to repeat the same show at 8:00 for West Coast listeners. In New York, the same routine meant working as late as 1:00 in the morning for the benefit of audiences living on Pacific Standard Time. (For years, the regulars on the popular programs originating from WXYZ Detroit—including *The Lone Ranger, The Green Hornet*, and *Challenge of the Yukon* with Sergeant Preston—had to perform each of their shows *three* times a day, for a

As in any workplace, the cast and crew became extended family. Here, at Detroit's powerful WXYZ, everyone gathers 'round to celebrate the birthday of The Lone Ranger himself, Brace Beemer, who's about to cut his cake. Extreme left with glasses is director Charles Livingstone; the woman with hat is actress Elaine Alpert; next to her is actor Bill Saunders; flanking Beemer are sound-effects man Don Davenport and actor-announcer Jay Michael. Partly hidden by the mike, with cigarette dangling, is Paul Sutton, otherwise known as Sergeant Preston of the Yukon. Smiling in front of him is actor Gilbert Shea, Mike Axford in *The Green Hornet*, then engineer Ray Spana. The handsome fellow in shirtsleeves and tie is announcer Fred Foy; next to him are actor Harry Goldstein and a scholarly-looking fellow in bow tie whom no one would ever guess was the voice of Tonto, John Todd. Kneeling in front are sound-effects men Bill Hengstebeck, Tony Caminita, and Jim Hengstebeck

trio of time zones. By the late 1940s this had been reduced to twice a day, but the schedule was such that one broadcast ended at twenty-nine minutes and thirty seconds after the hour, and the repeat show began exactly half-a-minute later!)

No question, the Angelinos had the best deal, but it came at a price: the peril of "drinking one's dinner," and being sloppy for the second performance.

"It was a curse," said William Conrad. "If you did a really good job, you had three hours to sit around and wait until you had to do it again. What do you do? You go out and have a drink, that's the first thing you do, so the second show was always hysterically funny compared to the first. Much more interesting in my opinion."

"My tendency was to drink with lunch, but I had to watch that," admitted Howard Duff. "We really were interested in the show; we didn't want to hurt the show." The situation was relieved when the networks allowed shows to be transcribed and rebroadcast. "I must say it was a lot better when we only did one show," said Duff. "I think we all felt better. We'd get to do that performance, then that was it."

One thing actors on both coasts had in common was an extraordinary camaraderie. Movie actors rose at an ungodly hour to go to work, which mitigated against socializing at night. Stage actors only communed at favored watering holes or actors' clubs after hours. But radio actors were together all the time.

"The fun of radio to me," said Elliott Reid, "was to walk into a studio not knowing whom you would see there. It was always a very happy feeling when you walked into a studio, and some were already there and some not, and we'd sit around and mark the scripts and banter about a little bit, and then the director would finally get us to shut up and do the first reading. It was about the most relaxed, easiest, nicest, and friendliest part of show business."

A cast reading for *Gunsmoke* in the 1950s. At left: assistant director Frank Paris. *Front row:* actors Harry Bartell, Howard McNear (Doc), Parley Baer (Chester), and William Conrad (Matt Dilion). *At right:* director Norman MacDonnell. *Back row:* secretary Ann Gaffney, actors Vic Perrin, John Dehner, Georgia Ellis (Kitty), and an unidentified cast member.

William Conrad—who in later life was a TV star on such shows as *Cannon* and *Jake and the Fat Man*—recalled the period in the 1940s and 50s when he was part of a CBS stock company, along with such colleagues as Parley

Baer, Howard McNear, Paul Frees, and Hans Conried. "We virtually lived together for fifteen years. These are all the people that you worked with day after day after day. You go in and you got five shows, let's say four shows to do that day, so you go in and you meet three of 'em on this show, two of 'em on the next show and then the last show you'd get all four of 'em together again."

New York–based Jackson Beck, for years the voice of Bluto in the Popeye cartoons, and still active as a commercial announcer in the 1990s, is not one for misty-eyed nostalgia; he simply tells it as it was. "There was a closeness in our personal relationships," he declares. "We saw each other a lot every day in the usual gathering places and at work, and we built up personal relationships. I've got friends that I met God knows how long ago and I'm still friends with them. There was a familial relationship; I mean, we were there when their kids were born, we were there when they got married, we were there in between because we entertained each other, visited each other, lived in pretty much the same area, so there was something that built up that there is not present to my knowledge today.

"Those were great days," said Beck, "because they're always great when you're young. You don't realize that till you're older. We didn't know we had it so good."

Fellowship wasn't the only quality that was bred among these journeymen; there was a kind of team spirit and unselfishness rare in any situation, perhaps even rarer in show business.

"There was a sense of trust in the other actors," said busy character actor Harry Bartell. "I never found that in any other medium, theater or film."

"We were very supportive; we had to be, because you are critical to me across the microphone, as I am critical to you, in a very special way," explained Mercedes McCambridge. "And we loved each other; we really cared a good deal about each other."

"People loved each other, and helped each other, and they were generous," recalled June Foray, who started in radio and later carved a busy career as the voice of such cartoon stars as Rocky the Flying Squirrel. "I worked with Steve Allen for three years; we did a show called *Smile Time*. I didn't know he existed, and apparently the show had been on a few days, or a couple of weeks, and they weren't happy with the gal they had. And one actress (Florida Edwards) said, 'June, I can't do a lot of voices, but I know you can, why don't you go over and audition?' How sweet and generous. I did, and Steve hired me immediately. It was just a different world."

The awkwardness of auditioning for a job in competition with close friends was mitigated, for the most part, by the fact that there was more than enough work to go around. Actors who in other circumstances might have been selfish were able to take the high road—noting the example set by their peers—and join in the spirit of comradeship. (Chicago actors feel there was more generosity among their ranks than was found in New York, and credit the "nicer" atmosphere in Los Angeles to the fact that so many Chicagoans wound up there.)

There were other unexpected niceties, from time to time. Elliott Lewis never forgot the first time he won a supporting part on a Jack Benny show. "About four days later in the mail was a letter from Jack and a check. And the check was two or three times more than we had agreed upon. The letter from Jack said, in essence, 'Thank you very much; the enclosed is because I never would have dreamed you could have gotten that big a laugh on the line. Hope to see you soon, Best Regards, Jack Benny.' And he was always that way."

Breaking in wasn't always easy. As in any business, there were so many people firmly entrenched in their jobs that newcomers weren't always welcomed with open arms. And there were certain prejudices. When Jerry Hausner moved from New York to California, "there was a group of local actors who had it all sewed up at that time, and they were called the Coast Defenders. And if you were from New York, they didn't like you 'cause you sounded a little different; your pitch was higher—you know, we're used to yelling, coming from New York." But before long he found his liability to be an asset. "Whenever they needed a fresh guy, a tough guy, New Yorkese or Brooklynese or Jersey, I did those accents—and they were always in demand."

Similarly, when Jeanette Nolan moved to New York in 1935, Shakespearean actor Louis Hector said, "I want to give you some advice: don't ever tell anyone you're from California!"

With so many shows to be produced and cast on a daily basis, directors and ad agency executives tended to use people they already knew, from a pool of steadily working performers. Writer E. Jack Neuman recalls, "A director would call and say 'What do you think of Byron Kane for that role?' And I would say, 'Well, he's my second choice. Who else you got in mind?' And if there was someone special you had in mind, you could try to request them and hope they were available. But when you had people like that—like a Hans Conried—you had it made."

Writer-producer Paul Henning remembers, "A lot of times, writers particularly would say to the producer, 'Let's audition some new people. Why do we use the same people over and over?' but they were absolute insurance, they were just so dependable and so talented. And they used to go from show to show; it was just incredible. Occasionally somebody new would get a chance, but not often."

In time, however, the real talents made themselves known, and managed to infiltrate the ranks of the "dependables." And just how much work was there? So much that an actor in demand often found himself juggling one show against another. "You finally arrived when you had a conflict," explained Parley Baer, one of the CBS stock company, who for nine years played Chester on *Gunsmoke*.

William Conrad had been announcing at local station KMPC in Los Angeles when he got a call to do the voice of *The Whistler*, then a West Coast show originating at CBS. "And from the day I started until the day I got out of radio, I worked seven days a week, everywhere, anytime. I'd go as high as twenty-seven shows in one week; can you believe that? I was so valuable to people they would tell me, I don't have to make the table reading, I don't have to make the first rehearsal, all you have to do is make the dress rehearsal. There were many times when they'd say, 'You sight read better than anybody anyway, so here's the script, everybody else is rehearsed' and it would go on the air."

Conrad wasn't the only actor whose talent got directors to bend the rules in order to accommodate their hectic schedules. Lurene Tuttle was already established as Effie, the loyal, lovestruck secretary on *Sam Spade* when she was hired to appear with Red Skelton as the Mean Widdle Kid's mother. She was so integral to *Spade*—though heard only at the beginning and end of each show—that the producers arranged for her to record her banter with Duff sometime Sunday afternoon, during rehearsals, so she could go on to Skelton show rehearsals Sunday evening.

As freelancers, actors never liked to turn down a job. The better ones seldom did. There were other conflicts, however, when a performer tried to pursue a career in theater and film as well as radio. Here, New Yorkers had the advantage: except for twice-weekly matinees, theatrical performances are at night. That meant an actor could work steadily on daytime radio, or evening shows that dovetailed with 8:00 curtains (providing he had an understanding stage manager). Or, as the prolific Raymond Edward Johnson says, "The more important you got to be, the easier it was because they made the way for you. Your way was made easy depending upon how much they wanted you."

Richard Widmark even managed to work on two daily radio shows in New York and make the nightly curtain for a play called *Trio*—in Philadelphia! "I used to finish my shows at 6:15, have an elevator and a cab waiting, catch a train at Penn Station and arrive at the Walnut Street Theatre in Philadelphia just in time to go on," he recalled years later.

Hollywood-based actors weren't as fortunate; moviemaking involves long days and unpredictable schedules.

For a busy actor like Frank Nelson, "You were running from show to show; you had sometimes five, six, seven shows in a day. You had to take a long hard look as to whether or not it was in your best interest to take a picture and go away for three weeks or six weeks and maybe lose a lot of these shows that you were on . . . I decided I was pretty much going to stay with radio. It would've taken a real good part to pull me away. So with the exception of a couple of things I did that were fairly good, I simply gave up the attempt to get into pictures."

Sheldon Leonard's career went in the opposite direction. "I came out here [to Hollywood] to do pictures, and I did pictures, but the market for the kind of character they had selected for me—a hoodlum, a Damon Runyonesque kind of hoodlum—became slimmer and slimmer." A friend wrote him a part on the Parkyakarkus comedy show *Meet Me at Parky's* and Leonard scored a hit. Soon he was a regular on *The Jack Benny Show* (as the racetrack tout), *The Judy Canova Show*, *Maisie* (as Maisie's Brooklynese boyfriend Joe Pulaski), and others. This left his film career in limbo. "The one kind of gave way to the other. I would not have been able to successfully exploit both at the same time, because I could not go off on location with a picture and leave these established characters hanging in midair; they were expected every week."

Rosemary DeCamp was already a radio veteran when she started making movies, and chose to favor the latter . . . with one exception. For fourteen years she played Nurse Judy opposite Jean Hersholt on *Dr. Christian*. This meant an occasional run-in on a busy movie set.

Jean Hersholt and Rosemary DeCamp enact a candid pose to promote *Dr. Christian*. DeCamp signed on as Nurse Judy and wound up playing the part for more than a decade! This was the closest thing in radio to a "steady gig."

"I had a good agent and they got built into the contract that I had to be off every [Wednesday] afternoon at a certain time to go to the studio," she explained. "When they sit around in an office, that doesn't sound too hard for them, so they agree.

Then when it comes time, and you're in the middle of a scene with a whole lot of people, it becomes very awkward [to leave], and it's kind of a fight."

Had *Dr. Christian* been a weekend offering, there would have been no problem, but for most of its run it was heard on Wednesday evenings. One particular Wednesday afternoon, DeCamp was working at MGM and left the set, as scheduled, but the person who was supposed to pick her up wasn't there. As she paced nervously, Katharine Hepburn—whom she'd never met—drove up in her convertible and noticed the actress' distress. "What's wrong?" she asked, and when DeCamp explained, Hepburn blithely tossed over her car keys and strode into the studio. Rosemary made her rehearsal on time.

Howard Duff had an unusual problem. It was during his run as Sam Spade that he started making movies; he was even billed onscreen in *Brute Force* as "radio's Sam Spade." When his film career suddenly took off, he found himself in a quandary unable (and unwilling, at that moment) to abandon his weekly starring show. When he went to shoot *Naked City* on location in New York, the *Sam Spade* show (including costar Lureen Tuttle) went with him. But when he was on location for a Western, *Red Canyon*, "I had to be taken every Saturday night over to the Twentieth Century Limited. I had to stop in the middle of a one-horse place, a station out in the middle of the desert near Utah; [the train would] pick me up and take me into the city so I could work the next morning at *Sam Spade*, and then they flew me back. I'll never forget that: being in that place all by myself till four or five o'clock in the morning because the train was late, in the middle of the goddamn desert with the coyotes and the jackrabbits."

Radio producers frequently elasticized schedules and juggled complex logistics to accommodate a star. While Robert Young was touring in a play, his costars on radio's *Father Knows Best* met him in each new city to do their regular broadcast. At the same time, stars were responsible for meeting the producers at least halfway. Gene Autry spent much of the year making personal appearances around the country, but wherever he was, by week's end he would have to check in to the nearest major CBS station in order to prepare and broadcast his *Melody Ranch* program. As it happened, many of his radio costars also appeared in his touring show, but those who didn't would have to make their way to Chicago or St. Louis or Minneapolis in order to be part of the broadcast. (Even when Autry stayed put, while shooting one of his popular western films, he had to make a weekly trek from the film's location site to Los Angeles.)

Courtesies were also extended to actors who weren't top-billed stars. Character actors who were in demand found that colleagues were willing to help them juggle increasingly complex schedules of rehearsals and performances. Sheldon

Leonard recalled that in rehearsal, "Usually the producers and directors had no objection to your coming in, reading your spot—the four or five pages that might constitute your spot—and getting the hell out the door, not to be seen again until dress rehearsal time. There were two shows I did that were on at the same time. With the cooperation of the writers, however, I would have my spot written in the first half of one show and the second half of another show, and we knew with stopwatch accuracy how long it took to get from the side door of NBC at Sunset and Vine to the back door of CBS, which was a block and a half away. Since everything ran by stopwatch, I knew that if I was off the air on *The Judy Canova Show* at 2:37, and I was due on the air on *The Jack Benny Show* at 2:41, I had a very nice, safe margin, because I could make it in a minute and a half." Another Benny regular, Phil Harris, eventually got his own weekly show, with wife Alice Faye, which aired immediately following the popular Benny program on Sunday nights. Because Benny was such a generous boss, he made sure that Harris' weekly spot occurred in the first half of the show so Phil would have ample time to leave and prepare for his own program. This continued even when Benny moved from NBC to CBS in 1949, and Harris remained on NBC.

Many members of the "actors' elite" found themselves working at this kind of pace. The proximity of NBC and CBS in Hollywood was a boon to every performer. New Yorkers didn't have it quite so easy, hopscotching from CBS at Madison Avenue and 45th Street to NBC at Sixth Avenue and 50th Street and (worst of all) Mutual/WOR at Broadway and 40th. It wasn't unusual for New York actors to tip elevator operators to hold a car for them, and hire ambulances to whisk them from one job to another with split-second timing.

Chicago actors were lucky that the Tribune Tower (housing WGN/Mutual) and Wrigley Building (home of CBS's WBBM) were just across the street from one another on Michigan Avenue. But getting back and forth from NBC (WMAQ) at the Merchandise Mart was a much trickier bit of maneuvering. The shortest and easiest route was over the bridge on Wacker Drive—but sometimes the bridge was up. This became the classic excuse for lateness in Chicago, even if the actor had only come from across the street (and, possibly, stopped at the Wrigley Bar on the way). In point of fact, a group of ex-Chicagoans who moved to Los Angeles named their informal meeting group "The Bridge Is Up Club."

Punctuality was the watchword for every performer. Says Patricia Hitchcock, who was active in New York radio in the early 1950s, "To this day I am twenty minutes early for everything; that's my radio training—knowing that if I was in a car and it broke down, I might have to take a cab." (Arnold Stang always carried a spare Band-aid with him; on rare occasions when he was late, he put it on his forehead

Three Chicago radio actors in costume: Willard Waterman (*top*), Barbara Luddy, and Bret Morrison. All three eventually forsook the Midwest, playing (respectively), *The Great Gildersleeve,* the leading lady on *The First Nighter Program,* and *The Shadow.*

and made up a story about an accident he was in en route to the rehearsal.)

Actors did their best to cover for each other, no matter what happened, but inevitably there were foul-ups from time to time. Frank Nelson liked to tell the story about the day he and Lou Merrill were both appearing on a show at KFWB. "We each had maybe three or four parts, and one that he had was Mulholland, the man who developed our water system [in Los Angeles]. Mr. Mulholland had a three-and-a-half-page speech, and as I started to dash out the door to get over to *Lux,* there's a rap on the window and the director said 'No, no, no—do it!' And I look around and Lou is gone, and [the director] is now throwing the cue at me. I had never even looked at this speech, and I read three and a half pages of a speech I had never looked at before and then went roaring over to *Lux,* and I am met at the door by Lou Merrill—who says, 'I've been covering for you. Where the hell have you been?' "

The level of professionalism in network radio was so high that directors had little to tell the actors they hired except when to come in, and whether to speed up or slow down their readings on the air. There was little or no "direction" per se, because it simply wasn't necessary. A director's principal job was to cast his show. (When an actor was still breaking in, things didn't always go so smoothly. "If someone was wrong, he would just be replaced," said Howard Duff. "I remember I got replaced on *Big Town*; I thought I probably would stay drunk for a week. I was inconsolable for a while. That guy didn't think I was cutting it.")

From the actor's standpoint, "You could almost tell the kind of part it was going to be by the director who called you," according to Parley Baer. "If you were specializing in this kind of part or that kind of part the director would say, 'Just do your regular hillbilly.' "

Indeed, some actors thrived on specialization. Jerry Hausner was an experienced radio actor, but became an expert at imitating a baby's cry. It got to the point where on some shows he'd show up just in time to do his specialty—which might take mere seconds—and leave as quickly as he came. Once he was hired to do the baby voice on a Jack Benny show. During rehearsal another actor was needed to read one line as a ballpark announcer, a running gag line that had been used before. No one had thought to rehire the actor who'd read the line on earlier shows, so Benny looked at Hausner—the baby-voice expert—and said, quite seriously, "Can you talk?" Hausner replied that he could, tried out the line, and Benny was both pleased and surprised.

For other actors, versatility was the name of the game. Accents and dialects were important tools of the radio actor's trade; the more they mastered, the more often they worked. On one single half-hour spy show Paul Frees played an Englishman, a Belgian, and a German. This was par for the course for any working actor. In the waning days of network radio, the dulcet-toned British actor Ben Wright found himself cast as the pidgin-English-spouting Heyboy on *Have Gun, Will Travel*—and was very convincing in the part.

Some performers specialized in colorful comedy characters; in this arena, few could compete with Mel Blanc. On one Judy Canova show in 1943, the indefatigable Blanc played five separate roles: Roscoe Wortle, aka Sylvester, Judy's driver (with the sputtering, sibilant voice of the cartoon cat Sylvester); a man on a streetcar (an ordinary voice); a dumb-sounding shopper; a department store salesman with a French accent; and Pedro, Judy's workman at the Rancho Canova. (Incidentally, neither he nor anyone else in the cast received credit on the air!) The following week, Blanc played Sylvester again, a Scottish-burred Mr. MacPherson, Loverboy the squealing pig, and a low, breathy-voiced elk (on a commercial).

Some actors' voices were so distinctive that they were hard to camouflage. William Conrad used to joke that he was known as "the man of a thousand voice." Yet even he could alter the pitch of his performance and become relatively unrecognizable, as on a famous episode of *Escape* called "Snake Doctor," in which he was cast as an ignorant Southern backwoodsman. On a *Sam Spade* episode called "The Dry Martini Caper," Conrad played an officious businessman who hires Sam and is then murdered. A few moments later he had one line as the man's chauffeur! And on a 1956 *Suspense* episode titled "Waxwork," Conrad was the entire cast, playing three principal roles and narrating as well.

It was repertory acting raised to the highest level. Satisfaction came from the work itself, and the convivial atmosphere. Said Hans Conried, "It's not that I love acting; I love actors. I liked the company. Amusing people, a warm life, a pleasant life, good fellowship."

To quote Ira Gershwin, who could ask for anything more?

11

The Hollywood Connection

I t wasn't the climate that brought big-time network radio to Los Angeles, as it had the moviemaking pioneers. It was access to Hollywood's most prized commodity: stars.

At first, radio was considered The Enemy by Hollywood's power brokers (who felt the same way about television a generation later). For a time, studio-contracted stars were forbidden from appearing on the upstart medium, lest those appearances diminish their box-office value at the neighborhood Bijou. As late as 1940, some exhibitors complained to the studios that allowing stars to appear on radio was giving away for free what theater owners were trying to peddle for a price.

But, as with television, Hollywood eventually made its peace with radio. Movies and radio not only established peaceful coexistence, they helped to support one another, as radio shows promoted new movie releases and actors' careers. Movies eventually provided a substantial source of radio fodder as adaptations of hit movies became a staple on the air.

The first person to break down the barriers of studio control was syndicated newspaper columnist Louella Parsons. In 1934 she launched *Hollywood Hotel*, a variety hour hosted by Dick Powell and featuring Parsons herself, conducting interviews and imparting the latest celebrity news. Louella was so powerful at that time, with a column read by millions in the Hearst papers every day, that no one could afford to snub her—and she knew it. She used that clout to get the biggest stars in Hollywood to appear on her show—*for free*—in return for generous plugs of the star's latest film. In many cases, those stars appeared in twenty-minute versions of those films on her program. Parsons wasn't above using a not-very-subtle form of blackmail to corral stars for her show. Organist Gaylord Carter vividly remembers overhearing Parsons telephoning a recalcitrant Olivia de Havilland to persuade her to appear on the show. "And I heard her say, 'Now Olivia, you get down here or I'll tell a hundred million people what a rotten actress you are.' I heard her say this." Some years later, Carter met de Havilland and mentioned the incident; the actress remembered it well, and told Carter, "She was really after me."

Even the voice of Broadway, columnist Walter Winchell, made his way to Hollywood in the 1930s, here presenting an award to his friendly rival, bandleader Ben Bernie, with the encouragement of Ruth Etting and Ginger Rogers.

Nor was Louella shy about dealing with the stars once they arrived. Child actress Marcia Mae Jones appeared with Bonita Granville and Miriam Hopkins in an adaptation of the 1936 movie *These Three*, and remembers that Hopkins complained about the children having a disproportionate amount of dialogue. When a satisfactory answer was not forthcoming, she stalked away in a huff; Parsons, without missing a beat, called for an understudy to take Hopkins' place on the broadcast, and the actress quickly returned.

Just because they showed up didn't mean they were going to "go over." Arch Oboler was then a writer-for-hire who'd been engaged to prepare a play for *Hollywood Hotel*. He remembered his first experience: "The very first broadcast, my star, so to speak, the man I wrote for, was Gary Cooper, who was certainly a top star at the time. And Mr. Cooper was terrible; he was a terrible actor for radio. There weren't any retakes; this was live radio. I listened to Mr. Cooper massacre my play, and I couldn't take it. Finally, I went to the director and said, 'Please, the man has no concept of radio. He doesn't realize that it's a different medium, that you're as close to the listener as he is to the microphone; it's an intimate thing. Please, talk to him.' The director said, '*You* talk to him. You direct him.' Glory be, I was going to be a director. So I went up to Gary Cooper and introduced myself as the author, and we sat down in a quiet place on the stage. From the part of my heart that was reserved for that part of writing I

Louella Parsons had no trouble attracting the biggest stars in Hollywood to appear on *Hollywood Hotel*. Here's a sampling: Warren William, Dick Powell, Mary Pickford, and Claudette Colbert.

told him my thinking, and when I got through with my peroration Mr. Cooper, who had listened very carefully, looked at me and said, 'You know, Arch, I've been thinking, if I raised the sight on my rifle when I'm deer hunting about a "quart," I'll bet I could get the deer about one hundred yards further.' That man had never even heard all the talking I'd done."

The studios may have had their misgivings about the show, but ironically, it wasn't studio opposition that killed *Hollywood Hotel*. It was the burgeoning Radio Guild (eventually known as AFRA) that protested the idea of actors appearing in any context without pay. The show breathed its last in 1938.

Lux Radio Theatre was the next major show to capitalize on star power. After two seasons in New York, the heavily bankrolled hour-long show made its Hollywood debut on June 1, 1936, and introduced its new host thusly: "As our Hollywood producer, a man who will not only bring you the greatest plays and players, but the very spirit of Hollywood itself, that outstanding figure of the motion picture world, Mr. Cecil B. DeMille."

Said the distinguished DeMille, "Greetings from Hollywood, ladies and gentlemen. There are two theaters in this town almost as famous as Hollywood itself. They are Grauman's Chinese and the Carthay Circle. Perhaps it's a

Cecil B. DeMille confers with a *Lux* guest star, Joan Crawford. From the beatific look on her face, you'd never know that she was petrified to appear on live radio, especially in front of a studio audience.

coincidence that a production of mine opened both of these theaters. *The King of Kings* raised the curtain at the Chinese, and *The Volga Boatmen* was the first picture ever shown at the Carthay Circle. And tonight it is my privilege to open a new Hollywood theater whose audience is greater than any four walls could encompass. The largest theater in the world, *The Lux Radio Theatre* . . . "

Famous as DeMille was—more recognizable to the public, it could be said, than any other moviemaker in the world—Lux wasn't banking on his name alone.* Said the producer-director that night, "Sitting before me in the Lux Radio Theatre is the most distinguished and perhaps the most critical audience ever assembled in Hollywood. I see a lot of familiar faces. There's Joan Blondell, Gary Cooper— he stars in my next picture, *The Plainsman*—Stuart Erwin and his lovely wife June Collyer, Al Jolson, Ruby Keeler, Franchot Tone, ah—and there's our mayor, Frank L. Shaw of Los Angeles, and I think I see Freddie March—I fed him to the lions the last time I directed him. And now, we ring up the curtain on the play of the evening, 'The Legionnaire and the Lady,' starring Marlene Dietrich and Clark Gable."

Gable! Who could ask for a bigger star to launch a risky venture? (Never mind that it was Gary Cooper whose part he was taking in this adaptation of the 1930 Dietrich hit *Morocco*.) *Lux* more than lived up to its sponsor's expectations,

*DeMille's already considerable fame was further enhanced by his weekly appearances on Lux for nine years running. Although he neither produced nor directed the show, that illusion was never broken for the listening public. Actors who appeared on the show were much less impressed, as DeMille never appeared until the actual broadcast, and then had little to do with the players on hand. Paul Henning remembers when they got C.B. to make a guest appearance on *The Burns and Allen Show*. "When DeMille was a guest . . . that was the strangest thing I've ever seen. We were all sitting around this table and he would whisper to his secretary, and she would say, 'Mr. DeMille wonders if he could . . .' He didn't speak to George, he didn't speak to anybody. He spoke only to his secretary, who relayed the message."

and over the years virtually every major movie name appeared on the show. Not only did the stars often re-create their parts from popular films of the recent (or distant) past, they also bantered with C.B. DeMille during the "curtain call." Nothing pleased movie fans more than hearing their idols out of character—even though these often-stilted passages were scrupulously scripted.

Lux presented other guests during intermission, ranging from comedy producer Hal Roach to a man who manufactured silk stockings for the stars. Most of them wound up singing the praises of Lux Flakes.

The show became a Hollywood institution, and ran for more than twenty years. Although drama was its hallmark, the producers were flexible enough to tackle comedy (with Bob Hope, Red Skelton, Abbott and Costello) and an occasional musical. They were even willing to bend the rules from time to time, casting Jack Benny and Mary Livingstone in "Seven Keys to Baldpate," which turned out to be more a one-hour comedy script for the popular duo than a bona fide movie adaptation. Every once in a while the show displayed a flair for original or novelty casting, putting Gene Autry in the role originated by Gary Cooper in *The Cowboy and the Lady*, for instance.

One time, *Lux* even aired a "movie" that hadn't been made. Barbara Stanwyck had come upon the stage play *Dark Victory* (which Tallulah Bankhead had headlined on Broadway) and realized it would be a great vehicle. "I had to do it, I had to say those lines," she later recalled. "It became an obsession." According to the actress, it was she who urged *Lux* to acquire the rights to the play, which were then held by David O. Selznick. The night they performed the show, writer-director Edmund Goulding chanced to hear it on his car radio, and persuaded Jack Warner to buy the rights from Selznick so he could direct the film. Stanwyck read the announcement in the trades and felt that she'd pulled off a coup and now would get to do the role on film. Then she read they'd assigned it to Bette Davis! The thought of it still smarted as she told this story fifty years later.

Lux was not above hopping on a bandwagon, either. When the biographical musical *The Jolson Story* (with Larry Parks as Jolson) became a surprise hit, the show attempted to obtain the rights for a radio version, but Columbia Pictures held back. So *Lux* hired Jolson himself to star in "Alexander's Ragtime Band" on April 7, 1947, and then had him back less than two months later to do "The Jazz Singer" on June 2. They didn't get to "The Jolson Story" until February 16, 1948, and then followed up with "Jolson Sings Again" on May 22, 1950. In these audio adaptations, Larry Parks would have been superfluous; Jolson played himself.

Lux Radio Theatre was one of radio's great success stories; the format, and the dedication to quality, remained remarkably consistent through twenty years on the air.

⁓

Orson Welles prided himself on mining the classics of literature and the theater for his *Mercury Theatre on the Air* broadcasts. When he chose *The 39 Steps*, in 1938, it must have seemed out of character, and Welles knew it; at the end of the broadcast he was careful to explain that his version was not derived from the movie. "Ladies and gentlemen," he intoned, "if you missed Madeleine Carroll in our stag version of *39 Steps*, the young lady in the movie, in common with almost everything else in that movie, was the child of its director's own unparalleled and unpredictable fancy. If you missed anything, you must blame Mr. Alfred Hitchcock. If you were surprised by anything, you must blame us." (Welles also adapted Daphne du Maurier's *Rebecca* in 1938, two years before Hitchcock made his movie, but again, he was faithful to the source material, and featured a considerably different denouement than Hollywood censors would allow.)

When Campbell's Soup assumed sponsorship of Welles' show, they encouraged him to integrate movie adaptations into his menu on a regular basis, and gave him enough money to hire actual movie stars to appear, as well. It didn't always work out. For "Beau Geste," in 1939, the program not only recruited Laurence Olivier, but had Noah Beery Sr. re-create the part of the villainous Sergeant LeJeune, which he had played in the famous 1926 silent film. Alas, neither he nor Olivier was terribly good. (Beery did contribute some interesting memories of shooting the silent film during an interview at the end of the show.) "It Happened One Night," with Miriam Hopkins and William Powell, and Welles in the role of the runaway heiress's blustery father, was remarkably flat in spite of the stars. (Oddly enough, the one moment from the film that depended on sound was thrown away in this production: the car screeching to a halt when the heroine lifts her skirt to attract a motorist. In the Welles radio version, the car simply stops—with no exaggerated sound effect.)

Two weeks later, Welles unwisely cast himself as Longfellow Deeds, the Gary Cooper part in "Mr. Deeds Goes to Town." For all his brilliance, he could not convincingly play an endearing hayseed. (That production does, however, include a wonderful inside joke. The Viennese doctor called upon to pronounce Deeds insane is that great specialist, Dr. Herman Mankiewicz. In real life, Mankiewicz would soon be collaborating with Welles on the screenplay for *Citizen Kane*.)

In truth, Welles was more preoccupied than ever with theater and potential film projects during this period, and it showed. *The Campbell Playhouse* was to ring down its final curtain in March of 1940.

Host Robert Taylor with two of MGM's brightest stars, Myrna Loy and Clark Gable, on *Good News of 1938*. MGM director George Sidney took this and the accompanying photos during rehearsals with his "spyglass" camera. He was given special dispensation to do so because his father, Metro executive L. K. Sidney, produced the show.

The idea of adapting movies for radio was now well established. *Sears Then and Now*, produced by William N. Robson in the late 1930s, did the first radio adaptation of *Gone With the Wind*, with Robert Montgomery and Constance Bennett—in seven minutes!

In 1937, MGM joined forces with Maxwell House Coffee to present *Good News of 1938*, an hour-long extravaganza hosted by a succession of MGM stars (James Stewart, Robert Young, Robert Taylor) and featuring dramatizations of upcoming Metro films as well as peeks into the process of moviemaking. ("Your ticket of admission is your loyalty to Maxwell House Coffee.") It was a big show, featuring Meredith Willson and his orchestra and a wide array of guests every week. Soon, Fanny Brice (as Baby Snooks) and Frank Morgan were part of the regular roster; they became the most popular and consistently amusing aspect of the program, and took it over completely in 1940.

Supposedly broadcast from an actual MGM soundstage (in reality, a theater on Hollywood Boulevard), the show is best remembered today for a surviving broadcast that provided the public with its first exposure to the story and songs of *The Wizard of Oz*, with most of the stars on hand. But in the best Hollywood tradition, that show—like most of the weekly installments—played fast and loose with the truth, using actors to simulate the voices of studio executives in its "behind the scenes" segments. There's a particularly funny moment on one episode in which Wallace Beery introduces MGM's fabled art director Cedric Gibbons. When actor Gale Gordon says his first line in the role of the designer, Beery says, *sotto voce*, "Oh, a *new* Cedric Gibbons."

MGM executives must have been taken aback when the show wasn't a huge success. There was constant tinkering and a cavalcade of ideas and gimmicks. (During the show's first season, Lionel Barrymore announced a contest awarding $5,000 to the listener who came up with the best title for his next picture.) Unlike *Lux*, a solid, one-hour drama, *Good News* was a variety show, which made the movie-studio connection less compelling than it should have been.

Gable, Lionel Barrymore, and Loy study their scripts; Frank Morgan is seated behind them, notably *not* studying his lines ahead of time.

There was another, more fundamental problem, which Arch Oboler alluded to earlier: movie stars were not surefire radio personalities, to say the least. In his experience as writer and director, Oboler found that some actors understood radio, and others didn't. "I never knew when an actor would be good for radio. I used tricks sometimes when there was no other way to get a performance. Dick Powell appeared one day with his wife Joan Blondell, and they were going to do a show together, and I couldn't get a performance out of him. It was just a little short bit he had to do, and I finally told him that the way he could get what I wanted him to have on the air was to use a very small amount of energy, a small voice, get close to the microphone and sort of breathe the lines. And you know, it worked. On the air he sounded like a passionate man."

Good News musical director Meredith Willson confers with MGM star Mickey Rooney.

Even movie actors with theater experience might not respond to the mike, according to Oboler. "It really had nothing to do with (the] stage, it had to do with a kind of an intelligence—a receptive intelligence. I remember sending an actor by the name of Walter Pidgeon home, telling him to leave the studio. Metro was furious because he was one of their big stars, but Walter Pidgeon simply couldn't get the idea of what radio was about. He simply couldn't. And finally, time ran out and the stop-watch was getting close to the hour of broadcast and there was no hope, and I told him to go home. And when he got angry I pointed out to him care-

Judy Garland introduced the score of *The Wizard of Oz* to radio listeners on *Good News*.

fully, that in all of his years on the stage, and all of his years in motion pictures, put together, he couldn't reach as many people as that half-hour broadcast that I was asking him to do. And I wouldn't do him the disservice of having him go on. He finally understood that."

Don Ameche, who was one of the few dyed-in-the-wool radio actors to achieve major screen stardom, said, "There was no way you could get Carole Lombard to go on the air with me. She knew that I had to make her look bad—not because I did it intentionally, I never did—I just did the best that I could. But she was that smart; she knew that she couldn't master that medium in one quick time." Others, he said, "were petrified; see, these are people who were used to if you made a mistake or this

Don Ameche enjoys a laugh with W. C. Fields, Edgar Bergen, and (yes) Charlie McCarthy during rehearsals of *The Chase & Sanborn Hour,* while costar Dorothy Lamour goes over her script.

take wasn't any good, you did it over. In radio that didn't happen. So they were really petrified, and in a sense, they were right, I think."

There was even a prop devised to help screen actors adjust to the rigors of radio. It was a ring that surrounded the microphone at waist level; an actor accustomed to moving about could hold onto it and remain in proper microphone position. Vincent Price said it was made for Bette Davis and Herbert Marshall after they drove the engineer crazy while roaming off-mike during "The Letter" on *Lux*. Gale Gordon said it was built for John Barrymore when he'd rehearsed *Richard III* and blown the engineer's ears out. Whatever the case, it was a useful crutch.

Margaret O'Brien, old enough now to be wearing braces (and tall enough to reach a microphone), makes one of numerous appearances on *Lux Radio Theatre*, with Cecil B. DeMille's successor as host, producer-director William Keighley.

(As late as the early 1950s, some actors were still having trouble acclimating to radio. Jack Lemmon, hired to appear on the soap opera *Road of Life* when he was still a novice, says today, "I screwed up more lines on live radio than I ever did in live TV or on the stage, ever, with a script right in front of me, because I couldn't use my body, and I had such a tendency to want to move and use my face, my arms. I'd walk away from the mike and they'd keep saying 'Get back! Just turn your head slightly, but you don't walk away, you stay there . . .' ")

Some actors had other handicaps. When Margaret O'Brien became a popular child star in the 1940s, she was much in demand for radio appearances. There was only one hitch: she hadn't yet learned to read, so unlike her adult colleagues, Margaret memorized all her lines. "They let me *hold* a script, to feel grown-up," she remembers. On the hour-long *Lux Radio Theater*, an actress was assigned to sit on the sidelines and read all of Margaret's lines silently, so that if the child forgot, she could look up and lip-read her dialogue. O'Brien says that she found radio much more challenging than moviemaking, because she had to rely so much on her own resources. When she had to cry in a movie scene, the director would take her aside and help her prepare, by reminding her of sad things that would get her in the proper mood. There was no such opportunity in the midst of a show like *Lux*.

(A child performer also had to have access to the mike; it wasn't always possible to assign a specific microphone to him or her for the duration of the show. In that case, boxes or steps had to be on hand.)

Character actor Edward Arnold was notorious for blowing lines on movie sets—seemingly a problem of memorization—but in fact he wandered from the script and managed to flub his lines on radio, too, as witness surviving episodes of *Good News* and *Jubilee*. By the time he headlined his own series, *Mr. President*, in the late 1940s, he seems to have gotten control of his reading skills.

Some performers found radio a safe haven. Vaudevillian Benny Rubin, who made many movies in the 1930s, became a pariah by decade's end because he was so closely associated with Jewish characters. With the rise of Hitler, that ethnic stereotype disappeared from the screen, and Rubin found himself looking for work. But he was a superb dialectician, and soon built a new career on radio.

Fanny Brice, who also trafficked in dialect comedy, had been a major Broadway star, but her few starring movies in the early talkie era were unsuccessful. When

Warner Bros. star Bette Davis obligingly addresses the KFWB microphone at the opening of Hollywood's Santa Claus Lane parade in December 1936.

she adopted the character of overgrown child Baby Snooks in the mid-1930s, she forged a new career on the airwaves, and never veered from it from that day forward.

One show had film performers actually volunteering to appear. The *Screen Guild Theater* was established at a time when the motion picture industry was

Fanny Brice introduced her popular Baby Snooks character on the *Good News* broadcasts, and eventually these skits overtook the program. Note that Miss Brice holds the all-important tool of every radio actor in her hand: a pencil. Photograph by George Sidney.

banding together to build a retirement home and hospital. Gulf Oil agreed to sponsor a program and donate all the stars' fees to this worthy cause. Studios agreed to make their contract players available, and waive their usual fees for use of older film properties as well. (Not that they were entirely unselfish; at the end of every show, an upcoming movie featuring each star was plugged, and if they didn't have a film to plug, some other film from their home studio was promoted in its place.)

The show started its life as a variety program, but after a year on the air became a half-hour film adaptation show instead. In fact, for many years it followed *Lux* on Monday nights, and according to John Dunning's book *Tune in Yesterday*, "When the show was scheduled on Monday nights, back to back with the famous *Lux Radio Theatre*, the producers of both agreed in a rare display of cooperation to space out their heavy and light productions. When *Lux* ran a heavy, *Screen Guild* did a light comedy. The result was 90 minutes of top Hollywood action, and a veritable corner for CBS on the cinema dramatics market."

Screen Guild Theater also had its own approach to movie properties. When *Lux* presented "Pinocchio," Walt Disney himself was on hand as a guest. When *Screen Guild* got around to it, several years later, it was hosted by Baby Snooks (Fanny Brice) and Daddy (Hanley Stafford) and Jiminy Cricket was played by Arthur Q. Bryan, the voice of Elmer Fudd.

Adapting feature-length films to short-story length was a daunting task, but producer-director Harry Ackerman got a handle on the idea fairly quickly. "I always chose one of the characters in the story to narrate, and carry us through . . . the most dramatizable areas, and it worked," he later boasted. "As a matter of fact, the first writer I assigned to do my first show, 'The Shop Around the Corner,' was Norman Corwin, who had no great radio experience in the commercial field. And he wrote a brilliant script in which the Frank Morgan character was the narrator, and the show played as well as it did on the screen."

(Not every radio adaptation worked quite so well. A would-be rival to *Screen Guild* called *Academy Award* made its debut in 1946 and folded after just one year. Trying to cram an entire screenplay's worth of story-telling into a half-hour wasn't easy. The "Foreign Correspondent" episode is a perfect example of how a great movie could be drained of all its dramatic value.)

Paulette Goddard appears on *Screen Guild Theater*—as indicated by the specially decorated microphone.

Ackerman was not prepared for some of the pitfalls he would encounter with his cast, however. "I remember my very first show as if it were yesterday, because I always liked a lot of rehearsal. I wanted to line up this show with a week of rehearsals, rehearsing part of every day until the show aired on Sunday. My first show was 'The Shop Around the Corner' with Margaret Sullavan, Jimmy Stewart, and Frank Morgan. We started rehearsing on a Monday, and Frank Morgan did not appear. So I called rehearsal again for Tuesday and he didn't appear on Tuesday. And that night when I said, 'I'll see you again at 11:00 tomorrow morning for rehearsal,' Jimmy Stewart and Margaret Sullavan conferred on the side of the stage by themselves and came over and said, 'We feel fully rehearsed and we invite you to direct Frank Morgan for the rest of the week. We'll be there on Sunday.' And I thought my world had fallen apart, because by then I had learned that Frank Morgan was out on a toot. He was getting drunk all over town and nobody was catching up with him. Well, Sunday came and I had signed an actor named Hans Conried to stand by and do the Frank Morgan role, if indeed he did not appear. And Hans was there and he was 'up' for the role, because Morgan was narrating the show and also playing a part in it.

"Suddenly, about an hour before airtime, Frank Morgan came in the stage door escorted by a couple of his friends, blotto drunk. We took him upstairs to one of the executive offices and put him in the shower, poured hot coffee in him, and I'll tell you, he came down and five minutes before we hit the air he took a script in his hand which he had never seen before and went out and was letter perfect. That was my introduction to 'star' directing."

The jaunty, delightful, but notoriously unreliable Frank Morgan, seen here while singing "The Man Who Broke the Bank at Monte Carlo." Photograph by George Sidney.

Like Arch Oboler, Ackerman realized that not every film actor would be ideally suited to the medium of radio. "I never knew until I heard them on the microphones [which ones] really didn't know how to act with their voices. I would take Clark Gable aside from the rest of the cast, after a rehearsal, and work with him, and explain the nuances we needed in order to convey what he would normally convey with his full physiognomy on screen. I did the same thing with Gary Cooper, and people like that who had limited acting experience. They had personalities, no question about it, powerful ones, but they had limited experience to convey through their voices what they were capable of conveying as human beings. And they accepted that help and welcomed it. Radio mystified them and they were a little afraid of it, I think."

One time, Elliott Lewis was hired to appear in an adaptation of *Command Decision* on *Screen Guild Theater* with Gable, Walter Pidgeon, Van Johnson, and John Hodiak. The show was on Tuesday evening, but Lewis' call began Monday night at 8:00. When he arrived at the studio, a number of executives were on hand, but no cast members. Then Gable showed up, mystified as to where everyone else was. Lewis recalled, "Bill Lawrence (the director] came out and said, 'Here's what we're gonna do. Clark, you're gonna play what you play, and Elliott, you're gonna play everything else.' I said OK. Gable said 'Why are we doing this? When do the other people come in? You're not going to go on the air that way.' He said, 'No. Tomorrow everybody else will be here. Elliott will play your part, then we'll take these two tapes and we'll cut Elliott out of both of them, and put the two tapes together and we'll have a show.'

"So Gable said, 'Why are we doing that?' Well, it seems he was so embarrassed he could have killed himself. Somebody said, 'He gets very nervous doing a radio show,' which he did. 'If he gets nervous in front of all his friends, he'll be very unhappy.' Which was untrue. So they embarrassed him by doing this, and that's how he did the show. Gable and I did the show, and I played every other part; the next day I went back and Hodiak and Pidgeon and Van Johnson are saying, 'Where the hell is Gable?' They said, 'He had to work, he's out of town, and Elliott will play his part and we'll fix it up later.' 'Oh, okay.' I was left over in one line called Second Gunner or something."

There were simpler ways of making a movie star feel at home. George Burns recalled, "Clark Gable did our radio show; he *had* to come on, because we talked about him for weeks and weeks and weeks, and Gracie was in love with Clark Gable. And Clark got nervous on our show, so I said to him, 'Would you like to do it sitting down?' He says, 'Jesus, George, that would be great.' [And I said] 'We'll all sit down; we'll get some stools.' "

Sometimes it just took the human touch to ease the way. Howard Duff recalled, "One time our guest on the Oboler show was Norma Shearer, and she was frightened to be at the microphone all by herself. So Arch asked me if I minded being on the other side of the mike even though I had nothing to feed to her, just so she had somebody to talk to, or some visual contact. I said sure. And she sent me a very nice letter afterwards thanking me for my help."

But for Joan Crawford, there was no comfort. She was terrified of facing an audience, or even a microphone. Actor-announcer Hy Averback remembers appearing on a *Suspense* episode ("The Ten Years") for which "it was just the two of us in the studio. She was so terrified that normally, the orchestra would be in the studio with us, but they had to pipe it in from another place. She was ripping at my arms."

On the other hand, comedy shows gave movie stars a welcome breather, and many of them warmed to the idea of appearing in that lighthearted context. Writer Paul Henning recalled of the *Burns and Allen Show*, "Cary Grant must have been on seven or eight shows; he got such a charge out of it. He said, 'I'll work for nothing; bring me back, bring me back.' He loved it; he was so good." Jane Wyman was a good friend of Gracie's and even filled in for her on some broadcasts when the star was suffering from migraine headaches.

Similarly, Humphrey Bogart and Lauren Bacall never refused Jack Benny when he asked them to appear. Says Bacall, "He was a darling, darling man. He was so generous always to his guests. He never would have anyone on his show unless he had a definite point of view, and he always featured the guest; he didn't dry to hog the limelight all the time, which was, of course, very rare."

For sheer novelty, however, nothing topped *Suspense*. In the mid-1940s, the show hit on the idea of inviting actors to play against type in their half-hour crime stories, and the stars couldn't resist. Danny Kaye, Mickey Rooney, Betty Grable, Ralph Edwards, Ozzie and Harriet, and Jim and Marian Jordan (Fibber McGee and Molly) were among the many incongruous performers who became involved in the sinister world of *Suspense*.

Writer E. Jack Neuman was a regular contributor to the series and remembers, "I tailored [the scripts] for the star. They'd call up and say 'We've got so-and-so coming up on the fifteenth, can you think of anything?'

"We always had the non-actors—Lana Turner and Victor Mature and whatnot. None of them could act, they couldn't even say hello without flubbing the line. And I learned how to write and make them look very good, without having to deliver a lot of lines." (On *Lux*, too, there were times when after the first rehearsal, the director and writer would huddle to figure out how to take lines away from their star-of-the-week and give them to others on the show.)

"I always looked forward to getting the comedians in different situations," says Neuman, "like Phil Harris, [who] was always drinking and clowning around and bragging. We did one [1951's "Death on My Hands"] where we had him whimpering and crying and begging, and he was a brilliant actor. He could do it!"

Harris's longtime boss, Jack Benny, so enjoyed himself on *Suspense* that he returned, year after year, and liked one episode in particular so much ("The Face Is Familiar," 1954, in which he played an accidental bank robber) that he later starred in a television adaptation of the same story.

Some of the more unusual—and less successful—ventures on *Suspense* took place when it briefly expanded to a one-hour format in 1948. Robert Montgomery now hosted the program, and bantered with its stars. The second hour-long program "borrowed" the *Sam Spade* show intact, with Howard Duff and Lurene Tuttle, and threw in a funny gag in which Spade called his colleague Philip Marlowe on the phone. Who should answer but Montgomery—who played Marlowe on screen in 1946's *Lady in the Lake*. On that same show, however, director William Spier hired two experienced actors (Joseph Kearns and Sidney Miller) to emulate, if not exactly imitate, Sydney Greenstreet and Peter Lorre in the roles of Kasper Gutman and Joel Cairo from *The Maltese Falcon*. How Greenstreet and Lorre might have felt if they'd known of this is anybody's guess.

Another program featured Montgomery's longtime friend James Cagney, a relative stranger to radio, in a production of James M. Cain's "Love's Lovely Counterfeit." Unfortunately, Cagney seemed ill at ease, and muffed several lines, though he was praised at show's end by the author himself.

The smart movie actors knew their own limitations and recognized the reality of the situation. Says Gregory Peck, who appeared on *Suspense* and *Lux Radio Theatre*, among others, "The best radio actors were specialists who would color the words with a great emphasis to help the audience to imagine, to see what they were hearing. And they usually played all the supporting roles and usually far better than the movie stars who came on the radio."

Some bona fide movie stars were also first-rate radio performers, however, and lived "double lives" in Hollywood. Ronald Colman, who possessed one of the great voices of the century, enjoyed radio immensely; it also happened that good film roles were becoming harder to find in the 1940s, and radio filled a gap in his career. He was a frequent guest star on a number of shows, and hosted the syndicated *Favorite Story* for Jerome Lawrence and Robert E. Lee. Then he and his charming wife Benita Hume became

Gregory Peck rehearses for "Nightmare," a 1949 *Suspense* episode, with Lurene Tuttle, one of the radio stalwarts who earned his admiration.

recurring guests on *The Jack Benny Show*, playing themselves—as Jack's exasperated neighbors. This quintessential British couple were more than willing to let their hair down on Benny's show, and had the time of their lives in a series of scripts that brought out the best from Benny's writing staff. Finally, Mr. and Mrs. Colman starred in their own genteel comedy series, *The Halls of Ivy*, created by Don Quinn; it also enjoyed a brief television run in the early 1950s. (Amazingly enough, this seemingly tailor-made series was not written with them in mind. It was originally cast with Gale Gordon and Edna Best, but NBC rejected Gordon because he was then costarring on the newly popular CBS series *Our Miss Brooks* with Eve Arden. The Colmans were, in fact, an afterthought!)

Other film actors found themselves in demand on radio because of their professionalism, and their adaptability. James Stewart brought the same conviction to every radio performance that he did to his classic screen roles; it wasn't until the 1950s that he undertook his own series, *The Six Shooter*, but he gave to it the same qualities listeners heard and enjoyed on guest appearances over the years on everything from *Cavalcade of America* and *Suspense* to Norman Corwin's celebrated *We Hold These Truths*, a tribute to the U.S. Bill of Rights on its 150th birthday.

Joseph Cotten had come to Hollywood as one of Orson Welles' Mercury Players, and made his film debut in *Citizen Kane*. Before long he was a genuine movie star of the first rank, and found himself in demand not as a radio player-for-hire, but as a movie "name." His lack of ego made him a popular last-minute fill-in whenever another male star took ill or couldn't fulfill a commitment (as when he stepped in for Clifton Webb on a 1945 *Suspense*). "I'd come around and they'd say, 'Who's sick?'" But he didn't mind the kidding. He claimed that one year's work on *Lux Radio Theatre* paid for his house.

In the late 1940s and early '50s, film production dwindled and term contracts expired as Hollywood adjusted to new realities brought on by television and the government's breakup of production and distribution monopolies. In this uncertain period, radio became a welcome haven for many stars. Humphrey Bogart and Lauren Bacall (*Bold Venture*), Dana Andrews (*I was a Communist for the FBI*), Joel McCrea (*Tales of the Texas Rangers*), Tyrone Power (*Freedom, U.S.A.*), Glenn Ford (*Christopher London*), Alan Ladd (*Box 13*), Brian Donlevy (*Dangerous Assignment*), and Adolphe Menjou (*Meet the Menjous*) are just a few of the actors who brought instant marquee value to radio series . . . but significantly, none of those shows enjoyed long-lasting success. Even with starpower on their side, the shows had to deliver the goods or audience interest waned.

⌐

By the mid 1940s, competition for movie properties to use on the air was keen, if not downright fierce. After a decade on the air, even *Lux* was running out of good material and started redoing old favorites. Newcomers to the adaptation sweepstakes had to settle for reusing movies that had already been produced on the air at least once, if not several times.

However, there were still opportunities to score an occasional coup, as Fletcher Markle discovered when he produced and directed *Studio One*, later known as *The Ford Theater*. "For 'Double Indemnity,' it was Billy Wilder [the director of the movie] who helped tell me where to go. It had not yet been on *Lux* or *Screen Guild*, or anywhere, and we got it in a breeze . . . and outraged *Lux*, and all kinds of other people who had obviously been after it, because it was a good radio piece. It has a narrator, for heaven's sake! The other one was *The Last Tycoon*, by Scott Fitzgerald. David Selznick felt that he had that sewed up in a dozen body bags . . . and *we* got it. There was a great deal of rattling of sabers, and a lot of telegrams and long-distance phone calls and hollerings." The canny Selznick had overlooked one item in his contract: he had not specifically purchased the radio rights. Markle recalled paying about $1,500 to get this radio "first."

Markle was more literary-minded than some other producer/directors, and regarded *Studio One* much as Orson Welles had his *Mercury Theatre on the Air* ten years earlier, as an arena for presenting great works from literature and the stage. When Ford took over sponsorship of the show, Markle suggested *Madame Bovary* for its debut broadcast, and the sponsor protested. They wanted something "more familiar."

Markle recalled, "I said, 'How can you argue with a great love story like *Madame Bovary* with Marlene Dietrich, Van Heflin, and Claude Rains at the top of the cast?' The word went back to Detroit . . . and it was okay, and we did it. [Composer] Cy Feuer said, 'Oh, God, let's have a choir and let's do the whole bit.' The Ford brothers wanted to have a premiere party at the Waldorf, which they had, and who could dress that more handsomely than Marlene? Along with Heflin, and Claude Rains, who had done a lot of *Studio One*'s with us. He was a great friend by that time, perfectly happy to work for nothing, just loved radio."

Markle even produced a radio adaptation of Jack Benny's notorious "turkey," *The Horn Blows at Midnight*. The film wasn't that bad, but Benny got twenty years of jokes out of its failure; in fact, the 1949 radio adaptation on *The Ford Theater* was a complete comedy rewrite, retaining only the bare bones of the story from the 1945 film and filling it with contemporary gag lines, such as a reference to the notoriously feisty head of the Musicians Union. (Claude Rains, as The Chief in heaven says to Benny, "Before you blow that horn be sure to check with Petrillo; I don't want any trouble with him!") The unexpected finale has a heart-tugging plea for world peace which is surprisingly effective. At the end of the broadcast, Benny promises Markle, "If I ever make another bad picture, you can have first crack at it."

(A *Hotpoint Theatre* production of *The Man Who Came to Dinner* on Christmas Day of 1949 with Jack Benny and an all-star cast was similarly rewritten to update its topical references and add a lot of gags. One of them included a wisecrack about the play's coauthors, George S. Kaufman and Moss Hart, calling on the phone to register their dismay!)

One of the last shows to join the Hollywood parade was *The Screen Directors Playhouse*, which debuted in 1948. Taking a page from their actor colleagues, members of the Directors Guild decided to stage a weekly program to benefit their pension fund. The series debuted (under the short-lived title *NBC Theater*). The kickoff show was introduced by Screen Directors Guild President George Marshall. "Stagecoach" reunited the stars of the nine-year-old film, John Wayne and Claire

John Wayne and Ward Bond re-create a moment from *Fort Apache*, originally fashioned on film by John Ford, for an episode of *Screen Directors Playhouse*.

Trevor, with their director, John Ford. Thereafter, each show was introduced by the director of the original film, who returned at the end to banter with his stars, as often as not the same leading actors who appeared in the movies. The lineup was most impressive: Ford (*Fort Apache*) and Alfred Hitchcock (*Spellbound* and *Lifeboat*) appeared several times, along with Billy Wilder (*A Foreign Affair*), John Cromwell (*The Prisoner of Zenda*), William Wyler (*Jezebel*) and Henry Hathaway (*Call Northside 777*), to name just a few.

Some of the half-hour versions of their movies were inadequate, to say the least, and the show improved immeasurably when it shifted to a one-hour format during the latter part of its brief, two-year run.

(Incidentally, Hitchcock, who gained such notoriety hosting his own long-running television anthology series in the 1950s and '60s, attempted to launch a similar radio program ten years before his TV debut in 1955. It was called *Once Upon a Midnight*, and while it featured one of Hitch's trademark stories of murder and suspicion, it didn't make full use of his droll sense of humor.)

Just as television was dawning on the horizon, one more Hollywood institution made a major foray into radio when MGM decided to capitalize on several of its durable movie series. Ann Sothern was recruited to reprise her role as good-hearted but wisecracking *Maisie* (which had already had a brief radio run in the mid-1940s), Mickey Rooney and company (Lewis Stone, Fay Holden) were brought back to star in *The Hardy Family*, and Lew Ayres and Lionel Barrymore returned to the medical world of *Dr. Kildare*. These syndicated shows, produced at NBC in Hollywood, were slickly made and called on top talents on both sides of the mike.

There was a certain irony in the fact that as far as movie work was concerned,

MGM had let Sothern's contract lapse, had a patent disinterest in Rooney, and no longer cared to employ Ayres on screen. But the actors involved were happy to work, especially in the relatively stress-free arena of radio. Sothern even recalls that when she got hepatitis, the producers arranged to record some episodes in her home, while she lay in bed.

⌐

Turnabout was not unheard-of in the Hollywood/radio connection. Radio was used as a backdrop for movie stories from the early 1930s onward, and radio stars were recruited for screen work after the first wave of talkie fever scooped up all the

stage and vaudeville headliners. In 1930, Radio Pictures signed the biggest radio stars of them all to make their screen debut. Amos 'n' Andy toplined *Check and Double Check*, and wisely never tried to do it again; the film was a dog, though it made a lot of money in its initial release. Even the studio must have recognized that the film's success was due to sheer curiosity on the part of fans, and that a sequel wouldn't draw the same response. Freeman Gosden and Charles Correll simply weren't movie actors; what's more, they left themselves in the hands of Hollywood "experts," surrendering the control they maintained over their popular nightly broadcasts, and learned a bitter lesson. They later agreed to lend their voices to a short-lived series of Amos 'n' Andy cartoons for the Van Beuren studio in 1932, and made a guest appearance in *The Big Broadcast of 1936* performing one of their own sketches.

Perhaps the ultimate radio-related movie was the 1932 Paramount picture *The Big Broadcast*, which starred Bing Crosby more or less as himself, and featured

Charlie McCarthy is given the star treatment on the set of *Look Who's Laughing* by Neil Hamilton, Lucille Ball, and Jim and Marian Jordan (Fibber McGee and Molly).

specialty numbers by such air personalities as Burns and Allen, Cab Calloway, The Street Singer (Arthur Tracy), Kate Smith, The Mills Brothers, and The Boswell Sisters. Bing and his acting costars filmed their scenes in Hollywood, but most of the New York–based radio performers shot their disconnected numbers at Paramount's studio in Astoria, New York.

In 1934, Universal brought the soap opera *Myrt and Marge* to the screen, but it failed to click, and Hollywood found it best to go after radio comedians and singers and leave the fictional characters to their studio mikes. Fred Allen made occasional forays to Hollywood, while his "rival" Jack Benny actually carved out a screen career. Lum 'n' Abner, Fibber McGee and Molly, The Great Gildersleeve, and even such incidental characters as Bert Gordon's The Mad Russian and Kenny Delmar's Senator Claghorn were featured in their own undistinguished movie vehicles (*How Do You Do?*, 1945, and *It's a Joke, Son*, 1947). Brenda and Cobina and Vera Vague, from *The Bob Hope Show*, landed comic-relief parts in feature films, and Vague (Barbara Jo Allen) went on to headline her own short-subject series for years to come. A number of radio announcers got to be momentary film personalities, although Bill Goodwin and Harry Von Zell actually pursued legitimate acting careers. (Von Zell, like Vera Vague, also briefly had a slapstick comedy series at Columbia Pictures.)

Take It or Leave It, People Are Funny, Queen for a Day, and other novelty shows made their way to the screen in one-shot efforts, while short-lived series were derived from *Big Town*, *The Whistler* (one of the better series, although it had nothing to do with the radio show), and *I Love a Mystery*.

Only a handful of successful radio plays made their way to the screen. Norman Corwin's adaptation of Lucille Fletcher's *My Client Curley*, about a dancing caterpillar who becomes an overnight celebrity, became a modestly successful movie with the unmemorable title *Once Upon a Time*, starring

Lum and Abner and Pine Ridge's Jot 'Em Down Store were visualized in a series of feature films in the 1940s. This scene is from *So This Is Washington* (1943).

Cary Grant, in 1944. Four years later, Fletcher herself adapted her radio classic *Sorry, Wrong Number* for producer Hal Wallis. Barbara Stanwyck took the part originated by Agnes Moorehead, but it wasn't the change of casting that caused some people to express a vague dissatisfaction with the finished product.

Fletcher herself comments, "Some of the value of the radio show was its intensity, and the fact that by the time it ended, you felt that this woman had dug her own grave. Whereas the [movie] was a complex set of circumstances which aren't as effective as an intense short story."

Radio catchphrases found their way into films, especially the Warner Bros. cartoons, which seemed to thrive on them. "T'ain't the way I heerd it," "I betcha," "Who's Yehudi?," "Wanna buy a duck?" and many others were copied and parodied, based on the audience's certain familiarity with the lines.

Cartoons not only used radio-inspired gags, but drew their voice talent from the realm of radio performers. Mel Blanc wasn't the only one to work both in radio and animation; the voice of Elmer Fudd, Arthur Q. Bryan, had the running part of Doc Gamble on *Fibber McGee and Molly*. Announcer Robert Bruce did narration whenever Warners needed an authoritative voice; Sara Berner performed her trademarked fast-paced, high-pitched characters on many an occasion; and Bea Benaderet was called on for a variety of female voices (most memorably the loud-mouthed Red Riding Hood in *Little Red Riding Rabbit*). MGM hired another *Fibber McGee* regular, Bill Thompson, to do the voice of Droopy, the understated basset hound, who sounded a lot like his radio character Wallace Wimple.

Even so ephemeral a radio "star" as Bert Gordon (right), The Mad Russian on Eddie Cantor's weekly show, was given a screen vehicle, *How Do You Do?*, albeit by low-budget PRC Pictures. Charles Middleton and fellow Cantor acolyte Harry Von Zell were featured.

As tough as it was for some stars to adjust to the demands of radio, the same was true in the opposite direction. Many radio actors wanted to work onscreen; not all of them were able to make the transition.

John McIntire explained, "There's a lot of mechanics in pictures: being conscious of the camera, and knowing that you shouldn't have a speech with your head down and all that you've got to learn." Some actors were said to have "microphone feet," because of their habit of planting themselves in front of the mike and never moving an inch.

Don Ameche knew about this first-hand. He had been one of Chicago's stalwart stock-company players, and based on his beautiful speaking voice and good looks, he was signed to a contract by 20th Century-Fox in 1936. (His brother Jim Ameche remained a radio performer, and a very successful one, for decades to come; he's best remembered today as the original star of *Jack Armstrong, the All-American Boy*.)

Director Henry King worked with Ameche in his second film, the outdoor romance *Ramona*, with Loretta Young. As King later said of Ameche in his Directors Guild of America oral history, "If he could stand and hold onto something he could give a great performance, but if he had to walk he couldn't."

The actor went to see King at the hotel on location and said, "Mr. King, if you could just tell me how to start, I think I can accomplish anything if I know how to begin. I don't know how to do the things that you're talking about. Will you just help me enough to know how to start and I'm sure that I can please you and you won't have to get someone else."

King replied, "It would be great if you could. I'll tell you, it's as simple as this, if you could just learn to do this. . . . Talking to him, I got up out of this chair, walked over, picked up a book on the table, walked back and put it down on a chair in the other corner, came back to him, came back around here, telling him all this story at the same time. I said, 'It's being able to coordinate your mind, your body, your voice, everything, so they all work together so it becomes natural.' He said, 'I get the idea. I'll guarantee tomorrow morning I can do the scene that you rehearsed this afternoon.' " And he was good to his word.

Others never gained that degree of confidence. Says Rosemary DeCamp, "It was terrifying to go from radio into film. I was always terrified that I wouldn't handle the props correctly, because I didn't have enough theater background. So when I'd get on a set, I'd get there very early and work with the props and get used to it, 'cause I knew that I was basically radio and I'd better learn."

On the other hand, said Howard Duff, acting "was what I really wanted to do. I used to approach things, when I was doing radio, from a visual side, too. I tried to imagine the visual side of things . . . so I didn't just become a voice, a disembodied voice, and I think that helped me a great deal. I'd always had my eye on film." Indeed, he was one of the lucky actors to succeed in film and television.

Some were even luckier. Frank Nelson recalled, "I had a friend who did just bits with me in radio shows, and one day he said, 'Frank, I have a chance to do some pictures; what do you think I ought to do? Do you think I should stay in radio or do you think I ought to do the picture thing?' And I was thinking, 'Boy, he reads in a monotone; if he can do anything in pictures'—and I didn't think he could—'he sure ought to take that.' Well, fortunately he did, and he did very well for himself; his name was Alan Ladd."

⌒

When television came along in the 1950s, Hollywood had a whole new series of decisions to make about its relationship with an upstart medium. Radio survived in the movie capital throughout the 1950s, although shows like *Gunsmoke* moved their tapings to Saturdays in order to free up its cast to work in movies and television during the week.

William Conrad, who starred in *Gunsmoke*, fondly recalled one of the more colorful traditions that crossed over from movie sets to radio studios when both industries were going strong. In recollecting his response to it, he echoed sentiments that other screen actors had expressed at different times.

Loretta Young brought a silver platter to work with her, and demanded that her colleagues drop money on it if a curse word passed their lips. More than a few leading men, like Robert Mitchum, had found this somewhat odious, not to mention presumptuous. Conrad finally said, "How much would it cost me to say, 'Why don't you go—— yourself, Loretta?' "

"And," he recalled years later, "I pulled out a $50 bill and put it on the table and walked out. The best $50 I ever spent in my life."

12

Music, Music, Music

Music was the mainstay of commercial radio when it began, and remains its principal raison d'etre today. However, the nature of the music, and how it is played and programmed, is a world apart from radio's salad days.

Jazz historian Gene Lees wrote in a 1994 essay in his *Jazzletter* publication, "I grew up, ear to the radio, on the sounds of the big bands in the 1930s. Network radio was an incredible cultural force, presenting—live, not on records—music of immense cultural diversity, almost every kind of music that America produced, and making it popular. Network radio made Duke Ellington and Benny Goodman famous, and a little later, Glenn Miller. It made Arturo Toscanini and James Melton household names. On Saturday afternoons, the broadcasts from the Metropolitan Opera could be heard everywhere from the Mexican border to the northern reaches of Canada."

Today, radio is a narrowcast medium on which records are played for specific listeners: country music fans tune in an all-country station, and hear nothing but, compiled from commercial recordings. The same is true for fans of heavy metal, so-called oldies, and even classical music. Live performance is a rarity. There is no effort to elevate or educate the listener, nor is there a forum where listeners might

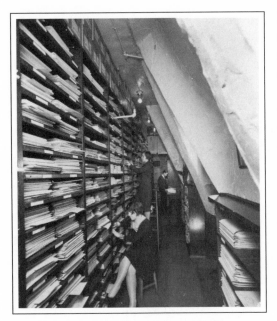

This is just one corner of the music library maintained by NBC's San Francisco headquarters in the 1930s. It was reckoned that more than 3,300 concert numbers were filed here, with a value of $100,000. Said the original photo caption: "Seven persons are kept busy classifying, filing and purchasing new music as it is required."

hear a broad range of music during the course of the day; there is only a determination to zero in on a consumer of precise demographic description.

Radio music, in the 1930s and '40s, offered what radio itself sought to give its listeners: variety. What's more, almost all of it was performed "live."

Classical music was a mainstay of radio stations large and small. At the network level, there was an active rivalry to obtain the services of the most renowned conductors, symphony orchestras, and operatic soloists. NBC scored one of its greatest coups in persuading maestro Arturo Toscanini to forsake his plans to retire to his Italian homeland and, instead, build his own orchestra at Radio City.

Such programs never broke any ratings records; many of them were in fact not sponsored, but presented by the networks on a sustaining basis. They represented a quality (and a goal) that's all too rare in contemporary communications: prestige.

In the earliest days of broadcasting, almost anyone who could sing or play an instrument found a home on radio. Local stations, with hours to fill every day, realized that music was the answer. It required no "production" other than a studio with reasonably good acoustics, a microphone, and a permanent piano or organ. Musicians were happy to play for a pittance (if that), just for the thrill of appearing on the air.

Even when radio became a more sophisticated business, musicians and performers were just as eager to get airtime—eager enough to sacrifice salaries. Bandleader Woody Herman recalled, late in life, "If we had to lose $2,000 or $3,000 a week, it didn't matter because we were getting the right kind of airtime." Radio was the lifeline for bands like Herman's, who made their name over the airwaves, and then made their money on the road—where customers turned out because they had heard those bands on the radio. What's more, adds Les Brown, "The record companies weren't interested in you at all unless you were on the air and you could plug your records."

Music was also useful when radio was young because it was so flexible. As *Radio's Best* reported in 1930, "Frequently a speaker or an orchestra will finish two or three minutes ahead of time. That's where a young lady like Virginia Arnold comes in handy. She can pick up the strains of an orchestra on her piano and fool you into thinking she is part of the program. Columbia keeps her around constantly to fill gaps and guard against the air being empty for any space of time over fifteen seconds."

As radio cut into record sales—particularly during the Depression—and started wearing out songs from overuse, some people in the music industry started complaining. Said Irving Berlin, "We have become a world of listeners, rather than singers. Our songs don't live anymore. They fail to become part of us. Radio has mechanized them all. In the old days Al Jolson sang the same song for years until it meant something—when records were played until they cracked. Today, Paul Whiteman plays a song hit once or twice or a Hollywood hero sings them once in the films and the radio runs them ragged for a couple of weeks—then they're dead."

Indeed, *Radio Daily* magazine compiled a weekly tally of "Network Song Favorites," to keep track of airplay on the most popular current tunes. On April 16, 1937, the publication printed the following list, for the week ending April 3, covering songs played from 5:00 P.M. to 1:00 A.M., on CBS and two NBC networks (Red and Blue). Only compositions played fifteen times or more were included:

"I've Got My Love to Keep Me Warm" 34 times
"Too Marvelous for Words" 33
"Boo Hoo" 31
"Trust in Me" 28
"Little Old Lady" 26
"Moonlight and Shadows" 23
"September in the Rain" 19
"You're Laughing at Me" 18
"Good Night, My Love" 16
"Swing High, Swing Low" 15

Faced with such statistics, one could certainly find oneself agreeing with Berlin. Many songs were literally played to death. But even the grand old man of

Tin Pan Alley had to be impressed when Kate Smith's debut performance of his "God Bless America" on Armistice Day, 1938 made the song an anthem overnight. Such was the power of radio.

Another impressive patriotic piece, "Ballad for Americans," by John Latouche and Earl Robinson, made its debut on November 5, 1939, on the *Pursuit of Happiness* program, supervised by Norman Corwin. Paul Robeson sang the powerful number with orchestra and chorus. On November 20, *Time* magazine reported, "In the studio, an audience of six hundred stamped, shouted, bravoed for two minutes while the show was still on the air, and for fifteen minutes later. In the next half hour 150 telephone calls managed to get through CBS's jammed Manhattan switchboard. The Hollywood switchboard was jammed for two hours. In the next few days bales of letters demanded words, music, recordings, another time at bat for 'Ballad for Americans.' " RCA Victor immediately arranged for Robeson to record it, and like "God Bless America," it became a sensation, thanks to its launch on radio.

Still, the medium remained a mixed blessing for songwriters. Tunesmiths who worked on Broadway were often approached to write for radio—the prestige they brought with them was unbeatable—but few if any could conform to radio's voracious appetite. For a time, operetta king Sigmund Romberg composed original songs (with lyricist Otto Harbach) for a series bearing his name. In 1935, NBC announced with great fanfare that Rodgers and Hart were going to contribute original songs to a new series called *Let's Have Fun*. The debut show (which survives on disc) featured Helen Morgan and Ken Murray, and introduced a grand total of two songs which were endlessly reprised during the hour-long broadcast. Neither one became a hit. (It didn't help that Murray initially forgot both the lyrics and the melody when it came time for him to sing "I'll Take a Little of You on Toast." He stumbled for several bars, and then caught up with the tune.) Howard Dietz and Arthur Schwartz (of *The Band Wagon* fame) fared somewhat better when they signed on for thirty-nine weeks of *The Gibson Family*. They survived the entire season, and wrote some eighty songs, but they were smart enough to use the show as a kind of proving ground. The popular ballad "If There Is Someone Lovelier Than You" later turned up in the score of their 1934 Broadway play *Revenge with Music*, while the series' theme song, warbled every week by Conrad Thibault, later became the title tune of the 1936 Lawrence Tibbett movie *Under Your Spell*.

Songwriters had another unexpected sideline during radio's live-music heyday: rewriting unacceptable lyrics to make them palatable to advertising agency czars. Sometimes the reasons for changes were mundane and self-serving. Stan Freberg remembers *The Railroad Hour* changing the words of "These Foolish Things" from "an airline ticket to romantic places" to, naturally, "a railroad ticket to romantic places." Just as often, the reasons were moralistic in nature. On a 1949 Bing Crosby show, two lines of Irving Berlin's song "Heat Wave" had to be altered for vocalist Gertrude Niesen. "She started a heat wave by making her seat wave" wouldn't pass muster, so it became "letting her feet wave." And "She certainly can can-can" was changed to the meaningless "she certainly can yan-yan." At least it didn't corrupt anyone's morals.

As far as exposure was concerned, radio represented a brass ring for every songwriter and publisher in America. That is why and how an unusual breed known as song pluggers came to be. They were hired by music publishing companies to place their latest tunes with popular singers and musicians. Some of them were savvy and likable guys who knew how to ingratiate themselves with the right people, and brought a lot of good songs to the forefront; others tried using various forms of payola in lieu of personality or good material. (In the 1945 movie *State Fair*, Frank McHugh plays a song plugger and laments, "You have no idea what a shnook like me has to go through to get a song on the hit parade. Last week I fell down in front of Dinah Shore's taxi just to get in a conversation. Every Christmas I've got to remember to send Sinatra a new bow tie. When a bandleader's wife has a baby, I gotta stay home with it on the nurse's night off. It's a big question whether 'Mairzy Doats' would have been a hit if I hadn't known how to change a didy!")

Popular singer Tony Martin remembers, "The song pluggers went after all of us at that time. First they'd go to Bing," he admits, laughing, "and then they'd go to Russ Columbo, or Jolson, and then they'd go to Lanny Ross, and then they'd get to me. But I had a few good buddies out here [in California] that were song pluggers at Paramount Music Company and Warner Bros., and they'd always give me a good hot song to do."

Says veteran bandleader Les Brown, "They romanced all the bandleaders, or anybody that had any airtime. Romanced 'em in many ways—gifts and things like that, which are now verboten. But I just wouldn't do that. I had a name; I had integrity, I thought. In retrospect, I think that maybe I was very foolish, because the other bandleaders were making them pay for the arrangements. I figured, hell, you're being a prostitute if you do that; you lose control, so I wouldn't do it. If I liked the tune, I played it, and I wouldn't take any money."

Brown organized his band at Duke University, and got his first airplay over WDNC (in *Durham, North Carolina*) in the early 1930s. "It was strictly a local station," he explains. "Later on, we went on to Richmond, Cleveland, Youngstown; practically everywhere we went, they'd put a mike in front of the band. This helped us get a record contract. Finally we got a job at the Edison Hotel in New York in 1938 and we were on the air every night for six days a week.

"In those days, all the hotels—that was their way of advertising, you might say. They allowed NBC or CBS or whatever to come in and put a wire there and record the band that they [were] paying for. So it cost them nothing for the wire, but they had to furnish the band. It helped us, and it helped NBC and it helped the hotel.

"Later on, when we started with Columbia Records, we went to the Black-hawk in Chicago in 1941. We were hired for a month; they kept us over four months, and there we had 50,000 watts. That was from WGN in Chicago, and we got to be known after that, and our records started selling."

But what about the challenge of supplying new material every night on the air? "We wouldn't do the same program every night," he responds. "We had a repertoire of, let's say at least eighty or ninety tunes. (Nowadays I'm up to the thousands. Just recently, we cut it down from carrying three hundred with us to about 110.) I'd hardly ever repeat a tune in the same week. But some bandleaders did the same program every night and NBC used to get madder than hell. Tommy Dorsey had his own publishing company; anything he recorded or published at the same time, he had on the air, and he said 'Okay, that's on Monday, Tuesday, Wednesday, Thursday . . .' They raged at him, and he said, 'If you want me, that's what you get.' Because you don't have the same listeners every night."

Those nightly band remotes sparked an entire nation, and enabled what is now known as the big band era to flourish. Many a budding musician was inspired by the sounds that came wafting over the airwaves from distant cities like Chicago and New York. Skitch Henderson, later a top pianist, composer, and conductor (and eventually music director of NBC during the television era), was then a precocious teenage musician.

"My father sent me to live with his sister in Minnesota, and I ran away and got a job at a radio station in Bismarck, North Dakota, and that's where I started, at KFYR. I played piano at night, for fifteen minutes or something, and then there was a 'territory band' there, Harry Turner and his Orchestra. I think it was about seven or ten men, and we played little gigs in those small towns and we broadcast twice a week on the radio station. [Lawrence] Welk was starting at Yankton at that time.

"I used to sit and listen to the monitor at the station, listen to the line, as you say. Fletcher Henderson was at the Grand Terrace in Chicago; I have total recall of that strange period. I remember hearing Ray Noble's band from the Rainbow Room. Ray and Gladys and I became very good friends in later years and I always told them that that was my inspiration to get the hell out of North Dakota. It damn sure inspired you to get away from the jackrabbits."

Guy Lombardo and His Royal Canadians, with Carmen Lombardo at the WABC mike, in an early 1930s broadcast. Radio helped popularize the Lombardo band, as it did innumerable others.

Billy May, then a top trumpeter, vividly recalls, "I was playing with Charlie Barnet and we were playing the Palomar [in Los Angeles] when Hitler invaded Poland. So they would put us on the air all the time, because they would be waiting to patch into Berlin for a news flash, or patch into London for a news flash. Meanwhile they had to have somebody standing by. It was very exciting in those days."

Many careers were boosted by this kind of exposure. Legendary jazz impresario and record producer John Hammond chanced to hear a sensational swing band one night in 1936 while driving in Chicago. He later told jazz historian George T. Simon, "I happened to tune in to an experimental radio station at the very top of the dial, just beyond the last station on the regular AM wavelength." He was so entranced by the sounds he heard that he followed up, discovered the band's name, and later tracked them down in Kansas City. Eventually he brought Count Basie to New York, where his career took off.

Music wasn't only heard on musical shows. Most of the top comedy shows featured music, as well, as if to say that a half-hour of comedy *without* a song would be unthinkable. The shows of Jack Benny, Fred Allen, and Burns and Allen subscribed to this theory, as did *Fibber McGee and Molly*, among others.

Along the way, music and comedy merged. In the 1930s, singers like Kenny Baker (on the Benny show) and Tony Martin (on Burns and Allen) were gradually pressed into service as comic actors, and learned how to deliver dialogue. "I had no experience," Martin admits, "but I had a sense of humor—everybody else's humor, not mine. So I got good lines to read, and George would make 'em much better with those wonderful takes he did with the cigar in his hand to the audience. We'd get tremendous laughs. He used to rehearse me in my lines very well."

In the 1940s, such fine singers as Harriet Hilliard (on Red Skelton), Frances Langford, and Doris Day (both with Bob Hope) turned out to have surprisingly good comic sensibilities. (Day, when asked what she learned most from Hope, replied with a smile, "Not to step on his lines.") Peggy Lee was a fine straight woman, as well, alternating one season between the Bing Crosby and Jimmy Durante shows, but never losing her stage fright. ("If I were given my preference of going in and singing or being shot just before the program, I would have taken the gun," she said years later with a laugh.) Perhaps the biggest surprise was when Langford stepped into the role, opposite Don Ameche, of loud-mouthed battle-axe Blanche

Frances Langford confers with Bing Crosby and musical director Meredith Willson for a *Command Performance* broadcast on Armed Forces Radio Service during World War Two. Note that Willson is in uniform.

Bickerson, in Phil Rapp's "The Bickersons" sketches; she was quite simply sensational.

Not surprisingly, Jack Benny topped the competition in this arena by hiring, and then nurturing, a young singer named Owen Patrick McNulty. An Irish tenor brought onto the show to replace the departing Kenny Baker, he was renamed Dennis Day, and as the 1940s went on (with a break for wartime service) he, like bandleader Phil Harris before him, became not only a

Dennis Day joins forces with Andy Russell, Dick Haymes, and Bing Crosby to form a formidable quartet for a 1947 Jack Benny show.

fine comedian in his own right but an invaluable member of the Benny stock company. (Eventually, both Harris and Day headlined comedy shows of their own.)

Bandleaders were another unexpected source of comic talent. Practically every comedy/variety star bantered with his conductor; some, like Ray Noble (with Edgar Bergen), Meredith Willson (on a number of programs, notably Burns and Allen and *The Big Show*), and John Scott Trotter (with Bing Crosby), showed a real flair, though none could come close to Phil Harris. Originally hired as Jack Benny's bandleader, he eventually became much more valuable as a comedy player, and left the musical direction of the show to others (although on the air it was still referred to as "his" band).

How exactly did shows fall into the habit of using their conductors as comic foils? Veteran composer-conductor-arranger Frank DeVol says, "I'll tell you why they did that: the orchestra leader would read the lines for nothing." He elaborates, "If you were an arranger and a conductor, you had it over somebody who was a conductor only, because he had to hire an arranger. Then, if you did comedy and you could do the arrangements and conducted, you got rid of some [other] people." DeVol parried with Rudy Vallee, Ginny Simms, and Jack Carson on their 1940s radio shows, and eventually exploited his comic know-how as a featured player in scores of movies and television shows. (Perhaps his finest hour came years later on television, as deadpan bandleader Happy Kyne on the late 1970s talk-show parody series *Fernwood 2-Night* and *America 2Night*.)

As much as music permeated the airwaves, most popular music shows stressed variety. There were relatively few shows in the Top 10 that presented music and nothing but. *Your Hit Parade* was an enduring exception to the rule. This bugged the restless and entrepreneurial music director Meredith Willson (who later wrote Broadway's *The Music Man*). After returning from wartime duty in the 1940s, he hatched an idea, which he later described in his book, *And There I Stood with My Piccolo*.

"I thought I'd toy with a musical show of my own and I ended up with a thirty-eight-piece orchestra featuring Ethel Smith's electric organ, Les Paul's electric guitar, and Burl Ives's electrifying folk-song singing, plus no talk or announcements at all, but instead a lot of sponsor-identification tricks, including the use of the Sono-Vox and a male chorus that chanted the commercial in unison . . .

"Anyhow, my program was a big success except for one small detail—nobody bought it. This was because it cost fifteen thousand dollars a week, and that was supposed to be too expensive for a musical show.

"It seems to be generally good practice in the radio business to pay not more than one thousand dollars per Hooper point* for a program—so if the show cost fifteen thousand dollars, you'd have to expect a Hooper rating of fifteen, which everybody said couldn't be done with a musical . . ."

Willson had to content himself with serving as conductor (and comedy foil) on *The Burns and Allen Show* and *The Big Show* with Tallulah Bankhead, while pursuing more creative and experimental projects on his own time.

⟿

For working musicians, radio was a godsend. Skitch Henderson, who earned his living as a freelance pianist in Los Angeles during the late 1930s and early 1940s, says the prime requisite for being a successful on-call musician was "being prepared, never saying no. I was so young I didn't have fear yet. I mean, panic is different than fear. Panic is paying your rent and keeping your collar starched, but fear is a whole different thing that came later, and still exists."

*An industrywide measurement of audience ratings in the days before the Nielsen company came along.

Then-trumpeter Billy May remembers that West Coast work was regulated. "In those days, there was a very strange thing going on in the musicians' union in L.A. I don't think they had it in New York. They had a thing called the quota system here, and there were only so many transcontinental broadcasts you were allowed to do. It was a make-work kind of a thing. Some of the musicians were so good that they could have taken [all the jobs]. In New York, there were musicians who would send substitutes who would work the rehearsals and then mark the parts for the ringers. The ringers would come in and play the shows, and then when the show was over, they'd run quickly down the hall to the next studio and play the next show. To avoid that, that's why they had the quota laws here. You were only allowed to do four half-hour shows as a sideman."

Band members served another important function on radio shows. As Billy May explains, "There was a guy in Jack Benny's band named Frank Remley. Phil Harris kept this guy on—an average guitar player, nothing outstanding, he held up the part. But he had one of those trigger laughs; in other words, the minute the [joke] was out of the comedian's mouth, he laughed. And he started the audience. They knew that and they kept him on the show for that."

Eventually, gags about Remley crept into the scripts—usually matching his drinking activities with Harris's. Soon, he was one of the regulars on the Benny show, though he was spoken about more than he was ever allowed to speak. When Phil Harris inaugurated his own show, he decided to make Remley his on-air foil, but after the first show, he realized that Frankie was no actor. According to Elliott Lewis, it was a chance meeting in the hallway at NBC that led to Phil recruiting him to play Remley on the air that night. "That night" led to a nine-year stint.

Many top comedians enjoyed playing to the band, aiming hipper jokes their way, and counting on them to crack up even if the audience might not.

A famous character among Los Angeles musicians was an imposing trombone player named—no kidding—Abe Lincoln. Says Billy May, "Abbott and Costello gave a quart—or a fifth—of whiskey to the band player who laughed the loudest. And Abe Lincoln won it every week, 'cause he had one of those automatic laughs, real loud."

Abe had a way of rankling people, as well. When Paul Weston was leading the band on *Duffy's Tavern*, Lincoln was in the trombone section, and had a habit of talking to his fellow musicians during the show, which drove Ed Gardner crazy. Weston warned Abe about this several times. Finally Gardner said to Weston, "Look, either he goes or you go." So, says Weston, "I went to Abe and I said, 'Abe, this is ridiculous; you gotta shut up.' And Abe said, 'Well, what does he care? I'm not talking about *him*!' "

Another of Lincoln's regular gigs was in Ozzie Nelson's radio band—until Ozzie, too, got fed up and fired him. (Except Lincoln wouldn't let him finish his sentence; he broke his trombone over his knee and quit.) Ozzie Nelson was a bright and ambitious man who'd made a success as a bandleader in the 1930s, and eventually married his vocalist, Harriet Hilliard. They were both appearing on Red Skelton's popular show in the 1940s. When Skelton was drafted, Ozzie and Harriet were given their first headline opportunity on the radio. This started Nelson thinking about broadening his horizons, and led to the creation of their hugely successful family comedy series, which he supervised down to the last detail.

Billy May had been playing trumpet in the band on the Skelton show, and Ozzie hired him to work on the new show as well. When Nelson and his arranger clashed, he gave May his first significant work as an arranger-conductor. "Ozzie always had a big band, so I had a pretty good-sized orchestra to experiment with there," May recalls. "We had close to twenty-two men; that's a little over the norm. We had five or six strings, and a 'toys' guy who played the xylophone and all the bells and clinks."

It was understandable that Nelson would want to have an especially good orchestra on his show, even if he was branching out into comedy. "He never gave up the idea of being a bandleader," says May. "I guess he was covering himself in case the show folded; he could always go back out on the road as a bandleader."

The atmosphere in radio was the same in the musical community as it was for all the others: great fun, pumped by adrenaline and the inevitable drinks that were consumed between the West Coast and East Coast broadcasts. Conductor-arranger Paul Weston remembered, "At NBC, Studio A would be *Fibber McGee*, and then we [Weston and wife Jo Stafford] would be in Studio B, Bing was with *The Kraft Music Hall* in Studio C and somebody else was in D; it was a ball. When we would have a break in our rehearsal we'd go in and sit in the audience, and talk back and forth; Bing would come into our studio to hear the band and Jo."

For singers, radio offered as much opportunity as it did musicians. Ray Charles, the choral director who has come to call himself "the *other* Ray Charles," started out as a boy singer in Chicago and eventually went to work for Bob Trendler, who did a lot of choral work there. "On some shows he had the band, some shows he just had the choir, and I was part of that seven- or eight-voice group that went from studio to studio. On *Chicago Theater of the Air* every Saturday night we did an abridged version of a light opera or an operetta."

In 1942, Charles went to New York and auditioned for Lyn Murray, Jeff Alexander, Ray Bloch, and Maya Rapaport, four of the leading music directors in town. On his first big show he got an eight-bar solo in a rendition of "I Left My Heart at the Stage Door Canteen," thanks to Lyn Murray, and that encouraged him to move to Manhattan. "I had a child already, so I was deferred a little, but the draft board was after me and they finally got me in June of '44. By the time I went into the Navy, I was doing ten shows a week."

What was it like for a working singer? "You'd come in and have an hour coach rehearsal, when you'd read the music; you'd have an orchestra rehearsal, and then you'd do the show. You'd pick up the music and read, like an instrumentalist would; there wasn't time to take it home and learn it, because the ink wasn't dry when they handed it to you. It was a very fast operation, all the time.

"I got out of the service in 1946, some place in Long Island or Brooklyn, and that night, I had to run down to the Jack Carter/Chuck Carson show to sing 'Mmm-mmm good, mmm-mmm good, that's what Campbell's Soups are, mmm-mmm good.' In those days, jingles were not recorded; every jingle that you heard was being done live, which meant that there was a lot of running around to do." At that time Lyn Murray asked him to take over choral direction on the Broadway-bound musical *Finian's Rainbow*, which was out of town in Philadelphia. "I had to go down to Philadelphia five days a week. I would get the train in the morning and I would rehearse and I wouldn't see the show because I had to be back to sing 'Mmm-mmm good' on *Bob Trout and the News* at 7:00 at 53rd and Madison. And I must say, I always made it . . . sometimes out of breath."

On the West Coast, one of the steadiest jobs on the air was won by a young woman who could whistle the theme of the mystery show *The Whistler* every week. Elliott Lewis recalled, "When we first went on [during World War Two] she was working at Lockheed. She would come rushing in for the dress rehearsal, because she had to get off from her job at Lockheed."

Another specialist who was never out of work in radio's heyday was the organist. Like other solo-instrument musicians, he was often called on to fill time in the early-morning or late-night spots with regular recitals, but he also found a niche on daytime soap operas.

Some stations were actually equipped with pipe organs, but the development of the electric organ—more compact and less expensive—served as a boon to this brand of music on radio. Master organist Gaylord Carter, who made his reputation playing for silent movies in Los Angeles during the 1920s (and was still at it in the 1990s), recalls his first experience at radio station KHJ in 1935.

"I remember they had a funny little organ there, a little Estey organ at KHJ and it was kind of decrepit. It's now residing in a little chapel in Forest Lawn, where it should have been all this time. But I remember the one time the thing collapsed, a Hammond organ had been sent to the station by the local Hammond dealer downtown. Now, this is when the Hammond organ first came out, and they didn't realize that they had something that had entertainment value. They thought they were God's gift to the churches, that they would supplant the church organs with the Hammond organ. Well, I discovered it was a good thing to play jazz on, and all kinds of little bright, sparkling pieces. So I was doing this, and I got a call from them and they said, 'Mr. Carter, please do not mention the name Hammond on your show; you're ruining our church sales.' "

A unique opportunity presented itself to Carter in 1936 when radio's institution *Amos 'n' Andy* moved to the West Coast. "They brought the show to California for Freeman Gosden's health. They started in Palm Springs, then they came in to L.A., and the orchestra they had in Chicago didn't come with them. I was hired to go on the *Amos 'n' Andy* show, and that was very prestigious for an organist, though your name was very rarely mentioned. But the show was enormously popular.

Gaylord Carter at the organ, age 21.

"They asked me, 'Where can we get a good organ for radio?' NBC at that time didn't have an organ. And there was one at Warner Bros. studios where KFWB was located. Well, Freeman Gosden knew Jack Warner, so that's how that happened." Carter's music was actually piped in from a separate building! "It was about a mile from where they were, so I didn't see them for the first year I was on the show. [Announcer] Bill Hay was with them, and there would be an engineer in the booth at KFWB. I'd get a signal from him and I'd start a stopwatch, which was hanging on a little hook on the organ, and then I'd go into the theme that's supposed to last a minute, and it did. At that time, to take a minute out of a fifteen-minute show for playing a theme was unheard-of, but that theme was very famous. 'The Perfect Song.'

Gaylord Carter, at the organ console, and announcer Bill Hay, seated, functioned in a separate studio from Freeman Gosden and Charles Correll on the *Amos 'n' Andy* broadcasts. A floor director, with stopwatch in hand, is ready to throw a cue. A commercial announcer waits at left.

"Then about a year after I had joined the show NBC got an organ in their studios at Sunset and Vine, and I moved over there.* [But] we never were in the same studio. We were on the first floor and they were on the second floor. They wanted to be by themselves, and for some reason, didn't want to be where the announcer was. Bill Hay and I were in the studio together, and they had their studio upstairs; and they'd always worked that way."

Eventually, Carter joined CBS station KNX, where as a staff musician he was occasionally called upon to play on such shows as *The Whistler* and *Suspense*, to augment the sound of the orchestra. (In later years, some dramatic shows like *Escape*, which were normally accompanied by full orchestras, saved money by using only an organ for the West Coast rebroadcast.) But the organ—and the organist—found their real home on daytime radio, accompanying quiz and audience-participation shows, and especially soap operas. Every soap opera needed a theme; in those days, recorded music was verboten on the networks, and

*Carter happily added this footnote: "The original organ that I played from the Warner Bros. studio, the studio finally sold it; it was bought by a radio actor by the name of Joe Kearns. He bought the organ and installed it in his home, and later on I made some recordings on it. After he died, it went for sale and has been installed in a theater in Mansfield, Ohio, and I played a concert there about a year ago, and the promotion said, 'Gaylord Carter comes to Ohio to meet an old friend.' Here was the organ and there was the little hole in the board right above the stops in the keys where I had had the little hook that held the stopwatch. And it sounds absolutely magnificent in the theater."

an orchestra would have been prohibitively expensive for a simple daytime series. The organ was a perfect solution, richer than a piano and better suited to the emotions of daytime dramas.

On soaps, a musician like Gaylord Carter was also the music director. One of his regular shows was *The Second Mrs. Burton*. "I'd get the script on maybe the day of the show, just as the actors would, and we'd all go through them and make little marks and where it says, 'Music under and out,' you'd make a little jiggly line

This photo of a *One Man's Family* broadcast from Hollywood illustrates the relationship of the organist to the cast. Notice the placement of the microphone, up high, to capture the sound of the organ.

along through the speeches being made and then a little terminus where you'd come out. The director, whom you had your eyes on all the time, where it says 'Music up' would give you a cue and then he'd gradually come down and wave you out. Or, if you were going under the dialogue he would just bring you down and then keep you under the dialogue, and then give you a little sign to get out." In other words, the director functioned as a conductor.

Playing in harmony with the actors, and helping to create a mood as they were, was part of the skill required of a radio organist. "Even in the studio when the actors are doing it, in my imagination I'm painting a scene of where they are or what they're doing—whether they're in the woods, or in a cathedral, or whatever it is. To stimulate the imagination, that's the greatest thing, and I think that's what radio did," says Carter.

As for writing those musical passages called bridges, "I got very adept at it. After I'd been out of it for a while, I was invited to come back and play a radio show and I had a terrible time fitting into it again. It is such a highly specialized thing, making a point in five to ten to fifteen seconds maximum. It's not like doing a whole score."

Writing those bridges and stings was a major part of every music director's chores in radio, including the leading prime-time shows which had full orchestras. Some of the

Bernard Herrmann runs through a score for his director, Orson Welles. (Note that Welles is having dinner during the orchestra rehearsal. So much for the glamor of radio.)

comedy show composers became quite punny in their choice of bridges from one scene to the next, such as Jeff Alexander on the later *Amos 'n' Andy* half-hour programs. In a 1951 episode, after Kingfish makes an appointment to bring Sapphire's ugly mother to a beauty salon, he plays "Lovely to Look At"; after Andy and Kingfish borrow lawyer Calhoun's car, "In My Merry Oldsmobile."

Others wrote their own mini-compositions. In comedy shows, they often had to indicate, in a lighthearted way, a transition from one location to another, or in some cases close out a scene. On the dramatic shows, there were different approaches to music. One of the pioneers in this area was Bernard Herrmann, who went on to a long and distinguished career in film music.

Herrmann started out in the 1930s at CBS in New York, where he had many opportunities ranging from conducting classical recitals to scoring the *Mercury Theatre* shows of Orson Welles. It was then that he and Welles formed a partnership; when Welles went to Hollywood to make *Citizen Kane*, Herrmann went along to compose the score, and never returned to New York. Yet even after he had established himself in Hollywood, Herrmann continued to write for radio. The reason is obvious: he enjoyed the creative freedom, coupled with the deadline challenge, that the medium afforded him.

Jerry Goldsmith cut his teeth at CBS Radio in the early 1950s, where as a music student he was admitted to a talent training program. In time, he got a full-time job—not as a composer, but as a script typist! He was promoted into the production department, where his job included scheduling announcers. "I'd sneak into one of the rehearsals and I'd be watching Bernard Herrmann and Lyn Murray and Jeff Alexander doing a show; it was great. I was drooling for a chance." His opportunity came through a fluke. Goldsmith became very familiar with the stock music library at CBS, and as shows started dropping their full-time orchestras, he won the assignment of scoring them with records.

Jerry Goldsmith conducts a five-piece "orchestra" for a *Suspense* broadcast of 1954. This picture makes it clear why musicians and composers felt a comradeship with the actors and others who put on a radio show.

"It was a period when live music was really down the tubes. So then I got the *Hallmark Hall of Fame*. They took the orchestra off the show, which Lyn Murray had been doing for years. They were very impressed with me and I did *Romance* that way, and then every once in a while I'd sneak in, they'd let me do a show with two or three instruments live. And then actually it got to the point where I was using the whole staff orchestra, where I was doing regular shows with an orchestra. And then we did *The CBS Radio Workshop* [when it] came back on the air; that was a very, very special time, that year of doing those shows. Particularly one show I did with Bill Conrad ["1,489 Words," 1957], which was poetry and music."

When Goldsmith branched out into television and then film (where he remains today one of the premier composers) he learned first-hand that there were significant differences between writing music for movies and scoring a radio show.

"When you do a film, [it's] up for grabs, where does the music go, where doesn't it go," he explains. "In radio it was always very much laid out, mostly in the script; it was the format. You started with a little ten-second overture and then you went under the opening narration, and as soon as the dialogue came in, you went out. Then when a scene changed, you played music. There was no such thing as a visual dissolve or cut; you bridged it with music. Music was your dissolve. And then you came to the end of an act, and you had to have a finale or a curtain to end.

"The time parameters were minuscule; you didn't have a visual image, either. And you were not really underscoring per se, because most dramatic radio shows were narrative anyway. What you really did is you were tying scenes together. I think it was just a matter of gluing the show together so it had some kind of dramatic impact to it. It was very much Mickey Mouse; there was nothing subtle about it."

That was the battle fought by the more intelligent directors, like Fletcher Markle, who declared, "You have to learn to train yourself not to let music enter at the obvious place, as is still done in films. When you are going to be told that something violent will happen, the poor man who's writing the score has been told to begin when the light goes out, or whatever—all that Western Union stuff. All that telegraphy is so depressing. But you had to be careful doing that in radio, and you quickly found composers who could make an entry innocuous, but it would enhance what you were doing, and what you were leading to, and once the dialogue had begun, then the orchestra was there, and could aid it or bridge it and make a transition out of it."

The better composers were inspired by imaginative directors. Arch Oboler recalled, "I would take a play in to Gordon Jenkins and we'd sit and talk about it, lightly, quickly. I would say, 'Here it's the heart of a man, here it's the thought of a woman,' that's all I'd say. And in a few days Gordon would come into the studio with the orchestra—small or large, depending on how much budget we had—and it would be great. If ever there was an unsung genius . . ."

Jack Johnstone remarked, "A *Hollywood Star Playhouse* with [Charles] Laughton had him push his wife down a flight of stairs. The sound effects man was very much puzzled about what to do with it. I consulted with Frank DeVol and we did it musically. And it was far more effective than it would have been with a sound effect." DeVol, a self-taught musician, observed his father playing for silent movies, and feels that this gave him an unconscious ability to score both radio shows and films in later years.

In the late 1940s and '50s network radio presented a growing number of daily quarter-hour music programs featuring headline singers. This meant even more work for musicians, conductors, and arrangers . . . and tighter deadlines than ever. Frank DeVol recalls, "I did Jack Smith's show for five years; that was a five-a-week, fifteen-minute show with Dinah Shore, Margaret Whiting, we had Martha Tilton at one time. Five years of radio. It was just lovely to be in a job and you know what you're doing every day."

But the workload was formidable. "With the Jack Smith show, I was writing—a lot of times—five numbers for a fifteen-minute show, on a daily basis. I used to get up at 4:00 A.M., start writing, and at five o'clock, I called the first copyist who took it down."

Composing and rehearsing a score on a tight deadline was one hurdle; the next was making sure it sounded right on the air. Director Elliott Lewis recalled how it was done on a dramatic program: "There's a point in that orchestra rehearsal where the arranger will conduct and the conductor is in the booth saying, 'I need more clarinet,' or 'The bass is too close,' or any of those things; they're moving chairs and they're moving stands. Now the engineer—live—is mixing all of this, what three people or more do in a dubbing room today." Composer/arranger Paul Weston recalled that there was one engineer at NBC who made the music sound so good that when he was hired by Johnny Mercer to help establish a new company called Capitol Records in the 1940s, he recommended bringing the engineer, Art Brearley, with him.

Overseeing the interplay of music and acting while the show went live on the air was the work of the director. Elliott Lewis recalled one particular show. "We did *The Mystery of Edwin Drood*, and Lud [Gluskin] wrote a score—because the guy's an organist in the story, a church organist—he wrote a score for organ and orchestra together. I'm in the booth; in the right corner of the studio is Lud and his orchestra; in front of me is the cast, to my left in the back corner of the studio is sound effects. And in another room is the organist, listening to all this. But Lud can't communicate with the organist; Lud has to turn to me and signal, and I [throw the cue] and he plays in the other studio."

In the early 1950s, producer-director Lewis sold a weekly show to CBS called *Crime Classics*. These were the waning days of network radio, and the budgets were small; music would suffer more than any other facet of broadcasting. The executives asked Lewis to use recorded music, and he said, "I don't want to use recorded music; it sounds terrible. We have no theme on this show; each show is in a different time period, could be 1500 or 1900, each show is in a different part of the world. Can I have a three-piece orchestra? They said, 'What are you going to do with a three-piece orchestra?' I told them, 'Whoever is going to write it, will write for any three pieces he wants.' "

Lewis lucked out and got Bernard Herrmann, who rose to the challenge in spectacular fashion. "He said, 'Any three pieces I want?' I said, 'Any three pieces you want; it depends on the show.' 'But one thing,' he said, 'when you break for the music rehearsal, you have to leave the studio. I don't want you to see—and I'm not going to tell you. I want you to be surprised when you start your dress rehearsal.'

"He had the damnedest collection of people," Lewis recalled. "He called me one week and said, 'Can I have a fourth person?' And I said, 'Yeah, we have some money in the budget. What are you using?' The show was 'The Assassination of Abraham Lincoln.' He said, 'I'm not going to tell you.' Okay. I got to the studio and you could barely enter the room; his four men were percussionists, and he had every percussion instrument known to man. I never knew there were so many drums: snare drum, field drum, bass drum, double bass drum, [plus] finger chimes, xylophone, tambourine, everything you can think of, and that's how he scored 'The Assassination of Abraham Lincoln.'

"One week—oh, it was so marvelous—he called one week and said, 'I need a fourth instrument.' I said, 'Okay, you can have it.' And this week, why he needed a fourth instrument fascinated me, so I stayed in the booth and turned the lights off. And as soon as everybody broke, the stagehand came in with four music stands and four chairs, then the guy from the music copying department and he put down the parts on the four music stands. And I waited to see how Bernard Herrmann had scored 'Jesse James.'

"Four men came in, and they were all trombonists! And each one was carrying a trombone case: a big trombone case, a little trombone case, a regular trombone case. And the expression on their faces when they came in . . . For the first time in their lives it was perfectly obvious they were the orchestra. They weren't the trombone section, they were it."

In 1958, CBS made a bold move, and hired satirist Stan Freberg to headline his own thirteen-week comedy series. It was an expensive show to do, not the least because Freberg held out for musical director Billy May and a full-sized band. By this time, virtually all surviving network radio series were using canned music, so the presence of a live orchestra signaled that this show was something special indeed.

May remembers, "Lud Gluskin was the music director at CBS for many years; he was still holding sway. They were just about gonna let him go, and Freberg came in, so he had a last gasp. We had to use what was left of the staff, which was about ten men. I think we added maybe two more outside guys. The band would be called at four o'clock and I'd go over and run the band down; we'd play the themes and play the bridges, and I'd tell 'em, 'Take a ten,' because I'd still be writing the show, because Freberg would be so late. So they'd have like an hour off, and then they'd come back and maybe I'd have the next part written.

"Gluskin heard that and he wrote a very salty memo to the producer, Pete Barnum, and he said, 'I understand that the band on the Freberg show was getting extraordinarily long "fives." ' The fives were the five-minute period of rest on the hour, see? And he wanted to know why that was so. And Pete Barnum wrote back and said, 'You know how bad the service is in the saloon across the street?' "

Looking back, he says, "I think everybody realized that we were kind of closing down a chapter of some sort of history." As in fact, they were.

Television took up much of radio's slack, both in terms of employment and exposure of a broad range of music. Even classical shows like *The Voice of Firestone* and the *Bell Telephone Hour* made their way to TV, in those halcyon days before commercialization took everything over.

But there were differences, just the same. Choral director Ray Charles vividly recalls that he was told to hire younger, more attractive singers to populate the chorus on the Perry Como TV show. This was never a consideration in radio. Singers who were accustomed to reading off sheet music (not to mention scripts) were suddenly forced to memorize their material, for the benefit of the cameras. The pressure of going live on the air was increased tenfold for all the participants.

Bing Crosby continued working on radio much longer than many of his colleagues. (For one thing, he'd fought and won the battle to pretape his shows, which wasn't yet possible on television except with film.) With an active schedule of moviemaking, he relied heavily on his musical director, John Scott Trotter, and such key musicians in his band as pianist Buddy Cole and guitarist Perry Botkin.

Says Hal Kanter, who wrote for Crosby in the 1940s, "Bing didn't need very much rehearsal. John Scott Trotter would go to the studio where Bing was working and in between set-ups or rehearsals, or at lunchtime, he'd run over things with him in his dressing room on just the piano. Then Bing would come to the studio, the orchestra would always have been rehearsed, and they would run through it one time and [he'd be] ready to do it."

Says Billy May, "John Scott Trotter was a very fastidious man; everything about him was very tasteful, and I always felt it was quite an honor to work for him. He always made sure that the music associated with Bing was of a high quality. There's a song called 'I'll Be Seeing You,' and the melody had been lifted from one of the Mahler symphonies. Well, John made an arrangement of that and he used every device in the book to [let you] hear Gustav Mahler. And very few people would understand that."

In 1954, even Crosby had to bow to economic realities. His weekly half-hour show went off the air. But Crosby wasn't ready to abandon radio, and vice versa. He continued taping a daily fifteen-minute music show for CBS—but without a studio audience, and, more significantly, without an orchestra. It was the Buddy Cole Trio backing up the Old Groaner for the duration of his radio career.

Eve Arden shares a moment with *Our Miss Brooks'* musical director, Wilbur Hatch.

As with actors, the musicians and composers felt a genuine loss when network radio faded away. Composer Jerry Goldsmith, who came in at the tail end of radio's golden age, remembers, "You didn't get this in any other [medium]: the cast was so excited when the orchestra came in. . . . When there was the orchestra there, they would all team together. That was the kind of electricity and energy you felt, that went through everybody. It became an ensemble piece. In radio, you were part of it.

"We'd all go out as a group afterwards, and a lot of times we'd all have dinner and drinks. There were always drinks; that was a constant. Half the cast was loaded when we hit the air, and sometimes the directors were, too.

"A social club is what it was."

⌐

Eventually, radio became more and more a medium of disc jockeys playing recorded music.

Today, there are occasional live broadcasts of rock concerts which earn a national hookup by satellite. National Public Radio and Public Radio International distribute a range of rarefied musical programming, much of it prerecorded (even in concert). Garrison Keillor's weekly live broadcast of *A Prairie Home Companion* brings an eclectic blend of music to a wider audience than any program on radio or television. *Riverwalk—Live from the Landing* features Jim Cullum's Jazz Band and an impressive lineup of guest stars from its home base in San Antonio, Texas. And, amazingly, the Saturday-afternoon broadcasts of the Metropolitan Opera are still on the air (although the revered announcer-commentator Milton Cross is long gone), maintaining a tradition that began in the 1930s.

In a medium—and a country—where traditions are scarce, it serves as a living link to a time when such programming was not an event, but a daily occurrence.

13

LIVE—On the Air!

Parley Baer remembers a movie actor whose radio debut left him a nervous wreck. "He was just petrified, and he went down in infamy when he went on the air. He walked through two or three doors that hadn't opened, and he kind of consummated his performance by waiting for the telephone sound saying, 'Alarmed, hello?'"

Someone once defined live radio as sitting on a limb, sawing on the trunk side of the tree for a half-hour, and praying that the limb wouldn't snap.

Given that almost all of radio broadcasting was heard in millions of homes just as it was happening in a studio, it's amazing there weren't more mistakes, not to mention catastrophes. But the people who worked in front of a mike, day after day, were professionals, and they learned to roll with a variety of punches.

Announcer Andre Baruch gave one example: "I used to do *The Shadow* at WOR, and I was playing in a golf tournament and the tournament ran overtime. (I was playing match play and we tied at the end of eighteen holes, so we had to play extra holes.) Finally I jumped in the car and we drove from White Plains, New York, down to WOR at 1440 Broadway and it was the maddest dash anybody's ever made to a studio. I got up to the studio and the director already had the script in his hand ready to go on the air, when I took the thing out of his hand and started that opening announcement."

No one was smoother on the air than Bing Crosby, but even his professional nonchalance was put to the test at least once. Writer Hal Kanter remembers one night in the late 1940s. "We were actually taping the show and while they were on stage, I was sitting in Bing's dressing room writing the tag, the good nights. And Bill [Morrow, the producer] would come in from the control room during the musical numbers and say, 'How's it going?' and 'Let's see it' and 'Change that' and 'Fix this' and 'Okay' and 'Hurry up' and so forth. Finally, Ken Carpenter was doing the last commercial when Bill walked out on stage with the script and carbon copies; he had made a change in one on pencil and was literally handing copies out to Bing, to the guest star and whoever else had something to say, and then slipped Ken's carbon copy under the copy he was reading.

"We never stopped doing that; it was done like a live broadcast, even though it was on tape. And they came to the tag and they read it, did the good-nights. The show was over, and I was standing out in the hall; Bing came out and fixed me with a glare. If it had been a laser beam, it would have left holes through my head and on the wall behind me, and he said, 'Don't you ever do that to me again.' That was the only time I ever saw that man really mad about the show. Also, I guess he and Ken were about the only two people I know who could carry a thing like that off and not be rattled by it."

Writer Larry Gelbart remembers how Ed Gardner handled an unexpected situation on *Duffy's Tavern* one night. "We had Monty Woolley on the show, and he was a prolific boozer. They went to Brittingham's, which was a fabled eating place at Columbia Square up on Sunset and Gower adjoining the CBS studios, between the two shows and they had something like twenty martinis. Monty Woolley fell down during the program, fell on the floor with his script, and Ed, the ever-thoughtful host, got down on the floor with him and they finished the program lying on their sides, both smashed."

Sometimes it was boredom, not booze, that prompted unscripted moments. Singer Bea Wain recalls, "Frank Sinatra got bored with singing 'Now Is the Hour' on *Your Hit Parade*. There's a soprano in the background doodling while he's singing 'Now Is the Hour,' and he said, 'Thank you, Marjorie Main' in the middle of it. Which is fun for all of us, but the next morning, there was a call from Vincent Riggio, who was then the head of Lucky Strike, and that was the start of the decline with Frank on *Hit Parade*."

Sinatra's wisecrack may have been immature, but it was harmless. Other radio veterans remember practical jokes born of boredom, and the desire to disrupt the daily routine. One standby was setting an actor's script on fire. Raymond Burr recalled doing this to an actor who was noted for his punctiliousness. In recounting the story, Burr said, deadpan, "It simply *had* to be done."

Orson Welles had a variation on this theme; just before airtime, he would lose control of his script, sending its pages helter skelter across the studio floor. Newcomers would be aghast; veterans knew that he was using a substitute copy, just to get a rise out of people.

Another favorite routine was setting the studio clocks ahead. The cast of *One Man's Family* pulled this on writer-director Carleton E. Morse one day, then started fluffing—and cursing—as if they were already on the air!

Steve Allen recalled many jokes from his tenure at a local station in Phoenix, Arizona, but his favorite was preparing a piece of announcer's copy and sneaking it into the continuity book. Because of its placement, he would know exactly what time the chosen announcer would read this bogus page. Allen would be home in bed, listening with gleeful anticipation for the moment when the unsuspecting fellow would begin a commercial announcement and then find, in the middle, that he was reciting pure gibberish.

Allen also remembers nailing newscasters by removing their clothes at the beginning of a fifteen-minute, commercial-free broadcast. The hapless victim would have no choice but to continue reading as if nothing was amiss. Announcer Jackson Beck has a similar story. "There was a time that Rosa Rio was playing the organ, and Dorian St. George, who was a real prankster, was the announcer at the show. She's at the Hammond organ, and she's a very attractive, talented lady, great sense of humor. And he went up and unbuttoned her blouse while she's playing; she had a blouse with buttons down the back. He unbuttoned the whole thing and then he undid her bra. She can't say anything, [and] there's an audience up in the visitor's booth at NBC watching this. She waits until his middle commercial comes up and she walks up, undoes his belt, unzips his fly and drops his pants. And then starts on the undershorts. And there's an audience up there! They go, 'What the hell is going on here?' "

In the early 1950s, a neophyte actor named Jack Lemmon got his first break working on soap operas. One day he got his baptism of fire on *Road of Life* when he turned over a script page and accidentally said a line that belonged to the show's star, Don McLaughlin. "So he just looked at me, [made a face] and went over and sat down, and left me. This is a live show; the sonofabitch left me there! So there was nothing I could do. Finally I said, 'Well, I know what you'd say . . . you know what I'd say to that? I'd say such-and-such . . .' Now he's getting in hysterics 'cause I'm actually doing it pretty good and I'm getting away with it. I snuck a look at the booth, to see what the director was doing, and there was nobody. All there was was a pair of feet sticking straight up; he was on the floor, and his feet were sticking up in the window, just shaking, he was laughing so hard."

Richard Wilson told Karen Latham Everson that even the august *Mercury Theatre* troupe wasn't above a bit of tomfoolery. "We had an announcer named Ernie Chappell, and they had a phrase at that time, 'Just as sure as you like chicken you'll like Campbell's chicken soup.' That was a phrase that was sort of constant, and we—particularly Orson—kept digging at Ernie and saying, 'Well, we read an ad in the *Poultry Journal* which said, "If you've got any old roosters, Campbell's will buy them," ' things like that. So whenever he would say, 'Just as sure as you like chicken . . .' we'd chime in and say, 'ROOSTER SOUP!' Until finally he said it one time, much to his horror. I forget where it was, or if it was just in a dress rehearsal, but finally it was, 'Just as sure as you like chicken, you'll like Campbell's Rooster Soup!' And I can remember the guffaws that followed that. It was a long, bitter campaign that was waged against this poor, hapless stuffed shirt of an announcer."

Even *The Mercury Theatre* troupe needed to blow off steam from time to time. Orson Welles *(top left)* enjoyed a joke as much as anyone in radio.

Orson Welles told Peter Bogdanovich of a time when havoc reigned throughout the studio, during a *Columbia Workshop* production of *Hamlet* in 1936. "We got one cue wrong in 'Hamlet'—one cue off with [conductor] Bernard Herrmann. He had broken his baton and thrown his script up in the air and walked out of the studio forty seconds before air time because of a quarrel with [director] Irving Reis. And I dragged him back. We didn't have time to get the notes back in order on his stand, so he was one cue off all through it. So we had fanfares when it was supposed to be quiet, approaching menace when it was supposed to be a gay party, and all live; it was riotous. Nothing to do—he just went on. It got funnier and funnier, because Reis was an emotional-type director and Benny is an emotional-type conductor . . ."

Inside jokes were also a part of the convivial atmosphere at some shows. Lurene Tuttle recalled that celebrities, among others Louis Armstrong and Sammy Davis Jr., regularly visited the control booth to watch her and Howard Duff perform *The Adventures of Sam Spade*. "Many times Howard and I would mention them. He would say, 'Did you see Dizzy Gillespie the other day?' and I'd say, 'What was he doing over there? I didn't see him . . .' and then we'd go on . . ."

Many of radio's most memorable goofs were entirely unplanned. One of the most notorious involved the night that Major Ramshaw, an eagle, got loose in the Fred Allen studio. The majestic bird was supposed to fly around briefly and return to his trainer, the British lecturer and raconteur Captain Knight, who was holding a piece of meat. But the eagle wouldn't come back, and keep swooping around the audience, screams and laughter increasing all the while. This impromptu bit of visual entertainment prompted a series of choice Fred Allen ad-libs.

Lurene Tuttle and Howard Duff fool around with their *Sam Spade* director, William Spier. Often the kidding spilled over onto the air.

Almost everyone who spent any time in radio has at least one story of disaster, or near-disaster. Herb Ellis was announcing a band remote in San Francisco in the late 1940s, trying to sound as smooth and debonair as possible. However, a mike that was supposed to be in place for bandleader Henry "Hot Lips" Busse wasn't there. He moved over toward Ellis, the unwitting announcer turned around, and knocked the trumpet into Busse's teeth, sending his mute—his all-important, trademark mute—flying out onto the dance floor! Live on the air, Ellis tried desperately to retain his cool, while Busse fumed and some poor fool went scrambling among the dancers trying to find the missing mute.

Rosemary DeCamp tells of one particular evening during her long run on *Dr. Christian*. "Art Gilmore said something [at the beginning of every show] and I had twenty or thirty seconds to get to the microphone. I got my sash caught in one of those folding chairs, and I tugged and wiggled around and couldn't get it loose. Finally I had to come right up to the microphone *with the chair* and say 'Dr. Christian's office.' Wild applause, of course."

Parley Baer remembers one of the most famous foul-ups on national radio, involving a *Lux Radio Theatre* broadcast. "Burt Lancaster was the star and Jeff Chandler (who was then Ira Grosell) was playing the second lead. During the break Burt went out to Universal—he was under contract out there—to change his clothes, and he thought the show was 6:30 instead of 6:00, so he came wandering in about 6:15 and we'd been on the air. Fred MacKaye was the director, and when Burt didn't show up he switched Jeff and Burt's part. [Director MacKaye played Chandler's part himself.] No announcement was made; they did the 'starring Burt Lancaster' and when he came, he went on and nobody knew the difference. He took over his part midway; Jeff returned to his part. Fred MacKaye was so easily becalmed; he had capable people. I think the studio audience might have been surprised that Burt Lancaster had changed for the first half of the show, but those things happened. You learned to cope in the days of live radio."

⌣

The three most famous goofs in the history of radio have become the Stuff of Legend. Yet there remains considerable doubt about how—and indeed, whether—they occurred.

The first was the utterance of radio's beloved kiddie show host Uncle Don (Carney), who reigned supreme at New York's mighty WOR from the late 1920s through 1949. The story goes that one evening, after signing off, Uncle Don, thinking the microphone was dead, muttered sotto voce, "That ought to hold the little bastards." The hue and cry that followed this accidental broadcast was tremendous, and has become part of radio lore. This writer has met people who swear, with equal conviction that, (a) they were present at the time and it did not happen, (b) it happened, but was not heard over the air, and (c) it never occurred.

A supposed recording of the incident was heard on Kermit Schafer's original recording *Pardon My Blooper*, a popular and hilarious compendium of fluffs and out-takes which used both genuine and re-created moments of radio mayhem.

The record also included a supposedly bona fide transcription of the second All-Time Great, from 1931:

In stentorian tones, announcer Harry Von Zell told a national audience over CBS, "Ladies and gentlemen, the President of the United States, Hoobert Heever." Von Zell later explained to radio historian Chuck Schaden that it was not an introduction of the President, but the final line of a lengthy summary of the statesman's life and career. "I must have mentioned in that opening the name of Herbert Hoover no less than twenty times," he recalled. "I was very young at the time . . . and was very nervous." At the end of this extended birthday tribute, Von Zell slipped up and garbled the President's name.

"I walked out of that studio—we were on the twenty-third floor of the Columbia Broadcasting System building—and fortunately the windows were not operative. They were fixed windows or I would have jumped out! And I thought that whatever career might have been a potential in my life began and ended right there in that one incident. It turned out not to be so." Von Zell went on to a long and prosperous career, but the story dogged him the rest of his life.

The final gem is one that has never been substantiated—and yet, refuses to die. The story goes that at the end of a prestigious Hollywood program, *Lux* or *Screen Guild Theater*, that week's star player was, as usual, billboarding the following week's guest stars. The star originally scheduled for the show, whose name had appeared in his script during rehearsal, had been hastily scratched out at the last minute, so cold, on the air, the actor read a typically hyperbolic build-up. But when it came time to read the guest star's name, the actor blurted out in amazement, "SONNY TUFTS!!!???"

For years it was said that Joseph Cotten perpetrated the act. In later years, he coyly refused to accept or deny responsibility. Graced with a delightful sense of humor, he certainly wasn't going to disavow a funny story.

The facts: on the March 23, 1944, episode of *Suspense*, Cotten *did* tell audiences to listen to Sonny Tufts the following week. He did so without any humor or exaggeration.

How did this story get going, then? Perhaps Cotten had his little joke at rehearsal and the story spread around town. Or perhaps he said it on the West Coast version of the show, which hasn't survived on tape. However this alleged incident passed into lore, the broad reading of Sonny Tufts' name has become infamous.

Of all the stories told, and retold, about unexpected incidents on the air, my favorite remains this anecdote, told in great detail by director Fletcher Markle about a *Studio One* broadcast of the late 1940s. His informal stock company at this time included character actors named John Merlin and Miriam Wolf, "two of the most alert people, who were ready to jump in in any kind of emergency. I kept the whole cast on stage with the orchestra, for that very reason. Let me give you one example.

"Paul Muni we wanted very much to have on *Studio One* and he turned down several properties; I've forgotten what they were. But he came up with a property he wanted to do, a worn old play called 'The Amazing Dr. Clitterhouse,' and I said, fine, because what we wanted was Muni. And we got one of our best writers to do an adaptation of it, which he largely narrated, and I began to appreciate why this was a vehicle he had chosen for himself.

"We came to the penultimate scene in which Muni's character, Clitterhouse, had an aria of some consequence, addressing a meeting of psychiatric people, or something. He was carried away by the studio audience and their response. We never had that in rehearsals, you see. And I looked up from the booth as it was finished, and the orchestra came in, ready to cue for the concluding scene, and I saw Mr. Muni's back disappearing in the wings of the theater! John Merlin and Miriam Wolf . . . followed immediately to get him back as soon as possible. He didn't have the first line of the next scene, the final scene, but he was in the second or third speech. I gave Alex Semler, who was then conductor, the stretch [sign], and he sustained the transition as it drifted away, as long as he could pull strings— literally—to sustain, and Muni did not reappear.

"Two other actors were in the final scene; one of them was Everett Sloane, and the other was a marvelous radio actor named Charles Gordon. Everett had the first line, then Charles had the second, and then Clitterhouse. Everett, one of the greatest radio performers ever, immediately assessed the scene over his shoulder: no star. And Everett [made a sign] to Gordon, and took his first line in his normal character voice; Gordon said the next one, and Everett went right into his Muni imitation. Impeccable.

"Everett had been fascinated by his behavior, his idiosyncrasies, his strange personality, and was a great mimic by training. It was about two thirds of a page; halfway through it, Muni is careening across the stage, Miriam Wolf hanging onto one arm, because his script he has thrown onto the shelf in the dressing room (it's over, it's finished, my great speech is done) and she had no idea what had transpired while she was offstage rescuing this absent-minded man. But Everett saw the arrival of the body over his shoulder, shifted his script, and then put his arm out and withheld Muni from screwing up the remaining four or five speeches of the scene. And Miriam quickly cottoned on to the fact that Everett had saved [the day].

"The audience was remarkably quiet. You can imagine how easy nervous laughter would be at this point, but Everett firmly put his arm right across Muni's chest, and finished the scene in this exemplary imitation, and the finale came up with the orchestra. Everett quickly went over and gave him a big hug, and got him off the stage."

People tell wild and funny ancedotes about mishaps in the early days of live TV, but that's one story television could never match.

14

The End of an Era

I t wasn't hard to see television coming. NBC's famous broadcast from the New York World's Fair in 1939 set the stage, but World War Two put plans for a new form of communication on hold. With war's end, America settled down once more and talk of television resumed.

At first, there were skeptics who refused to believe that television was a practical reality. But year by year, the new medium, and its enormous sales and advertising potential, became more genuine.

Eventually, the question itself changed. It was no longer, "When and how will television establish itself?" but rather, "What will happen to radio?"

Radio underwent one significant change in the late 1940s: the advent of recording tape, based on German technology brought home by Americans at the end of World War Two. Until this time, the networks had forbidden the use of recorded material of any kind on the air. (Local stations had no such constraints; syndicated programs and open-ended music performance shows had been distributed on transcription discs since the early 1930s.)

Now, a major star with clout tested the waters—and broke open a dam. Bing Crosby wanted to have the freedom to tape his weekly radio show where and when he wanted. NBC and the J. Walter Thompson ad agency refused, fearful that a star would have undue influence over the fate of a show. They also believed that audiences would reject recorded programs. But the newly formed upstart network, ABC, was badly in need of starpower, and was only too happy to accede to Crosby's wishes. Thus, Bing's *Philco Radio Time* was the first taped program on network radio, in 1946. The quality of recording was superior, and had no discernible impact on the listening audience. Bing could now spend a month in San Francisco and bring his guests there to join him, or stockpile several programs if his schedule was especially demanding. Once, a threatened strike by the musicians' union caused him to record six shows in a short span of time, just to be safe.

There was another decided

Chet Lauck and Norris Goff celebrate fifteen years on the air in the title roles of *Lum 'n' Abner*. In 1946 it was difficult to conceive that network radio's days were numbered.

advantage to tape: the ability to edit. Up until now, actors sweated out the recording of transcription discs, because a mistake meant starting all over again. Now, a show could be spliced if it was running long, in the case of a variety show like Crosby's, or if the actors flubbed their lines. The concept of editing had been pioneered by the Armed Forces Radio Service during the war, when staffers transferred network shows from one disc to another and figured out how to excise the commercials.

Soon, the term "transcribed" was being mentioned in the credits of many network shows. Concerned that it might be perceived as a negative factor by listeners, some buried the word in the midst of a greeting or slogan ("Now, transcribed tales of the Old West . . ."). It didn't take long for jokes to start popping up in comedy scripts. On a *Kraft Music Hall* of the late 1940s, Oscar Levant remarks to Al Jolson that he can't understand how Jolie could have retired for so many years. "You got that wrong, Oscar," Jolson replies. "I wasn't retired. I was transcribed for release at a more convenient time."

On April 17, 1946, an irreverent ABC comedy series from San Francisco called *The Jack Webb Show* (yes, the same) began its show with a pearly-voiced announcer saying, "The following is transcribed." After a moment's pause, another voice says, "No it isn't."

"LOVE BEGINS AT 30" SAYS FRANK PARKER

Radio Guide

THE NATIONAL WEEKLY OF PROGRAM   WEEK ENDING FEB. 6, 1937

10

JACK BENNY

WHO IS HOLDING TELEVISION BACK?
ANNE SEYMOUR'S ANSWER TO TROUBLE

The announcer, unperturbed, repeats, "The following is transcribed."

"No it *isn't*."

"Oh yes it is."

"It is not."

"Yes it is."

"It is not."

"It is too!"

"It is not!"

"It is!"

"It isn't!"

"Yes!!"

"No!!"

"Yes!!!"

"No!!!"

"Yes!!!!"

Then there is the sound of a gunshot. A moment later the second voice declares, "The following is *not* transcribed!"

A few comedy and variety shows deliberately ran long and pruned out the weak spots. An existing tape of the inaugural *Martin and Lewis Show* from 1949 runs about forty minutes long, but this was not part of the plan. Midway through the show, Bob Hope arrives for a guest spot. Jerry flubs a line, and Hope says "Start over; it's tape!" This gets a big laugh and applause from the audience, and Hope adds, "Crosby starts ten times a night; go ahead!" From that point on, Dean, Jerry, and Bob get looser and looser, muffing lines and cues and joking about their inability to stick to the script. All of this tomfoolery must have been fun for the studio audience, but the folks at home never heard it.

At least one show got on the air the way it did because of tape. Actress Eve Arden chanced to meet CBS boss William S. Paley. "I was coming back from New York," she recalled, "where I'd done a publicity trip for movies, and I met Bill Paley at the Ambassador in the Pump Room and he asked me to dance. He was a wonderful dancer, and he seemed to think I was too; a couple of weeks later

I got a request to do a record of *Our Miss Brooks*." According to her memory, other actresses had been tested already; she also expressed some displeasure with the original script, but after new writers were hired it improved tremendously and she said yes. But there was one condition. "They wanted to make a tape of it and put it on for a summer replacement, and I said all right if they would do fifteen scripts before I wanted to leave for Connecticut, where I was taking my children to spend the summer. They did, and at the end of that summer, I was at this friend's farm and I got a call from Frank Stanton saying, 'Congratulations.' I said, 'What do you mean?' He said '*Miss Brooks* is the number one show on the air,' and of course, there was no going back from that."

Beginning that fall, the show was performed live every Sunday, but had it not been for the flexibility of tape, Eve Arden would have turned down the job.

For dramatic shows, the move to tape took some of the spark out of performing live on the air. When director Jack Johnstone took over *Yours Truly, Johnny Dollar* in the mid-1950s, he insisted that each fifteen-minute recording session proceed from start to finish with no retakes. "A few actors resented this in the very beginning," he later remarked, "but most of them got to like it, because it got much better performances. If we were a third of the way through a program and somebody fluffed, we went back to the beginning, started all over again. As I say, it got good performances because everybody was on his toes."

But for actors like William Conrad, taped shows "never had the edge that they had before, and no matter how hard you tried to give [it] back, you're manufacturing an edge, and you can't do that. It's either there or it isn't." In fairness, one would be hard-pressed to find a better show in all of radio than *Gunsmoke*, which was recorded for almost the entirety of its nine-year run. Conrad's *Gunsmoke* costar Parley Baer became so accustomed to tape that while doing an episode of *This Is Your F.B.I.* he garbled a speech, but didn't worry about it, knowing he could record a pickup of the dialogue later on. Only after finishing his section of the script and sitting down did he realize they were already on the air! He was mortified.

⌐

Some executives and ad agency people saw the handwriting on the wall and switched allegiances to television early on. Pioneering syndicator Frederick Ziv made his first filmed TV pilot in 1947, and says, "This sounds very self-serving, but I knew it would put radio out of business. I knew TV would take over, even at a time when successful owners of radio stations did not go into television, because

Freeman Gosden and Charles Correll continued to ply their trade on CBS's *Amos 'n' Andy* well into the 1950s—even after the demise of the television series of the same name.

they said it was too expensive." Ziv continued producing radio programs for a while, but got in on the ground floor of television with such successful series as *The Cisco Kid* and *Highway Patrol*.

Top comedy writer Hal Kanter felt so strongly about gaining experience in television that he signed onto the Ed Wynn show at a cut in pay from what he'd been receiving on radio. (Wynn paid him $750 a week, which according to Kanter made him the highest-paid comedy writer in television.)

Stars were more reluctant to abandon the proven success of their radio shows, and stepped gingerly into the new medium. Bob Hope, Jack Benny, and other headliners made experimental forays into TV but stopped short of committing themselves to weekly shows. (Hope never did, but Benny finally succumbed.) Freeman Gosden and Charles Correll were in a quandary about how to present *Amos 'n' Andy* on television, and were finally persuaded to allow black performers to portray their characters on screen.

The zany team of Martin and Lewis had already made their television debut when NBC wooed them to headline a radio series in 1949. Radio was never their medium, and they knew it. "We hated it," says Jerry Lewis. "Dean hated it I think worse than I did, but he had a wonderful way of showing it. We were on the air for Chesterfield and he came in every night smoking Luckies."

⌐

Fred Allen, enjoying a premature retirement, and still reeling from the blow his program had received from a competitive cash-giveaway quiz show, was extremely leery of the new medium. He dropped in to visit his friends Paul and Ruth Henning at the Algonquin Hotel one day, and spied a basket of fruit the management had sent up and placed on top of the TV console. "You know," said Allen, "that's the best thing I've seen on television yet."

Allen's baggy, wrinkled face never made peace with the television camera, nor did his comic sensibilities. His talent was squandered as the host of panel shows.

Allen bemoaned another trend that started in the latter days of radio and flowered on TV: the ascent to stardom of hosts who had geniality to offer but no discernible talent. For a vaudeville veteran like Allen, who not only had a specialty (juggling) but had learned along the way to sing and dance a little, this was a terrible insult.

But, as one of those genial hosts, Art Linkletter, freely admitted in later years, "I wanted to *be* somebody, but I had no talent. I couldn't sing, I couldn't act. I was about to quit and go into the executive side of the business when the man in the street idea came along, and my whole life changed." Linkletter started in 1933 at KGB San Diego, and enjoyed ever-growing success as a radio, then television, personality.

But even he was surprised during the transition from radio to TV, when he learned a truth that others were doomed to discover for themselves. He explains, "You know, *People Are Funny* was one of the original stunt shows—that and *Truth or Consequences* were the first. We were dying for television to come along, so people could *see* the stunts—and when it did, we found it wasn't as funny. We thought, gee, give a woman a skunk on a leash and tell her to walk it to the Broadway Hollywood [store] . . . it just wasn't as funny when you could see it."

The literalization of entertainment, both comic and dramatic, was the greatest pitfall facing writers, directors, and performers who tried to adapt radio programming for TV. The excitement of seeing images on a TV screen couldn't make up for the abandonment of *imagination* that radio offered. Radio comedy indulged in many wild and wacky "images," on shows ranging from Jack Benny's to *Fibber McGee and Molly*. Even the fundamentally realistic *Our Miss Brooks* used outlandish exaggeration for gags (like a drunken frog hiccuping in Mr. Boynton's science lab) which could never be duplicated on television. Yet for many viewers, the novelty value of TV was great enough to compensate for any sacrifice.

The most successful early TV shows, however, were not picture versions of radio programs; they were television originals. Milton Berle had never enjoyed great success on radio, though he appeared on the medium in many formats over the years. It was TV that allowed him to become America's favorite *tummler*, dressing up in drag, horning in on acrobatic acts, and mugging for the camera.

Slapstick was one of the watchwords of early TV comedy; everyone from Berle to Lucille Ball indulged in pie-throwing. Perhaps it worked so well because it was strictly visual, in sharp contrast to radio comedy.*

Sid Caesar and his colleagues on *Your Show of Shows* downplayed slapstick in favor of satire, and called on a skill that no radio comedian could have possibly employed: pantomime. It also seems significant to note that while most top radio comedy writers made the transition to TV, the brain trust behind *Your Show of Shows* and subsequent Caesar vehicles included hot young talents who had no radio experience at all, including Neil Simon, Woody Allen, and Mel Brooks. They came of age with television.

Larry Gelbart, who made the transition to TV working for Bob Hope and wound up on Caesar's staff, still feels that they came up short. "At first we just did radio in funny costumes. We had no idea what to do with television, so we just kept writing radio-type material, and if it was a cowboy, he wore a twenty-gallon hat. We really weren't writing television. If you ask me now what television writing is, I'm not quite sure; maybe there wasn't any real television comedy writing until *Laugh-In* in a way. Good as *Your Show of Shows* and *Caesar's Hour* were, I think those were essentially theatrical pieces adapted to television; not to put them down, they were marvelous, but there was no electronic comedy when we first did it. So we did the monologue and the standup 'in one,' in front of the curtain, and then we would do a sketch, and if it was an eskimo, he'd have fish sticking out of his ears, but it was just to be visual because we were on television; there was no real appreciation of using the medium."

George Burns, crafty as ever, tailored his and Gracie Allen's radio series for television with one simple but ideal addition: he spoke directly to the camera. It was a stroke of genius.

Some situation comedies made fairly easy transitions to TV, including *The Life of Riley* and *Father Knows Best*, but star and coproducer Robert Young learned that simply dusting off radio scripts for television reuse wasn't going to work. A premise might be viable, but all dialogue and no visuals wouldn't sustain a successful TV series. Nor would he be able to continue touring in plays and having his supporting cast meet him in a given city to record that week's episode. Ozzie Nelson actually put his family into a theatrical feature film (1952's *Here Come the Nelsons*) to prove to the powers that be that they could play themselves successfully on TV.

*Oddly enough, there was one show that did engage in pie-throwing on radio: *Truth or Consequences*. What's more, the contagious laughter of the studio audience seemed to satisfy the listeners at home who couldn't see the actual gag.

Some of the most enduring kids' adventure shows, like *The Lone Ranger* and *Superman*, owed as much to the formats and production techniques of Saturday matinee movie serials as they did to their radio predecessors.

The format of the Jack Webb *Dragnet* scripts was so rigid, and so descriptive, that many of his radio shows *were* able to be filmed almost verbatim. What's more, Webb insisted on using his informal stock company of actors, giving many of them valuable TV experience at a time when some radio actors were worried about proving themselves on camera.

In the waning days of network radio, NBC turned to established movie "names" to help bolster ratings. Here, the network's detectives and crime fighters gather for a photo opportunity: Sydney Greenstreet, Brian Donlevy, Vincent Price, Steve Dunne, Gail Bonney as the damsel in distress, Herbert Marshall, and Frank Lovejoy.

Even when Milton Berle and Howdy Doody and Ed Sullivan and Friday-night fights made television desirable and successful, radio refused to roll over and play dead.

Proof that radio was still a potent medium, with a large and loyal audience, is evidenced by the fact that a number of early TV successes made a reverse transition onto radio! It isn't generally remembered that the early sitcom *My Little Margie* enjoyed a three-year run on radio, with its TV stars, Gale Storm, Charles Farrell, and Gil Stratton Jr. re-creating their roles, as did the casts of *Wild Bill Hickok*, *Space Patrol*, *Tom Corbett, Space Cadet*, and even the hugely popular *Howdy Doody*. As late as 1958, CBS found it worthwhile to translate its Western success *Have Gun, Will Travel* to radio, adapting its television scripts to suit an audio format.

In open defiance of conventional wisdom, NBC even mounted a major variety program in the fall of 1950. Its mandate was no secret: it was a bold attempt to steal both thunder and audience share from television, and it was called *The Big Show*. It also represented a departure from radio procedure in that it was produced by the network, and not by an advertising agency. This was program executive Sylvester "Pat" Weaver's idea, to wrest control of both radio and television away from the agencies (where he himself had worked for many years). Thus, *The Big Show* had no single sponsor, but sold its formidable ninety minutes of entertainment in half-hour chunks.

The Big Show was a wonderful program. It originated from New York, and offered every week a knockout lineup of talent, drawn from stage and screen, from nightclubs and recordings. Broadway stars even performed scenes from their hit plays and musicals. The host was "the glamorous, unpredictable" Tallulah Bankhead, whose deep, raspy voice and self-deprecating sense of humor made her unique in any medium. The guests on a single episode were Jimmy Durante, Bert Lahr, Margaret O'Brien, Ed Wynn, and Edith Piaf. Another evening offered Ethel Barrymore, Joan Davis, Judy Holliday, Bob Hope, Van Johnson, Groucho Marx, and Ezio Pinza! Fred Allen even came out of retirement to become a semi-regular. Clearly, the program was not misnamed.

At a rehearsal of *The Big Show*, Tallulah Bankhead chats with guest star David Brian while Groucho Marx and Fanny Brice carry on their own conversation. *The Big Show* was NBC's—and indeed, radio's—last gasp of large-scale variety programming.

Goodman Ace headed a topnotch writing team, and Meredith Willson served as musical director. Ray Charles, who supervised a choral group for Willson on the series, recalls, "There was real excitement for that show, because we were really in the presence of the cream of the entertainment world. One of the girls in the choir had an autograph book, every week, and she went and got everybody's autograph. We all kind of made fun of her; now, I wish I had done it! And Tallulah was fun; she brought a wonderful quality to the show. She was larger than life, and she was wonderful to all of us."

But *The Big Show* was an expensive proposition, budgeted at $100,000 a week. During the 1951–52 season, producer-director Dee Engelbach took Tallulah and company to London and Paris. But they were facing still-stiff competition from Jack Benny and Edgar Bergen, who'd been stolen by CBS a few years earlier. And they all succumbed to the growing popularity of *The Ed Sullivan Show* on television, well on its way to becoming a national institution. *The Big Show* died in 1952.

Radio veterans who made the jump to television soon discovered that they were now swimming in different waters. Says writer-producer Paul Henning, "Radio was just so easy; once you had an idea, you'd sit around and a script would build itself up. But television was an altogether different matter; you had to suddenly realize everything is visual. You can't just talk about it; you had to show it."

Performers who were used to reading their scripts suddenly had to contend with memorization. Peg Lynch and Alan Bunce, well accustomed to the rhythms of their daily quarter-hour *Ethel and Albert* radio show, suddenly found themselves doing several sketches a week on Kate Smith's popular TV show—in front of a huge studio audience. "The audience always bothered me," Lynch recalls, "because it was a quiet show, and I was not a stage person who was accustomed to performing in front of an audience, as comedians are; they're used to timing the laughs. And I always felt it spoiled my timing. I would have to hold up for the laugh. I was so nervous . . ."

The pressure was more intense in the new medium, where so much seemed to be at stake with every broadcast—especially the live ones. Says composer Jerry Goldsmith, "When I was doing radio, everybody was sort of laid back, and appreciative; it was all friendly, good ole boy sort of thing. All of a sudden I got on *Climax* and I was surrounded by ten charcoal grey suits from New York from the advertising agency, a couple of execs from the third-floor programming [department]; there was a producer, a director, a writer, and a roomful of people . . . and it was a nightmare. You'd finish a dress [rehearsal], you'd get this pile of notes: this is no good, that's not right, change this, add these again, more music there, less here. I tell you, how any of us survived those days is amazing."

The shift of importance to television did have one benefit for radio: an easing of pressure. The networks weren't going out of business; they still had hours to fill every day, and every night, but ratings were of diminished importance as the 1950s wore on. Many shows that debuted during that decade went sponsorless, or sold spot ads, which in either case meant that an ad agency was no longer pulling the strings. The network hierarchy was simplified immeasurably. And in that relatively free atmosphere, some excellent radio shows were created, like NBC's landmark science fiction series *Dimension X* and its mid-fifties retread, *X Minus One*, CBS's *Gunsmoke*, and the fifteen-minute daily version of *Yours Truly, Johnny Dollar*.

Soap operas continued to prosper, even as some of them switched over to television, and New York remained the home base for most of the enduring daytime shows. This meant a continuing source of employment for actors, including a new generation of actors who came to New York hoping to succeed in the theater. (One such hopeful was Jack Lemmon, who like so many others was grateful for the income radio offered. He worked for a year and a half on the daytime dramas *Brighter Day* and *Road of Life*.)

Successful actors on both coasts now had to juggle radio and television schedules, which wasn't always easy. CBS decided to tape *Gunsmoke* on Saturdays, to avoid such conflicts. The show's great success, as one of radio's pioneering "adult westerns," attracted a series of sponsors, and before long there was talk around CBS that it was a shoe-in for a switch-over to television. The stars of the radio series hoped they would be considered for the TV version, and to help their cause, rented Western costumes and posed in character on the Western street at Knott's Berry Farm for a series of stills taken by fellow actor (and stock-company regular) Harry Bartell. It was said that William Conrad even dieted in anticipation of the photo shoot.

In later years, Conrad denied that he even wanted the part on TV, declaring, "I don't look like Matt Dillon, goddammit! I got talked into making a test; it's pitiful. I was so bad; I was scared to death, the only time in my life that I really was ever scared to death. I was afraid I was gonna get it, which I didn't want, I really didn't, but I was committed to at least, for the sake of CBS, for them to look at me and say yes or no. But I was delighted not to have done it."

Conrad continued to make himself available for radio calls, and kept busy at CBS on a variety of shows, including *Escape*, for which he alternated opening-announcement chores with Paul Frees. *Escape* was *Suspense*'s stepchild at the network, never given a permanent time slot, bounced on and off the air, and unable to win a regular sponsor. Yet in many ways, it was the superior show. Unfettered by sponsor interference, the need for a name guest star, or strict adherence to a set format, *Escape* combed the short-story libraries of writers ranging from H. G. Wells to Cornell Woolrich for material, and produced some of the greatest half-hours ever broadcast, including "A Shipment of Mute Fate," "Evening Primrose," "The Diamond as Big as the Ritz," "Leinegen Versus the Ants," and the hair-raising "Three Skeleton Key," in which three men are trapped in a lighthouse about to be attacked by a swarm of rats. (More than once over the years, *Escape* swapped scripts with *Suspense* for encore performances of especially good stories. The two shows also employed many of the same writers, directors, actors, composers, and soundmen.)

Use of tape simplified some aspects of production, but created roadblocks as well. Prerecording musicians was a no-no (which, in time, led to the extinction of live, original music on the air). Elliott Lewis recalled, "You could record the actors with no extra fee, but you couldn't record the musicians with no extra fee, so I would record the actors and in my head—tape was still running—I would play what I thought was a good cue, and then I'd cue the actor. The composer would then write a cue to fit the hole I left on the tape, so when we went on the air, we rolled tape [with the actors], and then at the normal place the music would start, we'd bring the music in under the tape; the tape would finish, the music would come up." In other words, the live musicians would accompany prerecorded actors as the show went out over the air!

Resourceful men like Lewis, William Robson, and Jack Johnstone knew how to get the most out of their productions, even when budgets were cut. The area hardest hit was music. Jerry Goldsmith rose to a position of prominence at CBS because he became so adept at scoring shows from the network's record library.

"You'd actually get two engineers with four turntables," he remembers of this period, "and we'd pick out this music and you'd almost conduct like you would with an orchestra. You'd cue this guy and you'd cue that guy, and you put them together. We sort of devised this method where I'd sit there on a podium and conduct these mixers or turntables. This was fascinating to everybody."

He also remembers the atmosphere at CBS as the curtain started to ring down on a glorious era. "Now, people were playing to empty halls, more or less, and it was sad. Jack Johnstone was filled with stories of reminiscing; he would spend more time talking about the good old days, when we did this and did that. I kept saying, this just doesn't seem right; I mean, these men were superstars, they had everything going for them."

General Electric, which sponsored Bing Crosby's final season of weekly network shows, penalized him for not appearing on television and thereby hastened his radio show's demise. Jack Benny, never afraid of hard work, spent his last seasons on CBS doing both radio (weekly) and television (every other week) simultaneously. Mary Livingstone didn't share his work ethic, however, and during Jack's last season on radio, she pretaped all her lines.

In 1956, there was a last hurrah of sorts when CBS decided to revive *The CBS*

Radio Workshop, "dedicated to man's imagination—the theater of the mind." For this unsponsored series, the network's finest talents rose to the occasion and produced a series of challenging, experimental, one-of-a-kind broadcasts, beginning with an ambitious rendering of Aldous Huxley's *Brave New World*. William N. Robson wrote some especially memorable shows, including an adaptation of Sinclair Lewis's "Young Man Axelbroad" and "An Interview with Shakespeare," moderated by Dr. Frank C. Baxter and featuring remarks by Christopher Marlowe, Sir Francis Bacon, Richard Burbage, and others who claimed to have written the Great Bard's plays. William Conrad was especially fond of "1,489 Words," which was simply a recitation of three great poems set to original music by Jerry Goldsmith. Top actors, writers, directors, musicians, and soundmen gave their best efforts to this show, which earned a fair amount of print publicity.

Elliott Lewis recalled, "I was in television and I was working at NBC and Bill Froug, who was vice president of CBS Radio called me and said, 'We're still doing *CBS Workshop*; we're going to be doing it for thirteen more weeks, then it's finished and that's the end of all of this stuff. Want a half-hour?' So I said 'Sure.' 'What are you going to do?' 'I don't know yet.' He said, 'Do whatever you want. You have a half-hour.' So I wrote 'A Man's Nightmare,' [ultimately broadcast as "Nightmare"] and I played the man, and directed it, and it was thrilling. Fred Steiner wrote the score, and we talked about what we'd do, and what is a dream." They decided that they didn't want typical musical bridges, but wanted to create instead a kind of freeform stream of consciousness in which music would meld into dialogue which would be overtaken by sounds, as in a dream. Lewis' goal: "Really make use of the medium. And it was great." *The CBS Radio Workshop* signed off for the last time at the end of 1957, after a notable twenty-month run.

That same year, CBS again surprised the show-business community by hiring satirist Stan Freberg to headline his own, lavishly produced half-hour comedy series, replete with top-notch supporting cast, live studio audience, and an orchestra led by Billy May. This fifteen-week series inherited Jack Benny's time slot and studio, and has led Freberg to refer to himself as the last network radio comedian! "One of my big thrills," he recalls, "was looking out in the audience one night before my show went off and there was Groucho sitting in the third row."

CBS apparently fired up its Standards and Practices division in anticipation of Freberg's debut; after several set-tos, the network decided it could not allow him to broadcast live, as he wanted to. Freberg's stock-in-trade was topical satire, which then as now tested the patience and fortitude of censors and sponsors alike. His ultimate response was an unforgettable jibe at censorship, in which the network "suit" (played by Daws Butler) causes him to change so many lyrics in a classic American song that it winds up being called "Elderly Man River."

By the end of the 1950s, radio was an afterthought in the world of ABC, NBC, and CBS: still there, hanging on with a handful of original shows, but no longer a force to be reckoned with. Some of the finest talents behind the scenes in radio never left the medium, and their careers died with it.

Television never had a laboratory for experimental drama, or comedy for that matter; the concept of sustaining shows, where quality for quality's sake was the hallmark, never existed on TV. One is hard-pressed to picture the television industry banding together, as the four radio networks did in May of 1945, to broadcast a program like Norman Corwin's meditation on V-E Day, *On a Note of Triumph*. Says Corwin, "Television was born without a conscience."

Yours Truly, Johnny Dollar and *Suspense* were the last original dramatic shows produced by CBS, and they both met their demise on September 30, 1962.

⌐

The 1950s produced the last generation to grow up with any sense of what dramatic radio was all about. Says veteran producer-director Himan Brown, "The advent of television absolutely destroyed radio drama. Once people began looking, and having movies in their own house, it was very hard to get them to turn the set off and just sit down and listen. They lost the ability to listen. Nobody listens anymore."

But not quite.

The advent of tape has enabled radio shows of the past to have a new life, through redistribution to radio stations and the sale and exchange of cassettes. Old-time radio (or OTR) societies and conventions have sprung up from coast to coast, celebrating this golden age, and inviting many of its survivors to join them for panel discussions and re-creations.

Peggy Webber, one of the best "golden age" actresses, has formed CART (California Artists Radio Theatre), which stages new radio productions on a monthly basis, using veterans like Jeanette Nolan, Parley Baer, and Elliott Reid, as well as younger actors who want a taste of radio performing. Santa Monica–based L.A. Theatre Works attracts major stars from movies and television to perform classic plays and novels, as well as new material, on-mike, while the Wells Fargo Radio Theatre stages western-themed plays by Rosemary and Newell Alexander on a regular basis at the Autry Museum of Western Heritage in Los Angeles. Other companies, both professional and amateur, have launched

Radio's most enduringly popular duos, from the 1930s through the 1950s: Edgar and Charlie, Gracie and George, Mary and Jack. Radio made them all part of the fabric of American life.

similar ventures around the country. On public radio stations coast to coast, Michael Feldman plies his trade as a comic quiz-master, in the best tradition of Groucho Marx, for a popular weekly show called *What D'Ya Know*. In 1996, National Public Radio commissioned Norman Corwin, the poet laureate of radio, to write a series of new audio plays for nationwide broadcast. His first effort, *No Love Lost*, about a decade among Thomas Jefferson, Alexander Hamilton, and Aaron Burr, attracted no less a cast than Jack Lemmon, William Shatner, Lloyd Bridges, and Martin Landau—all of them eager to work with Corwin in this rarefied atmosphere. In England, where radio drama has never died, the BBC arranged with George Lucas to produce an audio interpretation of the *Star Wars* trilogy.

None of this will ever make a dent in the impact of all-pervasive television (which director Fletcher Markle called "the haunted aquarium"), but it does provide a stimulating alternative for many people.

Meanwhile, many of the best shows from radio's golden age are still with us; those voices in the air live on, to entertain new generations of listeners willing to open their ears, and inspire young writers, directors, sound-effects wizards, and actors to see what they can do when they simply use their imagination.

BASED ON WEEKS BEGINNING WEDNESDAY, OCTOBER 22, 1947 SATURDAY, NOVEMBER 1, 1947 SATURDAY, NOVEMBER 8, 1947 SATURDAY, NOVEMBER 15, 1947		**PACIFIC** **PROGRAM HOOPERATINGS**			**REPORT ISSUED** NOVEMBER, 1947 **AVERAGE CALLS PER HOUR** **IN EXCESS OF :** Evening = 1440 Daytime = 3600		

PROGRAM-TALENT-NOTES	ADVERTISER, PRODUCT AGENCY PLACING	Network, Day, Pacific Time # Checking Points	**Hooperatings**			Program Sets In Use*	Share of Audience**
			This Report	Last Report	Year Ago	This Report	This Report
GEORGE BURNS AND GRACIE ALLEN Bill Goodwin, Mel Blanc, Meredith Willson's Orchestra	GENERAL FOODS SALES CO., INC. Maxwell House Coffee Benton & Bowles, Inc.	NBC-Thursday 9:00-9:30 PM (6)	14.7	14.2	14.7	31.2 (-2.7)	47.2 (+5.2)
GIVE AND TAKE (Two Months) M.C. John Reed King (Figures include five minutes of miscellaneous programming on Nov. 1st only)	THE TONI COMPANY Toni Home Permanent Wave Foote, Cone & Belding	CBS-Saturday 11:30-12:00 N (6)	3.6	4.6	3.9∅	19.5 (+3.8)	18.4 (-10.6)
GRAND CENTRAL STATION (Two Months)	PILLSBURY FLOUR MILLS CO. Various Products McCann-Erickson, Inc.	CBS-Saturday 10:00-10:30 AM (4)	7.5	6.7	5.7	15.8 (-1.3)	47.4 (+8.4)
GRAND OLE OPRY M.C. Red Foley, Minnie Pearl, Wally Fowler, Red Brasfield, Oak Ridge Quartet	R. J. REYNOLDS CO. Prince Albert Tobacco William Esty & Co., Inc.	NBC-Saturday 7:30-8:00 PM (6)	10.6	12.8	15.3	30.0 (-3.4)	35.4 (-2.9)
GRAND SLAM Irene Beasley, Dwight Weist, Bob Downey, Organist-Abe Goldman	CONTINENTAL BAKING CO., INC. Wonder Bread, Hostess Cake Ted Bates, Inc.	CBS-MTWTF 8:30-8:45 AM (5)	3.7	2.6	4.0	13.2 (-1.9)	28.0 (+10.7)
GREATEST STORY EVER TOLD	GOODYEAR TIRE & RUBBER CO. Kudner Agency, Inc.	ABC-Sunday 3:30-4:00 PM (5)	2.6	3.7	∅∅	25.2 (+0.3)	10.4 (-4.5)
GREAT GILDERSLEEVE Harold Peary Jack Meakin's Orchestra	KRAFT FOODS CO. Kay Natural Brand Cheese Needham, Louis & Brorby, Inc.	NBC-Wednesday 8:30-9:00 PM (6)	14.2	14.2	19.8	36.8 (-1.1)	38.6 (+1.2)
GREEN HORNET	GENERAL MILLS, INC. Betty Crocker Cereal Tray Dancer-Fitzgerald-Sample	ABC-Sunday 8:30-9:00 PM (6)	3.9	4.5	∅∅	36.6 (-0.2)	10.6 (-1.7)
GUIDING LIGHT Hugh Studebaker, Betty Lou Gerson, Willard Waterman, Ned LeFevre (Not broadcast Monday, Nov. 17th because of Pres. Truman's address)	PROCTER & GAMBLE CO. Duz Compton Advertising, Inc.	CBS-MTWTF 10:45-11:00 AM (5)	3.7	3.5	3.5∅	14.5 (-1.9)	25.8 (+4.6)
HARVEST OF STARS M.C. James Melton, Frank Black's Orchestra	INTERNATIONAL HARVESTER CO. McCann-Erickson, Inc.	NBC-Sunday 11:30-12:00 N (6)	6.9	6.1	8.5	22.2 (-4.6)	31.1 (+8.2)
HEADLINE EDITION Taylor Grant	COOPERATIVE	ABC-MTWTF 6:00-6:15 PM (4½)	1.6	1.2	∅∅	29.8 (+0.8)	5.4 (+1.4)
HEART'S DESIRE M.C. Ben Alexander	PHILIP MORRIS & CO., LTD., INC. Philip Morris Cigarettes Cecil & Presbrey, Inc.	DLBS-MTWTF 2:15-2:30 PM (6)	1.5	1.1	∅∅	13.0 (-0.2)	11.9 (+3.4)
HENRY J. TAYLOR	GENERAL MOTORS, INC. Kudner Agency, Inc.	DLBS-W & F 9:45-10:00 PM (6)	1.8	2.9	1.7	23.7 (-1.5)	7.4 (-4.1)
HENRY MORGAN	EVERSHARP, INC. Various Products The Biow Company, Inc.	ABC-Wednesday 9:30-10:00 PM (6½)	10.4	11.1	6.6	29.3 (-2.8)	35.6 (+0.9)

Page 15

For Explanation of Symbols see Page 2

Index